P9-DYB-195

ENCYCLOPEDIA OF
EVENTS
THAT CHANGED THE
WORLD

Eighty turning points in history

ENCYCLOPEDIA OF
EVENTS
THAT CHANGED THE
WORLD

Eighty turning points in history

ROBERT INGPEN & PHILIP WILKINSON

VIKING
STUDIO
BOOKS

For M.W.

VIKING STUDIO BOOKS
Published by the Penguin Group
Viking Penguin, a division of Penguin Books USA Inc.,
375 Hudson Street, New York, New York 10014, U.S.A
Penguin Books Ltd, 27 Wrights Lane, London
W8 5TZ, England
Penguin Books Australia Ltd, Ringwood, Victoria,
Australia
Penguin Books Canada Ltd, 10 Alcorn Avenue, Suite 300,
Toronto, Ontario, Canada M4V 3B2
Penguin Books (N.Z.) Ltd, 182–190 Wairau Road,
Auckland 10, New Zealand

Penguin Books Ltd, Registered Offices: Harmondsworth,
Middlesex, England

First published in 1991 in the United States of America by
Viking Penguin, a division of Penguin Books USA Inc.,
and in Great Britain by Dragon's World Ltd.

10 9 8 7 6 5 4 3 2 1

LIBRARY OF CONGRESS CATALOGING IN PUBLICATION DATA

Wilkinson, Philip, 1955–
    Encyclopedia of events that changed the world/Philip
Wilkinson, Robert Ingpen.
        p.   cm.
    ISBN 0–670–84141–2
    1. Chronology, Historical. I. Ingpen, Robert R. II Title.
D11.5.W4Z 1991
902'. 02–dc20   91–50239

DESIGNER Robert Ingpen
EDITOR Michael Downey
ART DIRECTOR Dave Allen
EDITORIAL DIRECTOR Pippa Rubinstein

Printed in Singapore
Set in Garamond

CONTENTS

INTRODUCTION

People have always been fascinated by their past. Even pre-literate peoples would recount memories of their ancestors, tales of their heroes and heroines of long ago, stories that showed them how everyday life used to be lived. The writers of the early civilizations, from Sumer to Greece and Rome, chronicled the doings of their forbears, beginning a tradition of thinking and writing about the past that extends to this century. Today, if we are often bewildered by the pace of change in our own lives, we seem unable to resist looking back to previous times. In doing so we are often confronted by certain events that stand out – happenings that seem to change the course of history in some special, wide-reaching way. This book is about some of those 'great events'. It begins some two centuries before the birth of Christ at the time when Buddhism, one of the most influential of world religions, was beginning to spread across the globe. And it charts some eighty decisive events from the following two thousand years, ending with some of the most dramatic and important happenings of recent history.

The idea that certain moments stand out as significant, or that certain events seem to sum up a whole age, occurs in our own lives. Few Americans or Europeans alive in the 1960s can forget what they were doing when the news of John F. Kennedy's assassination reached them; still fewer people in eastern Europe in 1989 will forget the first breaches in the Berlin Wall or the initial unrest that led to the revolutions in Romania and Czechoslovakia.

It is the same when we come to the great events of more distant history. What stick in our minds are often important moments – from the crowning of Charlemagne to the dropping of the atom bomb, from the death of Caesar to Captain Cook's landing in Australia. There seems to be a deep human need to remember such crucial events and to make memorials to them. And so we celebrate anniversaries and erect monuments at the places where famous events – from the signing of a great charter to the death of a police officer in a riot – occurred.

Yet, compelling as these moments are, they are not isolated in history. Negotiations led up to the charter, the riots had a whole social context crying out to be understood, and much hard work had already been done before the demonstrators came out on to the streets of Prague and Bucharest. If we rightly remember the bravery of those making a public stand, we should also honour the efforts of the people who worked for freedom behind closed doors in situations equally life-threatening, to make the 'great event' possible.

Choosing the moments

It is not always easy to select the event that best sums up a particular historical movement or development. It is frequently not obvious, for example, which battle, if any, forms the crucial turning point in a war. And many developments take centuries. How can one select an event that characterizes them perfectly? A good example is the history of socialism and communism. Few would argue that these have not had a profound effect on our lives. In this book they are represented by the publication of the original *Communist Manifesto*, by Karl Marx and Friedrich Engels, and by the October Revolution in Russia and the Long March in China.

But it would be possible to take several different views. One could, for example, look at the history of labour relations, showing how the winning of the right to strike and to organize trade unions has been influential. To take this route, one could look at the earliest origins of organized industrial unrest. This might take us back as far as ancient Egypt, where the first recorded strike was held by workers on the tombs in the Valley of the Kings when their food supplies were delayed and their survival in the desert was threatened. Or one could recall the organization of the craft guilds in the Middle Ages. These organizations brought together large numbers of people with common interests, who frequently caused disruption to gain their ends.

However, since the ancient Egyptians are so remote in time and culture, and since the medieval guilds involved artisans and entrepreneurs more than unskilled workers, we would have to look to more recent history to find the origins of that strength in mass unity that has been the characteristic of modern trade unionism. There are still many events to choose from. Some of the strikes in England in the late 1880s could be seen as turning points, particularly the strike of the match workers in 1889. This was the one that showed a large number of unskilled workers that, powerless as they seemed as individuals, could gain great strength by acting collectively.

Quiet revolutions

So the great events of history are not always the obvious ones. Some of the most influential events have all but vanished from the visible record. We are used to thinking of battles as frequently being turning points in the history of nations. But the technological advances that changed the way battles are fought have been even more decisive than the conflicts themselves. Take the arrival in Europe, some time in the eighth century AD, of the stirrup. We do not know exactly how it arrived, though it probably came from China and Korea by way of India and Iran, and may have been introduced to Europe by Charles Martel, the grandfather of Charlemagne. We do not know who 'invented' the stirrup. But it certainly revolutionized a soldier's control over his horse, turning rider and mount into a single fighting unit and making cavalry warfare viable for the first time.

Another example is the introduction of gunpowder, apparently first used in China. Its early uses are obscure. It was once thought that the Chinese used it only for making fireworks. But recent scholarship has shown that it was probably used in weapons in the east before it reached the battlefields of Europe. It does not seem to have made a lasting impression on the warriors of China, however. So the turning point for this eastern invention could be said to have come in the west, when gunpowder was introduced into the fields of battle at Crécy and Calais in the fourteenth century.

If technological advances are important, we should also be aware that the conditions have to be right for their use. One technology that had to wait years to come into its own was food canning. The can was introduced some time before an efficient can opener, and before the social changes that made 'convenience foods' valued in the home.

7

Printing is another example. It is one of the most influential of all the technological inventions. Its importance in spreading the ideas of the Reformation and Renaissance, not to mention subsequent texts covering everything from poetry to propaganda, is obvious. Yet printing had been known for centuries before it became influential. What changed the world was Gutenberg's invention of a method of casting metal type, so that movable letters could be made in sufficient quantities to allow printing to become the force it was destined to be.

It is no accident that, like printing, many of the events described and illustrated in this book are connected with communications. The story of the way people have communicated with each other is one of the most important in history and chapters from that story rightly find a place here. From the introduction of the penny post in the nineteenth century to the invention of the television and the computer in the twentieth, such developments have changed our lives beyond recognition and will without doubt continue to do so.

Revolutions in thought

Technology has had a very tangible impact on history. Less concrete, but equally dominant, has been the influence of religion and philosophy and the established churches. From Buddhism to Islam, Christianity to Communism, these movements and institutions have provided complete world views and frameworks for great political influence. Their effect on methods of government and the attitudes of rulers, on who should govern and how, have been almost incalculably great.

In the Middle Ages, for example, the Church held the key to whole areas of life. Because education was run by the Church, everything from law to medicine, the production of books to the profession of diplomacy, was dominated by churchmen. Popes and bishops gained considerable political power and were able to compete with kings and princes for worldly power. In any case there was not the modern distinction between Church and state. In the medieval period kings ruled by the grace of God. Their political power was inextricably linked with spiritual power. Church and state were intertwined. Other cultures have seen religion and politics interact in different ways. It is well known how the tenets of Islam affect both everyday life and political policy. Less familiar in the west is the influence of Buddhism, something that was evident very early on in the history of that faith in the policies of the Indian emperor Asoka.

More recently, the influences of great social creeds have to some extent replaced those of the established religions. And so some of the important declarations of social philosophy also have a place in this book. In particular, the declaration of the Rights of Man, made in the aftermath of the French Revolution, and the publication of the *Communist Manifesto*, have been selected. The appearance of Jean-Jacques Rousseau's Social Contract or the signing of the United States Constitution might also have been chosen.

Making a choice

All history is selective. A history of 'great events', deliberately choosing decisive historical moments rather than attempting a broad, continuous narrative, is likely to be more selective than most. In concentrating on the 'great' and 'important' it can easily omit reference to the commonplace. And yet popular movements and everyday happenings are as worthy of consideration – and can be as influential – as the doings of the great and privileged. So studying great events should mean seeing the popular inspiration of movements like the Reformation, perceiving the human need behind inventions such as antisepsis, and taking on board the human effects of battles and wars.

Making an informed selection of events to cover in a book such as this also means attempting a balanced geographical coverage and a treatment that avoids the jingoistic. This book gives as much weight to the adoption of Buddhism by the Indian emperor Asoka, and to the unification of China under the First Emperor, as to events in Europe or America; it examines the spread of Islam as well as the spread of Christianity. For such events have had repercussions over centuries that affected millions of people. This book also looks at the global implications of events that happened in the west. For example, the victory of the English over the Spanish Armada had effects that went far beyond the shores of the two countries who took part in this episode.

Many other events, from the signing of Magna Carta to the storming of the Bastille, have had similar far-reaching repercussions. An event is often as significant for the way it is interpreted later as for its impact immediately after it occurs. Magna Carta itself forms a good example of this phenomenon. When it was signed, its significance was that it addressed a series of problems surrounding justice, government and social relations in medieval England – problems that badly needed to be addressed. This was important enough at the time. But in later centuries Magna Carta became a rallying point for many who campaigned on behalf of democracy and the universal accessibility of justice. So it is not fanciful to claim that an event that took place in thirteenth-century England could influence thinking in seventeenth-century Europe and America.

But when all is said and done, it is still easy to be aware of the omissions in a book such as this. Our coverage of the arts, for example, could have been much broader. For the great works of imaginative literature and the canvases of the world's most important artists have done as much, if not more, to shape our view of the world than rulers and politicians. The works of the great composers, too, while their effect has been much more abstract, have shaped our civilizations in unique ways. But our selection would have had to be ruthless, and we have decided to focus our attention mainly on events from the world of action.

Reaching a conclusion

What can we learn from this patchwork of events? Historians sometimes say that the only lesson of history is that we can learn nothing from history. Every situation is different and it is naive to propose simple parallels between happenings in the past and those today. It is naive, for example, to draw direct comparisons between the rulers of ancient Rome and those of modern Europe, or between politicians of Machiavelli's era and our own. There are similarities, to be sure, but these should not blind us to the different orbits within which these different groups of people move.

Indeed, the events of our own time can be even more difficult to interpret than those of the more distant past. It is still too early to judge the final consequences of the recent revolutions in central and eastern Europe, although they find a place in this book as a pointer to the future. As for another recent 'great event', the war in the Gulf, it is too early to assess even the details of the way the conflict was fought, let alone to guess the final effects in the Middle East.

And yet any serious study of the past tells us more about humanity and the way people behave, and this must contribute to our understanding of our contemporaries. What is more, we live in an age when we are becoming increasingly aware of the need to understand and respect our environment. Our past is as much a part of that environment as the present – it is an essential part of our humanity. We preserve the buildings of the past and visit them for enjoyment and to learn what life was like when they were first built. To think about the great events of the past, finding out what lay behind them and what their effects have been, is to undertake a similar journey, and to come a little closer to an understanding of ourselves.

ASOKA AND THE RISE OF THE MAURYAN EMPIRE

The unification of India and the spread of Buddhism

The Indian subcontinent has a long history as the home of civilization. The Indus Valley culture, represented by the cities of Mohenjo-daro and Harappa, flourished between 2500 and 1500 BC as the home of burgeoning agriculture, successful trade, and a sophisticated urban culture. After the downfall of these great cities, India went into something of a dark age. Some 1,000 years after the fall of the Indus civilization city life began to develop again, and northern India alone contained about sixteen separate states, mostly based around rich cities near the Ganges. There is little documentary evidence about these places, although we do know that the number of states was reduced to four during the following century, and finally to one – the state of Magadha – as northern India moved towards an uneasy unity.

Then the subcontinent's first great conqueror, Alexander the Great, appeared on the scene. The Macedonian leader arrived in the north in 327 BC, via the Indian provinces of the Persian Empire, which he was taking over. He took the city of Takshashila, known to the Greeks as Taxila, and continued a two-year campaign. He worked his way across the Punjab, but his soldiers refused to continue, so he went back down the Indus to the sea, and returned home via Babylon.

Alexander died young and, although he left Greek governors in India, they did not stay long – his conquests did not have a lasting effect on the country. But within India there was soon to appear a dynasty that would make a much more lasting impression. These were the descendants of Chandragupta Maurya, who came to the throne of Magadha in 321 BC. From the lands around the Ganges, Chandragupta moved west to take over the lands that Alexander's governors had left behind, before moving down to central India and occupying the lands immediately north of the River Narmada.

Chandragupta left his son Bindusara an

Stone head of Buddha, circa 200 BC

extensive kingdom when he died in 297 BC. And Bindusara built on his father's conquests, bringing almost the entire subcontinent into Mauryan control by the time of his own death in 272 BC. The only area that did not bow to his control was Kalinga, on the east coast of the Bay of Bengal. It was left to Bindusara's son, Asoka, to add this area to his empire.

Asoka was thus the first person to rule over practically the entire area we now know as India. Even though his empire did not last, this was a remarkable achievement. He set up a capital at Pataliputra on the Ganges, a large city that was well defended with wooden ramparts. And his empire thrived as be built up trading links with his neighbours and built roads along which his merchants could travel. But this success was not the only reason for Asoka's importance. Another is simply that we know a great deal about him. He was very good at leaving inscriptions about himself at prominent points around his kingdom, and his contact with Greek kingdoms such as the neighbouring Seleucid Empire meant that foreign writers have also left us information about Asoka's India. But most important of all, his conversion to Buddhism and his support

of the Buddhist faith set a trend that was to continue for centuries.

The position of Buddhism

Gautama Buddha, the young prince who left his leisured life for the way of asceticism, who sought the meaning of life and found nirvana under a pipal tree in the sixth century BC, was at first the inspiration of a relatively obscure sect. But at some point during the reign of Asoka, Buddhism became a prominent faith with a growing following spread far and wide. There is little doubt that Asoka was in many ways connected with its success.

To begin with, Buddhism was a somewhat disorganized movement. The primary duty of the followers of the Buddha was to seek their own enlightenment, not to encourage others to join the faith or to create the structure of a closely unified church. Poor communications encouraged this lack of unity. So there were numerous sects or schools within Buddhism existing side by side.

During the reign of Asoka, the Buddhists came together in their famous Third Council. At this meeting the important Theravada school of Buddhists elbowed out the dissidents, made strong efforts to remove corruption and attempted to unify the faith. They also embarked on a campaign of proselytizing.

According to some traditions, Asoka himself was behind these changes. The emperor is portrayed as the person behind its sudden flowering and spread across the subcontinent he ruled. Sadly, however, there is no actual documentary evidence for this. We would expect to find such a fact commemorated on the inscriptions set up by Asoka, but it is not. Yet there can be little doubt that the emperor encouraged the new development. He would be glad to see his new-found religion being adopted all the way across India – apart from anything else it would help to bind his people together.

Asoka's Buddhism

What do the documentary sources tell us about the emperor's faith? Much weight is given to his conversion, which is said to have taken place suddenly after the battle of Kalinga. This battle gave him the area of eastern India that took his empire to its greatest extent. In common with many propagandistic accounts of rulers throughout history, Asoka's response to his new faith is given in exaggerated terms. We are told that he undertook to build 84,000 stupas, or shrines, as well as embarking on a remarkable series of pilgrimages. Such claims are not necessarily credible today, but they show how important the faith was to Asoka and his ministers. They also indicate what a remarkable expansion there must have been at the time.

The inscriptions are also put into perspective when the many philosophical statements of Asoka are examined. For his relationship to Buddhism was not just to do with political propaganda. He tells the faithful how they should behave, and the vices they should give up (cruelty, laziness, hastiness, and so on) in order to attain heavenly bliss. And he tells how important it is for him that even the lowly of his empire should be free from taint and attain endless happiness.

As time went on Asoka acquired the qualities of a sage, someone with the power to lead others to heavenly bliss and to cause others to see extraordinary and supernatural visions (celestial chariots and heavenly processions). He was attaining a quasi god-like state, something which rulers are wont to claim but which in Asoka seems to have been particularly effective and powerful.

Buddhism, Dhamma and Asoka's rule

This special status had a particular value for Asoka. It enabled him to have a spiritual as well as a governmental influence, and the sort of spiritual teaching Asoka espoused was especially relevant to his political role, so one aspect of his personality fed off the other. Asoka's teaching revolved around the idea of Dhamma. This is a word with many meanings, from the concept of a universal law of righteousness to that of a social order. The concept was left intentionally vague since India was already a melting pot of different religious beliefs. If Asoka was to unify his empire he had to offer a philosophy that would appeal to as many of these as possible. But there can be little doubt that Dhamma was closely connected with Buddhism.

So the most important principle that Asoka laid down was that of toleration – both of other people and of their beliefs.

Mauryan lion symbol

Non-violence was another essential virtue – and this extended from a disapproval of unnecessary force in dealing with people to a restraint on killing animals. In common with Asoka's flexibility and tolerance, violence was not banned completely – there were circumstances in which violence would be necessary. But in any battle clemency was a prime virtue.

The concept of Dhamma extended into the area of social policy and planning. Asoka was proud that he had built and maintained an effective network of roads, constructing rest houses and watering places on the main roads for the benefit of travellers. He planted many trees to give shade. He had wells dug and initiated irrigation projects. He ran mines and manufacturing industries, and his government gave money to individuals and monasteries. Such actions gave the policy of Dhamma a tangible quality, making it concrete even for those who could not read Asoka's inscriptions on the subject.

In line with the missionary zeal that had become part of Buddhism since the Third Council, Asoka also publicized his policy of Dhamma with enthusiasm. First of all, there were the inscriptions themselves – on rocks overlooking the roads and on pillars in public places where they would readily be seen by a great number of passers-by. Next, officials were instructed in Dhamma. These men were given extensive powers to put the policy into practice and were told to teach any person who wanted to know about the emperor's policy of Dhamma.

The officers of Dhamma also took the word of the emperor beyond the formal boundaries of Asoka's empire. This was clearly in the Mauryan interest since tolerant, non-violent neighbours were less likely to be a threat to the borders of the empire. And thanks to this policy, the borders of the Mauryan Empire stayed relatively stable for the thirty-seven years of Asoka's reign.

Administering the empire

No empire the size of Asoka's could succeed without an efficient system of government and administration. In the Mauryan period the emperor held supreme power, but a council of ministers assisted him in government, advising him and discussing policy with him. Principal among the ministers was the chief priest.

Perhaps more important than the ministers were the administrative officers of the empire. These were led by the Chief Collector and Treasurer whose job it was to collect and account for all the income and taxes that came in from the whole empire. These officials had an extensive staff, including local officers. There were many departments looking after the revenue from areas as diverse as passports and prostitution, armour and agriculture.

This network of officials was very important to Asoka, both because they provided him with his wealth and because they forged a link between local and central government. Such a link was vital in a large empire, and the financial basis for it meant that Asoka could keep quite tight control of the provinces of his empire. But this system cost him dearly. For one thing, the officials were extremely well paid. Romila Thapar, the author of one history of India, has noted that a senior official earned an astonishing ninety-six times as much as a clerk. Such a system must have put a lot of strain on the revenue it was designed to collect.

Another weakness, and perhaps the greatest one, in Asoka's system of government was that it was too centralized. The senior officials were appointed by the emperor, and these senior officials were responsible for choosing their juniors, and so on down the hierarchy. A change of ruler therefore meant a change of top officials and this could easily mean change throughout each tier of the administration. The chances for continuity were only favourable when, as in the case of Asoka, an emperor ruled for a relatively long period.

There was another weakness in the system which seems to contradict the first. In spite of the centralization, the power of local officials was often very great indeed. The Mauryans did have a system based, like that of many early empires, on an extensive network of spies, to limit this power. But in a large empire with (for all Asoka's road-building) poor communications this only had a very limited effect. Briefly and simply, the strength and continuity of the Mauryan Empire relied much more than anything else on the strength, personality and longevity of the ruling emperor himself.

The contemplative expression on the face of the Buddha was an important presence in the Mauryan Empire in the time of Asoka. Buddhism helped Asoka to unite his empire. It also proved to be one of the most influential religions in the continent of Asia for centuries afterwards.

After Asoka

Asoka was an exceptional ruler. He owed his power to military conquest and yet was able credibly to renounce violence, to accept the tenets of Buddhism, and yet still to hold on to his power. Unlike the Buddha himself, who withdrew from the world of affairs, Asoka kept his grip on the state. For almost forty years he kept India stable in a way that that country has seldom known.

Asoka's empire broke up after his death. Areas such as Kalinga in the east and Andra in central India once more became separate kingdoms. Nomads from central Asia and Greeks from Bactria and Parthia invaded from the north. Rulers of Greek and Scythian origins also took over parts of central India, often taking up Sanskrit names and the local religion in order to give themselves credibility. The desire for greater unity in India did survive Asoka. The territories of later rulers such as Chandragupta II (AD 375–414), though not as extensive as Asoka's and confined mainly to the north, show some of the same aspirations.

But Asoka's influence was most important because of his Buddhism. The missionary zeal which he inspired and the officials he sent out to the borders to spread the policy of Dhamma led to the spread of Buddhist ideas and the Buddhist faith across northern India. Buddhism also moved outwards to Ceylon, Burma and Thailand, and towards the Kushan kingdom in the area we now know as Afghanistan. The development of Buddhism in the latter area was towards a more popular, even more widely attractive faith which, by the first century AD, had reached China. Trade routes like the Silk Road carried the faith still further in the north. Most of these developments owe their origins to the early flowering of Buddhism under Asoka.

ACCESSION OF THE FIRST CHINESE EMPEROR

The unification of China and the building of the Great Wall

China has not always been the vast, unified state that it is today. Although Chinese history can be traced back for many centuries in terms of the different dynasties, these influential families have rarely ruled over the entire mass of land that we now call China. During the seventeenth century BC, for example, the Shang or Yin dynasty came to prominence as a considerable political power based on a royal city in the northeastern part of the country. The Shang expanded through a vast geographical area, and to them the Chinese owed some of the hallmarks of their early culture – writing, bronzeworking, the use of wheeled transport and a strong political structure.

The Western and Eastern Chou dynasties were also considerable powers during the period between the end of the eleventh century and the fifth century BC. But, as their names suggest, these dynasties were limited geographically. At the end of the Eastern Chou period (481 BC) China was divided between a group of warring states: the Qin, Wei, Chao, Yen, Ch'i, Chu, Han and Sung. The Qin held one of the largest territories of these states in western China and, by means of a series of conquests, began to push westwards, annexing the lands of the other states, particularly the Ch'i (the other power holding extensive lands) in the south. By 221 BC the whole of China was unified under the Ch'in.

The person who presided over this success and set the pattern for Chinese unity in years to come was the ruler Shih Huang Ti, whose name means simply 'the First Emperor'. With his adviser, Li Su, the First Emperor realized that, in order to maintain the unity he had achieved by force, he would have to impose some far-reaching reforms on the country. Standardization of money, currency, weights and measures and cart sizes (so that the contents did not have to be continually unloaded and weighed), were among the most important of these unifying reforms.

The First Emperor also built the Great Wall of China, joining together various stretches of existing barriers to make the largest fortification ever conceived. The wall kept out the northern nomads who were perpetually threatening any Chinese frontier in that part of the country. It also kept the Chinese people within their borders, reducing the likelihood of fraternization between the Chinese people and their neighbours. This policy weakened any opposition within the country to the First Emperor's power.

The resettlement of large numbers of

The Great Wall of China

people in the south and near the wall was another policy intended to have this effect, breaking up potential opposition to the emperor. Shih Huang Ti was ruthless when it came to suppressing opposition. There are many stories about the large numbers of workers who died during the building of the Great Wall. Intellectuals were also treated brutally: many were buried alive for their views.

These were sweeping policies of great – if ruthless – vision. The building of the Great Wall involved a labour force of thousands and extraordinary logistical

problems of getting men and materials to the border, particularly in the mountain regions. The resettlement policy was also on a scale that was amazing for the time. And the reforms of weights, measures and currency must have needed formidable organization to bring into effect. These achievements were very impressive. They also led to the deaths of a great number of innocent people.

Such a ruthless regime could not last. It died with the emperor who inspired it. And, ironically, the First Emperor is now remembered above all else for his death – in particular his astonishing tomb at Mount Li with its terracotta army. But if the vast Chinese state that he created could not be held together, the First Emperor at least set the pattern for the large Chinese empires that were to continue long into the future. And some of the changes he made had effects beyond those he intended. For example, the standardizations in coinage and weights and measures were brought in mainly to unify the emperor's territories. But they also encouraged trade, which in turn fostered China's contacts with her neighbours, something of which the First Emperor would not have approved. Trade routes across Asia towards Europe developed and the setting up of colonies and trading posts meant that the influence of China was, by the Han period (202 BC to AD 220), felt right across Asia. China's power and influence grew in a way that the First Emperor could not have foreseen.

The First Emperor is shown against the background of the Great Wall, the structure for which he is remembered and which symbolized the strength and unity of China during his reign. In fact the Great Wall was probably much less elaborate in the time of the First Emperor. Subsequent rulers extended Shih Huang Ti's fortifications and made them more sophisticated.

DEATH OF JULIUS CAESAR

A transformation of the Roman power structure

It is ironic that the most famous son of the Roman Empire is remembered above all for his death. But his life was nothing if not eventful. Gaius Julius Caesar was born into the patrician (aristocratic) class in about 100 BC, a time when the Roman republic was in crisis. As a result of the Second Punic War, the Italian peasantry had been left poor and dispossessed. The governing class was reviled and there was a series of revolts and counter-measures which left the republic demoralized. Meanwhile, the nobility themselves, continually vying for power and office, lacked the unity to pull the republic together. It seemed that the only chance for reform lay with some new system, probably led by someone with autocratic power.

Julius Caesar was the person destined briefly to play this role. He began his career by steadily climbing the political ladder from one public office to the next, very much as one might expect an ambitious young Roman politician to do. The path led from the office of quaestor (held by Caesar in 69–68 BC), to his eventually being elected a praetor for the year 62, governor of Farther Spain for 61–60, and consul for 59. During his period of consulship he moved quickly to form the first triumvirate – the governing trio comprised of himself, Pompey and Crassus – in the same year.

The following years saw Caesar's achievements as a general, with his conquest of Gaul, bringing numerous small states under Roman control. These conquests, which Caesar himself described in his books on the Gallic Wars, greatly increased his power. They gave him wealth and – most important – the potential to raise still larger armies.

This increased military power was invaluable to Caesar in the following years. Between 56 and 45 BC he had to deal with opponents at home and abroad. He embarked on a civil war with Pompey, famously crossing the river Rubicon in 49 BC from his territory in Cisalpine Gaul to Italy, to open the hostilities. This was as much a conflict about how Rome should be governed as a personal dispute between the two men. Caesar saw himself as the single person with enough power to successfully unite Rome together. He was vigorous and unstinting in pursuing this goal. As a result, he was elected Dictator for ten years and given the office of Prefect of Morals – a position that gave him control over almost every aspect of Roman life for three years. He had managed to garner supreme power for himself.

Gaius Julius Caesar

But this power was threatened. Enemies abroad occupied much of Caesar's time. He had to crush opponents in Spain, Anatolia and North Africa. Yet Caesar was not ruthless with all his enemies. At home, particularly, he was merciful to many opponents. This proved a weakness since there were many left to plot against him. The conspiracy resulted in the assassination of Julius Caesar on 15 March (the Ides of March) 44 BC.

The killing took place in the Senate House. So famous was the death of this most celebrated of Romans that it is not surprising it has been surrounded by myths. Spurinna, the soothsayer, is supposed to have told Caesar to beware the Ides of March. Caesar's wife, Calpurnia, is said to have had nightmares the night before; and the ceremonial armour of Mars, which Caesar as Pontifex Maximus kept in his house, was supposed to have fallen from the wall with a terrifying crash. Doctors and soothsayers advised Caesar not to go to the Senate that day.

The conspirators sent Brutus to persuade Caesar to go to the Senate, which, in spite of the inauspicious auguries, he did. The conspirators, acting like petitioners begging favours of Caesar, stood around him in a semicircle and stabbed him repeatedly – twenty-three stab wounds were later counted on his body. His last words 'And you too, my child!' were addressed to Brutus, whose career he had fostered, and whom he finally recognised as one of the conspirators.

Julius Caesar's brief life saw a transformation of the power of Rome. His reforms spread from the top of Roman society (which would henceforth be ruled by an emperor, but which would also have a larger and more representative senate) to the bottom (he resettled the proletariat and his discharged soldiers). He swept away much of the power of the nobility, giving the empire new stability – it was to last some 400 years in the west, still longer in the east. And he spread the influence of Rome far and wide, bringing Roman civilization to Gaul in the north and spreading Hellenism in the east. The death of Caesar came just late enough to ensure that his influence could live on in his empire.

The most famous murder in the ancient world took place on 15 March 44 BC. It brought to an end the life of one of Rome's most successful rulers.

DEATH OF JESUS CHRIST

The execution that inspired the Christian faithful

The death of Jesus Christ is an event that is familiar to us from the accounts in the Gospels – and indeed from mentions in Roman historians such as Tacitus. It is of such importance for Christians that it is often assumed that, when it happened, it sent shockwaves across the world. But this was not so. The Crucifixion happened in a far corner of the Roman Empire and concerned what was then an obscure cult involving only a few adherents.

What happened to change this state of affairs? The Bible tells us that after the crucifixion and the death of Judas Iscariot, the eleven remaining apostles, together with Matthias, who had been chosen to replace Judas, were brought to trial. They were accused of preaching the life, death and resurrection of Christ. They offended the Sanhedrin, the guardians of Jewish law, by saying that they had to obey God rather than men, and that the Holy Spirit spoke directly to them.

The result was that the apostles were beaten, ordered not to preach again in Christ's name, and released. Afterwards, the Bible tells us, the apostles continued to preach, basing their work on the city of Jerusalem and predicting the return of Christ to herald the kingdom of heaven. They set themselves apart from their contemporaries in this belief in the return of Christ and their conviction that with him a new era had dawned. They were also distinguished by their ceremonies of baptism and the breaking of the bread at communal meals.

From its small base in Palestine the new faith, not initially referred to as Christianity, began to spread around the Jewish communities of the Mediterranean. As well as Galileans and Judaeans, new converts came from the ranks of Greek-speaking Hellenist Jews. These people were to play a major part in preaching the faith. Spread around the eastern provinces of the Roman Empire, they were already used to sustaining their law and their way of life in a hostile environment. As the mission of Christ's original followers spread its influence, communities of followers grew up in many of the cities of the eastern empire – such as Damascus, Antioch and Alexandria – before the faith spread to Rome itself.

At first, these early followers of Christ were either Jews who observed the laws of the Torah regarding ritual and diet, or non-Jews who did the same. But some of the early missionaries, including the influential St Paul, preferred to eliminate these obligations, making the faith more attractive to non-Jews. The final separation of Judaism and Christianity came in around AD 70, when the Jews were in revolt against Rome. The Romans destroyed the church at Jerusalem and at the end of the war the Jewish loyalists took a heroic last stand at the fortress of Masada in the Judaean desert. The Romans captured the fortress and some 1,000 Jews took their own lives.

In his *Annals* the historian Tacitus (AD 51–117) gives the Roman point of view of the Roman reception of the Christians during the reign of Nero. The emperor 'charged and tortured some people hated for their evil practices – the group known as "Christians". The founder of this sect, Christ, had been put to death by the governor of Judaea, Pontius Pilate, when Tiberius was emperor. Their deadly superstition had been suppressed temporarily, but was beginning to spring up again, not just in Judaea but even in Rome itself, where all kinds of sordid and shameful activities…catch on.'

There is a hint here that Tacitus was noticing a phenomenon that often occurs when a set of beliefs meets with widespread disapproval. Burn a book and it begins a flourishing life underground. Kill a religious leader and he becomes a martyr around whose memory the faithful will rally. Christ's opponents unwittingly connived in the success of Christianity.

By the time the emperor Constantine converted to Christianity and made it the religion of the empire, the faith was established as a gentile phenomenon and had spread further. But it was still a marginal faith that seemed unlikely to become one of the major religions of the world. If the death of Christ did not inspire an immediate expansion of the Christian religion, it was certainly influential in other ways. Above all, it emphasized the cruelty of the opponents of Christianity, to which the new religion opposed an ethic of gentleness and compassion even in the face of violence exemplified by Christ's doctrine of 'turning the other cheek'.

The Crucifixion also served to bring home to Christians the essential humanity of Christ during his time on earth. He could suffer just like ordinary mortals, a fact which perhaps had not been obviously demonstrated during much of his life but which the gruesome manner of his death made very clear. And so the Crucifixion became the Christian symbol of God's own sacrifice: Christ was sacrificed in order that humanity might be saved. As such, the Crucifixion has remained a potent, if at times disturbing, symbol. It became a recurrent subject in Christian art, a focal point in countless churches, an icon to be set up in the home or worn in the form of jewellery. Even in today's secularized world, it remains recognizable.

We do not know for sure exactly how the Romans crucified their victims. The exact shape and construction of the cross is unknown – and in any case varied from one crucifixion to the next. The bodies would have had to be supported in some way, either by being tied to the cross or by resting on a wooden ledge, otherwise the nails would have simply torn through the flesh and bone. But however it was actually done, crucifixion was a gruesome form of execution that has long inspired sympathy for the victims.

THE CONVERSION OF CONSTANTINE

The spread of Christianity through the Roman Empire

Christianity spread quite rapidly after the death of Christ. Before AD 38 it was already established at Antioch and Damascus and it had reached Asia Minor by AD 45. In another five or six years the faith would also be established at Corinth and at Rome. This was due to enthusiastic missionary work, most famously by the apostle Paul. But the spread of the Christianity was not without incident – public disorder followed Paul on his journeys, and if the early church was often persecuted, this was usually because the local authorities wanted to restore law and order.

As the stability of the Roman Empire was increasingly thrown off balance, the Christians seemed to some of the emperors and their military leaders to pose a more fundamental threat. Persecution became more widespread, more legitimized, and more severe. Christians from the farther reaches of the empire were thrown to the beasts; those from Rome itself were beheaded.

Such a state of affairs was understandable, but it did not bring about the unity the authorities hoped for. For one thing, the Christians alone were not responsible for the divisions in the empire; for another they were traditionally loyalists anyway. Even so, the turning point in the fortunes of Christianity must have come as a surprise to most Christians. Early in the fourth century no less a person than Emperor Constantine the Great converted to the faith and proclaimed religious toleration.

Constantine was an exceptional emperor. He it was who finally set the pattern for the divided empire, with its second capital at Constantinople, the city named after him. He was a successful general, with a string of victories to his name and a streamlined army that made much use of troops from his Germanic and Frankish territories. And he streamlined the

Gold coin of Constantine the Great

government of the empire too, increasing the number of officials but decreasing their chances of creating a rival power-base to his own.

The new religion

Roman historians give us a dramatic account of Constantine's conversion to Christianity. Important as this was to the emperor himself, it was less important to history than the way in which Christianity could fit into Roman society. Clearly, the moment of the new religion had come. The units of local government were by this time small enough to become sees – each the headquarters of a bishop. The way in which the emperor himself had been worshipped and the ceremonies that had been adopted at his court could easily be altered to accommodate the worship of the Christian God. And in the basilica, the Romans had an architectural form – a rectangular hall with aisles – which would serve well as a basis for church design in the ensuing centuries. What was more, the fact that Christianity had already spread around the northern and eastern Mediterranean meant that there

were established churches and practices (such as the regular holding of meetings known as synods) which gave the newly legalized church a platform on which to build.

From Constantine's point of view, when freedom of worship was proclaimed in AD 313, the new faith helped to draw together an empire that was threatening to disintegrate. But he remained an emperor in the traditional Roman mould. There is no evidence that he valued greatly what we now see as the Christian virtues of humility or brotherly love, or that he was interested in God's mercy or man's sin. But Constantine did encourage the spread of the faith, even if he had to do this by actively discouraging paganism. In the end the burden of persecution was turned the other way and the internal splits of the church meant that it was far less of an effective force for unity than the emperor wished.

Christianity was not a cure-all for the ailing empire. Rome was falling anyway. But the long-term legacy of Constantine had repercussions that have lasted until the present. Christian Europe began when a vast tract of the continent was admitted to the faith and given the power to organize the church. Many of the turning-points of history described in this book, and many of our attitudes in the west today, stem from Constantine's decision.

The conversion to Christianity of the world's most important ruler represented a great step forward for the followers of Jesus Christ. What had been a minor cult became an accepted religion. It was not until later that the effects of Constantine's reign would be felt. His decision to divide the empire allowed the eastern part to live on after the fall of Rome. The Christianity of the eastern empire became the dominant religion for hundreds of years.

FALL OF ROME

The end of a unified Europe under a single emperor

In AD 410 the Visigoths, having established footholds around the western Roman Empire, captured Rome itself. Although the great city was no longer the capital of the western empire (this distinction belonged in turn to Ravenna and Milan), the loss of Rome, the establishment of the Visigoths in southern Gaul and Spain, the setting up of a kingdom of the Vandals in northern Africa and Sicily, and invasions by the Huns from the Danube basin in 451 changed western Europe for good. From this time on the Roman empire lived on only in the east, ruled from its capital at Constantinople.

Why did the mighty power of the Roman empire give in to attack from apparently minor forces from outside? It is a question about which entire libraries have been written: here only a few of the possible reasons can be suggested.

We are used to hearing of the peoples whose arrival precipitated the fall of Rome as 'invading barbarians'. Yet in many cases they did not have to invade: the Germanic peoples were already there, serving the imperial army. The problems in the army, indeed, made up one of the major causes of the fall of Rome. In theory, the empire had a large and well organized army of almost half a million men. In fact, this figure was unequally divided between a frontier force and a much smaller and more mobile elite fighting unit. Moreover the army was not as big as it might have been. Regular conscription was not enforced properly. Evasion of military service by self-mutilation (the amputation of thumbs, and so on) was not uncommon. And many people exempted themselves by paying for soldiers to be 'bought into' the army. Large numbers of these mercenaries came from Germany: a poem in praise of Emperor Constantine says: 'Your Rhine furnishes you with armies.'

Although the army offered an interesting career to Roman and German alike, the soldiers of the emperor were far from contented. Pay was poor. Even the soldier-emperor Septimus Severus, who was criticized for excessive generosity to his troops, was probably only bringing their pay up to an acceptable level.

And yet the army did have great power. Every emperor needed the support of the army to rule and this meant that the generals in particular were often influential when it came to promoting and supporting a new candidate for the imperial throne. And of course it was tempting for generals to put themselves forward for the title. During one period of 150 years before the reign of Constantine the Great, some eighty generals were put forward as emperor at different times. Such threats to imperial power divided the empire and led to civil unrest that weakened Rome's ability to defend itself from outside. The emperors depended on the generals, but despaired of ever being able to use them effectively to defend their own interests.

Since the late emperors were so

Coin of Alaric the Visigoth

vulnerable, it is not surprising that they cut themselves off in a rather defensive way from the empire that they were trying to rule. The late emperors had large and sycophantic courts which indulged in elaborate ceremonies. They relied on propaganda (much of which appeared as slogans on their coins) to bolster their position as much as on real power.

Shifting the capital to Ravenna in northeastern Italy did nothing to make the court more accessible. The emperor Honorius had moved there in 402, precisely because his capital at Milan had been attacked by the Visigoths. He chose Ravenna because it was surrounded on three sides by swamps and on the fourth by the sea. Almost as inhospitable to the court as to invaders, it allowed him to stay aloof and protected.

If the generals held and abused great power, so too did another class, the lawyers and bureaucrats. By the time of the fall of Rome, the civil service was huge and powerful. This large bureaucracy was essential: the Roman Empire was vast and diverse. But the civil service had a hereditary appointments system, which meant that the best candidates for officialdom were unlikely to be selected. On the other hand, there was continuity, and the Roman civil service was responsible for maintaining the status quo, if for nothing else. The legal system was little better. Many laws were passed and many imperial pronouncements were made. But these have a repetitive air that suggests they were neither enforced nor obeyed. Together with an unhealthy dose of corruption, such problems must have made the empire almost impossible to run effectively.

The ordinary people

How did the population of the empire

respond to these changes and deteriorations? This is a vast question, but a few broad answers can be suggested. There can be little doubt that ordinary people were alienated from the classes above them and from the emperor. This was not a simple matter of the emperor and his court being secluded at Ravenna. The people of the empire were hit where it hurt hardest – in the purse. They were subjected to high taxes in order to pay for the army. Their cash was further depleted by inflation, a tendency that the authorities fuelled by issuing more and more bronze coinage as a temporary solution, a coinage which only became worth less and less. The rural poor payed taxes on land; they also had to pay taxes in the form of produce, losing much of the grain they had worked so hard to grow.

The people also had to pay by service, donating their labour on imperial projects from the maintaining of roads and bridges to the felling of trees for timber. If the poor were discontented, it was hardly surprising. Valentinian, probably the shrewdest of the late emperors, instituted a scheme in which officials called 'Defenders of the People' were appointed in every town. They were empowered to deal with grievances. It was a brave scheme, but its chances of success were ruined by subsequent rulers who gave the city councillors (who collected the taxes) the power to appoint their own Defenders of the People. The old corruption reasserted itself.

It is not surprising that many people dropped out of conventional society altogether. Banditry was common, and in some areas, such as Gaul, outlaws organized themselves into nationalist movements, posing a real threat to the power of the empire. This was not the only way to 'escape' from society. In the era after Constantine, monasticism became an increasingly attractive way of life. Churchmen such as Jerome and Augustine did much to popularize the monastic movement in their writings. Monasticism was never a truly 'escapist' solution. Augustine, for example, laid stress on the importance of manual work in the monk's life. Yet it can be argued that simply by removing so many able-bodied males from society and making celibacy fashionable the fund of potential soldiers was once more being depleted – leading to still greater reliance on people from outside and on the taxes that were needed to pay them.

The middle classes

The backbone of the Roman Empire was its cities. From here came the middle classes, who provided the men to run the civil service and the law. The cities also defined much of Roman culture. And they were centres of power from which outlying areas could be controlled.

But after the wave of invasions during the third century, the cities were left in disrepair. It became the main concern of city people to rebuild their walls and look after their own interests. These developments had two important effects. They turned the city people away from Rome; and they meant that in any case, with the cities in decline, the actual numbers of the middle classes fell, leading to a polarization of society into rich and poor with few in between. Neither of these effects was good for the unity of the empire.

The upper classes

The Roman senate was the body most representative of the upper classes. It was very large (4,000 people divided equally between the east and the west) and many of its members were very rich both in terms of property and cash. And, although they were supposed to play a part in government, they frequently did not, preferring to sit back and enjoy their wealth, taxing their tenants heavily to pay their own dues. Many of these men saw their main priority to be hanging on to their own wealth. But this did not necessarily mean maintaining the imperial status quo. They were just as likely to get on with the Visigoths and Vandals when they became the ruling class.

Broader divisions

It was at once a great strength and a great weakness that the Roman Empire had been divided into two. It made sense to rule such a large empire from two separate centres. Apart from helping to run an area of such size, the split also helped when a ruler died: there would always be continuity in the other half of the empire, providing some stability until the succession had been confirmed.

But there were frequent political differences between the two halves, and they often did not come to each others' aid when they were attacked. When border disputes took up the attention of the eastern army, for example, they could not or did not rush to the help of the west when there was an uprising in Gaul. Sometimes there was active hostility between the two halves of the empire. This happened when Emperor Honorius died, leaving his two young sons and their guardians Stilicho and Rufinus in charge of the divided realm. Stilicho was convinced that it was his right to care for both of Honorius' sons, and thus to reunite the empire. Such a bid for power only weakened the empire, allowing Alaric the Visigoth to create a power-base in Greece.

Another division in the empire was religious. Rome was officially Christian, but Christianity was still the religion of a minority. Because state and church worked closely together, the state could

Military forces played a crucial part in the fall of Rome. Combats between the empire and the 'barbarian' peoples who were to take over involved some of the most powerful armies in the world, and the conflicts could be bloody. But it was not a simple matter of Roman fighting barbarian. For one thing, the Roman army itself contained soldiers from the dependent territories of Rome. For another, even key commanders and imperial advisers were often 'barbarians'. So the battles were as frequently struggles in the realm of power politics as they were campaigns on the battlefield.

△1 Huns
△2 Visigoths/Ostrogoths
△3 Vandals
△4 Franks
△5 Jutes/Angles/Saxons

Roman Empire
AD 400–500

coerce people to become Christian, a movement that was the ancestor of numerous inquisitions and religious coercions in the medieval period and beyond. The implications for Rome were gloomy. Religious coercion only divided the people; the new prosperity of the church did not help the wealth of the state; and the message of Christianity in any case tended to devalue the temporal, so that Christians – with certain notable exceptions – tended not to be overly concerned with the problems of the empire.

With so many influences threatening the unity of such a large empire, there is perhaps little wonder that the emperors missed the opportunity to integrate the Ostrogoths, Visigoths, Huns and other peoples waiting to step into their shoes. The number of Germanic people in the Roman army, and the power of men such as Stilicho, showed how much these people were part of the society of the empire before the fall of Rome. Many of these people were highly Romanized and willing to share power with the citizens of Rome. Instead, with the empire breaking up in disunity, they seized power by more violent means, and divided up Europe between them.

THE BEGINNINGS OF ISLAM

The start of a religion that would change the lives of millions

In the twentieth century about one sixth of the world's population are followers of Islam. The Islamic nations are among the most influential in world politics. It is the youngest of the great religions of the world, its prophet Muhammad being born in the seventh century AD.

Muhammad was born into the tribe of Quraysh who, by the time of his birth, had settled in and around Mecca. Mecca, situated in a barren valley some fifty miles inland from the Red Sea in what is now Saudi Arabia, relied for its prosperity on trade. Merchants of Quraysh travelled widely from Mecca and had trading agreements with Persia, Yemen, Ethiopia and the Roman Empire. Muhammad's father died before he was born, and Muhammad was placed with foster parents. His mother died when he was six years old. As a young man he gained employment from a rich widow for whom he acted as agent in her trade with Syria. So successful was he that she eventually married him.

Revelations to the Prophet

It was a common religious custom in Muhammad's time to spend one month on Mount Hira each year. It was during one such visit that the event was to happen that changed Muhammad's life and, eventually, the lives of millions of others. One night Muhammad was visited in his sleep by the angel Gabriel who began to reveal to him the series of fragments that were to make up the Islamic scripture, the Koran. This was the first of a sequence of revelations during which the principles, rituals and morality of Islam were explained.

Islam is a monotheistic religion: there is one god, Allah, and Muhammad is his prophet. Muhammad is therefore seen as the final member of a group of prophets stretching from Adam, Noah, Abraham and Moses, through Jesus, to Muhammad. The first four figures play similar roles to those they have in the Old Testament; Jesus is portrayed as God's messenger

Koranic script representing the one God

rather than his son, although in other respects most of the details of his life are similar to those given in the New Testament. The God of Islam is all-powerful and all-knowing. All believers must submit to God: the literal translation of Muslim is 'one who submits'; Islam means 'submission to the will of God'.

The Koran also establishes the rituals of Islam. The faithful are to make themselves ritually clean by washing. They are to pray five times each day. They are to give alms. They should fast between dawn and sunset for one month (the month of Ramadan) each year. They should undertake the pilgrimage to Mecca.

These precepts were written down in the Koran, which was a record of the things the Prophet said (or that God said through the Prophet) when he was visited by the angel Gabriel. The word Koran means 'recitation'. The sayings were written down piecemeal as they occurred, on any materials that came to hand – from stones and palm leaves to fragments of pottery – and collected together later. But in spite of what was to begin with a rather haphazard approach to the actual recording of the words spoken through the Prophet, the words themselves have remained an inspiration for millions.

Islam did not spread immediately. To begin with it was a faith shared by Muhammad and members of his family. But after about three years, God ordered his prophet to make his religion public, and Muhammad started to find converts in Mecca.

The beginning of the spread of Islam brought a problem for the early converts. Although Mecca was a relatively tolerant place, the faithful still needed some form of protection. The reason for this was that the town was already a centre for pilgrimage to the shrine of the Kaa'ba, the Black Stone. The people of Mecca feared that Islam would pose a threat to the shrine and began to persecute the Muslims. For some time Muhammad enjoyed the protection of a pagan uncle, Abu Talib, but when he died the problem was raised once more. One group of Muslims travelled as far as Ethiopia to benefit from the protection of the ruler.

The journey to Yathrib

Muhammad himself undertook a short, but more momentous journey, to the city of Yathrib, now called Medina. Yathrib was a city torn by civil strife. A number of its people recognized in Muhammad and his new religion a force that could unite the city, and the Muslims were offered protection there.

Muhammad's flight (known as the hijra or hegira) from Mecca to Yathrib in 622 was an event of the utmost importance in the history of Islam. It is from this date that Yathrib became Medina, the city of the prophet, and 622 was later decided on as the first year of the Muslim era. The hijra was important because it ensured the safety of the prophet and his followers, and also because what happened immediately afterwards set the trend for the history of Islam in the subsequent centuries.

The call to prayer is the regular reminder to the faithful of their submission to God.

Muhammad had two key tasks to fulfil if he was to ensure the safety of the Muslims and Medina. He had to establish a constitution, to provide a framework within which the Muslims and the existing community could coexist. And he had to wage war on his enemies outside the city, for his own protection, and to foster the spread of the faith.

The first of these requirements was fulfilled by the Constitution of Medina. This defines the community of Muhammad's followers, the umma, and lays down many directions about the running of the community. In particular it is interesting that the Jews are said to belong to the community, and to fight alongside the Muslims, although they follow their own religion. Disputes within the community are ultimately referred to God and Muhammad.

In spite of this apparent unity with the Jews, it is not surprising that there was much resentment on the part of many Jewish tribes in and around Medina about the arrival of the non-Jewish Muhammad. Such resentments led to open strife, and the Muslims frequently found themselves fighting against, rather than alongside, their Jewish counterparts.

The Jews were not the only enemies of Islam. Muhammad had to contend with opposition from Mecca, the city from which he had fled. The whole concept of war against unbelievers is very strong in the Koran. It is not merely sanctioned – God actually orders that war should be waged until the unbelievers have been defeated or until a favourable peace agreement can be secured.

War took up a great deal of the decade left to Muhammad between the flight to Medina and his death. It was not until the eighth year of the hijra that hostilities were ended with Mecca and Muhammad

was welcomed back to the city in triumph, to remove the idols of the Black Stone and to establish the city as the centre of Islam. Meanwhile he had fought successfully against two Jewish oases (Khaybar and Fadak) and he was subsequently also to win the oasis of Ta'if. Most significantly of all, before he died he was planning campaigns against the Romans' territory in Palestine. The scene was being set for the Muslim domination of the Middle East.

By the time Muhammad died in 632 the seeds were sown for a transformation of the Middle East. To his predecessors it

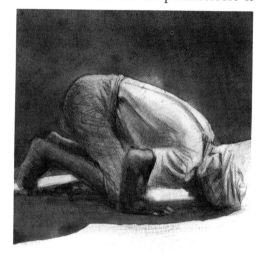

At prayer

must have looked as if one or other of the two great empires – the Roman and the Persian – would keep their hold on the area and take over more of its lands. And in religious terms it would have been thought that Christianity had the best chance of becoming the dominant faith – albeit with substantial Jewish and pagan elements remaining.

But it was evident that the young faith of Islam had a strong chance of sweeping across the area, bringing political as well as religious consequences. And so it was. In

the century or so after the prophet's death Islam expanded rapidly. Abu Bakr was appointed caliph, or successor, to lead Islam after Muhammad.

From the heartlands in western Arabia the early caliphs pushed out in every direction. They moved north and east through the rest of the Arabian peninsula. They went northwards through the Persian Empire and westwards along the coast of North Africa. There was further expansion under the Umayyads (660–750), the dynasty founded by the third caliph, Uthman, when Islam reached Spain in the west and the Indus eastwards.

At the height of the Umayyad period the Byzantine Empire was surrounded to the west, south and east by Islamic lands. But the Byzantines stood firm against the advance, defending their border with northern Syria. It was to be many centuries before their capital Constantinople would fall to the Muslims.

The empire of the Umayyads did not last. The vast territory was eventually split, with a substantial area centred on Baghdad held by the Abbasid Kings and other lesser dynasties holding on to lands on the eastern and western edges of the old empire. But the faith had been spread and would continue to be defended. The members of the Abassid dynasty in particular fostered large-scale conversion of the people they ruled.

The heartland of Islamic civilization had been established, from which that faith would be taken still further across the world. A formidable and characteristic Islamic culture would develop. Certain arts in particular, such as the calligraphy used for the text of the Koran, would flourish and acquire particular Islamic characteristics. And even when the political boundaries of Islam were contracting the spread of the faith continued.

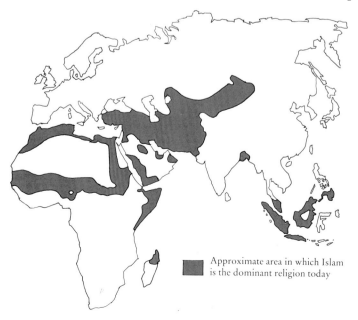

Approximate area in which Islam is the dominant religion today

CHARLEMAGNE'S CORONATION

A new concept of kingship and empire comes to Europe

After the fall of Rome in AD 410 Europe was divided up amongst the various so-called 'barbarian' kings who took over from the Roman emperor. One of the most powerful of these kingdoms was that of the Franks, who occupied the area that the Romans knew as Gaul. They were sufficiently far north to avoid the forces of the eastern Emperor Justinian when he reconquered parts of the old western empire at the beginning of the sixth century. The Franks remained a considerable power in Europe during the following period.

They still held large territories when Pepin the Short was crowned King of the Franks in AD 754 and appointed his two sons, Charles and Carloman, his joint heirs. The Frankish kingdom by this time included much of what we now know as France, Germany and the Netherlands, together with all of Belgium and Switzerland. Just before he died in 768 Pepin divided his lands between his two sons. But Carloman was to die in 771, and his people transferred their allegiance to his brother Charles. The great Frankish kingdom was intact again under a ruler who was in his own time called Carolus Magnus, Charles the Great, and whom we know as Charlemagne.

From the beginning Charlemagne was ambitious. He saw himself as the heir of the great Roman emperors (and indeed he took over much of the old Roman administrative system to run his extensive empire). He also claimed descent from the kings of ancient Troy. And he brought to the west a new concept of kingship: the idea of the Christian ruler with authority over both the state and the church.

Charlemagne made his base to the north of his kingdom, at Aachen, close to the borders of modern Belgium, Holland and Germany. From here he set out on an awesome series of military campaigns to expand his kingdom and make its borders more secure. His many campaigns against

Coin of Carolus Magnus, Charlemagne

Saxony, to the northeast, alone would have been enough to occupy a life of warfare for many a leader. He undertook at least ten major Saxon campaigns, involving the deportation of 7,000 Saxons in 794, the expulsion of one in three Saxon householders in 797, and the removal of some 1600 of the Saxon upper classes in 798.

As if this was not enough, he annexed Bavaria. He besieged the city of Pavia to give him control of Lombardy, and he crushed a revolt in Aquitaine. In addition, he pushed into many other areas on the edges of his kingdom to create the 'marches', border zones such as Brittany, Slovenia, Friuli (in the east, to the north of Venice) and the 'Spanish march', to the north of Barcelona. The result of all this activity was to give Charlemagne control of the bulk of Europe, from the west coast of France to Bavaria, from the Danish borders to parts of Tuscany.

Charlemagne's contacts with foreign peoples were not all warlike. He had diplomatic relations with rulers as far apart as Offa, King of Mercia and Harun al Raschid of Baghdad. And his most important diplomatic links, as for any European ruler in this period, were with the pope. Charlemagne himself visited Rome four

times, including the occasion at Easter 774 when he was triumphantly received by Pope Hadrian I and the visit in 800 when, on Christmas day, he was crowned emperor at Rome.

It was no accident that Charlemagne cultivated the pope, or that he went to Rome on important dates in the Christian calendar. The relationship of the emperor with the pope, and with the church in general, was crucial for the development of European politics over the following centuries. In the eastern, Byzantine, empire the idea of the emperor's authority over all Christians had survived. But this had not happened after the fall of Rome in the west. Charlemagne undertook to revive this concept. He saw it as his right and duty to guard and administer divine law. He did this by conquering pagan powers such as the Saxons. The emperor therefore considered that he could and should supervise the church: he was not a priest but he could oversee the priests, intervene in theological matters, and interpret the law of the church. Although the term 'Holy Roman Empire' was not actually used in Charlemagne's time, this later title sums up his aims.

In conceiving of his role in this way Charlemagne was setting the scene for a series of claims and counterclaims between the empire and the papacy which occurred throughout the Middle Ages, with the Pope and emperor involving themselves in what to modern eyes would seem like each others' affairs, and with the victory going to whoever was most powerful on each occasion. For Charlemagne himself the system worked well. He had established his supremacy on the battlefield and his power over the church gave him the scope to increase his power through diplomacy too.

Charlemagne also presided over legal and administrative changes. Perhaps the most significant of these was his alteration in the way he raised his army. Originally,

When Charlemagne wanted to be crowned, the ceremony was carried out on Christmas Day 800 in Rome. By going to the headquarters of the church and choosing Christmas Day, the emperor was signalling the importance of his relationship with the church. The relationship between empire and papacy would remain a vital one throughout the Middle Ages, wherever the emperor or the Pope was based. The visit to Rome was important in another way. Charlemagne wanted to underline his links with the former Roman Empire (something also shown by the way in which he dressed). It is not surprising the that Holy Roman emperors of the later Middle Ages looked to Charlemagne for a role-model.

unable to afford a standing army, specific vassals were charged with providing troops for the king. But after he was crowned emperor, Charlemagne changed the law so that the military obligation was vested in land. Whoever held a particular piece of land had a specific military duty. This system was reliable and influential. It would be used all over Europe for centuries to come.

Some four hundred years before the area ruled by Charlemagne had displayed a whole series of disunities that had together led to the fall of the Roman Empire. The emperor was aware of the dangers that his own empire might split up again. He responded to this threat by creating divisions that worked to his own advantage. He put his sons in charge of the separate kingdoms of Aquitaine and Italy; he treated Bavaria in a similar way, making it a prefecture under his brother-in-law. And he set up a network of aristocrats known as *missi* who were to act as his agents, travelling around the empire and reporting back.

The empire did not last long after Charlemagne's death. His son Louis the Pious had to contend with a dispute about the division of territory between the bishops and his sons, and finally went to war against his sons himself. As a result, after Louis' death (in 840) the empire was divided into three parts in 843 as a result of the Treaty of Verdun. A further division (into five parts) was to follow in 855.

In what sense was Charlemagne's apparently short-lived empire influential? Was his coronation really an event that changed the world? If Charlemagne's empire did not live for long after him, his idea of kingship, with its very special relationship with the church, did. And his concept of a European empire remained throughout the Middle Ages in the form of the Holy Roman Empire, which was to have such an effect on the history of the continent. What is more, Charlemagne was claimed as a forebear by both the Germanic Holy Roman Emperors and the kings of France, so his influence was felt in the two great European secular powers.

Charlemagne also had a cultural influence. Himself an illiterate, he nevertheless had great respect for learning and gathered many scholars around him at his court. One of the most notable was the English cleric Alcuin. He it was who organized the palace school. This was based at Aachen, but travelled around with the imperial court.

The scribes at the school were responsible for writing down much Latin literature (particularly poetry) which would otherwise have been lost, an important legacy in itself. Add to this the masterpieces of architecture and the visual arts that came out of Charlemagne's court and one can see something tangible of the civilized side of the great warrior emperor – and something else that lived on to influence European culture.

NORMAN CONQUEST OF ENGLAND

A new direction for the island race

We are used to thinking of William, Duke of Normandy, as the Conqueror of England. But he would not have seen it like that. He believed he had a legitimate claim to the English throne and that he was coming to England as its rightful ruler. He was not the only one. Harald Hardrada, King of Norway, also had a convincing claim. Harold of England, the reigning king, was thus beset by enemies, the Norwegians coming from the north and the Normans (themselves Scandinavian in origin, but settled in Normandy in northwestern France) from the south.

It was difficult to predict who would attack first. In the end it was the Norwegians who landed on the river Humber, gained a tremendous victory over the Mercians, and marched confidently to the city of York. Harold of England was in a difficult position. He could either stay in the south, hoping to defend himself successfully against a Norman invasion that had not yet materialized, or he could head north and attempt to cut off the progress of Harald Hardrada and his ally the Earl Tostig, Harold of England's own brother. In the end he opted to go north and, early in the morning of 25 September, defeated the Scandinavians at Stamford Bridge, near York. Both Tostig and Hardrada were killed and the victory was decisive.

But meanwhile there was trouble in the south. William of Normandy had set off for England, ignorant of the result of the Battle of Stamford Bridge but spurred on by a favourable wind in the English Channel. He already controlled the sea ports of northeastern France so his passage across the sea was unimpeded. He arrived to find the English unprepared.

Both parties wanted an early battle. William was conscious that he was less secure once he had landed; Harold wanted to surprise the Normans as he had the Scandinavians at Stamford Bridge. But the English king was far too quick for his own soldiers, many of whom arrived in the south exhausted by a rapid journey so soon after a major battle.

William was ready for the fight. He also had excellent cavalrymen at his disposal and Harold's axemen were no match for these. William's spearmen and cavalry forces were able to break up the massed ranks of the English axemen and score a decisive victory at the now-famous battlesite near Hastings in southern England. After this, William was secure. He moved at a steady pace through the countryside, finding enough support amongst the English lords to be crowned king at Westminster Abbey on Christmas Day 1066.

After the battle

But the situation was not totally secure. There was a pronounced nervousness about the actions of the Normans in the following decade and one medieval chronicler describes the English lying in wait for groups of Normans, ambushing them, and killing them secretly in woods and lonely places. And there were more organized rebellions in Kent and Exeter, as well as in the north in 1070, when the Northumbrians, in alliance with the Danes and an English claimant to the throne, captured York. William had to respond drastically, burning villages and stretches of land in the north, resulting, if we are to believe the chronicles, in the death of many people and more farm animals. Similar action was taken fifteen years later, when a Danish invasion was threatened.

It was activities such as these as the victory at Hastings that earned William the reputation of an oppressor. The churchmen who wrote the *Anglo-Saxon Chronicle*, the year-by-year history of the events of the Saxon and Norman periods, voice some of the frustration of people forced to pay high taxes while trying to eke out a living from the land in the face of a scorched-earth policy.

The short-term effects of the Norman victory were dire for many English people. But what of the more profound results? These are difficult to analyse. One view looks at the Normans as bringing institutions such as feudalism and strong bureaucratic government, social structures represented on the ground by towns and castles, and reform of the monasteries to England.

But it is equally possible to argue that trends such as these were already appearing in Anglo-Saxon England. In many cases it is clear that the Normans took over perfectly adequate Anglo-Saxon institutions and that these were better than anything they might have devised themselves. For example, the taxation and coinage systems were taken over; and the organization of local government, with its counties and smaller hundreds, was maintained. On these terms the Norman conquest remains something of an enigma. What is more, the idea that 'foreigners' were ruling England for the first time would not have been widely held in a country that had undergone a series of Scandinavian invasions.

Our main visual source for the Battle of Hastings is the famous Bayeux Tapestry. But this great work, probably made by people who had no direct knowledge of the fighting, has a graphic beauty that gives little idea of the helter-skelter confusion of the battle. The English, in particular, would have been confused, their tired axemen scattering in the face of William's fearsome cavalry. The battle initiated a new dynasty of English rulers, but whether it brought about decisive changes in the way the country was governed or in the life of the people is still a matter for debate.

VIKING RAIDS AND CONQUESTS

The confidence of Christian Europe is shaken

By the eighth century a number of the kingdoms of Europe had attained a certain stability. The Franks, for example, ruled a large expanse of the mainland and welded it together into an empire under Charlemagne. In Britain, the Mercian rulers controlled a large kingdom. These were Christian kingdoms with numerous monasteries and plenty of wealth. Their riches came mostly from trade, and neither their religious communities nor their towns and trading posts were heavily fortified.

The wealth of these places was therefore an attractive target to any aggressor, particularly a non-Christian one, who might come along. In one sense the Franks and Mercians were not easy targets. They were both capable of defending themselves on the battlefield. But since much of their wealth – in the form of portable property made of precious jewels and metals – was housed in the monasteries, it was relatively easy prey to raiders who avoided the formal conflict of pitched battle and went straight for what they could carry away.

The Scandinavian seamen we know as the Vikings were masters of this art. From their homelands in Denmark, Norway and Sweden they covered impressive distances, their fast, well-built ships taking them by river as far as Constantinople and by sea to the coast of North America. But it was places nearer home – Ireland, Britain and mainland Europe – that were to suffer from the raids that made the Vikings feared throughout the continent.

Denmark was the centre of the Viking homeland – at least in a strategic sense. From anywhere in Jutland, or the islands surrounding it, you could reach the sea in a day or less. From their lands in Skane and Halland (now parts of Sweden) the sea was also easily accessible. The Scandinavians also had a foothold in the area now called Schleswig, on the borders with Charlemagne's empire.

The Viking seafarers were not all mindless raiders. They had a well organized society headed by a king who was both a religious and a military leader and whose main aim was to keep the peace and allow his merchants to trade freely. There was a system of taxation and a legal framework that allowed, for example, a woman the right to divorce and to manage property in the absence of her husband.

Chess-piece representing a Viking warrior

The raiders often came from the ranks of the disaffected – lesser branches of one of the two families from which the king was normally elected, or men who had been exiled for misdeeds. But it was not only the Viking outlaws who pillaged the Christian communities of Europe. Apart from the fact that the kings took their share of the raiders' booty and were thus implicated in the attacks, the raiders were followed by more organized assaults that had the direct sanction of the king – a second wave of Viking attacks by a great conquering army. The attractions of conquering were not purely those connected with

easily accessible portable property. An island like England contained land that could be taken over and worked with far less effort than much of the land in Scandinavia. And a ready supply of labour was at hand in the conquered territories.

The first assailants were the Norwegians, who plundered the monastery on the island of Lindisfarne, off the Northumbrian coast, in AD 793. The following year the monastery at Jarrow was attacked, although this time the English were better prepared and the raiders were seen off. Soon after, in 802, another coastal monastery, at Iona, was raided and destroyed. Another popular target were the offshore islands around Scotland – the Hebrides, Orkneys and Shetlands – together with the Faroes. The Vikings had found a weak spot in the British defences, far away from Offa of Mercia's centre of power, where the pickings were rich.

Raids on Ireland began in 795 and continued until the first Viking settlers came to Dublin in 836. This was the pattern of attacks – a series of raids followed by settlement and conquest. There were also attacks on the European mainland. These were mainly carried out by the Danish Vikings. Charlemagne's lands in Frisia were attacked in 810 by Gottfrid of Denmark. The defences were destroyed and the Vikings came away with tribute. But on the whole the empire had a better system of defences than England and some attacks were held back. The turning point came in 834, when the Vikings sacked the important trading city of Dorestad.

In the following years, particularly after 840 when the empire was split up on the death of Louis the Pious, attacks continued unabated, with Viking ships penetrating up the Seine and Scandinavian forces ranging inland from a base on an island in the Bay of Biscay. It was an awesome series of assaults, with cities as important as Paris, Hamburg and Rouen being damaged, and targets attacked as far afield as Portugal, the Balearics, Tuscany and Provence. Indeed Paris itself was burned by a force that arrived in 120 ships, while the force that attacked Hamburg needed 600 ships to carry it. As well as pillaging and burning, the Vikings extorted tribute – protection-money in modern terms – the notorious 'Danegeld'. This system of extortion probably had the effect of institutionalizing the raids, making them less opportunistic expeditions of pillage, more a source of regular income. And from this it was a short step to outright conquest of the lands the Vikings invaded.

Viking trade

But it was not all extortion. Trade was another vital source of income for these great sea travellers. It was probably this motive that led them to explore the rivers that led through Russia from the Baltic to the Caspian and Black Seas. Vikings known as the Rus founded the first Russian kingdom; other Scandinavians reached Constantinople, and some of these men made up the élite guard of the Byzantine emperors. Perhaps too much has been made of these, the most wide-ranging of the Vikings' contacts, which took them to the eastern fringes of Europe. Some of the artefacts that have been taken as evidence of Viking activity may have been traded several times before they got this far east. Nevertheless it is certain that some of these intrepid travellers got through to Russia and Byzantium, making journeys as remarkable in their way as those made by their compatriots across the Atlantic.

In later years they made still greater journeys. For example, they colonized Iceland around 900. Isolated as it was, it was allowed to become a free state, governed by its own parliament. From here explorers sailed on to Greenland and colonized once more. From Greenland, in 1002, Leif Eriksson sailed to 'Vinland', the eastern coast of America. Vinland had its

own natives, and although the Vikings made further voyages, there was no sustained effort at founding a colony. If they were going to have to fight for land, it was best to do this nearer home. And so, in 1016, King Canute conquered England, ending for good the round of pillage in favour of more sustained, politically stable domination.

Looking at the superb quality of Viking art, and at the preference of the later Vikings for conquest followed by a more peaceful rule of their new subjects, some historians have sought to make the Vikings respectable. They have pointed out that the accounts of the Scandinavian attacks come from churchmen, who would naturally be appalled at the pagan destruction of their churches and religious communities and who would be quick to attack their assailants in their writings.

Yet these were tough times. Monks who had to contend with the problems of setting up and running a religious communities in isolated places like Jarrow and Lindisfarne knew how hard life could be. It took a lot to shock them, but the Vikings succeeded. When Alcuin, at Charlemagne's court, bewailed the fact that 'Out of the north an evil shall break forth upon all the inhabitants of the land,' he was not exaggerating.

What was the legacy of the Vikings? In some ways their influence was short lived. Soon after the reign of Canute an Anglo-Saxon king was again on the English throne. On the European mainland, the Frankish Empire had been weakened, but this would have happened in any case as the lands of Charlemagne were divided up amongst his successors.

A number of towns owe their existence to the Vikings, to whom trade became increasingly important. Irish towns such as Cork, Dublin, Limerick, Waterford and Wexford became places of consequence – first as fortified settlements and

then as trading ports – under the Scandinavians. Other cities, such as Rouen and York, also expanded as a result of Viking settlement. Further afield, places such as Kiev and Constantinople, not themselves Viking cities, nevertheless were affected by the Viking influence, even if we do not know how many Vikings actually made the great journeys along Europe's rivers to these far-flung places.

Much of the hard archaeological evidence of the Viking presence has long dis-

Compass dial from a Viking ship

appeared, although in their native Scandinavia remarkable finds have shown us at first-hand how superbly designed their ships – in many ways the key to their success – really were. But their presence lives on in more subtle ways. In England, for example, where half the country was under Danish rule for some considerable time, place names (ending in suffixes such as -by, and -thorp) mark Scandinavian territory to this day. A further legacy was the granting of Normandy to the Danes in 911. These north men, or Normans, were to have a further conquering influence on England. This was to prove decisive.

First the Vikings came to plunder and pillage. Later they settled in places such as England and Ireland to form more settled communities and to trade. This pattern is not unusual. Many expanding powers begin with expeditions that are mainly opportunistic robbing parties, before launching more determined campaigns and settling down. But the Vikings were exceptional in the severity of their raids and their visits left a clear imprint on the history of Europe.

Viking voyages of the ninth and eleventh centuries

FIRST CRUSADE

The beginning of a series of wars with repercussions stretching into the future

The Mediterranean world in the early medieval period was made up of many separate states, but there were three particularly significant power blocs. First there were the states of western Christendom, diverse in size but broadly similar in outlook, and Roman Catholic in religion. Next there was the Byzantine Empire centred on Constantinople, with its Greek Orthodox faith. And finally there were the Islamic states, occupying a great arc from the Holy Land, through Egypt and northern Africa, to southern Spain. This pattern, particularly the conflict between the Islamic and Christian areas, was to influence many aspects of history during the eleventh to thirteenth centuries, and the events that bring this out were the series of wars between the Christian and Islamic powers – the crusades.

It is difficult today to assess the importance of the crusades. In western and English-speaking countries we are used to hearing of them as heroic escapades in defence of Christianity. From this point of view they are part of the western historical mythology, led by monarchs who are often key figures in their nation's history – Philip Augustus of France, Richard the Lionheart of England, and Emperor Frederick Barbarossa. But from the Islamic viewpoint they have a different significance, as episodes of land-grabbing which were so poorly organized that they had little permanent effect on the Islamic world, particularly when compared to the more devastating campaigns of Genghis Khan. From this perspective the most significant product of the crusades was a long-lasting resentment between Christian and Muslim.

The crusades did not begin until centuries after the Arabs took over Jerusalem. From the capture of the holy city in AD 637 to the arrival of the Seljuk Turks in 1076 pilgrims were allowed to go peacefully to the Holy Sepulchre. But with the arrival of the Turks and the threat by Islamic forces to the Byzantine emperor, the balance of power seemed to be changing. The Byzantine emperor appealed to the pope, Urban II, for help. Urban's response, at the Council of Clermont in 1095, was to preach the first crusade, a holy war against the forces of Islam with the avowed aim of recapturing the city of Jerusalem and making it safe once more for Christian worship. It was to be a response that was repeated several times during the following two centuries.

Crusader's cross

Two broad groups of people responded to Urban's call to arms. The first were a poor and disorganized group led by Walter the Penniless, a French knight, and Peter the Hermit. The second force had a more aristocratic leadership, made up of Godfrey de Bouillon, Duke of Lower Lorraine, Raymond, Count of Toulouse, Bohemund, Lord of Otranto, and Robert, Duke of Normandy.

The leaders chose different routes to the Holy Land. Godfrey travelled from the empire southeastwards through Hungary to Belgrade, before crossing Bulgaria. Raymond went from Lyon to Trieste, before following a line parallel to the Adriatic coast and then turning eastwards through Thrace. Robert followed a more southerly route through Italy before crossing the Adriatic and northern Greece to follow a similar route to Raymond. All three parties, together with others who joined along the way, met up at Constantinople, where a mass of some 150,000 crusaders gathered.

To call this group an army would be somewhat inaccurate. It included the followers of Peter the Hermit, a large number of ordinary men who travelled as pilgrims rather than as soldiers and who were massacred on arriving in Asia Minor. Even those who made up the true fighting forces were a poorly disciplined lot. There had been atrocities even before they arrived at Constantinople.

One striking example of this was the crusaders' treatment of the Jews. The Christian crusaders, sworn to fight Muslim persecutors of Christianity, soon realized that they would find other 'enemies' of their religion along the way, none sooner than members of the race who had persecuted Christ himself. Furthermore, many individual crusaders were indebted to individual Jews – there was bound to be a certain amount of resentment that could easily build up into open hostility.

One of the crusaders from the Rhineland was Count Emich of Leisingen. His army contained members of the German and French aristocracy and their followers and made up a formidable force. Emich told his men that their crusade was against the Jews as well as the followers of Islam. There followed massacres at the cities of Spier, Worms, Mainz and Cologne. At Worms some 500 Jews were killed; at Mainz the number was nearer 1,000. Other German commanders, such as Gottschalk and Volkmar, added to the death toll, in spite of the fact that influential leaders such as Godfrey de Bouillon renounced the concept of crusading against the Jews. Fortunately Emich and his followers broke up after reaching the border between the empire and Hungary.

Another group who fell foul of the crusaders' misplaced zeal were the Greek people of the Byzantine Empire. The Byzantines were caught between two opponents. The Muslims gave them no support for trying to restrain the crusaders; the crusaders were frustrated not to find support from the leaders of this Christian empire. The result was that the less scrupulous crusaders found ample excuse to attack Constantinople – the suburbs of the city were ravaged by Peter the Hermit's followers when they arrived.

Even Godfrey of Bouillon and his better disciplined army fought the Byzantine forces. This happened because Godfrey rejected the emperor's diplomatic overtures. The emperor wanted to make Godfrey sign an oath of allegiance to him and to get the crusaders away from the city as quickly as possible. Godfrey responded by attacking Constantinople. But the imperial armies were well organized and on their home ground, and they were primed for action after the skirmishes of Peter the Hermit. Godfrey was defeated, after which he still had to defer to the emperor's requests. It was this mixture of humiliation and wasted lives that became the hallmark of the crusades.

At the same time as the emperor was defeating Godfrey, the other bands of crusaders were arriving at Constantinople. The emperor had to negotiate – and sometimes fight – with each of these. It required both strength and diplomacy. But ultimately a united army left Constantinople to march together with imperial forces through Asia Minor towards Jerusalem.

The road to Jerusalem

The crusaders were now in the territory of the Seljuk Turks, whose capital was at Nicaea. The Seljuk sultan, Kilij Arslan, quickly dispatched the followers of Peter the Hermit, and it may be that this made him somewhat complacent about the quality of the crusading army – Godfrey and the rest certainly seem to have taken him by surprise by quickly attacking Nicaea while the sultan was away from the city. The sultan was unable to defend the city from outside and, after inflicting heavy losses on the crusaders, retired. With the help of the imperial army Nicaea was then taken.

Nicaea was the first of a string of cities that the crusaders had to attack before they reached Jerusalem itself. The first town they had to pass through was Dorylaeum. When the first half of the crusading army approached this city they camped on the plain outside. They were attacked by the Turks who surrounded them and seemingly were about to defeat them before they had even reached the Holy Land. But a messenger was able to get away before they were completely surrounded and galloped off to warn the other half of the crusaders. By the time the rest of the Christians arrived, things were looking desperate for their comrades, who were not really prepared for an attack. But neither were the Turks ready to meet Christian reinforcements so soon. When these arrived the Turks were thrown into disarray and the crusaders were victorious.

Buoyed up by their victory, and by the sudden acquisition of Turkish riches, the

Crusader at prayer

crusaders pressed on across Turkish territory. Some followed a northerly route through the interior of Armenia, others went south on a route parallel to the Mediterranean coast. They met up again outside Antioch. This was a vital city at the entrance to the Holy Land. It withstood a lengthy siege and various assaults, eventually falling to the crusaders but not before a terrible slaughter had taken place. No Muslim remained alive, the corpses rotted in the streets in the heat – even the houses of the Christians of the city were looted.

From here the crusaders followed the line of the cities on the coast – Tripoli, Beirut, Tyre and Acre – before turning inland just north of Jaffa to head towards Jerusalem. Many of the leaders of these cities were more deferential to the crusaders. The Arab leaders were pleased at the eclipse of Turkish power at Antioch and were prepared to treat with the crusaders to save their skins. This happened at Tripoli and Beirut, Tyre and Acre, although there was some opposition at Sidon to which the crusaders responded with more looting and pillaging.

They finally reached Jerusalem on 7 June 1099 and began immediately to besiege the stoutly walled city. The defenders knew that there were allies on the way from Egypt, and if they could hold out until these men arrived they could defeat the crusaders. But the existing garrison of the Holy City was small, and it was Christian reinforcements who reached the city first. The crusaders were hampered, however, by the lack of wood to make scaling ladders and siege engines and could not mount a successful attack on Jerusalem until over a month after they arrived. The final assault was bloody, and all but a few of the Muslims – together with all the Jews, who were alleged to have given them aid – were slaughtered. But the city was at last in Christian hands.

With the success of the Christians a group of crusader kingdoms was established in the Holy Land. The County of Edessa, the Principality of Antioch, the County of Tripoli and the Kingdom of Jerusalem were effectively Frankish colonies enjoying an uneasy existence next to the inland Muslim territories. More than one writer has called these small states the first attempts at western colonialism. But their ruling classes in many cases became more attuned to the local culture than many an imperialist, wearing Syrian clothes, eating local food, and tolerating the religion of their Muslim neighbours. This last fact annoyed many pilgrims newly arrived from the west, but suited people who had seen both the atrocities of the crusading armies and the similarities between Islam and Christianity – both, after all, are monotheistic religions.

What was the impact of the First Crusade and the sequence of crusades that followed it? First, the fact that other crusades were necessary showed the fragility of the western hold on the Holy Land. In spite of the work of military orders, frequent expeditions were needed to renew the Christian hold on the area. Ultimately, Jerusalem was lost to the crusaders and, worse, the Christian power of Byzantium

An important stage of the journey of the first crusaders was reached at the Turkish stronghold of Antioch. The city was well fortified and withstood the crusaders' siege for months. When the Turks sent reinforcements from Aleppo these were defeated, but still Antioch did not fall. Finally a Turkish traitor allowed some of the crusaders to slip through the wall so that the gates could be opened to the crusading army. The result was a bloodbath, with no Muslim spared. The victory gave the crusaders credibility with the Arab leaders they would meet on the final stage of their journey (the latter wanted a Turkish defeat) and so was important in helping their passage on to Jerusalem.

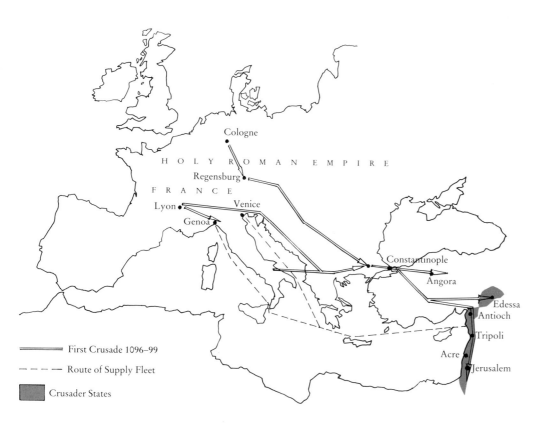

was weakened, particularly by a crusading attack on Constantinople in 1204. What was more, links between east and west were weakened. To the detriment of Europe this resulted in the relatively slow filtering westwards of the great technological sophistication of the Arab peoples.

But crusading would not have been seen as a negative activity to the men who responded to Pope Urban's original call. He presented the crusade as a way of leaving behind the petty local battles that engaged so many of the European nobility, of taking part in a just war, of perhaps indulging in some of the heroics worthy of the chivalrous knights of whom they had read in the romances, and in giving their lives for the sake of the church. If there was something reassuringly normal to the medieval mind about the call to arms, there was something uplifting in the cause.

In another way, Europe gained from the crusades. Before the crusades, the core of western civilization had been the Byzantine Empire, which had managed to inherit the mantle of Rome and nurture Christianity. Now the way was open for western Europe to become dominant. In the wake of the European fighting forces came another army, of merchants intent on making money in a way more acceptable than the looting soldiers who had preceded them. It was they who did more than anyone to maintain links between Christian and Muslim, but they could not repair the breach that had been made.

APPEARANCE OF AQUINAS' SUMMA THEOLOGICA

A restructuring of western thought that looked forward to the Renaissance

In medieval Europe the centre of intellectual life was the church. Education and scholarship, medicine and philosophy, the production of books and the provision of diplomats – the church held the key to functions as diverse as these, and to many more besides. The early universities were also essentially church institutions, run by priests and attended by people in minor orders. And the information handed down in these universities, and the ideas discussed in them, were naturally viewed from an essentially Christian perspective.

But the priestly scholars of the Middle Ages did not live in an intellectual vacuum, isolated from outside influences. Even the monks in their monasteries, some of the greatest scholars of the period, travelled much more widely and participated more in the broader community than is often realized today. They were also the men who produced the books, painstakingly copying manuscripts by hand to preserve and transmit knowledge and ideas.

Naturally, these men came into contact with views from far outside the Christian orbit. Some of the most persistent were in the classical texts of Rome and, especially, Greece. These were survivors of once-great civilizations. Their quality was obvious and as the texts became more widely available it became difficult for scholars to disregard them. Philosophers such as Aristotle, for example, seemed to offer a complete and often convincing picture of the world. Yet they did so without any reference at all to the Christian God. Muslim writers, such as Averroës and Avicenna, often working within an Aristotelian framework, posed a similar challenge. What was the churchman of the Middle Ages to make of these ideas?

It was not an easy question. Aristotle's philosophy was couched in terms that involved flux and transience – form and matter, act and potentiality, movement and change, coming into being and going out of existence. Such a philosophy could be applied to this world, but to the medieval mind it seemed impossible to apply it to an unchanging, eternal God.

There was also the question of the scientific approach of Aristotle. He and his Muslim followers talked about the world as they saw it. The perceptions of the senses were thus valued highly. This approach seemed at odds with the ideals of the medieval world, in which the senses were usually looked down on as a distraction from spiritual matters.

Since the classical and Muslim writers often described what they saw, the problem was part of a larger one that continually engages any thinking Christian. How can one reconcile or synthesize one's knowledge of what actually happens in the world with the 'revealed' knowledge present in the Bible? It was a problem that the churchmen of the Middle Ages were to turn to again and again.

St Thomas Aquinas

The man who was to make more effort to address this point than any other of his time was an aristocrat from central Italy whom we now know as St Thomas Aquinas. Born in the family home at Roccasecca in 1224, Thomas was placed at the age of five in the Benedictine monastery at Monte Cassino, where his uncle had been abbot. His family hoped that he too would rise to the same position. But before Thomas had finished his education there the monastery was turned into a battleground by the troops of the Pope and emperor.

Thomas' response was to withdraw and enrol at the University of Naples. Here he came under the influence of a new order and, in 1244, became a Dominican friar, a member of the order more than any other known for its preaching and teaching. He would henceforward work unceasingly for the Dominicans, spending two extended periods teaching in Paris and the rest of his life in Italy. When he died in 1274 he was head of the Dominican *studium generale* (house of studies) in Naples.

During his thirty years as a Dominican, Thomas wrote a formidable array of books – theological treatises, general philosophical works, commentaries on several books of the Bible, and commentaries on the works of Aristotle. He also encouraged other scholars to do work complementary to his own, for example encouraging his fellow Dominican William of Moerbeke to translate Aristotle's writings from their original Greek into Latin, the language of the church, making them immediately more accessible to medieval Europeans. Thomas' greatest work, written between about 1265 and 1273, is the *Summa Theologica*, the Summary of Theology, a vast (and unfinished) treatise. In it, Thomas said that he aimed 'to set forth briefly and clearly the things which pertain to sacred doctrine...for the instruction of beginners.' While to the modern reader Thomas' book looks neither brief nor especially clear, it does provide a new account of Christian thinking which influenced many contemporaries.

Body and soul

Christian philosophy before Thomas had taught that a person was made up of two parts, a rational soul inside a powerless,

From a modern point of view, a monk like Thomas Aquinas, working in a monastery, seems an obscure figure, away from the mainstream of life and thought. But in the medieval period it was different. The monasteries were centres of learning and education, melting-pots of ideas. A monk might find tranquillity in such a place, but he would also find the opportunity to influence the minds of Europe. From Naples, Aquinas' theological ideas spread out across the continent through the extensive network of the Dominican order.

material body. This is a concept which comes from the Greek philosopher Plato and was made current again in the Middle Ages largely through the writings of St Augustine. Thomas, on the other hand, took a view closer to Aristotle's. The human being is seen as a *union* between soul and body. Even this change made one thing clearer. Medieval Christians believed both in the survival of the soul after death and in the ultimate resurrection of the body. If the body was imperfect and material it seemed unfitting it should rise again. But if it was at one with the soul, the resurrection seemed more appropriate.

Holding the body in greater esteem than before also meant that the perceptions of the senses could be taken more seriously – they need not be merely fleshly apparitions which the believer should do his or her best to shun. And since human knowledge and science are based on the perceptions of the senses, then they too can be taken seriously.

Faith and reason

So Thomas is always drawing ideas together into one great whole. The soul and the body, human knowledge and Christian revelation, all are part of one greater truth. Even faith and reason are not seen as polar opposites by Thomas, although, of course, he does draw clear distinctions between them. Faith comes from revelation: it deals with divine truths. Reason deals with what can be known through human experience and demonstration.

But the two are not disconnected in Thomas' mind. He uses reason to support faith and revelation. And his reason is based soundly in human experience: he says that 'nothing exists in the intellect unless first in the senses.' Perhaps the most central example of the relationship between faith and reason is shown in Thomas' attitude to the existence of God. For him, this is not simply a matter of faith. God's existence, he asserts, can actually be proved.

Thomas sets down in the *Summa Theologica* five 'proofs' of God's existence. They all start from God's effects on the sensible world, the world we can perceive. For example, the first proof begins

with the concept that everything in the world is moved by another being. This can either be explained by some sort of infinite chain of cause and effect or by a first cause. There can be no infinite regression, so a first cause, God, must be the cause of all movement.

Thomas' other 'proofs' operate in the same way, moving from the world of the senses to the world of God. It does not matter that subsequent philosophers have taken the proofs apart. They work within their own theological framework and demonstrate the relationship between faith and reason, the spiritual ideals and the human experience, which was to mean so much to Christian thinkers in the following centuries. Like Thomas' annexation of Aristotelian thought, they exemplify a blend which was new and influential.

Men and morals

What effect was all this supposed to have on actual human behaviour? The high

St Thomas Aquinas

value placed on reason was important to Thomas because reason permits us to have free will. Reason gives us the ability to make moral judgements, and thus to choose how to act. Thomas insists in the *Summa Theologica* that the will tends generally towards good anyway, but that we should nevertheless use our reason to come to judgements leading to good

rather than evil actions.

However, to stay free of sin, Thomas asserts that we need to be infused with the divinely given quality of grace. Thus there are some virtues (such as prudence) which can be achieved through simple moral choice, others (such as faith, hope and charity) that are given by God through grace. So again, a combination of human and divine qualities is required if we are to live our lives the way Thomas asks.

The influence of St Thomas Aquinas

But what exactly was Thomas' importance? In his own time it was great. The sheer volume of his writings was impressive. But the novelty of his ideas was still more so. He brought about a change in Christian thinking, altering the prevailing view of mankind and changing the emphasis in the relationships between world and spirit, body and soul, faith and reason. At the same time, by taking Aristotelian thought on board, he helped to legitimize the great body of classical thought that was rapidly becoming available to the scholars of his time, fostering the spread of classical learning and literature that might otherwise have been lost.

Some have seen Thomas' influence last much longer. In his high valuation of reason, some have found a precursor of the French Enlightenment, the 'Age of Reason' of the eighteenth century. But the world of Descartes and the other philosophers of his time seems far removed from that of Thomas.

A more reasonable view sees Thomas as a precursor of the Renaissance. Renaissance thought was based on humanism – on a placing of extra value on the human experience (from the scientific evidence of the senses to the artistic appreciation of the human body) within a still-Christian context. The movement also relied heavily on classical thought (both the ideas of Greek and Roman writers and the influence of classical art and architecture). This engagement with the human in the context of the divine and this acceptance of classical learning were clear and consistent themes in the writings of Thomas. Without him, the Renaissance, and the modern world that followed it, would have been very different.

SIGNING OF THE MAGNA CARTA

An early bill of rights with a lasting influence

It is one of the most well known documents in history. Alluded to and quoted during discussions about justice, democracy and the rights of man, Magna Carta, the agreement drawn up between King John of England and his barons, has had a remarkable influence. It lays down the law about most areas of life in thirteenth-century England and its details refer very specifically to the feudal society that created it – from the barons to the merchant class, from taxation to the duties of the king's officers, from the church to the family, from towns to forests. But it does not mention parliament or democracy, and its scope, even by the most liberal interpretation, is limited to a restricted part of society. To assess the importance of the charter, and its relevance to later developments, it is helpful to look at the events leading up to its signature.

The historical setting

King John came to the English throne during a struggle between England and France. His predecessor, Richard I, had died at Châlus on the Limousin Plateaux, a vital strategic area for the control of southwestern France. Many of John's actions during the early part of his reign were connected with gaining control over this area. For example, in 1200 he married Isabella of Angoulême to make an alliance with the area to the west of the Limousin. And by holding on to the important castles at Chinon and Loches, south of the Loire, he maintained his domination over this part of France. This region, Poitou, seemed to be the key to France. Both John and the French king, Philip Augustus, knew they had to win it.

John launched an expedition to Poitou in 1206. He was not successful and so tried again in 1214. This time his barons, particularly those in the north of England, objected when asked to pay yet another tax to subsidize a military campaign far away from home. In spite of this John had

some initial successes on his campaign. He took the important cities of Nantes and Angers, and was spoiling for a battle with Philip Augustus himself. But Philip was miles away at Bouvines in Flanders where he decisively defeated John's general, William Longspee, and his ally Otto of Brunswick. This lost northern France for John and meant that Otto's rival Frederick II became emperor.

By this point in John's reign the barons were disaffected and the king demoralized. Expensive wars had led to a decrease, rather than an increase, in the king's power. Moreover John's style of government often did little to win the favour of the aristocracy. Apparently capricious

The Great Seal of King John

gifts to nobles were revoked with equal caprice. It was an attempt to purchase loyalty, but it was unsuccessful when there was such a heavy tax burden on the barons. The result was a revolt during which the grievances of the barons – and indeed of all free men – were spelled out in some considerable detail.

At the beginning of 1215 the barons started to put pressure on John to redress their grievances. They threatened to go to war against the king if he did not grant them their rights. John stalled, promising at answer at Easter and assembling his mercenaries. Then he sought papal privileges by taking up the cross of the crusader, but the barons did not relent and started the march on London. John tried to persuade them to submit their claims to arbitration, but by 17 May 1215 the barons occupied the whole of the capital except for the Tower of London.

John was in a difficult position. He had little money, and his main source of funds was fighting against him. More and more people were joining the rebels. He had to negotiate. During the month of June 1215, in the meadow at Runnymede between Windsor and Staines, this is what he did. Out of these meetings came a document, the 'Articles of the Barons', followed by Magna Carta, the great charter itself.

The charter and its provisions

We do not know exactly what the stages were by which the barons gradually arrived at the final document. But it was neither so revolutionary nor as surprising as is sometimes thought today. For one thing, the men who framed the charter had been discussing its content for a considerable time. For another, they looked back to charters granted to the nobility by previous monarchs, particularly Henry I (1100–35), in putting together their own document. Nevertheless, the great charter was an impressive piece of legislation.

Magna Carta contained laws covering a

The document that King John put his name to at Runnymede was directed specifically at righting the wrongs of the time. But it was far more influential than its role as a piece of crisis-management might suggest. The potent myth of the barons bringing their king to order for the sake of justice and the rights of individuals lived on, even if those rights were in reality closely limited. Magna Carta's influence was thus far greater than that of its thirteenth-century context. It was cited by seventeenth-century republicans and American constitutionalists alike.

wide range of grievances. Most of its clauses were designed to define the rights of the people (meaning the 'free men') and to protect them from the king's possible abuse of his authority. So the law of custody, wardship and marriage is written down to protect the vassal rather than the king; distraint for debts due to the crown is abolished; tax law is reformed (the tax of scutage to be levied only at the consent of 'the common counsel of the realm', for example, to discourage the king's tendency to make it into a regular levy).

The charter also outlined more general principles of legal practice. The most famous is chapter thirty-nine which states that 'No freeman shall be arrested, or kept in prison, or disseised [have his lands taken away], or outlawed, or banished, or in any way brought to ruin unless by the lawful judgement of his peers or by the law of the land'. Even this pronouncement, which sounds like a fundamental principle of justice today, emerged from specific abuses of the time: John had repeatedly punished his barons without recourse to a fair trial. Another general clause resulted from the high cost of writs, limiting the availability of justice. So the king was made to promise that he would not sell his justice, nor deny or delay justice to anyone. Further clauses were intended to make justice more accessible. Justices were to visit the shires four times a year and the court of common pleas should not follow the king around, but should be held in a fixed place.

In clauses such as these, it is clear that the barons were acting in as practical a way as they could to reform contemporary wrongs. Another way in which they responded to the developments of the time was in their clauses protecting the emergent merchant classes and protection of the rights of cities, towns and ports. The fact that many of the barons had served as justices and that many were or had been involved in lawsuits of one sort or another

at some time made Magna Carta a practical legal document.

And yet it was not as practical as it might have been. This can be seen in many details. For example, there was not nearly enough time for the justices to visit the shires four times a year. But there was a more general weakness. There was no supreme court to make sure that the clauses of the charter were enforced. What the barons proposed was a council of twenty-five barons who could select four of their number to listen to complaints against the king and obtain justice on the part of the injured party. In principle this was too one-sided: the king was not represented at all; in practice it was unworkable because the barons appointed the king's enemies to the council.

The influence of Magna Carta

If Magna Carta had its limitations, this did not stop it having a lasting influence. In the range of its regulations and in the fact that it applied to all free men it was unusual, if not unique. And it was reissued in the following years in a variety of different versions. The text of 1225 eventually was accepted as the version that stayed on the statute book.

Invaluable to the barons of thirteenth-century England, the great charter was also seized upon by lawyers in the seventeenth century. The opposition to the early Stuart kings used Magna Carta as an anti-royalist weapon, as a way of attacking economic monopolies, and an exemplar of the liberty of the individual.

And its influence did not stop in seventeenth-century England. As a result of the commentaries of lawyers in the Stuart and Cromwellian periods, the ideals of Magna Carta were taken to America where they would ultimately help to shape the Constitution of the United States. King John's document of desperation still influences those who espouse justice and democracy today.

CONQUESTS OF GENGHIS KHAN

The Mongol Empire spreads across Asia

Most westerners, when asked to name the empire that reached the greatest extent, would choose one of the great powers of antiquity – the Roman Empire or the lands of Alexander the Great. But in the Middle Ages the Mongol Empire had boundaries even wider than these. At its height it included much of the continent of Asia apart from India and the far north of the continent. Its founder was the most feared military leader of his time – Genghis Khan.

So great were his conquests and his influence that Genghis Khan was able to achieve an almost mythic status during his own lifetime. This often makes it difficult for historians to disentangle fact from fiction when writing about him. We know that he ruled from 1206 to 1227 and that his empire steadily expanded across Asia in a series of ruthless military conquests. But his actual life is shrouded in confusion. This is particularly true of his early life because we rely heavily on a single source, a book called the *Secret History of the Mongols*. This was written in 1240, some thirteen years after Genghis Khan's death, probably by the Mongol Chief Justice. It was called a secret history because it was intended to be read only by members of the Mongol royal family and their high officials. But its image of the great conqueror's early life is the one which has lasted.

Genghis Khan was born in the twelfth century. His people, the Mongols, were not the only nomadic tribe of the Asian

When Genghis Khan and his hordes began to arrive outside the fortified cities of Russia in the 1220s, the Mongol Empire already stretched across much of Asia. Well defended as many of these places were, they could not withstand the force of the Mongol armies. A whole string of cities, from Tashkent to Bolgar on the River Volga, were sacked or pillaged by the armies of Genghis Khan.

The horse – a symbol and source of Genghis' power

Steppes and they were far from the most powerful. The family of Genghis, or Temüchin as he was originally called, held high rank but were not exceptionally influential – his father, Yesügei, was a minor chieftain. Yesügei died while Temüchin was still a boy and the youth lost what followers his father had. So as he grew older Temüchin had to start again, building up a group of followers who were soon impressed by his leadership ability and his success as a brave, audacious warrior.

Defeating the Mongol rivals

As Temüchin began to challenge and defeat his rivals in the struggle for domination of Mongolia it became clear that there were certain tribes who would have to be defeated if he was to fulfil his ambition of becoming leader of the Mongol peoples. Foremost among these were the Tatars, the Keraits and the Naimans. All these were nomadic peoples, but the Tatars seem to have been strongest in the east, where they had frequent battles with the emperors of China – the other two tribes were more active in the west, where they came under Turkish influence. Temüchin's decisive step against the Tatars came when he was able to make an alliance with Toghril, leader of the Keraits, the greatest opponents of the Tatars. Together, and with the support of the Chinese emperor, they were able to defeat the Tatars.

Henceforward, Toghril was given the title of Wang (king) by the Chinese and became known as the Wang-Khan. It may have been from this time that Temüchin was first given his new name. The Mongol word Chingiz, which we usually write as Genghis, means 'oceanic' and was probably meant to indicate that he was a universal ruler.

But Genghis was not to maintain his alliance with the Wang-Khan. He knew he had to defeat the Kerait ruler if he was to gain domination of the Mongol peoples. After one indecisive battle Genghis sent spies to the Kerait camp, allegedly to ask if they would accept the return of one of the followers who had turned against them. The agents discovered that the Wang-Khan was not ready for battle and, according to the *Secret History*, Genghis quickly gave the signal for a renewed attack. For three days the followers of Genghis attacked their enemies unceasingly. Many were killed and, although the Wang-Khan escaped death, he was later to perish in obscurity.

Immediately afterwards Gengis campaigned against the other rival tribe, the Naiman. Success here meant that he was effectively leader of the entire Mongol peoples. In 1206 a great meeting was called at which Genghis was publicly proclaimed universal ruler of the scattered nomadic peoples of Mongolia. All the chieftains present were subservient to him. Those who had done well in battle were rewarded. And Genghis' standard, a pole to which were attached nine yak's tails, was raised. From this point he was always known as Genghis Khan. The Mongol state was founded and the history of the world had reached an important turning point.

Mongol expansion

The ambitions of Genghis did not stop here. Although he spent the next few years consolidating his position in Mongolia and defeating such local opposition as remained (for example some of the Naimans who had survived his earlier attacks), he was already planning his first major campaign of conquest outside the Mongolian heartland. The obvious prize was the Chinese Empire to the east. This was dominated largely by the Qin, but there were other peoples, such as the Tanguts of Hsi-Hsia to the south of the Mongolian heartland, that also offered tempting targets.

Genghis went for Hsi-Hsia first. There were probably two reasons for doing this. First, the state and its army were run in a similar way to the Chinese. Conquer the Tanguts and they would be prepared for the greater challenge of the Chin. Second, if they could take Hsi-Hsia they would have an easier route eastwards to China.

Hsi-Hsia was brought under Mongol control in 1209. The way was thus opened up for a series of assaults on the Chin. They proved a more resilient enemy, and campaigns were to continue from 1211 until 1234, some years after Genghis himself had died. Part of the problem for the Mongols was that previously most of their battles had been against other nomadic peoples. In such conflicts their cavalry forces had been supreme.

But these methods were no good against well established Chinese walled cities. The Mongols had to withdraw and modify their tactics, taking on board some of the methods of warfare used by the Chinese themselves and adopting the use of siege engines. They also had to cope with the Great Wall of China which, although it did not exist in the same form as it does today, was still a formidable blockade. But in the end the ruthlessness and persistence of the Mongols meant that they succeeded. Mongol power did not depend solely on the charismatic character of Genghis Khan.

The qualities of ruthlessness and persistence, so important in the conquest of China, were also revealed in the Mongol campaigns at the other end of the empire, in the west. Here Genghis Khan's neighbour was Khwarazm-shah, who ruled the area around the modern Soviet Republic of Uzbekistan. At first, the two rulers existed in uneasy peace side by side. But in 1218, some merchants from the Mongol Empire were suspected by the governor of Khwarazm's border city of Otrar of spying and were put to death.

When Genghis heard of this he sent ambassadors to seek an explanation, but one of these met his death and the others were humiliated by having their beards removed. Such an action was a signal that hostilities were now open. Genghis launched a merciless three-pronged attack on Khwarazm, killing and wrecking everywhere he went and driving Khwarazm out of his territory. As a result, the Mongols acquired another large area of land although this time they did not rule directly, but through a series of viceroys.

Once more, the final benefits of this conquest were not to be reaped until after Genghis' death, when a full-blooded campaign against Russia and eastern Europe was to be mounted. Meanwhile, Genghis had to return eastwards and fight the Tanguts once more, this time bringing them under complete subjugation.

By the time of his death in 1227, Genghis Khan was in control of an empire stretching from the Caspian Sea to Peking. In the style of his leadership and life he was little different from the Mongol leaders who had gone before him. He was still a nomadic chieftain happier in the saddle than in any sort of palace. But he had a unique determination and a sure strategic sense. He resisted the temptation to go chasing after conquests in China without creating a sound Mongol confederacy at home. His successors to some extent inherited this ability. After Russia had become a vassal state and the Mongols were close to taking Vienna they turned back to sort out troubles at home. Fortunately for the people of Europe, they were not to return.

What are we to make of the effect of Genghis Khan's campaigns? For the conquered, the results were often unambiguously disastrous. Yet it is difficult to be sure about the casualty figures, which contemporary sources often put so high that it is difficult to believe them. At the fall of Harat, for example, over 1.5 million people were supposed to have been killed. Even given the fact that people would rush to a city for refuge in times of war, this seems a high total – could such a city accommodate so many?

Whatever the actual figures, there can be no doubt that they were high and that the map of Asia was redrawn by Genghis and his immediate successors. But for the Mongol peoples themselves, Genghis had a different significance. He was a protector of the people and gave them an identity and a cultural focus. Under him, a loose body of nomadic tribes became an organized (albeit still a nomadic) confederacy. After his death the various Mongol Khanates, from the empire of the Great Khan in the east (covering most of China and having control of Tibet), through the land of the Golden Horde (taking in much of Russia), and down to the country of the Ilkhans (south of the Caspian Sea), dominated the entire continent of Asia.

The ethos of loyalty that is still a feature of life on the Steppes dates from the time of Genghis. From this period also come key ideas in Mongol law that have survived until recently. It is for reasons such as these that many people in central Asia still look upon the universal rulers as heroes. They show us that even such an apparently unambiguous character can be seen in diametrically opposing ways.

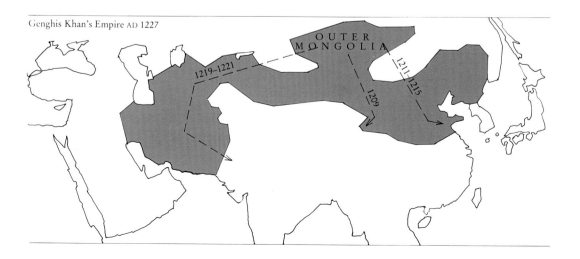

Genghis Khan's Empire AD 1227

MARCO POLO'S JOURNEY TO CHINA

New links are established between east and west

The Venetian Marco Polo has gone down in history as the greatest traveller of the Middle Ages. Although not the first westerner to reach Peking he was the first to describe it in detail, the first who was to tell of the great Khan as more than simply a military leader whose might was to be feared, the first to speak of Java and Sumatra, Burma and Siam. He has left his own vivid account of his journeys, and those of his father and uncle, Niccolò and Maffeo Polo, before him. He is thus the person most responsible for what understanding the west had of the east in the medieval period and for opening up trading and cultural links that were to last for centuries.

It was the city of Marco Polo's birth that sealed his fate as a traveller. Venice was Europe's trading capital in the thirteenth century. Merchants and ships from there set out for destinations all over the Mediterranean and beyond. The city is also towards the east of Europe. It would be an obvious starting point for Europeans wanting to open up trade routes with the fantastic eastern empire of which rumours were starting to circulate – the empire of the great Mongol Khans.

Two such Europeans were the brothers Niccolò and Maffeo Polo. Even they were not going into totally uncharted territory. Two Franciscan friars, Giovanni di Piano Carpini and Guillaume de Roubrouck had visited the Mongol capital Karakorum in the middle years of the century. And the town of Sudak in the Crimea had a colony of Venetians and could be used as a jumping-off point for travellers going farther east.

The brothers set off in 1255, following the trail blazed by these earlier travellers. From Constantinople and Sudak they travelled to the base of Barka Khan, the ruler of the Golden Horde, on the lower Volga. Here they had profitable trade and secured a trading concession that promised to stand them in good stead later. And here they might have stayed, trading with the Mongols of the 'Russian' khanate, had not a war amongst the Mongol factions cut them off from the west and pushed them on eastwards to the court of the great Khan himself. On the way they encountered one of the great Khan's ambassadors, himself riding eastwards towards Peking. The diplomat, knowing that his sovereign would not want to miss a meeting with two people from so far west, persuaded the brothers to travel with him.

The Venetians found a remarkable place, with its concentric walls enclosing the different zones of the city and the imperial palaces at its centre. They were impressed by the hospitality of the Khan and by his curiosity about all things western – particularly western religion. At the end of their year-long stay the brothers were asked to visit the Pope and to return with a retinue of 100 learned men from the Christian church. They were to take a Mongol emissary with them, the Khan's chosen representative. He, however, became ill and was left behind *en route*, leaving the brothers to act on his behalf as emissaries from the Khan to the Pope. Poor weather, including snows and floods, delayed them still further and the brothers arrived in Acre in 1269. But their mission to the Pope was to be cut short. The pontiff who had been on the throne when they left was now dead – the cardinals were unable to decide on a successor.

The return of the Venetians

Niccolò's teenage son Marco was amongst those who welcomed them back to Venice. He persuaded his father to take him on the return journey. But with no Pope to provide the required Christian representatives what were they to do? They decided to set off anyway, taking with them a sample of holy oil from Jerusalem, another of the Khan's requests. They had not got far when they received the news that their friend Theobald of Piacenza had been elected Pope under the name of Gregory X. They were at once provided with two papal representatives and continued again their journey.

It is hardly surprising that Gregory acted so quickly to support the travellers. It was in the interests of the spread of Christianity to send priests into the unknown lands of the east. It was also in the interests of the papacy's expanding power-base for the Pope to have representatives spread as far as possible across the globe. Like the Venetian merchants, the Pope had the scent of an opportunity here, and the reported interest of the Khan must have made it all the more enticing.

The rigours of the journey's three and a half years are memorably described in Marco's account of his travels. Rejecting the leaky-looking ships they found at Hormuz they travelled over land north through Kerman and then northeast across the mountains of the Hindu Kush and Pamir. From here they reached the city of Kashgar, something of an oasis after such hard country, before passing southeast to Yarkand (a city where goitre was rife because of poor drinking water). After crossing Tibet they had to confront the difficulty of crossing the Gobi Desert, where they were beset by mirages and haunted by the sound of the shifting sands. Having made it across the desert they were finally met by a messenger of the Khan and escorted safely and slowly to Peking.

Perhaps the aspects of Marco Polo's accounts of his travels that are most remembered today are his descriptions of the splendours of the great Khan's court. He marvelled at the sheer size of the palace, with its hall so vast that 6,000 people could sit down and eat there. He admired the assemblage of arms and armour kept there by the Khan. And he was awestruck by the New Year celebrations, with the gifts to the Khan of thousands of white horses and the appearance

The Venetians of the Middle Ages had a strong reputation for travel and commerce. But even for a Venetian, to travel across Asia to the city of Peking was to make a journey of almost unimaginable length. The Polos, in making such a journey, passed between two markedly different cultures, and fostered connections between those cultures that would continue as trade between the two continents increased.

of his staggering 5,000 elephants 'all covered with rich and gay housing of inlaid cloth representing beasts and birds, and each of them [carrying] on his back two splendid coffers; all of these being filled with the Emperor's plate and other costly furniture.'

It was not only architecture and ceremony that impressed Marco Polo in Peking. There were also technological developments that showed China to be ahead of the west. One of these was the exploitation of asbestos, another was the widespread use of coal – not unknown in Europe but strange to Marco Polo, coming from the southern city of Venice. Perhaps still more significant were his noticing of the imperial paper currency system and the complex postage system, with its three tiers of service for second class, first class and royal mail.

But Marco Polo did not limit his explorations to Peking. He went far and wide as an emissary of the Khan – Tibet, Yunnan, northern Burma, Karakorum, India and the Andaman islands. He passed through them all and left us his observations. He also served the Khan as governor of Yangchow, northeast of Nanking. Meanwhile his father and uncle were also in the service of the Khan, taking part in battles on his behalf and designing siege engines. Only after sixteen years in China did they return to Venice, via a hazardous sea journey and overland through Persia.

Marco Polo was notorious for his exaggeration, and many of his statements cannot be taken at face value. But no other person travelled as far as he did in the Middle Ages or brought back as much information. Together with his father and uncle he was the major contributor to an opening up of trade and dialogue with the countries of the east that has lasted until the present. He helped to make his city of Venice richer, consolidating a prosperity that was to grow until, along with the other rich Italian cities, it would result in the Renaissance.

Marco Polo's journeys also confirmed the place of Venice at the centre of the world of trade. Venice was already linked by land trade routes to the rich towns of France and the Hanseatic trading centres of northern Germany and the Netherlands. The city was also connected to the rest of the Mediterranean by sea and by overland routes across northern Italy. Now boats came up the Adriatic bringing goods from farther east. Carpets, silk and spices came in from the far east. Furs and precious metals were brought down from the north. Luxury foods such as sugar started to come westwards, as did staples like corn and rice. And many of these items were bought and sold by the merchants of Venice.

This would probably have happened anyway, even if Marco Polo had not made his epic journey. The Khans had realised that there was as much to be gained from trade as from military conquest. They had goods that were in demand in the west, and the west was setting up markets at which they could be traded. The rise of the European towns made this process inevitable.

But the long-distance impetus supplied by explorer–merchants like the Polos and the encouragement from powerful churchmen who saw the opportunity to convert people and increase their power speeded up the process. Moreover, the failure of the Christian aspect of the Polos' journey inspired other missionaries to follow in their footsteps. Many of these men, often Franciscan preachers, also left accounts of their travels, contributing further to the west's understanding of the Asian world.

INVENTION OF GUNPOWDER

A new technology that changed the pattern of warfare

People have always fought each other, and have always sought new ways of gaining the advantage. Apart from simple hand weapons like clubs and swords, there is a long list of ways of avoiding or supplementing hand-to-hand fighting. Some of the most successful in the Middle Ages were siege engines, from battering rams that pounded away at city walls to trebuchets that catapulted missiles over the top. Fire was an obvious adjunct to these weapons. A flaming missile launched by a trebuchet could be highly destructive, especially in a town made up largely of wooden buildings. And fire-ships, flaming boats set adrift amongst an enemy fleet, could decide a naval battle.

But in the Middle Ages people began to find ways of making fire yet more deadly. It was discovered that certain substances, such as sulphur, bitumen, saltpetre and what was known as 'naphtha' (various petroleum products) could make fire flame more vigorously, spit more menacingly or spread more devastatingly. One of the most effective of these extra ingredients was saltpetre. And as early as 664 an Indian monk who had travelled in China identified it and described how it produced a strong purple flame when put into a fire. The birth of gunpowder, which involved adding a higher proportion of saltpetre to carbon and sulphur, was even then quite close.

We do not know exactly who came up with the successful formula. But it was certainly arrived at by the thirteenth century, probably in China as a result of an extended dialogue between the Chinese and Islamic worlds. We know that thirteenth-century Arabs, for example, had a trebuchet that used counterweights enabling it to hurl quite heavy items over relatively long distances. Amongst the missiles that it hurled were primitive explosive bombs.

In this period a weapon called the fire lance was also developed. This was a tube (of bamboo, wood or metal) mounted on the end of a lance. The tube was filled with a mixture of low-nitrate gunpowder and toxic chemicals or simple 'shot' such as lead pallets or potsherds. It spouted sparks and flames for several minutes after ignition at the mouth of the barrel. Thus it was not a true gun, which is ignited at the other end of the barrel and is designed to produce a short, sharp explosion that expels all the shot in one fatal blast. Fire lances were common in the Islamic world. The peoples of the middle east were well placed to develop them, having access to Greek and Byzantine knowledge of chemistry, and having good supplies of naphtha.

Meanwhile, in the far east, gunpowder was being developed. Recipes exist from at least as far back as 1044, when one Chinese text records a mixture involving sulphur, saltpetre, charcoal, pitch and dried varnish. This may have been a recipe for a firework. Indeed it used to be thought that the Chinese development of gunpowder was exclusively for fireworks, and that the hand gun and cannon were western inventions.

Late medieval cannon

The coming of firearms

Some time towards the end of the thirteenth century a significant change in weapons technology seems to have taken place. Writers from the eastern Mediterranean region begin describing a weapon using a high-nitrate explosive roughly equivalent to gunpowder, ignited at the base of the barrel. These weapons were too big to be hand guns, and were not proper cannon since they did not fire cannon balls. But guns they were, and their descendants were to change history.

Although first described in the Mediterranean, these weapons almost certainly appeared first not in Europe, as was once thought, but in China. One of their barrels has been found on the site of a battle in Manchuria that took place in 1288. By 1326 or 1327 such guns were also known in Europe, and recipes for gunpowder written down by western writers (such as Roger Bacon, once credited with the invention of gunpowder) appear.

Although one cannot be certain that the gun spread from east to west rather than the other way round, it is very likely that it did. In particular, the characteristic design of the gun barrel, bottle-shaped with a pronounced swelling at the base, is similar in the early Chinese example and appears in the first European drawings of guns. It is unlikely that such a similarity would have occurred if the invention had been made independently in the east and the west. There is also a tradition that knowledge of guns passed from China to the west via Russia. This is quite likely. Chinese officials would have gone to the Russian cities regularly during this period to collect taxes. It also accounts for the lack of finds of guns from this period in the Islamic world, and puts into perspective a find of an early gun barrel in Sweden.

Oddly, it is possible that these early guns were used to fire arrows. The first European drawing certainly shows this happening, although whether from fact or

Firearm designed to fire a dart like an arrow. From a medieval manuscript.

from the ignorance of the artist is impossible to say. It is strange that, if fire lances had been used to fire shot, guns should not also have been. But if shot was not used to begin with, it was soon adopted. A document from Florence, contemporary with the drawing, shows the city authorities buying both cannon and shot. It may well be that in Europe, where siege warfare against substantially fortified cities was common, the cannon developed quicker and grew larger than in China itself. Soon the references to firearms in Europe come thick and fast. We hear of guns in Rouen in 1338, firearms using iron shot in Lucca in 1341 and in England in 1346, and of cannonballs in Toulouse in 1347.

The limitations of early firearms

But this was just the beginning of the story. Early firearms were inaccurate, dangerous to the operator as well as the target, and unpredictable. The problems began with the gunpowder itself. For a start, different recipes were needed for small arms and cannon, and it took people some time to work out the best proportions. Second, gunpowder, a loose mixture of carbon, sulphur and saltpetre, was difficult to use because saltpetre was much heavier than carbon. So the saltpetre tended to fall to the bottom of the gun barrel, leaving the carbon at the top. It also resulted in an uneven distribution of air spaces in the powder, making a strong, uniform explosion unlikely. This led gunners to come up with a method ramming the powder in with a wooden block before packing the shot in with rags to allow the correct amount of gas to build up in the barrel. It was not until the invention of 'corned gunpowder' in the fifteenth century that an equal distribution of ingredients and air spaces really became the norm.

These were not the only problems. Early firearms were costly both to make and to fuel. They were slow to load and fire. And they were impossible to aim accurately, with the result that it was difficult to keep firing at the same spot in a castle or city wall with the intention of breaching it.

Under the circumstances, it seems surprising that firearms caught on at all. After all, the medieval general had a range of weapons at his disposal, from highly developed siege engines to ranks of archers, all of which could be deadly when well deployed in the right place. But this is to ignore the psychological aspect of warfare. To have the latest military technology is in itself to score the first blow on the enemy before open hostilities have taken place. But more than this, when the latest military technology is something as spectacular as a high-explosive, the impact can be nothing short of terrifying.

Early firearms reminded contemporaries of thunder and lightning, powerful natural forces that were regarded with fear and thought of as portents of danger and destruction. Add to this medieval ideas about the fires of hell and the kind of supernatural magic apparently attendant on fire and explosions seeming to appear from nowhere, and we have perhaps some idea of the effect of gunpowder on its first victims. It must have been awesome.

Gunpowder in context

But why did guns develop so quickly in the fourteenth century, after such a slow development in earlier centuries? One answer is that there were many wars in the fourteenth century, both in Europe where the Hundred Years' War raged, and in the east where, in the mid-century, Chinese factions began to rebel against Mongol rule, ousting the Mongol emperor and establishing the Ming Dynasty in 1368.

The foundation of substantial empires defended by the new weapons technology was a trend that was to continue in the later medieval period. Amongst the peoples who began to expand their power with the help of gunpowder were the Portuguese, the Ottoman Turks, the Mughal Indians and the Persians, all of whose states have been called 'gunpowder empires'. Links between many of these empires, particularly between Ottoman Turkey, Persia and India, meant that knowledge about the techniques of gunmaking passed with relative ease between them; and although each empire had its own centres of manufacture, experts travelled widely and passed their skills around across the imperial borders.

The spread of firearms was helped by their apparently supernatural power, by their association with large successful empires, and by their use during some of the important battles of later medieval history. One such conflict was the siege of Constantinople, in which Ottoman fire power played a crucial part. This was an important example, since it happened at the junction of Europe and Asia. Knowledge of the effectiveness of firearms could thus spread far both east and west.

Some of the battles of the Hundred Years' War were also important for diffusing knowledge of guns and of establishing their importance. Two such examples were the Battle of Crécy in 1346 and the Siege of Calais in 1347 – two English victories over the French in the Hundred Years' War. Although Crécy is now remembered for the triumph of the English longbowmen, showing their skill in another new military technique, Edward III took with him three cannon, which he placed near his archers. After the English success at Crécy, the cannon followed Edward to Calais, where the combined threat of the English archers and the cannon, together with the English strength at sea, made the town surrender.

Firearms were not decisive at either Crécy or Calais, but they undoubtedly added to the psychological threat. Since it was at Crécy that England established itself as a military nation, her reputation

ensured that cannon would form a key part of European battles in the ensuing decades and indeed centuries. The creation of the great 'gunpowder empires' was linked to this development. It was to continue beyond the continents of Asia and Europe as nations such as England, Spain and Portugal expanded their influence into America.

And it was to mean a change not only in the way war was waged, but also in how people lived. For castles and city walls, at first improved and strengthened to withstand gunfire, were eventually overtaken by the power of cannon. Gunpowder would eventually be one of the factors in the end of the fortified city and the 'impregnable' castle. It would have its effect in the change in the balance of power, make military strength resident in technology rather than manpower. In so doing it would have its part to play in the decline of feudalism and rise of compact nation states at the end of the Middle Ages. And offering as it does a method of instant death and destruction, it would also have a profound effect on the status and vulnerability of human life.

A heavily fortified medieval city faces its first attack from gunpowder. The cities of Europe had been built with substantial stone walls to resist the advances of potential enemies. Soldiers had designed ingenious siege engines, from battering rams to catapults, to attack city walls. But the citizens could still expect to hold out for a long time against such an assault. With the coming of gunpowder, however, such fortifications were far more vulnerable. Cities, together with the castles from which rural lords held sway, had to find new methods of defence if their walls were not simply to tumble as a result of enemy bombardment.

BLACK DEATH

A lasting blow to the population and social structure of Europe and Asia

Bubonic plague spread to Europe from the far east. It travelled along the routes of trade and pilgrimage, originating in China in the early 1330s. From there it followed sea routes through southeast Asia and around the coast of India, picking up the pilgrimage route from the east to Mecca. It also travelled inland, along the Silk Road and other routes across Asia, from China all the way to Constantinople. From the Byzantine capital and other centres of the middle east such as Mecca, Baghdad and Trebizond it once more travelled inexorably along the trade routes through eastern and western Europe and northern Africa. It reached France and England in 1348.

The epidemic of 1348–9 was the worst, but not the only one. There were further outbreaks in 1361–2 and 1369. The succession of visitations cast a cloud over the fourteenth century. To the medieval mind, death was always a tangible presence. But the black death brought it even closer, as the period's cadaverous paintings, cults of flagellation, and the increasing use of chantries (instituted to perform masses for the souls of the dead) demonstrate. There were also sweeping economic results, inevitable when such a large proportion of the population was removed. The plagues of the fourteenth century set off a whole chain of events that were some of the most influential in the Middle Ages.

Today we are familiar with the notion that the spread of the plague was caused by a micro-organism carried by rats, a micro-organism known to biologists as *Pasteurella pestis*. But it was only in the last hundred years or so that medical scientists discovered the connection, as a result of work done on recent outbreaks of plague in southern Russia and China. To the medieval mind the plague was looked on as divine punishment for the misdeeds of mankind, similar to the plagues of Egypt in the Old Testament. It is reasonable to suppose that the micro-organisms that caused the plague, and the rats that carried it, had existed at least as long as mankind.

Why did the plague spread when it did? Largely because of improved communications over the great distances involved – the thousands of miles across Asia and Europe. The group of people who were mainly responsible for opening up these routes were the Mongols. Genghis Khan

The carrier of the bubonic plague

and his successors ruled over an enormous empire, covering China, central Asia, Iran, Iraq and most of Russia. In order to keep this empire together the Mongols developed a communications network along which both speedy messengers and slower caravans bearing goods could travel with ease. The records of Marco Polo's travels show how easy it was to travel long distances in this way. And Marco Polo was only one of many travellers during this period.

More significant still, the Mongol trade routes followed more diverse routes than had been common before. They revived the old Silk Road across central Asia, connecting China with Syria. But they also developed a more northerly route across the Steppes. This meant that the plague bacillus infected a burgeoning population of rodents for the first time, in an area where the micro-organism could survive summer and winter and gradually spread westwards.

William H. McNeill, a historian who has studied the impact of the plague in more depth than most, believes this development to be crucial. There had been plagues in Europe before, most notably during the sixth and seventh centuries. But the disease never seems to have got a firm hold. McNeill suspects that this was because the plague bacillus failed to find a lasting home, a stable ecological niche in which it could survive for long periods. The Asian steppes, with their many burrowing rodents and clement climate, provided just such a niche.

Once the black rats had established themselves here, the plague seemed to spread very quickly, from the earliest outbreak in China in 1331 to the height of the epidemic in western Europe a mere fifteen years later. The reason for the speed of this spread was that humans started to take part in the distribution of the plague bacillus. First there were the fast-moving Mongol horsemen, who could carry the disease as far as 100 miles in a single day. Then there were the recently developed shipping links between the Mediterranean and northern Europe, instigated in 1291 and becoming stronger as time went on. The final blow came in 1346 when some Mongol troops were besieging the city of Caffa on the Black Sea coast in the Crimea. Plague broke out amongst the Mongols and the infection spread into the city. The disease forced the Mongols to withdraw, and, through Caffa's trading contacts with the Mediterranean, the plague soon spread to Europe.

At the best of times medieval people were well aware of death. Plague brought death even closer, making medieval artists' preoccupation with corpses and skeletons all the more understandable.

The death toll

Some idea of the damage the plague could do can be gained by considering the outbreak in China in 1331. The population of China in 1200 was approximately 123 million. By 1393 this figure had almost halved to 65 million. Plague was not the only cause of this decline. The Mongol invasions occured during this time and these resulted in many casualties. But plague certainly accounted for a large proportion of these deaths.

In Europe the effect was devastating, although casualty figures varied widely from one region to another. The population of the city of Bristol, for example, was decimated; whole villages disappeared. On the other hand, Milan escaped the plague altogether. Taking Europe as a whole, probably one third of the population died of the plague during the period 1346–50. Deaths were likely to have been higher in southern France and northern Italy, lower in central Europe.

Any figures concerning population in the Middle Ages are at best estimates, at worst guesses. In England, the country on which the most research has been done, it seems that the population continued to decline for over 100 years after the outbreak of 1348. What was more, medical science could do little to combat the disease. Medieval medicine had various techniques to offer but none of them was appropriate for the black death. Primitive surgery, using some of the gruesome instruments illustrated in some medieval manuscripts, would have done more harm than good. Medicines concocted with herbs worked for some illnesses, but even the complex recipes of the medieval herbalists could not combat the black death. So the population continued to fall. This sustained drop had a marked effect on those who were left.

The economic impact

First, there were the economic effects. Before the black death, improvements in agricultural techniques had led to greater productivity and an increase in the population of Europe in the early Middle Ages. Forests were cut down to provide more land for agriculture, while the reclamation of land in England and the Netherlands also began at this time. The result was a higher capacity for food production – and a further increase in the population.

The black death transformed this picture. The expansion of agricultural land stopped as the plague hit the countryside. But much more badly affected were the urban areas, where disease travelled quickly amongst the poor of the towns. So country people moved away from the bad lands and concentrated on cultivating those best for agriculture, or they moved to towns to fill some of the gaps left there.

The drop in population, particularly amongst the poor, meant that labour was scarce and was valued more highly. There

was also more food to go round, so, after the initial onslaught of disease, the lot of the poor improved somewhat. But these benefits were largely offset by laws that prevented wage rises and restricted the degree to which workers could benefit from the availability of land. Nevertheless, the dramatic change in the size of the population meant that the feudal system, which had been the social and economic basis underpinning medieval society, was under threat. It took centuries to disappear completely, but such a drop in population would shake the foundations of any system based on service rendered in return for land.

The psychological impact

Medieval writers and artists have left us much information about the way in which the black death dominated peoples' lives and thoughts. The plague seemed to be everywhere, taking away thousands, especially from the lower classes. One writer, William of Newburgh, summed up the ubiquity of the disease and the uphill struggle for those who were left: 'Day after day it seized so many and finished off so many more that there was scarcely to be found any to give heed to the sick or to bury the dead'. The trouble was relieved only in the winter, when the cold conditions were less favourable for the transmission of the disease.

The visual arts of the time make the horror all the more clear. Images of cadavers and skeletons, often shown next to richly dressed men and women, suggest how quickly life could be taken away. The figure of death – either as an angel or a ghastly figure with a sickle – appears in countless paintings of the period to take away the living or to open the coffin ready to accept the corpse.

How did people make sense of all this? The poet William Langland expressed the only view that could fit the plague into the medieval scheme of things: 'These pestilences were for pure sin'. In the light of this, it is not surprising that there was something of a religious revival. It took different forms in different places. In some parts of northern Europe the cult of self-flagellation became fashionable, men scourging themselves in an attempt to replace the suffering caused by the plague and to persuade God to take away the burden of disease.

Another religious practice that became common was the setting up of chantries. Under this arrangement one would leave a sum of money to the church to pay a priest to say masses for one's soul. In a society in which death was the dominant fact, such a provision seemed prudent. It also gave consolation to the living. Evidence of the amount of importance attached to chantries can still be seen in the magnificent chantry chapels that still exist in many churches and cathedrals.

There was also charity. The papacy, even though it was going through its own trials and tribulations during this period, led the way for at least some of the time. Pope Clement VI, who was pope from 1342–52 and ruled from Avignon, was a lavish dispenser of charity. This was also a period when many hospitals were founded. Most of these were very small by modern standards, but St Leonard's hospital in York housed some 220 of the sick and poor in 1370. It was a help, even if all they could do was to ease the passage of the sick into a shallow grave.

BATTLE OF ORLEANS

Behind the banner of Joan of Arc France finds a new identity

The Hundred Years War, although it did not represent a century of continuous fighting, dominated the relationship between England and France and thus a large swathe of western Europe between 1337 and 1453. England was successful at the great battles of Crécy (1346) and Poitiers (1356), but the Treaty of Brétigny (1360) gave France the chance to recover. A further challenge came from England in 1415 under Henry V when they gained control of northern France as far south as the Loire. On Henry's death in 1422, his brother John, Duke of Bedford, ruled as regent in France on behalf of the young King Henry VI. He revived the parliament of the Norman Estates and married Anne of Burgundy, cementing an alliance between Burgundy, enemy of the French king, and England.

In 1422 the French king died. This was a clear opportunity for the English to press Henry's claim to the French throne. But there was a threat in the south. The dauphin Charles ruled beyond the Loire, and the English had to fight the French at Cravant (1423) and Verneuil (1424). On both occasions the English and their Burgundian allies were victorious. Verneuil in particular was a triumph for the English: they captured two of the French leaders.

But all was not well for Bedford in Normandy, where opposition was showing signs of rallying to the cause of Charles. There was also opposition in Brittany, and Bedford had to declare war on John, Duke of Brittany, to bring him to heel. Meanwhile the Earl of Salisbury was moving south through France, and the Anglo-Burgundian council ordered him to challenge Charles' power, striking at the city of Orléans on the Loire. It was an important city, heavily fortified (there were seventy-one large cannons), and success here might mean access to the heart of Charles' kingdom.

Orléans was defended by a garrison under the command of the illegitimate son of the assassinated Duke of Orléans, known as the Bastard of Orléans. To begin with, he had to contend with successes on the part of the English. They arrived in October 1428 and quickly took Tourelles on the south bank of the Loire, although Salisbury was killed there. Early in the following year they concentrated on cutting off the city from the north, building a series of forts (or 'bastilles') around the city at the various approaches. Orléans was now effectively cut off, and the people in the city gradually grew short of food. They hoped to intercept some of the incoming English supplies, but were unsuccessful – little help came from Charles.

Yet there were local risings against the English, and beyond the city things did not look as bad for the French as they did within. But these uprisings lacked a leader. At this point, the most unlikely leader in the history of warfare appeared. Joan of Arc came from peasant stock. She was brought up in the village of Domrémy, near Vaucouleurs in Lorraine. Since the age of thirteen she had heard 'voices' that told her to go to Charles and tell him that she had been sent by God to defeat the English at Orléans and take him to Rheims where he would be crowned king of France.

Joan of Arc

After various interviews she was allowed to speak to Charles at his court at Chinon. The dauphin was convinced by her and she was allowed to leave for Orléans with supplies and a relief army of three to four thousand men. By the time she arrived at the city, on 27 April, the Burgundians had left, leaving the English with too few troops to carry on the siege effectively. Joan's supplies were floated into the city on barges and the French were able to enter Orléans through a gap in the English lines and relieve the city.

Although Joan was keen to persuade the English to surrender they refused, and the French set about preparing for an attack on one of the English bastilles so that communications could be restored with the outside world. They chose and took the Bastille de Saint Loup to the east of the city on the road to the town of Jargeau. Soon the French had crossed the river and taken two of the southern bastilles, St Jean le Blanc and Les Augustins.

The English had to retreat to Les Tourelles, their bastion on the drawbridge across the Loire that they had breached to cut off the city. On 8 May the French repaired the bridge and attacked Les Tourelles from both sides. The English boldly defended their last bastion, pushing back the French each time they tried to throw up scaling ladders to attempt to storm its walls. Much of the fighting took place in the deep ditch around the bastion. During the fighting Joan was wounded, and there was a short break in the attack. But finally the bastion was taken and the English were forced to surrender. The city was saved, communications were restored, and the English were humiliated.

On 13 May Joan met Charles at Tours. She urged him straightaway to make for Rheims, where he should be crowned king of France. But the French generals realized the importance of consolidating the victory at Orléans by pushing the

English away from the Loire. This they did in a series of successful battles, culminating in the routing of the English at Patay. The way seemed to be clear for Charles to go to Rheims.

Here he was anointed King of France. Immediately he was granted spiritual credibility, just as the victories at Orléans and Patay had given him temporal credibility, as the ruler of France. Whole areas of the country submitted to his rule.

It was not over. The English opposition had not been entirely quelled and the war would go on until 1453, after which the only English possession in France was Calais. Joan, meanwhile, would be captured by the Duke of Bedford, tried, and burned as a witch in an attempt to discredit Charles and to vitiate his spiritual authority. But Joan's triumph at Orléans was still a turning point for the French. After this they acquired a national identity and a belief in their power to gain victory that they had lacked before. Joan gave the French a new symbol of nationhood, and the courage to act in a way that was worthy of this new role.

Leading the French before the Battle of Orléans, Joan of Arc cut a unique figure. The only surviving contemporary sketch of her shows a woman with long hair, giving the lie to the accounts that portray her shorn like a man. Whatever her appearance, however, she gave the French what they needed: an inspiring battle leader and a symbol of their nation.

FALL OF CONSTANTINOPLE

The end of the Byzantine Empire

One of the effects of the crusading movement was to isolate the Byzantine Empire from the west. The Byzantines, Christians like the crusaders, ostensibly shared their sense of purpose – to further Christianity, in particular by returning the Christian 'Holy Places' to Christian control. But in fact the relationship between the two powers was uneasy, with the Byzantine emperors doing their best to shepherd the crusaders through their territory with a minimum of controversy, fighting and looting. By the time of the fourth crusade of 1202–4, Constantinople itself was a target. The religious aim was to reclaim it for western, Catholic Christianity; the secular aim was to foster the trading power of the city of Venice, where the crusade began. But the underlying motive was jealousy of the riches of the Byzantines: there were probably more holy relics in Constantinople than in Jerusalem.

The sorry result was a city looted and pillaged, with large areas set on fire, and a distribution of the holy relics of the city between the Franks and the Venetians, who took the lion's share. The hold of the Latin west on Costantinople did not last. By 1261 a Greek Orthodox emperor, Michael VIII, was on the throne again. But the power of the eastern empire was curbed. The once vast empire was divided between Balkan, Frankish and Italian lords. And Byzantium was torn by civil wars: one emperor, John V Palaeologus, reigned for fifty years during the fourteenth century, having been deposed and restored three times.

More important than this, the empire relied on outsiders for support. It was the Genovese who rescued Byzantium from Frankish hands and helped to restore the Orthodox emperors. They too needed to be paid. However, another power was appearing which was to prove still more influential in the great area over which the Byzantine emperors once ruled: the Ottoman Turks.

Sultan Mehmet II, the Conqueror

The first recorded member of the family who were to rule the long-lived Ottoman Empire was called Ertoghrul, who came from the town of Sögüt in western Anatolia, near the border between the Byzantine Empire and the domain of the Seljuk Turks. His son, Osman, gave the dynasty its name. The charisma of these early leaders, plus the excellent strategic position of their lands, brought many followers to the Ottomans. The result was probably something of a population explosion which led them to expand their domains. This they did in the name of Holy War against the non-Muslims, and their expansion continued through the fourteenth century and into the fifteenth.

The Ottomans were formidable soldiers. Their famous fighting corps of janissaries, first levied and trained at the end of the fourteenth century, were soon feared throughout the Balkans. But fear was not the only emotion aroused by an Ottoman attack. In many areas the heavy demands of the feudal system (high taxes and hard labour) were replaced by a more liberal system under the Turks.

The Byzantine emperors did not look upon the Turks as outright enemies either. In past centuries Byzantine rulers had married Turkish princesses. The Seljuks, the ascendant Turkish dynasty of the twelfth century, had been friendly towards their Byzantine counterparts. And when it came to the time of the Ottoman expansion, civil wars meant that the Byzantines were diverted from the new challenge. In fact, the Turks themselves were sucked into this conflict.

During the struggle between John V and the supporters of the child emperor John Cantacuzenus in 1344, the younger John's regents hired Turkish mercenaries to help them out. Cantacuzenus' side was victorious and the new emperor called once more on Turkish troops to fight for him against the Serbs. Meanwhile the Turkish expansion continued. By 1354 the Ottomans had crossed the Dardanelles and conquered Gallipoli. It was as if the fall of the western Roman Empire was being played out again. A foreign force was simultaneously making itself necessary to the empire and beginning to take some of its power.

Another symptom of the empire's dependence on the Turks came in 1373 when the emperor John was forced to recognize the Ottoman leader Murad I as his overlord. Murad was instrumental in defeating John's enemies in the next round of Byzantine civil wars and the reliance of John on the Turks was confirmed. The new-found power of the Turks enabled them to move on to take Bulgaria in 1393. They also pushed their boundary eastwards into Anatolia, although here they met fierce opposition from the Mongols who defeated them at Ankara in 1402, checking their advance for some years.

By this time the Turks, under Murad's

A medieval view of Constantinople, with its strong walls and the church of Hagia Sophia prominently portrayed, shows how well defended the city was. In front stand the Sultan, a janissary wearing elaborate head-dress, and a royal falconer.

son Bayezit, had already planned to take Constantinople, the one remaining representative in the east of Byzantine strength and Christian civilization. But fears of a European coalition helping the Byzantines, and the defeat in the east by the Mongols, put paid to his plans. The work of Bayezit's immediate successors was therefore in re-establishing Ottoman power in Anatolia. The final blow was left until the mid-century reign of Mehmet II, known as 'The Conqueror'.

Mehmed came to the throne in a strong position. His power in Anatolia and Bulgaria was confirmed; he had no rivals for the throne – a strong advantage for a new, young ruler. He liked to strengthen his position further by alleging that his mother, who was probably a Turkish slave-girl, was a Frankish princess. He was going to make Ottoman Turkey into a world power.

By contrast, the Byzantine emperors were weak. To the last of the line, Constantine, the weakness of the capital was so evident that, in an extraordinary break with tradition, he was not even crowned there. Constantine's coronation was in the tiny city of Mistra in the Peloponnese, the last bastion of Greek Orthodox culture. It was another example of how the Byzantines had to look beyond their own local resources to hang on to their position.

The conqueror's progress

To begin with, Mehmet cultivated peace. He warmly received ambassadors from neighbouring kingdoms and from the emperor Constantine himself, promising to respect the boundaries of what was left of the Byzantine Empire. But it was a deceit. Mehmet used the years of peace at the beginning of his reign to prepare for the the great blow – an attack on Constantinople itself. Why did he concern himself with the city when the power of its emperors was so obviously at its lowest ebb and when he held so much of the surrounding land anyway? The capital of the eastern empire had immense symbolic value. But more than this the Byzantines, weak as they were, had long shown their ability to plot with the enemies of the Turks: what was left of their stronghold had to be broken.

Mehmet began by attacking the cities on the Thracian coasts of the Black Sea and the Sea of Marmora. There were also attacks in the Peloponnese to distract Byzantine princes there from coming to the aid of the emperor. Nearer to the capital, Mehmet already had a great fortress at Rumeli Hissar on the Bosphorus. From here he could control sea traffic coming to Constantinople from the north. His victories on the Marmora coast gave him control in the south. He could have cut Constantinople off from these bases and let the city die slowly. But Mehmet decided to go for a full-scale attack.

A great army assembled outside the land walls to the west of the city on 7 April 1453. Those walls must have seemed daunting even to the determined Turks. Their designers could not have imagined such a large army equipped with cannon, but the walls' solid double construction, their many towers, and the endurance of the defenders enabled the Byzantines to hang on.

For seven weeks the cannon pounded away at the walls, and the defenders were gradually worn down. Meanwhile, realizing the great strength of the land walls, Mehmet decided to attack at another point too. He wanted to bring his ships out of the Bosphorus into the Golden Horn, the stretch of water that constitutes the northeastern boundary of the old city. But the Byzantines prevented this by stretching an enormous chain across the channel. Audaciously Mehmet transported his ships overland from the Bosphorus, across the wedge of land where the 'new' city now stands, to the Golden Horn. He had Constantinople surrounded.

On 29 May the final assault came, with Mehmet stretching the defenders by attacking at three different points around the city. One of the greatest blows came when the Genovese general Justiniani fell. He led a substantial force of Byzantine allies who lost heart when their leader was killed. Then in the confusion one small gate was left unguarded at the time when Mehmet's crack troops, the janissaries, were brought into the battle. This small loophole gave them the advantage they needed. The walls were soon swarming with the Turkish forces and the last Byzantine emperor fell in the vain attempt to defend his city. According to the contemporary laws of Holy War, a city taken by storm could be looted by the victorious army, and three days of terrible bloodshed and trophy-taking duly followed the Turkish victory.

The Ottoman Empire was already well established when Constantinople fell, but the fall of that city ensured its survival. In one form or another it was to last until 1924, an Islamic empire to replace the old Christian one, with the old capital, renamed Istanbul, at its hub. At its height in the sixteenth century, the Ottoman Empire stretched from the Adriatic to Kurdistan, from the Crimea to the Red Sea. It was only at the sea battle of Lepanto in 1571 that the seemingly unstoppable advance of the Ottomans into Europe was halted.

As a result of this expansion there were great changes. Many Turks, for example, moved into the Balkans permanently changing the cultural mix of the area. But it was not all change. Mehmet, for example, was relatively tolerant when it came to religion. He did not ban the bishops, but organized them into a synod and gave them the church of the Holy Apostles as their headquarters. The greatest church in Constantinople, the Church of the Holy Wisdom (Hagia Sophia) was turned into a mosque and became the architectural model for many another. And so the balance of power remained tipped well in favour of Islam, leaving western Christianity even more out on a limb than it had been after the crusades.

INVENTION OF PRINTING WITH MOVABLE TYPE

A quantum leap in communications

The process of printing that today we take for granted has been in widespread use for around five and a half centuries. During that time it has ushered in so many changes, publicized so many new ideas, borne so much propaganda, and described so many innovations that the invention of the modern printing process has a good claim to be the most influential in any list of great 'world events'. And yet we know surprisingly little about the birth of this bringer of knowledge, and have little information about the first of the great information technologies.

Of course the idea of 'printing' is an ancient one. Potters in many cultures have used small stamps carrying decorative motifs to adorn their wares for thousands of years. In the Middle Ages, probably taking the cue from wooden blocks that were used to make prints on linen and silk cloth, pictures started to be printed on paper. They were often religious subjects intended for instruction in the same way that the poor could be instructed by the wall paintings and stained-glass windows in the great cathedrals.

It was possible to print texts in this way, too, but the process of engraving each word by hand on the wooden block was laborious and slow. It did not look likely to catch on as a means of disseminating literature. But if a way could be found of quickly producing individual letters that could be reused, so that one did not have to go through the engraving process each time, the potential of the printing process would be far greater. As wood-block printing became common in Europe, it seems that a number of people started to think about developing movable, reusable printing type.

They were not the first. As with so many good technological ideas, movable type seems first to have been conceived in the far east. In China in the 1040s the alchemist Pi Sheng was printing texts with movable type. He developed a process of sticking metal or hardwood characters on to a metal plate with wax and resin. The letters could be moved after printing by heating the plate and the type could be reused.

It was ingenious, but it did not catch on.

Johannes Gutenberg

The Chinese language, with its thousands of characters, did not lend itself to movable type. But movable type did have a successful history in Korea, where the king subsidized the printing of various books in the early fifteenth century. And the Uighur people (Turkic nomads who used a language with an alphabet) seem to have invented movable type independently around 1300.

No news of any of these developments seems to have reached Europe – or at least, if it did, written records have not survived. But Europe in the middle of the fifteenth century was a place ripe for easier distribution of information. The stirrings of religious discontent that were to lead to the Reformation had begun – and had begun to stimulate a demand for a wider availability of the Biblical text – preferably in the vernacular. Literacy was on the increase, too. And a method of book production that took responsibility away from the hands of the church would be welcome as religious changes gathered pace.

The people who developed movable type do not seem to have been associated with the existing wood-block printing industry. This is understandable. The next obvious step in the evolution of printing, making movable type from small wooden blocks, did not take off because wood wore out too quickly: the type would be useless before it was even reused. So the impetus came from men involved in metalworking, in particular from a goldsmith working in Mainz, Johannes Gutenberg.

Briefly and simply, four processes had to be mastered before modern printing could succeed. Good-quality, smooth, white paper was required; a fatty based ink was needed; movable type had to be perfected; and some form of press was required to get the ink from the type to the paper evenly and efficiently. Paper posed few problems: by Gutenberg's time, rag-based papers were common. It was quite easy to make existing ink sticky enough for printing. Presses were already in existence – not only for printing but also for operations such as crushing olives for their oil. So the main hurdle was the production of type.

What was needed was a method that allowed type to be produced both quickly and accurately. It had to be quick to give the new method the edge on wood-block printing; the type needed to be accurate so that it would fit together properly and give an even impression on the page. The solution was to engrave each letter in relief on one end of a hard metal punch. This could then be used to strike a piece of softer metal to create an impression called a matrix. The matrix in turn would be inserted in a mould into which molten metal could be poured to produce a letter in relief as on the punch.

The hundreds of pieces of type so made would then be distributed letter by letter in a wooden tray so that the typesetter

A compositor sets type, taking each letter from the appropriate compartment in the type case and lining the letters up on a composing stick. Next to him another worker is operating the press, pulling the lever to bring the paper into contact with the inked type. Behind the press a man is checking the printed sheets. Other recently inked sheets hang up to dry.

could pick up the ones he wanted and set them in lines and, ultimately, pages. When a satisfactory page was set, the dozens of pieces of type were locked in position and the resulting metal block or forme would be inked and printed at the press. When sufficient pages were printed, the type would be broken up and redistributed in the tray for reuse.

We are not sure of Gutenberg's exact methods of typecasting, though it is likely that by modern standards the process was slow, and that the type wore out rather quickly. The few documents about the process that have survived are tantalizingly brief and unsure in their terminology. We know only what we do because of a lawsuit that resulted when Gutenberg's business partners elbowed him out. The image of the great inventor being deprived of the financial rewards of his ideas is a familiar one and seems to be true in Gutenberg's case: he died in obscurity with very little money.

The same obscurity now surrounds another pioneer, Procopius Waldvogel of Prague, who was working at the same time as Gutenberg. And there are further shadowy figures in the story, such as Jan Van Zuren, Dirk Volkertroon Coornheart, and Laurens Janszoon, Dutch humanists and printers of whom we know little but who may have been using movable type before Gutenberg's first printed books appeared around 1453.

But it little matters to us now whether one or all of these people originated the idea of movable type or if, as seems more likely, they came up independently with similar systems. What is significant is that amazing speed with which the invention caught on, and the way in which printing presses set up throughout Europe and started to pour out their productions. By the end of the fifteenth century there were important centres of printing at Paris, Cologne, Deventer, Leipzig, Nuremberg, Augsburg, Basle, Lyon, Milan, Venice,

69

Bologna, Florence, and Rome. Each of these centres had produced over 500 books. And there were many other towns with one or two presses with smaller outputs. Altogether it has been estimated that the printers of Europe produced between 35,000 and 40,000 titles before the end of the century. In fifty years the literary world had been transformed and the age of the manuscript book was left behind.

What kind of books were produced by the early printers? Printers in Mainz, where Gutenberg worked, produced Bibles, prayer books, psalters, and other religious works. In particular, the famous forty-two-line Bible, attributed to Gutenberg himself and regarded as the first book printed with movable type, is considered a masterpiece of the printer's art. The success of these works inspired other printers and stimulated the great demand for the religious works which occupied most of the early printers' time, particularly in northern Europe.

If this does not sound a particularly revolutionary output today, it has to be considered in the context of late medieval Europe. The Bible had been the preserve of the church and the rich layman – only they could afford the expensive handwritten volumes. Now religious works could gain a wide circulation: one could expect to see books appear in editions of 500 rather than in individual handmade copies. And before long, the revolutionary ideas of reformers such as Martin Luther would be circulating alongside traditional religious works.

The demand was there and printers followed it. Soon printing presses were being set up in university towns. And this trend, together with the realization of the almost limitless scope of the printing press, led to a broadening of subject matter. Law, the classics, science, all were in demand. Series publishing began when the great printer

Aldus Manutius, working in Venice, began to produce his superb editions of the classics to a uniform format. The structure of the book trade developed with printers both selling their own wares and taking part in a continental network of trade in texts and ideas. (The Frankfurt book fair, still the international marketplace of the book trade, began in the sixteenth century.)

The rise of nationalism, stimulated by

Woodcut showing a printer's workshop

the Reformation, gave added impetus to another development. Although the majority of the books produced were in Latin, the language of the Roman church and of international scholarship, more and more were produced in the various European vernacular languages. So while printing contributed to a breaking-down of international boundaries as thought travelled across the continent, it also fostered the re-erection of new linguistic borders as the nations of the early modern world began to take shape.

But this was not on the whole a retrograde step because the sixteenth century was a great age of translation. Famously,

the Bible began to be translated into the vernacular languages. Other texts soon followed. Greek classics were often rendered into more accessible Latin for printing. Modern Latin works, such as More's *Utopia* and the works of contemporary historians, were also translated. And as soon as they were erected, the boundaries of nationalism were crossed in literature as the modern literatures of one European language were translated into the other tongues of the continent. To give one example, the Spanish play *Calisto* by Fernando de Rojas was translated into Catalan, French, Italian, German, Dutch, English and Latin.

Scholarship was well served. The Humanists could foster the recovery of the knowledge written down by the classical writers. Scientists, with the coming of the illustrated book, could instruct others about their findings and theories. The fields of law and history were afforded a wider readership. And, above all, religious writings reached a new and vast audience.

But did the printed book actually speed up the acceptance of new ideas? This is a complex question that can only be answered simplistically in a short article. But the technology of printing was not responsible for the ideas it conveyed. Printed books could contain either new ideas about religious reform or old prejudices about the position of the Earth in the solar system, new accounts of human anatomy or old myths about monsters. What the printed book did was to speed the *transmission* of these ideas, speeding up the passing of the intellectual initiative away from the church, hastening the demise of the oral culture, having a complex interaction with the rise of nationalism in Europe, and shaping the way people found out about things and passed on their opinions. This shaping has lasted until the present day.

COLUMBUS' VOYAGE TO THE NEW WORLD

A new chapter in the history of the expansion of Spain and Portugal

The fifteenth century was one of the great ages of European exploration and expansion. For the first time Europeans crossed the Equator, and the first significant exploration by Europeans of America and Africa began. India was reached by sea via the Cape of Good Hope and the first circumnavigation of the world was achieved.

From the perspective of the east, it was also an era of exploration. The Chinese admiral Cheng Ho commanded thousands of men in fleets of junks which sailed all over the seas of southeast Asia, through the Indian Ocean, along the eastern coast of Africa and around the Cape.

The fleets of the Chinese were great and their ships far bigger than those of the west. But it was the Europeans who did most to open up sea routes around the world. For the most part the Chinese sailed around, explored, and went back home. Why did the west press on when the Chinese, with their great resources and sophistication, drew back? In many ways it was precisely *because* the Chinese had such resources and sophistication that their explorers made less of a mark. They had their riches and did not need to trade or to conquer.

By contrast, the west was under pressure. In the Middle East there was the great Islamic power bloc, represented principally by the Turks. The Christian states, by comparison, were smaller and individually weaker. True, they had built up trade over land with the far east. But this meant crossing difficult territory for often meagre profits. And the disasters of the crusades had put further barriers between west and east. It looked increasingly as if the way forward was to explore by sea the unknown areas to the south and west, and to find sea routes to the east to avoid the difficult Middle East altogether.

The great European sea powers at the beginning of the fifteenth century were Spain and Portugal. It was these two countries – with some contribution from England, France and Italy – that were to provide the inspiration and funding for much of the exploration that was to take place. Explorers needed backing, but the impetus to start an expedition often came from an individual. One such individual was Christopher Columbus. He was from northern Italy, born in Genoa and educated at Pavia. But he lived in Lisbon and was eventually to find favour with the Spanish. Columbus was an internationalist before he even set sail.

Columbus' ambition was to reach the far east by sailing westwards. This seems a high ambition indeed given the small size of fifteenth century ships. But it did not seem so great to Columbus. He knew the world was round and had a rough idea of its size. He also presumed that he could sail directly eastwards because he did not know about the barrier provided by America. Moreover, from reading Marco Polo, who exaggerated or overestimated the distance from Europe to the far east over land, he imagined the sea route to be much shorter than it is.

For Columbus, the prospect of the journey was less of a problem than the backing he needed. Both his native state of Genoa and his adopted monarch, João II

Christopher Columbus

of Portugal, refused him. In the end, he went to Ferdinand and Isabella of Spain and they gave him the support that he needed. By the beginning of August 1492 Columbus' three ships were ready. The largest was his flagship the *Santa María*, which had a crew of fifty men and weighed about 280 tonnes. The other two craft, the *Pinta* and the *Niña*, had crews of thirty and twenty-four respectively. They sailed from Palos in August 1492. The voyage was not without setback. Only three days out of Palos the rudder of the *Pinta* was found to be malfunctioning – Columbus suspected sabotage. Fortunately they did not have far to go before they reached the Canary Islands, where the rudder was repaired and stores were taken on board.

From then on it was the uneasiness of the crew rather than damage to the ships that posed problems. All were anxious to find land. It may have been this anxiety that resulted in false sightings, including one on 25 September that was witnessed by several crew members but turned out to be a false alarm. Such dashed hopes bred discontent. Columbus insisted that they were to press on and did his best to reassure his crews.

Finally, a genuine sighting of land came in the early hours of 12 October. Columbus was vindicated, even though the place they had come across was not 'the Indies', as Columbus had hoped. They had in fact arrived at a place inhabited by people who called themselves Lucayan. When they gathered on the beach to meet the admiral, they were bewildered to see Columbus bring ashore banners of the Green Cross and to claim their home for Ferdinand and Isabella of Spain. Columbus renamed the island after the Saviour, San Salvador. It is difficult to work out from Columbus' log exactly which island in the Bahamas he had found, but the most likely candidate is the one now called Watling Island, some 250 miles northeast of Cuba.

Columbus also visited other islands in

Columbus' flagship, the Santa Maria, took him as far as Haiti before she ran aground and had to be abandoned. When he returned to Spain with his other ships, the Niña and the Pinta, it was a triumph for the united Spanish kingdoms of Castile and Aragon, under whose flag Columbus sailed, although he himself was born in Genoa.

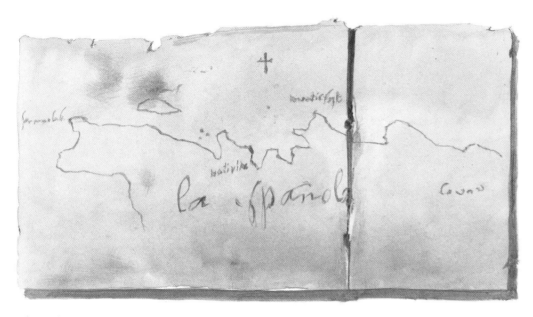

the Bahamas. Modern Rum Cay he named Santa María de la Concepción; Long Island he named for his king Fernandina; another island was named for Isabella. He was also told of a much larger island nearby, which he thought must be Japan, but was in fact Cuba – he still did not know that he was far away from the Indies that formed his original goal. He explored the Cuban north coast before sailing eastwards to modern Haiti, which he named Hispaniola.

It was off Haiti that Columbus met his one serious setback. The *Santa María* ran aground and he was unable to save her. He was able to rescue his men and stores, however, and they transferred to Columbus' new flagship, the *Niña*. In January 1493 the *Niña* and the *Pinta* set sail for home. In March Columbus was received at Tagus by the king of Portugal and at Barcelona, in triumph, by Ferdinand and Isabella. It was the beginning of a new era in the history of the Hispanic peoples.

Other explorers followed in the wake of Columbus. John Cabot, for example, an Italian who sailed on behalf of the English, discovered Labrador in 1496–7. Vasco da Gama sailed to India via the Cape

in 1497–8. In the following century the Portuguese navigator Ferdinand Magellan found the route south of South America to reach the Indies that eluded Columbus. Hernán Cortes sailed to Mexico in 1519 on behalf of Spain. The Spanish general Francisco Pizarro invaded Peru in the early 1530s.

Settlement and conquest went hand-in-hand with exploration and discovery. Columbus left behind men on Española in 1493. Panama began to be settled in 1519, to be followed by Mexico, Peru, Guatemala, Granada and central Chile. The incoming Spaniards began to mine precious metals and to farm, and by the 1560s silver was being exported to Spain in substantial quantities. Cochineal, tallow, hides and sugar were also prized commodities that were brought back to Spain.

The value of these imports gave Spain still greater power – and made her ships vulnerable to attack. The Spaniards organized a system of protection for the vessels and an increasing supply of silver and other precious goods flowed across the Atlantic. By 1580 Spain and Portugal came under a common ruler and the vast empire seemed all but unassailable.

THE SPANISH TAKE GRANADA

The end of Moorish Spain

After the decline of the Roman Empire, Spain was ruled first by the Visigoths, then, after the eighth century, by the Muslim Umayyad caliphs of Cordova. The Umayyads were highly civilized and in many ways successful rulers, but they were cut off from the eastern centres of Muslim power and the Christians gradually won back their Spanish lands. By the early thirteenth century Spain was a patchwork of Christian kingdoms – Castile, Leon, Navarre and Aragon – which tussled with each other for power for more than 200 years. Only Granada, in the south, was to remain for long as a representative of Islamic civilization.

Castile and Aragon

The most influential of the Christian states was the central-northern kingdom of Castile. It was gradually able to ally with and absorb the northwestern kingdom of Leon and expand southwards towards Granada. By the beginning of the fifteenth century most of central and northern Spain was in Castilian hands. The other strong state, that of Aragon, was in the east. And it was from here that the king who was to preside over some of the most important events of Spain's early modern period, Ferdinand II, was to come to the throne.

The first crucial event in Ferdinand's reign was his marriage. By marrying Isabella of Castile in 1479 he gave the joint crown control over almost all of Christian Spain. Moreover his own state, Aragon, had been suffering something of a decline. It had been a trading power, looking to the Mediterranean. But trade had slackened off and in the previous century Aragon had suffered badly because of the Black Death. An alliance with the more vigorous – and more warlike – Castile had clear advantages.

The fall of Constantinople in 1453 had renewed the idea of crusading in the minds of the Christian west, and it was this spirit that fired the desire of the Catholic monarchs to rid southern Spain of Moorish domination. They began in 1482, systematically attacking the kingdom of Granada piece by piece. Among the mountains of southern Spain the technique of warfare was based mainly on sieges. The endurance of the Castilian soldiers paid off as Moorish towns began to fall. Soon

Ferdinand of Aragon and Isabella of Castile

only the city of Granada remained in Moorish hands.

The disunity of the Moorish ruling class also helped the Christians. Ferdinand took advantage of this by reaching an agreement with Boabdil, one of the sons of the king of Granada. He agreed to go to war against his father in return for Spanish help. At first things went well for Ferdinand, with the important city of Málaga falling in 1487 to give him control of the western part of the Moorish area: Granada would soon capitulate too.

But Boabdil then decided to renege on his agreement and fight for Granada. This only served to bring things to a head. Ferdinand drew up a formidable army outside Granada, housing it in an impressive makeshift city. The preparations looked too much for the inhabitants of the city and eventually, towards the end of 1491, they agreed to negotiate with Ferdinand. By 2 January they had surrendered.

Agreement and disagreement

Terms were agreed that were not too unfavourable to the Moors. They were allowed to stay and practise their own religion, use their own customs and abide by their own laws. Hernando de Talavera, the archbishop of Granada, seems to have honoured this agreement. But trouble brewed. The Spaniards feared a revolt, and Talavera suffered opposition to his policy of tolerance. Forced conversions of Muslims were followed by revolts, and finally most of the Moors were expelled to northern Africa.

The taking of Granada was seen by Ferdinand and Isabella as the culmination of centuries of Christian reconquest in Spain. At last the country was completely Christian again. The refined Islamic civilization that had held on in southern Spain for so long was finally crushed. With it went a whole cultural tradition – that of learning and scholarship, of art and architecture – which was unique in western Europe. But the reconquest was also a new beginning. It acted as a confirmation that the new united kingdom could continue to expand – this time outside the Iberian peninsula. Soon the voyages of men like Columbus would instigate Spanish conquest and influence across the world.

The city of Granada was the last stronghold of Moorish Spain. With its superb buildings, such as the Alhambra, it had also become the symbol of Islamic civilization in Spain. The force Ferdinand gathered outside the city was formidable, and it was enough to push the holders of city towards negotiation and final surrender.

APPEARANCE OF LUTHER'S THESES ON INDULGENCES

The beginnings of the Reformation

The Protestant Reformation was one of the most important and wide-ranging movements in human history. Most obviously, it changed the way people thought about religion. It opened up and widened the gaps in Christian unity that were being felt in Europe in the fifteenth and sixteenth centuries. It led to a fragmentation of the power and influence of the church of Rome. It also had essential political results, being related to the cause of nationalism and the growth of towns and cities. Ultimately, it changed the map of Europe.

It was first of all a movement for religious reform. A growing group of people were unhappy with certain beliefs and practices in the Roman Catholic church. The most notorious practice was the purchase of 'indulgences' – the idea that you could buy your way out of punishment for your sins after death by giving money to the church. Such a practice clearly invests great power in the priesthood, particularly the Pope. And one of the wellsprings of the Reformation was a revolt against papal power – whether it came through in the reaction of a king like England's Henry VIII, who broke with Rome so that he could divorce his queen but who remained head of a church essentially Catholic, or whether it was manifested in a reformer like Martin Luther who pressed for doctrinal changes that took him farther away from Rome.

The position of the papacy

By the fifteenth century the popes were powerful figures – both politically and within the church. There had been popes at Rome since the first century. In spite of trials and tribulations, by the time of Pope Innocent III, in the thirteenth century, the papacy had a crucial political influence on what happened in Europe. Emperors and kings were often made to follow papal policy, and people spoke of the two 'swords' – of political and spiritual authority.

But papal power did not go unchallenged. In the fourteenth century popes were forced to flee to Avignon, where they lived under the protection of the French kings during disturbances at Rome. It was also during this period that rival popes, with the support of different political backers, sometimes ruled at Avignon and Rome. The open political struggles with which the papacy was involved, together with episodes such as the massacre of heretics and involvement in dubious military adventures such as the fourth crusade, made the papacy look far from infallible; the diversity of the Christian world began to look like disunity.

Martin Luther

The early reformers

It was against this background that movements towards religious reform began to take place. Three vigorous heretical movements appeared in the fifteenth century to challenge the Catholic Church: the Hussites in Bohemia and Moravia, the Lollards in England, and the Waldensians in France. In particular, the Hussites, behind their leader Jan Hus of Prague, provided a blueprint for the Reformation. The central principle of Hussite teaching was apparently simple: Hus wanted the congregation to partake of the wine (which was reserved for the clergy) during communion. But even here a questioning of the special position and authority of the clergy can be seen. What is more, Hus preached widely against abuses in the church and gained much popular support. His views led to his being burned as a heretic in 1415.

The Hussite movement did not die with Hus. An uprising and a civil war after his death led eventually to the Bohemians being granted their participation in the communion wine, although the Pope did not ratify the judgement. The Hussite cause, then, illustrates the way in which the Reformation relied on the interaction between inspirational individuals and popular opinion. Hus was in one sense a leader; but he was also following up and responding to discontents that already existed around him.

And these discontents were not confined to Bohemia. On the matter of indulgences, which so preoccupied Luther, criticisms had long been made. In the village of Montaillou in southwestern France, the community exhaustively studied by historian Emmanuel le Roy Ladurie, indulgences were thought of as a racket in the early fourteenth century. The Pardoner in Chaucer's *Canterbury Tales* (written in the same century) is a cheating purveyor of spurious 'relics'. Anticlericalism has a long and popular history, on which the leaders of the Reformation could draw. What is true of Hus can also be said of the Reformation's most famous figurehead, Martin Luther.

Luther's early development

The political position of the vast swathe of central Europe we now know as Germany has always been a key factor in European history. In Luther's time, despite being under the general rule of the longlasting Habsburg dynasty, it was disunited and the German Reformation was to feed on this disunity and exacerbate it. Social tension, together with a long tradition of questioning the Pope's authority, provided a good breeding ground for change.

Martin Luther, the son of a miner from Saxony, studied at the German university of Erfurt. By the time he took his master's examination in 1505 he would have absorbed the academic traditions of the university. He would have a training in the traditional skills of disputation, textual analysis, the formation of theses (themes for debate), conclusions and proofs, and rhetoric that would stay with him. He would also have been influenced by the nominalist philosophy at Erfurt, with its stress in theology on faith and scripture. He had also undergone his first spiritual crisis.

After taking his master's degree, passing the examination with flying colours, it was expected that Luther would continue his studies. This he did, choosing law as his subject. But with apparent suddenness he broke off his advanced studies to become an Augustinian monk. In spite of stories about his being required to clean latrines and go on begging expeditions, Luther remained an academic. On taking Holy Orders in 1507 he began to study theology and by 1511 he had a teaching post at Wittenberg.

Luther could not fail to be aware of the reform movements that had already gained ground in Bohemia, England and elsewhere. As an academic he would now become increasingly alert to another powerful force for reform: the teachings of humanism philosophers such as Erasmus of Rotterdam. Both the social and intellectual climate were appropriate for a new initiative for reform.

The issue of indulgences

It was on the subject of indulgences that Luther took his first stand. The way indulgences were used by the church seemed to Luther to be far away from the concept of repentance and change of heart that the gospel asks of a sinner. So Luther began to clarify his ideas by writing them down, in the form of a *Treatise on Indulgences* and a set of theses.

Luther's command of language ensures that his theses come across as strong assertions; but it should never be forgotten that their form means that they were primarily intended as starting points for debate. But not dry debate. The theses are impressive because they are based on knowledge of humanity and a feeling for Luther's fellow humans. For example, it is proposed that one's first duty is to support one's fellow humans rather than giving money to the

church: 'Christians are to be taught that he who gives to the poor or lends to the needy does a better deed than he who buys indulgences.' The Pope should himself gives alms to the poor rather than spending money on embellishing St Peter's – in fact, he should sell St Peter's to give alms to the needy, and so on. The same practicality pervades Luther's interpretation of spiritual matters. The sinner should be

The Wartburg castle, Luther's refuge

repentant. But this repentance must be shown by 'outward mortifications of the flesh' if it is to be worthwhile.

Luther did not immediately publish his theses. He sent copies to Archbishop Albrecht of Mainz, the local senior cleric; he also sent copies to his local bishop, the Bishop of Brandenburg and to various friends. There is also a story that Luther nailed copies of the theses to the door of the church at Wittenberg. Whether or not this is true, they soon became public knowledge. Very quickly, printers got hold of them and the theses were circulating widely.

Luther was disturbed – he did not want to circulate the theses. And the response from many recipients was one of alarm – the Prior at Erfurt, for example, worried that Luther would bring shame on his order. But more progressive thinkers, such as Erasmus and the artist Albrecht Dürer, received the theses more warmly – Dürer praised Luther for saying publicly what everyone else thought.

Why did the theses, concerning a single aspect of church practice, inspire such controversy? Because they hit at the heart of what the established church stood for, threatening its economic foundations, its authority, even its political power and the power of the Pope. When the Dominican friar Fr Tetzel formally denounced Luther as a heretic and asserted that he would be

burned within a month, it cannot have been a total surprise.

The issue of faith

It was not only his ideas about indulgences that made Luther a controversial figure. Luther had come to believe that the vital route to a person's salvation was through faith, and that the essential religious teaching was contained in the Gospel. The effect of this was to deny the importance of good works (it was possible to do good works but to remain sinful, Luther saw) and, with the primacy of the Gospel, to devalue the priesthood. The importance of the priesthood was also reduced in the light of Luther's belief that it is God himself who through the Holy Spirit offers salvation by arousing faith in a person. Such ideas led to the concept of a 'priesthood of all believers', something quite alien to Rome.

Moving away from Rome

The appearance of the ninety-five theses and the spread of Luther's ideas about faith around the German states led the established church to pursue Luther and to demand that he take back what he had said. Members of the priesthood could see that, if Luther's ideas caught on, the formation of a new church would be likely if not inevitable.

A series of assaults on Luther took place. He was denounced by Archbishop Albrecht of Mainz late in 1517. The following year the Pope sent Cardinal Cajetan to try to make Luther retract. In 1520 the Pope produced a bull, entitled *Exsurge Domine*, condemning forty-one of Luther's theses; Luther was urged to retract within sixty days. He did not retract and, on 3 January 1521, was excommunicated. The break with Rome was complete.

But the pressure did not stop there. The new emperor, Charles V, called Luther to the Diet of Worms later in 1521 where he was again asked to retract and again he refused. The result was that Luther, already exiled from the church, was exiled from his country: he was forced to leave the empire and his writings were ordered to be burned.

The spread of Luther's ideas

Even before the final break, Luther's ideas spread quickly. Soon some fifty of the eighty-five free cities of the empire had taken up the Reformation. Once the theses had been put down he continued to write, and his books became popular. One text, *On good works*, was published in June 1520. By the end of the year, eight editions had been printed. Another work, the *Sermon on indulgence and grace*, went

Although he was outspoken, Luther was often a still point in the turning world of Reformation Europe. He did not seek publicity – indeed it is not even certain whether the famous episode of his nailing the theses on indulgences to the church door at Wittenberg actually took place at all. But he did stick steadfastly to the task of writing and preaching about his views, not only in the theses, but in innumerable other letters, books and sermons. As the turmoil went on around him, Luther worked frantically. During his voluntary exile in the castle of Wartburg he translated the New Testament into German in eleven weeks. Both his concentration on the word of Scripture and his sheer hard work were important influences on Protestantism.

through twenty-two editions in two years. Historians often see the new technology of printing with movable type as a key cause of the Reformation, spreading the reformers' thoughts across the continent like wildfire. This is certainly true, and Luther had published a vast number of works before the imperial ban in 1521. In Luther's lifetime his books went through a total of some 4,000 editions.

But the Reformation was also spread through preaching, so that the illiterate were not excluded from Luther's message. Many former monks, taking their cue from Luther himself, took to the road to preach the Reformation. This allowed the Reformation to spread to smaller towns and villages where books did not find their way and where literacy was lower.

By this time a formidable array of other reformers had appeared, for example the Swiss Zwingli, whose first book appeared in 1522. Such men fostered the spread of reform across Europe. It was quickly established in Austria and Scandinavia, while in the Low Countries, with the preparation of humanist writers like Erasmus, it soon took root.

In England Luther's books were studied at Oxford and Cambridge and burned (a sure sign of success) in London. William Tyndale followed in Luther's footsteps by studying at Wittenberg; he was to begin translating the Bible into English in the early 1520s to bring the words of the gospel to more English people than before. Although Henry VIII was no supporter of Luther, he too was to break away from Rome a few years later as a result of the dispute about his divorce. And in

1536, the General Council at Geneva voted to take up the reformed discipline.

The effects of the Reformation

The map of the world has continued to follow the religious divisions mapped out in the sixteenth century – religious trends begun during the Reformation have continued for centuries. A primarily urban movement, it also fostered and was fostered by the growth of towns and the rise of the bourgeoisie throughout Europe, particularly northern Europe. What is more, democracy has frequently followed Protestantism around the world.

In cultural terms, the divisions of the Reformation have produced their own characteristic art – from the writings of Bunyan to the paintings of the Dutch seventeenth-century masters. Protestantism, founded on a fresh scrutiny of scripture itself (a scrutiny often based on the need to translate the Bible into the a modern language), also had a tradition of scholarship. This was begun by Luther himself and his colleague at Wittenburg, Philip Melanchthon, as well as by generations of Biblical translators from Wyclif on.

Some historians have taken this tradition further, pointing to the formidable scientific and technological traditions of the Protestant nations and attributing movements such as the Industrial Revolution to Protestantism. If this seems too fanciful today, the important role of the church in education must be remembered, as must the town-based nature of the Reformation. The movement sparked off by Martin Luther and his contemporaries affected every area of human life.

CONQUEST OF MEXICO BY HERNAN CORTES

The end of Aztec rule and the start of Spanish domination in Central America

By the beginning of the sixteenth century the native people of what we now call Mexico had built up a successful and sophisticated civilization. The Aztecs, as these people were called, had their capital at Tenochtitlán, on the site of modern Mexico City. According to tradition the city had been founded in 1325 and in less than 200 years had grown into a metropolis of at least 150,000 people (although some authorities put the figure nearer 600,000), housed on a network of islands and sandbanks, criss-crossed by canals and causeways in the vast area of water called Lake Texcoco.

From this unlikely centre the Aztec kings ruled a region that took in the central area of modern Mexico, a strip of land several hundred miles long stretching from the Pacific to the Atlantic coasts. It was not a large area, but the Aztec influence went further and there was trade with the other pre-conquest peoples. The Aztecs also pushed into southern Mexico, where the Maya peoples (who once too had a great civilization but had now reverted to a more rural culture) accepted their domination. This move provided the Aztecs with a supply of foods, textiles, pottery and other necessities, something that the growing ruling and administrative class in the capital needed to supplement the food already grown by the army of peasants in the central Aztec region. In addition, wars with neighbours provided captives who could be sacrificed at the Aztec temples. The kingdom of the Aztecs was successful and rich. It was also ruthless.

The expansion of Spain

The voyages of men like Columbus has fired the Spanish enthusiasm for exploration. The church relished the idea of further converts to Christianity. The prospect of wealth brought back from newly discovered territories made this all the more enticing to the laity. The voyage of

Hernán Cortés

Columbus to Hispaniola provided a starting-point. The island became a base for further expeditions to the areas beyond. The first explorers assumed that from here they would be able to trade with China, which they imagined to be a short distance to the west of the Caribbean. Although they did not find China, the Spanish did reach the coasts of central America, an area that provided them with pearls and gold objects – and a source of slaves.

The first Spanish settlement on the mainland was in Panama. This was established in 1519 and gave Spain its first base on the Pacific coast. But this was not to be as important as two of the conquests that came after – the conquest of Mexico very soon afterwards and that of Peru in the 1530s. At these centres an urban network was already in place for the Spanish to take over. Here also were ample supplies of precious metals to make conquest enticing and financially worthwhile for the invaders.

Hernán Cortés had reached Hispaniola in 1504. So by 1519 he knew what there was to know about the Spanish New World and the riches that could be obtained there. But it is unlikely when he set off for the coast of Mexico in 1519 that he

realized the splendour of what he was going to find. He took only 600 men and sixteen horses, but the force was to be large enough to defeat an empire.

We do not know a great deal about who these early invaders actually were. It is thought that many were members of the Spanish lower nobility – Hidalgos, as they were called. Cortés himself was one of these, from a noble but badly off family: he had little to lose and much to gain from adventures abroad. Many were younger sons, unmarried and with a limited inheritance, but with a fair amount of military experience and the ability to withstand hard conditions at sea and on the battlefield. Cortés himself praised the way his men could overcome hunger and hardship and still perform heroic deeds of war. But if they were hard-nosed, they also had a romantic streak, fired by romances like *Amadis of Gaul*, a work of chivalry particularly popular in Spain at the beginning of the century.

The arrival of Cortés

Cortés and his men landed on the central American coast at Tabasco. The locals tried to defend themselves, but the persistence and weaponry of the Spaniards were too much for them. Accepting defeat, the people of Tabasco did homage to Cortés and showered him with gifts. It was not long before news of the Spanish arrival reached the Aztec emperor Moctezuma II at his capital of Tenochtitlán.

Moctezuma's reaction seems strange. He sent lavish gifts to Cortés but tried to discourage him from coming to the capital. As far as Cortés was concerned the source of these gifts had to be the place to aim for. He started off on the difficult trek westwards towards Tenochtitlán.

The journey took several months and the Europeans often met with opposition on the way. But this opposition was not united and, although fighting was often fierce, victory fell to the Spanish each time and Cortés acquired new followers from among the forces he defeated. Historians have asked why, with such a small force, the Spanish could win so easily? Some have suggested that the Europeans' weapons were superior. Yet the Spaniards managed a decisive victory at Otumba when they had lost all their guns. The most convincing explanation is the differing fighting methods of the two empires. For the Aztecs, war was inextricably bound up with ritual. The aim was to capture live victims who could later be sacrificed at the temples. Consequently, few of the Europeans were killed in battle with the Aztecs. The Spanish, on the other hand, had a ruthless European attitude to war: they went for the kill. While the Aztecs were trying to secure captives they were picked off by the conquerors. And the result was one-sided.

The Spanish leader arrived at the capital on 8 November 1519. Some of the auxiliary troops acquired must have told Cortés what the Aztec capital would be like, but these descriptions did not fully prepare him for what he saw. Cortés' companion, Bernal Diaz del Castillo, who recorded his impressions for posterity in his *History of the Conquest of New Spain* described their amazement when they saw Tenochtitlán and the other Aztec cities. Some of the men thought they were dreaming. Apart from the architectural style, which would have been like nothing they had seen before, the sheer size of the capital overwhelmed them: it was several times larger than the biggest contemporary Spanish city.

The arrival of Cortés saw the coming together of two very different cultures. Spain was ancient; the Aztec Empire had risen quickly and the capital must still have had the pristine quality that new buildings quickly lose. Their social structure, art, religion, methods of warfare and customs were all different. And their aims were opposed. Moctezuma wanted to be left in peace; Cortés wanted either to take over the empire or to find some other way of getting wealth out of it. But somehow the emperor and the conqueror came to an understanding. The Spanish made themselves at home in the city, as much in awe of their surroundings as the Aztecs were of their military prowess.

But soon there was trouble. When Cortés had to leave the capital his deputy Alvardo quarrelled with the Aztecs. The Aztecs tried to expel Alvardo. Cortés returned and forced the emperor to restrain his people but, in trying to put down the rebellion, Moctezuma merely directed the hostility against himself – he was stoned and put to death.

The loss of Moctezuma meant that Cortés had lost the chance of peaceful control. He withdrew from Mexico, unable to decide whether to bow to the persuasion of his companions and undertake a full-blown military conquest or to return as a trader. In the end he came back as a conqueror, cutting off the city's water supply and going for all-out victory. The Spanish hold on central and southern America was confirmed.

The new Spain

In many ways Cortés took over where Moctezuma left off. The transition was surprisingly smooth, given the great differences between the two distinct cultures involved. But, as Nigel Davies, archaeologist of the pre-conquest civilizations, has pointed out, the two cultures did have something in common: 'in both empires plunder and piety went hand in hand.' Moreover, many of the people who had been under Aztec domination had been ruthlessly exploited by their overlords: with little to do, they thought it worth their while to give the Spaniards a chance.

And perhaps there also lingered the idea that the arrival of Cortés was the fulfilment of the old prophecy of the return of the old Toltec god Quetzalcoatl, the plumed serpent deity.

So Cortés received local support when he set himself up like an emperor. He ordered the capital to be demolished and a new city to be constructed on its site. Catholic churches were built with the stones of the Aztec temples. The new city of Mexico would be as much of a tribute to Spain and the Christian God as the old had been to the Aztec leaders and their deities. But outside the capital changes were slower and the people had time to adapt to the new ways of their leaders.

Cortés himself could afford to be proud of his success. The Hidalgo had achieved his ambition – effectively a move up the social ladder to a position where his children would marry well. But there were objections from Spain. The authorities worried about being able to control their new territory, and the church seems to have been concerned about the well-being of the locals.

This concern was well-founded. Even Cortés, respectful in many ways as he was to the indigenous people, took vast quantities of goods as tribute from them. Worse still were the officials who were installed between the leader and the people, whose demands for tribute were still greater. Finally, the emperor Charles V ordered Cortés to remove the officials. Cortés refused and Charles had him replaced with a viceroy, Don Antonio de Mendoza. But the abuses continued. Well they might, when it was in the interests of Spain to use the wealth removed from America to fund expensive wars in Europe. The people of the Mexican empires had for centuries been compelled to provide for the glorification of their overlords: it was nothing new.

The greater Spain

Mexico was important as the first extensive Spanish conquest on the American mainland. But it was not the only one. Guatemala (1523–42), Peru (1531–33), Granada (1536–39) and central Chile (1540–58) were all to follow. Of these, the conquest of the Incas of Peru under Francisco Pizarro was as devastating as that of Mexico and, in its way, as important since it provided the Spanish with their second major centre in America. Peru, for all its riches, was a less attractive destination as it was much less accessible than Mexico.

These conquests have affected the history of central and southern America ever since. Much of the area became, and still is, Spanish speaking – the Spaniards were excluded from Brazil by a treaty granted to the Portuguese. The resulting blend of civilizations – European-Catholic with indigenous – has developed into a unique group of cultures. Moreover, the Spanish invasions in America constituted the biggest overseas settlement by any European power up to that date, perhaps influencing other European settlers elsewhere in the world in later centuries.

Two cultures confront each other near the great temple at the centre of Tenochtitlán. The Spaniards could hardly believe their eyes when they saw the size of the city, its extraordinary site criss-crossed with canals. Seeing how new most of the great buildings were must also have been a shock for people from Spain. At first relations between the Aztecs and the new arrivals were good and Cortés seemed to want to get peaceful control. But violent conflict would be almost inevitable when it became clear that the Spaniards had come primarily to exploit a new territory.

MAGELLAN'S JOURNEY AROUND THE WORLD

The first circumnavigation

Of all the great journeys that were made across the seas of the world during the fifteenth and sixteenth centuries, probably the most impressive was that begun in 1519 by the navigator who signed himself Fernão de Magalhães, and whom we know as Ferdinand Magellan. Alone of all the explorations undertaken up to that time, Magellan's fleet sailed all the way around the entire globe. Magellan was born around 1480 in northern Portugal. He came from a family of travellers and adventurers, and it was no surprise that when still a youth he volunteered to sail to India with Francisco de Almeida, Portugal's first viceroy there.

So it was in the east that Magellan began his career. Although we do not know much about what he did there, stories have been passed down that indicate that he served with distinction and that he won the confidence of the men under his command. On one occasion, when sailing home from Cochin China in 1510, the ship on which he was sailing and another in the convoy struck rocks and were virtually wrecked. The civilian passengers and captains were sent on ahead in boats and Magellan was given the task of staying in command of the two hulks and their crew. Under a lesser officer it would have been a case of 'every man for himself.' But Magellan preserved order, shored up the wrecks, organized a watch to guard against pirates, rationed out the available food and saved his men and cargo.

Magellan had proved himself by the time he was in his thirties. But the strength of character that served him so well also

On 28 November 1520, the small ships of Ferdinand Magellan crashed out of the straits that would be called after him to enter the Pacific Ocean. Soon the waters would be much calmer, as the ships carried on through the voyage that would effectively join together the two halves of the world.

got him into trouble with the Portuguese authorities. He was accused of selling surrendered cattle to Portugal's enemies and, although the charge was eventually dropped, he got into a dispute about pay. In addition, he was trying to persuade the Portuguese to back him in an expedition to find the spice islands (the Moluccas) via a westerly route. The king of Portugal was not interested in Magellan's scheme and so Magellan turned to the king of Spain. Here the reception was better and in the autumn of 1517 Magellan formally renounced his allegiance to his native country and signed the papers that gave him Spanish citizenship.

It took Magellan two years to prepare for his journey. Finally on 20 September 1519 he was ready to depart. He took with him five small ships, the *San Antonio*, the *Trinidad* (Magellan's flagship), the *Concepción*, the *Victoria* and the *Santiago*. All were small by modern standards, with the largest, the *San Antonio*, weighing in at 120 tonnes and the smallest, the *Santiago*, a mere seventy-five tonnes. The crews came from all over Europe. Irish, Greeks, Cypriots and Sicilians jostling with numerous Genoese, who were valued as the most skilled seamen. Sadly for Magellan there were also a number of people on board who were not to pull their weight – well connected officers and idlers whom he was politically obliged to take along. Yet to one of these upper-class passengers we owe more of a debt than any save Magellan himself. Antonio Pigafetta kept a comprehensive diary of the journey, and from this more than anything else we know the details of their extraordinary journey.

The small ships were heavily laden with cargo with which to barter, including large amounts of cloth, knives, mirrors, 500 pounds of glass beads, some 20,000 hawk bells. We also know that Magellan took various objects of much greater value that could be given to those of high rank.

The start of the journey

The first leg of the journey was relatively straightforward and took the explorers over familiar waters. From the mouth of the Guadalquivir at Sanlúcar de Barrameda they sailed southwest to the Canary Islands where they took on additional provisions and men. But from here, after sailing southwards along the bulging coastline of West Africa for some way, they struck out into unfamiliar seas, heading across the Atlantic in the direction of the northeasternmost point of the Brazilian coast. When they eventually made it to Brazil they continued southwards, resting for two weeks at Rio before sailing south again towards the cold, unfamiliar waters of the far south Atlantic where the strait into the Pacific Ocean would eventually be found.

By the end of March 1520 Magellan's ships arrived at San Julián Bay. Here their leader decided to spend the winter: conditions farther south would be unbearable as winter fixed its grip on the South Atlantic. But waiting is often more difficult than pressing on through difficult conditions and Magellan had to suppress a mutiny amongst his Spanish officers before the winter was over. Magellan prevailed over the mutineers, but this was not to be the last of his troubles on this long and hard voyage.

With winter over, the five ships continued south. Finally, on 21 October 1520, Magellan discovered the stretch of water that was to take him and his men from the Atlantic to the Pacific – the strait that was to bear his name henceforward. By now, with conditions still cold and scurvy rife amongst the men, life was hard on board. What was more, progress was frustratingly slow. They did not know that they had found the passage they needed, and their progress was often impeded by following inlets that led nowhere.

So one or two ships were always being sent ahead of the main party to check out the way forward, watching out for any potential dangers and searching for safe anchorages. It was too much for the officers and crew of the *San Antonio*, who forcibly took over the ship from their captain and headed back for home the way they had come. Reluctantly, after searching for the ship, the rest of the group went on, entering the Pacific Ocean on 28 November.

The Pacific provided much better conditions for travelling. By the end of January 1521 they had passed the islands of Pukapuka and were nearing Caroline Island, but at neither could they find an anchorage. Thus their progress was good but they paid the cost in dwindling supplies as food ran out and they were forced to chew on hides and eat stewed rats, with only the occasional banquet of fresh fish. How relieved they must have been when on 6 March 1521 they finally arrived at the first Pacific island, Guam, on which they could find an anchorage.

The island provided them with their first fresh food for 100 days, but their stay was not without trouble. The islanders appropriated one of Magellan's longboats, and his men had to kill some of the local people in order to retrieve this essential item of equipment. Magellan and his crews named the place the island of thieves in commemoration of this incident.

Their arrival amongst the outer Philippine islands was a closing of the circle of navigation for Magellan, for he had come at last to a place he had visited before on a previous trip via the traditional eastern route. At first he and his men were well received with gifts of bananas and coconuts, which they reciprocated with items from the holds of their ships. The sick could rest and the diet of fruit must have done something to relieve the less advanced cases of scurvy. It must have seemed a place of recovery and hope, but

little did Magellan know that his journey was soon to come to an untimely end.

It was in April 1521 that the explorers arrived at the Philippine island of Mactan. Here they became embroiled in a dispute with the local leader. Magellan tried to make the chief recognize Humabon, a local leader whom Magellan had converted to Christianity, baptized, and made

Ferdinand Magellan

into the representative of the king of Spain. But the people of Mactan would have nothing of this and took the Europeans by surprise by proving more formidable opponents than expected. They fired poisoned arrows and hurled metal-tipped spears at Magellan's men in such profusion that they decided to send raiding parties to burn the houses of the Mactan people. But far from disheartening the locals, this only made their opposition more fierce. Magellan fought bravely, defending his men and standing his ground so that many of them escaped back to their ships. But in doing this he tragically lost his life.

This sorry episode left the remaining members of the European party to make it to the Moluccas, fill their ships with cloves

and return home across the Indian Ocean and around the Cape of Good Hope. They were a sorry group. Of the remaining ships, the *Trinidad* was so battered it had to be abandoned. So it was in the *Victoria* that the new leader of the group, Juan Sebastián del Cano struggled home. Some seven months after leaving the Moluccas and three years after the original embarkation, the *Victoria* arrived home. Only eighteen of the original crew survived on board, although about the same number were to turn up via other routes later.

Samuel Eliot Morrison, the historian of exploration, summed up Ferdinand Magellan's achievement by saying that he stood supreme amongst the navigators of the Age of Discovery. He crossed the difficult waters of the southern Atlantic, 'and overcame mutiny, starvation and treachery to cross the Pacific Ocean, which he named.' Although he did not live to finish the great voyage his was the plan, and his survivors saw to it that it was completed, connecting the two 'halves' of the world that had until then seemed so completely separate.

More than this, Magellan's journey put a seal on the global scope of Spanish sea power, following in the tradition of the other explorers who had sailed on behalf of Spain. It was at once sad and oddly fitting that he lost his life in a petty struggle that centred around an attempt to get local people along the way to submit to the power of Spain. Yet in spite of his death, that power was increased by what he achieved.

But Magellan's was not only a great political achievement. More than any of the other great navigators of the period, he is an inspired example of the power of human skill, courage and determination, and an inspiration to all those who have explored the earth's unknown regions since his time.

PUBLICATION OF MACHIAVELLI'S THE PRINCE

The beginnings of a new secular style of government

Nowadays the adjective 'Machiavellian' is used for any sort of amoral scheming. It has been applied to ruthless aristocrats of the Renaissance period who would kill to achieve their ambitions and to the more metaphorical back-stabbing of modern politicians and businessmen – to anyone, in fact, who is prepared to let their ends justify their means. The Italian statesman, diplomat and writer Niccolò Machiavelli (1469–1527) gained this considerable reputation through several books, the most famous and influential of which was *Il Principe* (*The Prince*). Amongst the powerful and their cohorts this was one of the most popular books of the Renaissance. It contained much more than the cut-throat philosophy with which its author is so often credited, covering the topics of statecraft in a manner that was both to reflect and to shape the way in which states were governed in the early modern period.

Niccolò Machiavelli was born in Florence. His father was a lawyer and his family was prosperous, if not high-ranking. Florence at this time was enjoying a heyday under the head of the great banking family, Lorenzo de' Medici. But Italy as a whole, and even Florence after Lorenzo's death in 1492, was having a troubled time. There were five powers of consequence in Italy at the end of the century: Florence, Venice, Milan, Naples, and the Papacy. In the 1490s first France and then Spain made their claim on Naples. It would have been in the interests of the Italian states to ally together and fight off these invaders, but they only succeeded in playing one foreign power off against another. The result was that Spain took control of much of Italy, particularly the south, but also Milan and even Florence itself.

Machiavelli was very much part of this world of power struggle. For some fourteen years he worked for the Florentine government as a senior civil servant, employed mainly on diplomatic missions.

Niccolò Machiavelli

He worked principally for Piero Soderini, who was the effective head of state of Florence during a period when the Medici family were absent from 1502 to 1512. This work sent Machiavelli to courts and governments all over Italy and the rest of Europe, and he became astute at assessing the power and success of whatever states he was visiting and the reasons for their success or failure. This work gave him much of the background information he needed to write his books on government, although it is unlikely he would have written them had the downfall of the Florentine Republic and the return of the Medici family in 1512 not left him out of a job.

Instructing the Renaissance ruler

The out-of-work diplomat wrote many books, but the one for which he is remembered is *The Prince*, in which he summarizes all his knowledge and opinions about kingship. Today, it seems a ruthless text: its main subject is how the prince can gain control over the territory he wants and how he can keep hold of it. Yet it bore a clear parallel with the way a Renaissance ruler had to act if he was to succeed. Much of its advice was purely practical. It covered the different types of state, why states

fail or succeed, the methods princes can use to acquire lordship over a state and to retain it, and the way states might organize themselves to attack enemies or to defend themselves. It also deals with the character of the ideal prince, the personal qualities that make a good ruler.

The book is firmly rooted in political reality. For Machiavelli, that means first of all that the prince should be a skilled warrior – from successful soldiering comes the opportunity to expand one's territory and the means to hang on to it. Mercenary troops and auxiliaries (soldiers of a foreign power) are no good to achieve this, says Machiavelli, because of their divided loyalties. *The Prince* traces the fall of Rome to the employment of barbarian mercenaries by the emperors. The ruler should keep his own carefully selected militia. The care with which one selects one's troops should also be exercised in choosing officials in peacetime. Machiavelli counsels against taking notice of flattery and points out the importance of delegation and choosing staff wisely.

So success is not just a question of force. The usefulness of settling your conquered territory is stressed, along with the importance of winning the favour of the conquered people. Often this can be done by deception. Ferdinand of Aragon is cited as someone who had a reputation for faith and goodwill, but whose actions belied this. The good ruler should seem to do one thing while actually doing another.

Many details of the ideal prince's character and conduct are drawn from Machiavelli's view of one man, Cesare Borgia. Borgia was the illegitimate son of Pope Alexander VI. On his father's election to the papacy in 1492, he became a cardinal, but he gave up this position to marry the king of Navarre's sister. In alliance with France he won the Romagna region of Italy in a series of battles at the turn of the century. But he continued to rely on his father's influence for his position and

Do one thing while apparently doing another: Machiavelli's approach to government involved the prince concealing his thoughts behind a series of masks in order to stay several steps ahead of those around him. Machiavelli's ideas about the role of the prince came from his observations of the people he met as a Florentine civil servant. Probably the most influential were Cesare Borgia and his family, members of which ride by in the background.

when Alexander died in 1502, Cesare had to relinquish his dukedom and flee to Navarre.

Sometimes Machiavelli's admiration of Cesare is explicit in *The Prince*. For example, when he is discussing the personal qualities of a ruler, Machiavelli points out that cruelty can sometimes be necessary. Cesare's apparent cruelty reformed and unified the Romagna and re-established law and order. Thus his cruelty could be seen as a disguised compassion towards his subjects, who benefitted from good government. Borgia is also cited for his skill in arms, and it is noted how his success increased when he stopped using mercenaries and auxiliary troops.

Elsewhere his references to Cesare are more ambiguous. Towards the end of the book, for example, he mentions a ruler 'in whom some spark seemed to show that he was ordained by God to redeem the country' but who was rejected by fortune for that role. This is almost certainly a reference to Cesare and his sorry end.

But Machiavelli was not motivated solely by his admiration for one man. He was commenting on a broader trend, describing and arguing for a new type of kingship which fitted what he saw as the needs of his time. It was ruthless because Italy needed a ruthless, single-minded approach if it was to attain anything like stability. It was secular, because arguments with the church and power struggles with the papacy had weakened rather than strengthened recent rulers' hands. And it concentrated on the state rather than on some broad concept of European empire, because this was the political unit with which the Italians of his time had to deal.

The contrast between the type of ruler Machiavelli describes and what had gone before has been stressed by those who have compared his book with medieval manuals of kingship. These earlier manuals deal with states that exist to further Christian ethics as well as political success; the morals of the ruler are seen as inseparable from the success of the state. And the glory of the Christian state is seen in the context of the universal glory of the kingdom of heaven. Machiavelli, on the other hand, separates politics from religion, ethics from success, and looks at the problems of the state only in the larger context of its relationship with outside allies and enemies. *The Prince* is an attempt to come to terms with the political realities of the time.

In so doing, Machiavelli's book comes close to describing the modern states that were appearing at the end of the medieval period. At the end of the Hundred Years' War France and England had already emerged in this form. Under the catholic monarchs, Ferdinand and Isabella, Spain had also established itself as a 'new monarchy'. *The Prince* ends with a plea for a new prince for Italy. But Italy remained in disunity. Ironically, this made all the more appropriate as the forming-ground of modern statesmanship. Here, if anywhere, the arts of diplomacy and the ruthless determination to rule were necessary if any monarch was to survive.

But it is noticeable that many of these developments were already happening before Machiavelli's book appeared in 1516. It is incorrect to state that his was a crucial influence on events in contemporary Europe – Machiavelli was describing an ongoing process. And yet the prescriptions he laid down for the effective ruler – be it his view of an essentially secular monarchy, or his divorce of ethics from good government, or his regard for the ends as opposed to the means – have all found favour with later politicians. Parallels have been drawn between the views of Richelieu and Napoleon and those of the Italian writer. And, nearer still to our own time, Mussolini was interested enough in *The Prince* to write an introduction to the book. It does not lose its fascination.

GALILEO'S OBSERVATIONS WITH THE TELESCOPE

The birth of modern astronomy and confirmation of Copernicus' theory of the solar system

Observation is the key to science. Looking closely and carefully at the world around us, and analysing what we see, we create the building blocks of science and discover the clues that can tell us more about our world. Galileo Galilei is important because he was one of history's great observers, the first man to use the telescope effectively to look at the skies.

Galileo was born in Pisa in 1564. He received his education at a monastery near Florence and at Pisa University, where he began by studying medicine. His early career is surrounded by legend. One story says that his interest in mathematics was awakened by watching a swinging lamp in the cathedral at Pisa. He noticed that the lamp – in effect a pendulum – took the same amount of time to complete each oscillation from one end of the swing to the other, no matter how far it actually travelled. Another story tells of Galileo dropping objects of different weights from the top of the leaning tower of Pisa to see how fast they fell.

These stories are legends (the second is almost certainly untrue). But they do relate to Galileo's work: he wrote about pendulums later in his his life. And he researched the behaviour of falling solids, disproving Aristotle's contention that objects of different weights fall at different speeds.

Galileo was not rich. Soon after he gained his first degree he was forced to leave the university of Pisa through lack of funds. So in 1592 he applied for a job as professor of mathematics at the University of Padua, a post he was to hold for eighteen years. It was here that he completed his work on falling bodies, showing how falling objects speed up and slow down uniformly with time. And it was here that he did his work with the telescope that was to earn him lasting fame.

Working with the telescope

The contemporary view of the universe was quite different from our own. Most people, including the church, followed the view of the universe put forward by Ptolemy, in which the Sun, Moon and planets revolved around a central Earth. Polish astronomer Nicolaus Copernicus, on the other hand, propounded the theory that the Earth rotated on its own axis once each day and that it moved in orbit around the stationary

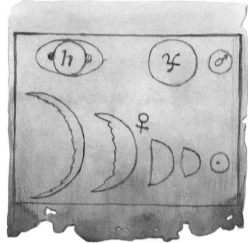

Galileo's sketches of Saturn, Venus, Jupiter and Mars

Sun. Most of Copernicus' followers kept their views quiet. They feared ridicule and the wrath of the church, which wanted to keep the Earth at the centre of things, and of the professional academics who had a vested interested in the Ptolemaic view.

Galileo saw the opportunity he needed in 1609, when a Venetian aristocrat returned home from a trip to Flanders with a telescope. Galileo wanted to use such a telescope to look at the planets and test Copernicus' theory. But the instruments available at that time were poor in quality and were not powerful enough for Galileo's purpose. One of the problems was that the glass

of the lenses was simply not ground accurately enough: it seemed impossible to produce lenses with a consistent curvature. So Galileo came up with an improved technique for checking lens curvature and was able to make vast improvements to the telescopes of the time. He soon achieved magnifications of over thirty times (ten times better than the capability of most previous telescopes). He found both that his instruments were in great demand and that he could use them to make new observations in the sky.

Impressive as all this was, it should be remembered that Galileo must have faced great problems with his telescope. For a start, the magnification he achieved was small by today's standards. Next, the optics of the time only permitted quite small lenses to be made. This, combined with the long, narrow tube made the field of view very small. In addition, there was no fixed mount or stand, so the telescope was difficult to hold still. In view of all these limitations it is surprising that Galileo saw anything interesting at all. Such problems also go some way to explain why contemporaries found it difficult to verify Galileo's findings. They lacked his rare combination of tenacity and acute powers of observation.

Galileo's first observations caused excitement in the scientific world. In 1610 he published a book, the *Sidereus Nuncius* (or *Starry Messenger*) recording his work on the telescope itself, and his observations of the Moon, the stars, the planets and, in particular, four of the moons of Jupiter. It was the discovery of these four satellites of Jupiter that

Galileo and his leather-covered telescope. Without this instrument he would not have been able to make the advances in astronomy that he did. Also on the table are proofs of his book Sidereus Nuncius.

caused the greatest sensation. Such a phenomenon – a planet with several bodies encircling it – seemed to parallel Galileo's view of the Earth and the other planets circling the Sun.

Among many scientists Galileo's book was received with enthusiasm. It had an immediate effect on the astronomer's life – the fame it brought enable him to leave his job at Padua and accept the post of 'philosopher and mathematician' to the Duke of Tuscany, a position that allowed him more time to do research. In Prague the astronomer Kepler, at first sceptical, managed to verify Galileo's discoveries. Galileo could also see practical consequences coming from his observations. For example, the working out of latitude at sea was a problem in this period because observable changing phenomena (such as eclipses) needed to be seen in the sky. The moons of Jupiter, with their rapid orbits and frequent eclipses, offered the possibility of a solution to this problem.

The visit to Rome

It was natural for an Italian scholar of the Renaissance period to want to share his discoveries and methods with some of the most learned and powerful people of his time – the men at the court of the Pope. So in 1611 Galileo made the journey to Rome. He was well received. Perhaps it was this positive reception that emboldened Galileo to publish explicitly his beliefs about the revolution of the planets around the Sun and to come out firmly on the side of the Copernican as opposed to the more widely held Ptolemaic view. In 1613, therefore, Galileo published his findings on sunspots, asserting that the movement of the spots across the Sun's surface showed that Copernicus was right.

Galileo decided to publish his findings in Italian, rather than the more usual academic language, Latin, which assured that they were widely read and debated. He found widespread support, although the vested interests of many who wanted the old ideas of Aristotle and Ptolemy to prevail meant that there was also opposition. The Aristotelians sought the backing of the church, pointing out that Copernicus' view of the universe was incompatible with that portrayed by the scriptures, and the Domenican friars preached against the abominable new 'mathematics'.

Galileo fought back. He pointed out that the church usually resorted to an allegorical interpretation of the Bible when its text described things that were found to be not literally true: could they not do the same this time? Many churchmen thought that they could. As educated men themselves, they could see the value of Galileo's observations. But at least one churchman did not agree: Cardinal Robert Bellarmino, the chief theologian at Rome. Bellarmino feared that if the church was seen to uphold Galileo's views it could fall into discredit. So in 1616 Galileo was told that his book would be banned. He retired from public life in disgust and did not publish anything for seven years.

It was at this point that Galileo came to an agreement with the Pope. He would be allowed to publish again if he put forward a clear and unbiassed account of both world systems, without coming down in favour of either. So he set to work. The result, his *Dialogue concerning the two world systems*, appeared in 1632. But it was not what the Pope wanted. Galileo could not resist the evidence of his eyes and his

Microscope from the time of Galileo

reason: the main body of his book showed him still to be a supporter of Copernicus, even though there was a conclusion at the end of the book along the lines that the Pope wanted.

At this point the church authorities produced their trump card: a document that purported to show that Galileo had been expressly forbidden to discuss Copernicanism in 1616. This meant that he had broken his earlier agreement and, despite his protestations to the contrary,

was tried and condemned as a heretic in 1633.

Fortunately for science, Galileo was not killed or put in a conventional prison. He was merely put under house arrest and was thus able to continue his work for the last nine years of his life. During this time he did further research on mechanics, worked out in more detail the idea of the pendulum (which the Dutch scientist Christian Huygens was to apply to clockwork a few years later), and used his telescope to make more minute observations of the Moon, including the way it wobbles from side to side during its orbit of the Earth.

Shameful as it was that Galileo should have been persecuted at all, there was something unsympathetic, something extreme and uncompromising about his character. It was not just that he stuck resolutely to his guns against the power of the church and the academic authorities. He also took the attitude that he had a God-given monopoly on astronomical discoveries. He writes in one document, 'It was granted to me alone to discover all the new phenomena in the sky and nothing to anybody else.' Yet his scientific success cannot be doubted now.

Galileo deserves to be remembered for his achievement in applying the telescope to the observation of the sky. The phenomena that he observed – Jupiter's satellites, the features of the Moon, the sunspots, Saturn's rings – are all profoundly important. Galileo also made valuable contributions to the field of mechanics.

But it was Galileo's method, as much as what he discovered, that remains important. His telescope brought home the key role of observation in science. Galileo was also a devotee of the experiment as a lynch-pin of scientific method. And he looked forward to many future developments. He foresaw the need for better telescopes, micrometers and devices for time measurement. And he predicted that with the aid of equipment like this we would be able to make accurate measurements of the size and position of the planets and the stars. Finally, he foresaw that physics and mathematics would come closer to offering combined ways of explaining the world. In this, as with much else, he was ahead of his time. It was an idea that Isaac Newton, born in the year of Galileo's death, would explore.

BIRTH OF WILLIAM SHAKESPEARE

A dramatist whose works changed our view of the world

William Shakespeare was born in the English midland town of Stratford on Avon some time in April 1564. His father was an influential town tradesman who held various offices in the town council, including that of High Bailiff, and his mother was the daughter of a local landowner. We know very little of Shakespeare's early life, but we can assume that he was educated at the local grammar school and we know that he married a local woman, who bore him three children. For some reason, some time before 1592, he went to London to become an actor and dramatist.

During the next twenty or so years he was to write a string of plays that, together with those of the other dramatists of the time and immediately afterwards, were to transform the English theatre and to provide a lasting inspiration for writers thereafter. Arguably, his influence has shaped the whole history of English literature – and that of other western cultures too.

If we know frustratingly little about Shakespeare's early life and how he came to London, we do know that his timing could hardly have been better. In the 1590s English theatre was starting to blossom. In the Middle Ages there had been a strong tradition of religious theatre, with regular and popular amateur productions of 'mystery plays' (reenacting scenes from the Bible) in major cities. The mystery plays, and the popular dramas that followed them, were not all high religious seriousness. They could include slapstick as well as solemnity, and were designed to appeal to ordinary people.

In the sixteenth century there was another dramatic tradition, more academic but equally influential, of verse translations from, and adaptations of, classical plays – the bloodthirsty tragedies of Seneca and the comedies of Plautus. This was a class of drama that was more likely to appeal to the educated classes. From these two broad categories of theatre the

Shakespeare's birthplace

English playwright had a rich fund of source material and inspiration: theatre could be serious or comic, religious or secular, its language could be down-to-earth or high-flown.

Theatre could also take place in a variety of locations. From churches to inn yards, great halls to market squares, the English had been used to seeing plays in many different contexts. And when the theatrical profession became organized enough to create purpose-built theatres, towards the end of the sixteenth century, it is not surprising that one of the most popular of these early locations should have been taken as a model.

The early public theatres in which Shakespeare played were modelled on the old inn yards and were influenced by the arenas used for bear-baiting. They were centred on a stage jutting out from one side of a courtyard surrounded by galleries. The rich could sit in the galleries, the less-well-off members of the audience could stand in the yard (or the 'pit' as it was known) in front of the stage. Again, the popular and prestigious aspects of the

theatre were coming together.

Plague was common in sixteenth-century London. When it struck, the theatres, breeding grounds for infectious disease, were closed. There was one such attack of plague quite soon after Shakespeare arrived on the theatrical scene. When the theatres reopened, in 1594, a change occurred which was to alter Shakespeare's position. The theatres were taken under the wing of the Lord Chamberlain. He himself assembled the best actors and writers he could find into his own theatrical company, the Chamberlain's Men, and Shakespeare was one of their number.

Under the auspices of the Lord Chamberlain, Shakespeare did well. In 1598 we hear of him as a 'principal comedian', in 1603 as a 'principal tragedian'. In the latter year the prestige of his company was given an enormous boost when the new king, James I, became their patron: from then on they were known as the 'King's Men'. In his later years with the King's Men Shakespeare was also a 'sharer' – rather like being a working director and shareholder in a company today, with an entitlement to a portion of the profits.

Throughout his career with the Chamberlain's and King's Men Shakespeare continued to act and to write for the company. Indeed he was the company's principal playwright. During his time in London he wrote some thirty-seven plays and acted in many more. His work has a variety that is surprising when compared to that of most other writers of the time. It is not simply that he wrote in many different genres (tragedy, chronicle play, comedy, and so on), but that a single play can encompass a multitude of moods. Thus a comedy such as *Twelfth Night* can embrace both mirth and deep sadness; an elemental tragedy such as *King Lear* also includes moments of grotesque comedy; and plays that seem to start with the simplest of actions can end up meditating on the profoundest of issues.

The shape of the Elizabethan playhouse derived from the near-circular arenas used for the popular 'sport' of bear-bating. Shakespeare called the theatre a 'wooden O', although since the building was made of straight wooden timbers it was probably in fact polygonal. There was a yard giving standing room (the cheapest accommodation), and several galleries with seats (progressively more expensive as you got higher and the view improved). The stage had minimal scenery – the rich language of Shakespeare and his contemporaries had to do the scene-painting.

Shakespeare's success was not only artistic. He earned a significant amount of money from his work in the theatre and he was able to buy a large house in Stratford. He was one of the more successful dramatists of his time if what we know of frequency of performances and comments by contemporaries is anything to go by. He won the respect and perhaps love of his colleagues, two of whom took the unusual step of collecting his dramatic works after his death and publishing them in the famous edition we call the First Folio.

Shakespeare was not the only great dramatist working in London at the end of the sixteenth and start of the seventeenth centuries. His exact contemporary Christopher Marlowe, as well as colleagues such as Ben Jonson, John Webster, and Thomas Middleton all produced great work. So Shakespeare's contemporaries, though respecting him, would not necessarily have seen him as the towering genius that people sometimes think of today when they consider his achievement. What is more, it is often difficult to speak of one dramatist directly influencing another in this period because the chronology poses so many problems. We rarely know when plays were first performed and dramatic works were often not published during the author's lifetime.

And any influence that Shakespeare might have had on seventeenth-century drama was in any case limited by events outside the control of the theatre companies. The Puritan element of the population had always been against the theatre. Throughout Shakespeare's career and afterwards there had been frequent attacks on the loose morals of the people who went to the theatre and the dubious moral content of what they could see there. So it was of little surprise that when the Puritans became more powerful the theatre would be threatened. London's theatres were closed during the interregnum and were only to open again when Charles II was restored to the throne. By this time a very different form of entertainment was required.

So why has the influence of Shakespeare proved so decisive? In the English-speaking world it has perhaps been the power and variety of his language that has inspired writers to the present day. Similar qualities have penetrated German and Russian culture too (his work seems to translate well into these two languages). Elsewhere other qualities, such as the vividness of his images, have caught on, and inspired the imaginations of writers and theatrical professionals.

And there is another quality that has appealed to people from many cultures and influenced writers who have followed Shakespeare. This is what one might call his democracy – his ability to write in a way that can be appreciated by the widest possible range of spectators or readers. So, if there are depths and enigmas in his work that repay lengthy study, there are also gripping characters and situations that explore issues with which almost everyone can find something engaging. Most ages and most cultures continue to find something of interest and value in Shakespeare's writings.

DUTCH REVOLT AGAINST THE SPANISH

A new identity for the Netherlands and the beginning of the end of
Spanish domination of Europe

The area that we know today as the Netherlands lies at the edge of Europe but has long had close connections with many of the states at the heart of the continent. It was not always the unified, autonomous nation that it is now. During the second half of the fourteenth century and early fifteenth century large parts of the area were ruled by the Dukes of Burgundy. Subsequently, when the French crown obtained some power over Burgundy in the late fifteenth century, France gained control of the Low Countries too. Even then there was a strong independence movement, but it only won concessions not freedom from the foreign yoke.

In the second half of the fifteenth century the fate of the Low Countries was bound to another great European power – Austria. This link was forged when Charles the Bold's daughter Mary of Burgundy (who ruled from 1477 to 1482) married Maximilian of Habsburg. In 1504 their son Philip the Handsome took over the government, and in the same year he and his wife Joanna inherited the crown of Spain. This created a link between Spain and the Netherlands, a link that took many years of struggle to break.

The Habsburgs put the Netherlands under the rule of a series of governors. Resistance to these overlords brought the towns of the Netherlands closer together and, ironically, the various administrative councils imposed by the Habsburgs made opposition still more unified. Philip II of Spain provoked further resentment by imposing his own church appointments, and resistance grew under Prince William of Orange (1533–84). The Calvinists offered fierce resistance against Spanish Catholicism, breaking images in churches and provoking the Spanish to send the Duke of Alba in 1567 to impose a stricter rule on the area.

Alba's policy of prison, torture and death for the religious rebels fanned the flames of opposition in the discontented provinces of the Netherlands. Alba's soldiers were sent to the main centres to suppress rebellion, impose law and order, and set up a 'council of troubles' to deal with the guilty. He also installed a new church hierarchy and imposed new taxes. None of this endeared him to the Dutch people.

Meanwhile, William of Orange rallied supporters overseas. The French Huguenots gave their support, and help was also forthcoming from England and Germany. At home, the rebels also gained important victories and gained William's support. And as successes began to come their way on the battlefield, so the Calvinists in the Dutch cities put pressure on the authorities to cooperate or step down.

In July 1572 representatives of the states of Holland met in Dordrecht to proclaim William of Orange Stadholder of Holland and Zeeland. He became a Calvinist in recognition of the importance of this revolt but supported the idea of a state in which both Catholic and Protestant could live and worship.

The first turning point came on 1 April 1572 when Den Briel was taken by the 'watergeuzen', water-borne troops fighting on the side of the rebels. This became a rallying point and soon the towns of Holland and Zeeland turned against Spain. Alba responded with a military campaign against the towns, sustaining heavy losses but gaining victories at Mechelen, Zutphen, Naarden and Haarlem. But the Spanish forces were stopped short at Alkmaar because of the rising water level and instead turned south to Leyden, the key to the rest of Holland.

Because of the number of troops he had already lost, Alba decided to go for a long siege at Leyden rather than risk a quick attack. So he surrounded the town. Fortunately for the people of Leyden, they had a good store of supplies. They had been keeping grain for Alkmaar (which that town did not need) and had much cattle from fields within the city walls.

On 21 March 1574 there was a sudden respite for Leyden. The Spanish left to fight another battle in the south and the population relaxed and celebrated. But their joy was short-lived. Towards the end of May the Spaniards were back in their old positions and the food supply in the town had dwindled. Plague was also rife and one third of the population died.

By 30 July the situation was so bad that the States General of Holland decided to act. They ordered the dykes to be cut so that the country would be flooded and the Spaniards forced to leave. At first, low water levels conspired with an unfavourable wind: the hoped-for floods did not come. Meanwhile, more people in the town were losing their lives. It was not until the beginning of October that enough water had built up around Leyden to threaten the Spaniards and allow the watergeuzen to reach the city. Finally, on the night of 23 October, pressurized by both the water and the troops, the Spaniards withdrew and Leyden was relieved.

After the Spanish troops had left Leyden in 1574, a young Dutch boy made his way gingerly towards the enemy camp. He was the first to realize that the Spanish had suddenly and quietly abandoned their position. Amongst the things they had left behind was a pot containing a savoury stew (known to the Dutch as 'hutspot', or hotch-potch). The same recipe is used for the dish which is eaten every year at Leyden to mark the anniversary of the Spanish departure.

DEFEAT OF THE SPANISH ARMADA

A triumph for British sea power and a blow to Spanish expansion

Philip II of Spain had extraordinary ambitions to extend his power and influence in Europe. He poured vast sums of money into his campaigns in the Low Countries. He waged war with France. And he wanted to further his inroads into the Protestant north by gaining control of England. England, he believed, would be a good jumping-off point for defeat of his powerful enemy, France. And it would be expedient to remove the threat posed by Englishmen such as Francis Drake to his ships sailing home laden with treasure from the New World. Philip's wars were expensive: he was coming to rely more and more on this source of wealth to finance his foreign policy.

In fact Spain and England were allies for much of the sixteenth century. Henry VIII had married the Spanish Catherine of Aragon in 1509. Henry's divorce with Catherine and his break with the church of Rome threatened the alliance, which was nevertheless held together by both countries' enmity towards France. The daughter of Henry and Catherine, the Catholic Mary Tudor, was betrothed to Emperor Charles V before she became Queen of England. And soon after she ascended to the throne in 1553 she married Philip, Charles' heir. This seemed to make the alliance firm, but Mary died in 1558, leaving the throne to Elizabeth who was to return the country to Protestantism and to be a resolute opponent of Spain.

Meanwhile, events in Europe were moving on at great pace. Continuous wars in the Low Countries did not seem to bring the Spaniards nearer to decisive victory, although they continued to use up enormous amounts of money. But Spain's support of the Holy League against the expansion of the Ottoman Turks was more successful, with victory at the Battle of Lepanto in 1571. Wars of religion also raged in France where, notoriously, in 1572 on St Bartholomew's Eve, thousands of Huguenots (French Protestants) were

Philip II of Spain

massacred at the hands of a Catholic mob. It seemed to the Spaniards that control of England would further their cause in the Low Countries and give them a basis on which to attack France.

But Philip did not go for England straight away. He was anxious that, in removing Elizabeth from the English throne he would leave the way open for her cousin, Mary Queen of Scots, a staunch ally of the French and heir to the childless English queen. Philip's commitment to campaigns in the Netherlands also delayed him. Ironically it was Elizabeth herself who removed the final obstacle by having Mary executed for her complicity in plots against the English queen in February 1587.

The rival forces
Philip's plans were typically ambitious. A large fleet of 151 ships with an army of some 20,000 men would sail from Spain. They would call at the Netherlands and pick up a further 17,000 troops of the Duke of Parma. This force would then be taken to England to invade the country. The commanders would be Parma himself and the leader of the Armada, the Duke of Medina Sidonia.

Meanwhile in England the defences were drawn up. A force was detailed to guard the queen, and another army was stationed at Tilbury to guard the Thames. Troops were also mobilized in the southern counties – the English did not know exactly where the Spanish would strike or what their invasion plans were.

But it was to be the English fleet of 226 vessels that was to take part in the decisive action. Although Elizabeth's ships were more numerous than Philip's they were on the whole smaller – modern naval historians believe the two fleets were evenly matched. In weaponry, however, the English probably had the edge. This was not because they carried more arms – the Spaniards, as an invasion force, carried large quantities of artillery. But the English guns had the distinct advantage of being easier and quicker to load. It may also have been critical that the English ships were smaller, making them more manoeuvrable in tight battle situations.

The two powers were also well matched when it came to their commanders. England had several experienced seamen and military leaders including Charles Howard, Sir Francis Drake, Lord Henry Seymour, Sir Martin Frobisher and Sir John Hawkins. Philip of Spain's chief commanders, the Duke of Parma and the Duke of Medina Sidonia, were also both highly experienced.

The progress of the Armada
It was on 30 May 1588 when the 'invincible Armada', as the Spanish called it, set off from Lisbon. As the Spanish ships sailed northwards up the west coast of the Iberian peninsula they experienced their first problem. Bad weather caused damage and scattered the ships, necessitating a stoppage at La Coruña on the northwestern tip of Spain for repairs. The English hoped to head off their rivals and a fleet of their ships left Plymouth on 22 July, the same day, as it happened, that the Spanish

left La Coruña. But like Medina Sidonia, Howard and Drake fell foul of bad weather, which forced them back to Plymouth to lie in wait for the enemy.

A week later the Spaniards were sighted off the Lizard, the southernmost point of England. News was sent to the British fleet at Plymouth which was readied to engage them. Another English force, under Seymour, waited in the Downs to guard the coast against Parma's troops from the Low Countries. On 31 July the two fleets met for the first time. There was a skirmish, after which the English followed the Armada on its way along the Channel. The following day the first victory went to the English when two Spanish ships, the *Rosario* and the *San Salvador*, were captured.

On 2 August the Spanish took the initiative. Medina Sidonia tried to board one of the English vessels, the *Ark Royal*, but her crew defended her well. In general, the English avoided boarding actions, probably because they knew how skilled their opponents were at this sort of fighting.

The next few days saw further inconclusive skirmishes. Medina Sidonia now realized that the English were going to avoid boarding actions but were intent on tracking the Armada. His best hope was to get word to Parma and send for further ships. These might distract the enemy, allowing Medina Sidonia to board some of the English ships. 6 August therefore saw Medina Sidonia anchored at Calais waiting for Parma's help.

But Parma was not ready. Even if he had been, several Dutch ships had left Flushing with the intention of stopping him getting through. So at this point it was the English who acquired reinforcements

– in the shape of Seymour's squadron who arrived from their position defending southeastern England to join the rest of the fleet anchored off the Calais cliffs.

The English leaders decided to take advantage of their new-found strength. On 7 August eight fireships (ships full of burning materials set adrift among the enemy) were used to attack the Armada. The ships were set off in a row, sailing very close together so that the only way for the Spanish to stop their approach was to pull the outer pair of ships away with grappling hooks before returning to pull away the next and subsequent pairs. They managed to divert the two outer fireships, but the other six came on quickly in the strong wind with the result that the Armada had to scatter rapidly in order to avoid complete disaster.

As they started to do so, the artillery on board the floating infernos exploded in the immense heat, and the Spanish were panicked into thinking that they were being attacked by enormous floating bombs. On the whole the Spanish ships escaped with little damage, although there were some collisions in the night-time confusion. But by morning the Armada lay scattered, many of the ships far north of their hoped-for meeting point with Parma, and their ordered formation at last broken up. For the first time the ships were truly vulnerable to attack from the English.

The English response was to attack with renewed vigour. A battle off Gravelines lasted from nine o'clock in the morning until the early evening of 8 August. There were many Spanish casualties and a number of Medina Sidonia's ships went down. The following night it became clear

the surviving Spaniards were in disarray. The wind blew them farther away from Calais and the English fleet were in any case set on preventing them from making for the port. So they had to flee north, with the prospect of returning home defeated, via the long, unfamiliar and chilly route around Scotland and Ireland. They were defeated by a combination of bad weather, English skill and lack of reinforcements.

But the English did not leave them alone. They could not be sure that the Armada would not turn around and attack once more. So Howard chased his opponents northwards as far as the Firth of Forth, before turning away confident that he had seen them off. Then the bad weather that had given the Spanish so much trouble struck again. They often had to seek shelter along the coasts of Scotland and western Ireland where they were far from welcome: many of those who did not die in shipwrecks were killed ashore. By the time the last Spaniard arrived home 11,000 of his compatriots had been left behind and one third of their ships had been lost.

The aftermath

The defeat of the Armada did not end the war between England and Spain. An abortive counter-armada, poorly prepared and badly led, commanded by Drake and Sir John Norris, led to the loss of almost as many lives as the original Armada. English expeditions against Spanish ships continued, and Spain made further attempts to invade England and Ireland. But other affairs, particularly the wars in the Netherlands, held the attention of both powers. After Elizabeth died and James I came to the English throne in 1604 both sides were ready for peace.

But if the events of 1588 did not immediately put an end to Spain's ambitions in northern Europe, they did mark a turning point. After 1588 Spain's role in Europe declined as the religious and political map of the continent began to be redrawn. In 1598 Spain withdrew all claims on France; the Peace of the Pyrenees in 1659 would confirm France's ascendancy. Between 1621 and 1648 further wars with the Netherlands were to accelerate the decline of Spain's power. The Netherlands and England were to remain Protestant and independent.

In other parts of Europe the situation was more complex. France remained predominantly Catholic: the Huguenots were pushed south and west and by 1685, Protestantism would be forbidden in France. In the empire, by contrast, the Protestants were limited to the northern lands; Bohemia, Austria, Styria and

The British flagship the Ark Royal

Poland were regained by the Catholics. Norway, Denmark and Sweden remained Lutheran strongholds.

These developments have little directly to do with the defeat of the Armada, except for the fact that defeat for Spain increasingly restricted her influence on European politics. But they provide an important context for the defeat. The European wars that took place at the end of the sixteenth century and during the first half of the seventeenth century resulted in a reordering of Europe's political and religious boundaries. The series of skirmishes and battles in the English Channel in August 1588 played a vital part in this process of reordering.

One of the decisive moments in the defeat of the Armada was when the English unleashed a group of eight burning ships and sent them sailing into the ranks of the Spanish fleet. The use of these fireships was shrewd, but the English were helped (not for the last time) by the weather – a strong wind ensured that all but two were blown hard among the Spanish ships. They caused considerable damage, but the confusion they wrought, as Spanish ships moved quickly to get out of the way, was just as important. It began the movement that would send the Armada home the long way around Scotland – through yet more treacherous weather.

DEFENESTRATION OF PRAGUE

The flashpoint of the Thirty Years' War and of decades of change in Europe

In the early seventeenth century the central European state of Bohemia (now part of Czechoslovakia) was ruled by Ferdinand of Habsburg, who would soon become the Holy Roman Emperor Ferdinand II. Ferdinand was a Catholic and his style of ruling veered toward the absolutist. Neither of these facts endeared him to the people of Bohemia, where a tradition of independent Protestantism had continued since the days of the reformer Jan Hus in the fifteenth century. Bohemia was not the only state in the empire in which there was potential conflict between the Catholic crown and local Protestantism. There had been religious wars in Germany before, most recently terminated by the Peace of Augsburg in 1555.

The peace lasted for over half a century. But then tensions surfaced again. And they became part of a larger struggle for power in Europe, one which would turn into the series of conflicts now collectively called the Thirty Years War, leading in turn to extensive alterations in the political map of the continent. The tension broke first of all in the capital of Bohemia, Prague. The Archbishop of Prague had ordered two of the city's Protestant churches to be closed down. The Protestants appealed first to the local imperial officials, then to the emperor, but their wishes were ignored. Then a group of powerful Protestant Bohemian noblemen had a meeting with three imperial officials in Hradcany Castle in Prague. When it became clear that the officials would give no ground, the noblemen hurled them through the upper-floor windows in disgust at their meddling in local affairs, bringing the hostilities literally out into the open.

The two imperial ministers and their clerk who received this treatment lived to tell their tale. Although they had a long journey down to the ground their fall was broken by a rubbish heap at the bottom of the castle walls. But if they kept their lives they had lost their dignity, and such treatment could not pass without a response from the emperor. Meanwhile, the locals took it as a signal that their grievances could be aired with violence: the Bohemians had used the gesture of defenestration before as a way of publicizing grievances and bringing them to a head. Soon there was rioting on the streets of Prague.

But the Bohemians were capable of greater defiance than this. They removed Ferdinand from the throne of Bohemia, replacing him with Frederick, the Elector Palatine, a Protestant sympathetic to their cause. They also sought other allies, notably a Protestant Transylvanian prince, Gabor Bethlen, himself an enemy of the Habsburgs as he had a claim to the crown of Hungary, which was in Habsburg hands. They also hoped for support from England and Holland.

Ferdinand, as emperor, could also draw on wide support. Spain was ruled by a Habsburg monarch, Philip III, while Ferdinand's cousin, Maximilian, Duke of Bavaria, would also fight on Ferdinand's side. Maximilian it was who dealt the Bohemians the first blow when his general, Graf von Tilly, defeated them at White Mountain, near Prague, in 1620. Frederick quickly lost his crown and the future began to look still more uncertain for Bohemia. But it would not be a continuous war. Armies were expensive. They were kept small and only occasionally put at risk. However, the risk to local populations was grave: if the amount of formal fighting was limited, the scope for pillage was not. In the ensuing decades many civilian people in Bohemia and the German states would lose their lives, many more their possessions.

The expanding war

The uncertainty was increased because the war was expanding. In the following year the Dutch and Spanish renewed their long-standing conflict. The Dutch had a much smaller population than Spain, but their country was rich. So they sought to win the war by sponsoring military allies. The first of these was King Christian IV of Denmark. He had much to fear from Habsburg expansion.

Denmark did not have lasting success in the war. Oddly, the person who dealt the Danes their most decisive defeat was a Bohemian, an ex-Protestant general called Albrecht von Wallenstein. Wallenstein, who first commanded imperial forces between 1625 and 1630, raised an army of some 24,000 on behalf of Ferdinand. This was a larger army than usual for the time. But Wallenstein, by opening up still further the possibilities for pillaging, was able to maintain such a force. The idea that 'war sustains war' had been born. Wallenstein's army met Christian's at Dessau Bridge in April 1626. Then Christian was defeated again by Tilly at Lutter am Barenberge. Denmark had withdrawn completely from the war by 1629.

The imperial success persuaded Ferdinand to issue an Edict of Restitution, restoring all that property taken by Protestants since 1552 to the Catholic Church. It seemed that the emperor had won his goal.

Political gestures often seem trivial, but they can have long-lasting effects. So although the men who were pushed out of the castle windows survived, the offence to the emperor they represented was enormous. Nevertheless, the defenestration of Prague did not cause the Thirty Years' War. Decades of political and religious tension led to the conflict and these effects were felt over a much wider area than Bohemia. What the defenestration did was to act as a rallying call for further Protestant defiance, a signal to many that the absolutist rule of the Holy Roman Emperor was not the only alternative for his dissenting subjects.

Sweden enters the war

No sooner had Denmark withdrawn, than another Scandinavian nation entered the field of conflict. Sweden, under its king Gustavus Adolphus, would play a key role in the early 1630s. The Swedes made a truce with their erstwhile rival Poland, and concentrated their aggression on areas to the west of their old adversary. The Swedish army landed in Pomerania in July 1630. There was a string of victories as they pushed southwards towards Brandenburg and Saxony. Tilly was defeated at Breitenfeld (1631) and at the Lech River (1632), where he met his death. At this point the emperor brought back Wallenstein to lead his army. The general recruited another large army, but the Swedes defeated him at Lützen (also in 1632), although Gustavus Adolphus was himself killed in this battle.

But the Swedish victories did not continue unabated. They suffered a crushing defeat at Nördlingen in 1634. The emperor suspected that Wallenstein was trying to negotiate with the enemy and had his general arrested. When he attempted to escape, Wallenstein was assassinated. But even if the imperial side was in some confusion as a result of this, it had become clear that the Swedes could not overcome the imperial forces alone.

The French involvement

But another major European power, France, would soon enter the war. Louis XIII was a Catholic monarch who had fought the Protestants in his own country. But he was concerned about the imperial expansion. France, therefore, entered into an unlikely alliance with the upholders of Protestantism in Europe: Sweden, the united Dutch provinces, and several of the German Protestant nobles. From now on the war would be essentially a struggle between France and the empire. Religious

motives would take second place to this political struggle.

France and her allies won a string of victories in the later years of the war. The prospects of the Protestants in Bohemia and the German states began to look much better. But large areas of Europe had paid a high cost for this: the toll of death and devastation that came as a result of the Thirty Years' War was particularly heavy. So in the 1640s, the states of Europe began to look for peace.

Steps towards peace

Peace conferences began in 1643 in the Westphalian cities of Münster and Osnabrück. But negotiations were difficult and long-winded because the war had not been formally ended and each party jockeyed for the best position in the discussions. Final agreements were reached between most of the countries involved in 1648. First of all in January Spain and the United Provinces came to an agreement. By October France, Sweden, the Empire, and the German states had also made their peace. But France and Spain continued their enmity for a further eleven years. There would also be wars between Sweden and Poland, and Sweden and Denmark in the following decade or so.

In political terms, the main result of the Peace of Westphalia was that it switched the balance of power in Europe from the emperor or Spanish ruler to the king of France. France gained Alsace and the bishoprics of Metz, Toul, and Verdun. The sovereignty of the German states, the Netherlands and the Swiss Confederation, all of which had been subject to the Empire, was recognized. In religious terms, Lutherans and Calvinists won equal rights with Roman Catholics. People who ended up in a state where the religion was not of their persuasion were allowed to emigrate.

The peace agreement, then, embraced both the religious and political issues that prompted the start of the war. It was clear that the political issues would now dominate the future of Europe. The war and the Peace of Westphalia also influenced the political pattern of Europe for the coming years. France would be the dominant power, and the strength of the empire would switch away from the German states. France would continue her expansion through the latter part of the century (annexing territories such as Burgundy and Strassburg), and further expansion was only prevented by intervention from England, Holland, Sweden and Russia.

Germany would remain a mosaic of some 300 separate states (principalities, bishoprics and free cities). These would prove impossible to unite as an empire. One state, Austria, stood out as larger and more dominant than the rest. This strength was increased because of the Habsburgs' other possessions, particularly in Hungary and Italy. Austria and Hungary would form the basis of the new European empire. These were long-term developments, and they involved a host of other factors. But the war helped to set their agenda. In the Baltic, the war saw the emergence of Sweden as an international power. Sweden would remain dominant in the region for the rest of the century.

If the political effects of the Thirty Years' War were far-reaching, so were the social consequences. Although the fighting was not continuous, the loss of life was enormous. Whole villages and communities disappeared. Some areas of the Germanic states lost more than fifty per cent of their population. This loss was made worse because the late 1620s saw one of the worst outbreaks of plague Europe had seen since the Middle Ages. Both socially and politically, the war was long remembered by those who survived.

ARRIVAL OF THE MAYFLOWER IN AMERICA

The beginning of European colonization of North America

One of the most influential of the series of exploratory voyages that took place in the sixteenth century was that of Sir Walter Raleigh to North America. In the 1580s he sailed across the Atlantic and founded the first British colonies on the American continent in what he called Virginia (now North Carolina). These colonies were not successful, although a settlement at Jamestown, established after peace was made between England and Spain in 1604, did survive. But for a while it looked as though, from the English point of view, the main benefit of the North American connection was the introduction of tobacco and potatoes to Europe.

But in 1620 something happened that was to change the emphasis of the English colonization of America. A small ship, the *Mayflower*, carried 102 English people to America where they would begin a new life. They were aiming for Virginia, but the ship was blown off course and they landed further north in December 1620. Their landing place, now in the state of Massachusetts, they called Plymouth after the English town of their departure.

These early settlers were different in their aims from the people who had sailed to America before. Their main motive for travelling so far to a new home was not economic success. They were idealists. They wanted to leave behind a country that seemed less and less to offer the sort of life they wanted. In America they hoped to build a new sort of state, a place where they could live the Christian way of life according to their Puritan interpretation of the Bible in a way that had proved difficult, if not impossible, in England. They were to be followed by thousands of others in the next twenty years who shared the same ideals.

The world they left behind
Why did these people take such a drastic step? They would undergo a long journey on which disease or storm might carry

The Mayflower

them away. They would be crammed uncomfortably on a small vessel. They would risk attack by pirates. They were travelling to a distant land of which they could have at best a hazy notion. It seemed a desperate thing to do.

It was. Life was not easy in early seventeenth-century England. It has been estimated that about half of the population lived on or below the poverty line. This made infectious diseases likely to be passed on quickly. Vagrancy was common. In the countryside there was more work and food at harvest-time, but for the rest of the year life was hard and the women often had to take work, if they could get it, as strenuous as that done by the men. As for leisure or education – these were at a minimum.

In the towns and cities the standard of living was often higher, with much prosperity coming from trades such as cloth-making. But women found it difficult to take advantage of this wealth. Only spinsters were allowed to be apprentices. There were problems in the cities. Law and order were frequently difficult to enforce. This was one of the chief objections to the theatre which, apart from any moral objections the Puritans had, tended

to produce an unruly rabble that was hard to control at closing-time.

Religion posed another problem. It was difficult for the increasing number of people who were drawn to the Puritan outlook to lead their lives as they wanted to. This was not necessarily a problem with the established church. A substantial minority – perhaps as many as ten per cent – of the English clergy were themselves Puritans, men who wanted to remove or distance themselves from the elements in the church that were reminiscent of Roman Catholicism. But this still left many of the laity unable to reach the sort of spiritual leadership they wanted. And even amongst those who could, it was hard to lead one's life in the way one wanted when the actual organization of society prevented it. For the beliefs of many Puritans went beyond church liturgy and doctrine. They believed that the only way they could achieve what they wanted was to found a better society. And the only way to do that was to start again, from scratch, in a new country.

In the new country
To begin with, the settlers had to concentrate on survival. They had to learn what the chances were of beginning some sort of agriculture and what the sources of timber and other materials were so that they could provide themselves with shelter. They had landed in winter and there was no obvious staple crop. It soon became clear that the people who had given them financial support for their journey would not gain any profits. They had to learn what they could about the land from the local Indians, and try to produce food as best they could.

They also had to work out how their community was to be organized. As they landed farther north than they had expected they were outside the legal remit of the Virginia Company. They therefore made their own declaration of political

The men and women who arrived on the coast of New England in the Mayflower *faced daunting prospects. It was winter and they dropped their anchor farther north than they had hoped. They had little financial backing and no information about how to cope in their new home. They were cut off from their homeland and their relatives. They had to survive on their own. But in many ways that was what they wanted. At least they were free of the religious persecution they faced in England. They could worship in their own fashion. And they could organize their community in the ways that they wanted. So if these early settlers faced a hard life, they also faced an exciting challenge. It was a challenge that led to the ethics of democracy, freedom and individualism that have been fundamental to North American life ever since.*

organization by drawing up an agreement to 'enact, constitute and frame such just and equal laws, ordinances, acts, constitutions and offices, from time to time, as shall be thought most meet and convenient for the general good of the colony, unto which we promise all due submission and obedience.'

Although they were still British citizens, their enterprise undertaken 'for the glory of God, and advancement of the Christian faith, and honour of our King and country', they needed this spirit of independence more than they knew. In seven years their backers would withdraw completely. They were truly on their own.

The later settlers

The people of Plymouth remained isolated until the end of the decade when the next, more substantial wave of British immigration to America began. The first of them came with John Winthrop. He had been made governor of a new company, 'The company of Massachusetts Bay in New England', formed by backers who wanted to trade with the new world. For all his alliance with the traders, Winthrop was motivated as much by religious motives as by any other reason for leaving England; as he wrote in one letter: 'Evil times are coming when the church must fly into the wilderness.'

Winthrop's company sent out an advance party in 1629 to found the town of Salem, just north of Plymouth. Winthrop himself followed, with a fleet of ships containing about one thousand men and women, the following year. These were the people who settled on the Charles River, in the place they called Boston.

The arrival was something of a replay of that of the first settlers in New England. They came in winter (a particularly hard winter, at that) and had to struggle before they could feel that they had a food supply on which they could rely. But they benefitted from the advice of the Plymouth settlers and in time prospered. They realized they could transfer the management of the Massachusetts Bay Company from England to Boston, and this they did, to give themselves a measure of independence. As more colonists arrived from England their position was stronger – at least there was land for every settler and a freedom from the restrictions that hampered both social and geographical movement back home. By 1640 some 14,000 had settled in the area.

There were five English settlements in North America: Virginia, the original pilgrim settlement at Plymouth, Massachusetts Bay, Connecticut and Rhode Island. They were united in that they survived mainly by trade and fishing. They were also united against common prospective enemies: the French, who had taken over the upper St Lawrence River, and the Dutch, who had established a colony at the mouth of the Hudson, which was later to become New York.

So the English settlement at Massachusetts Bay grew and Winthrop proved an able leader who engineered alliances with the settlers in Connecticut. Isolation was impossible, all the more so since the New Englanders depended on outside sources for many goods. This caused a problem, however, since they had little to export in return, so the purchase of items such as textiles and iron goods took cash away from America. This was less of a problem initially because new immigrants brought cash with them with which the economy was revived. Eventually it was to lead to the development of a 'triangular' trade, sending foodstuffs to the West Indies from where sugar was sent to England, from where manufactured goods were brought to New England.

Meanwhile, the New Englanders had to expand at home. They developed a system of town-founding that granted land to groups of people rather than to individuals, and tried to underpin the religious basis of the colony by making each of these groups the congregation of a particular church who undertook to found a new church on the new site. The church members, once their new church was founded, supervised the division of lands amongst the congregation and appointed

John Winthrop

church elders and a minister. They also formed the government of the town and sent two representatives to the central government of the colony. Already some of the roots of American democracy were beginning to be put down.

People were given responsibility in proportion to their abilities and the size of their family, as well as to their social status. Some skills, such as blacksmithing, were in demand and those who could offer them could benefit from generous grants of land. But only a few people held disproportionately large amounts of land. There was also land that was held in common.

The most powerful men were the church leaders and the magistrates. They had the difficult job of imposing a rigorous code of behaviour – although most of the colonists were there because of their beliefs, enforcing a demanding moral code is always easier in principle than in practice. But in the early decades at least they were successful.

In a society that was used to thinking about religion, however, religious differences were bound to occur. Indeed, the presence of the colony at Rhode Island was due to the casting-out of 'heretics' from the main community. Already the tendency for the American individualist to head for the uncolonized land of the frontier was beginning. This tendency also demonstrates the trend towards intolerance that typified Puritanism in New England as the century continued.

The developing colonies

By the end of the century the British colonies in America had multiplied. In addition to those already mentioned, Maine and New Hampshire were settled from 1622, Maryland from 1632, Carolina from 1663 and Pennsylvania from 1681. New York, settled by the Dutch from 1623, was seized by the English in 1664. The Swedes settled in Delaware from 1638 and the French settled in Nova Scotia from 1604. In 1682 the French also claimed the Mississippi area.

The domination of English-speaking settlers was clearly a marked one. But the very reason these settlers came to America – to escape from oppression at home – set the tone for future immigrations and helped to shape the polyglot nature of what were to become the United States. Such motives also shaped the high value placed both on the freedom of the individual and the proper structuring of an equitable government that has typified this part of the world ever since. The isolation which the Puritans in North America felt from England during the English Civil War strengthened their independence and reinforced their institutions. And if there was also intolerance (of religious opponents and of the native Americans), the foundation provided by the Puritans nevertheless gave the settlers a good base on which to build their state.

EXECUTION OF CHARLES I

England's experiment with regicide and revolution

The English revolution, which culminated in the trial and execution of King Charles I and the suspension of the monarchy for eleven years, is one of the most famous and most controversial phases in English history. It was to be one of the pivotal events of English, and even European, history.

Charles was an unpopular king who ruled in difficult times. Considering the potential problems, he did not do badly. In economic terms, the crown had a high income and a low national debt compared with other European countries. Social problems, such as rioting and vagrancy, were less frequent than under the Tudors or James I. The king was able to use his power to sort out disputes and, by ruling with the consent of the élite classes in the towns and shires, maintained stability.

But there were difficulties. Although the income of the crown was high, taxes (particularly Ship Money) were unpopular. Charles himself was disliked – for his remote personality, for his religion (highlighted by his alliance with Archbishop Laud, a 'popish' version of Protestantism), and for his high-handed and arbitrary style of government (represented by his adherence, like his father James I, to the idea of the 'divine right' of kings to rule). If the times did not seem ripe for revolution, they were ripe for discontent.

In the end, aside from the sheer financial burden of life under Charles, objections to his rule centred on three main areas. The first was constitutional: people saw that individual subjects were having their freedom eroded by the crown. The second was local: Charles was taking away the power of local élites. And the third was religious: 'popery' at court seemed to be driving out Protestantism.

These misgivings became much more clear during the early parliamentary sessions of Charles' reign. The House of Commons, dominated by the puritans, objected particularly to the views of Charles' adviser the Duke of Buckingham, who had been a favourite of the king's father James I. Buckingham was blamed for the failure of a naval expedition to Spain in 1626 and parliament tried to impeach him for treason. Charles responded by dissolving parliament to prevent this.

The next parliament met in 1628, by

King Charles I

which time there had been another military defeat, again brought about by Buckingham when he sent forces to aid the French protestants at La Rochelle. With the king's position vulnerable, Parliament forced Charles to sign a document called the *Petition of Right*. In it, the crown undertook not to impose taxes without the consent of Parliament; not to imprison subjects without cause; not to quarter soldiers on civilians; and not to enforce martial law in peacetime.

But taxes – and 'popish' religious practices – continued. Parliament condemned the king's actions in the following year. Charles realised that revolution was in the air and dissolved parliament. He did not call another parliament for eleven years, thus abandoning the framework of consent on which his government relied.

By making peace with France and Spain Charles reduced his expenditure and lessened the need for taxation. But by the time of the famous 'Long Parliament' of 1640–1, the old grievances were still there. And this time the commons were not to be put off. They managed to get Charles to agree not to dissolve parliament without its consent and made him change his advisers; he appointed more moderate, Calvinist bishops; they made arbitrary taxation illegal. But they could not make Charles surrender control of the army, which they feared he would use against them. What was more, the religious objections to Charles' rule were as strong as ever. There were increasing calls for a new ecclesiastical order, with a church devoted to preaching, discipline and moral reform. It was clear, for all the efforts of the Long Parliament, that Charles would not preside over a Puritan transformation of the English church.

The early months of 1642 saw both king and Parliament assembling their troops. Two phases of civil war followed, the first centring on 1642, the second on 1648. Decisive in the military progress of the war was the New Model Army, the highly disciplined and professional force led by Sir Thomas Fairfax and his deputy Oliver Cromwell. Their first victory over the royalist forces was at Naseby in 1645. Further victories followed, leaving Charles to rely solely on his Scottish allies. The Scots were finally defeated in August 1648, and the demand was heard that the king should be put on trial.

Charles was accused of high treason. He refused to recognise the legality of the court and refused to plead. But the outcome was predictable. He was found guilty and sentenced to death. Charles was beheaded outside the Banqueting House in Whitehall on 30 January 1649.

English kings had been put to death before. But the medieval kings who were executed had not been given the public scrutiny of a trial before they lost their lives. There had never been such an open questioning of the monarch's divine right to rule. This public, legal scrutiny of king by people was something new and would influence the thinking behind other revolutions in other places in years to come.

But what were the more immediate causes of Charles' execution? Some of the crown's despotic institutions, such as the court of Star Chamber (a court that Charles used to impose some of his unpopular policies) were removed. But the new regime was hardly the republic of saints that many hoped for. And in eleven years the monarchy would return. But it was less despotic: the veiled threat of what had happened to Charles I would always be there, tempering the crown in its responsibility to parliament.

The events of the English Civil War may also have speeded up a still more significant change that was beginning to be felt in English society and would continue to be felt in the west. Ultimately the church, which had played such an influential role in government in the past, was marginalized by the changes of the revolution. The wish of Oliver Cromwell, who wanted to unite religious leaders and the New Model Army to bring about a new moral order, was not so different from those of Charles who had wanted to unite with archbishop Laud to exercise both religious and political power. But when the new king came to the throne it was the country gentry and the powerful citizens of the towns to whom he had to bow. England was well on the way to becoming a secular state.

On 27 January 1649 King Charles I was condemned to death at Westminster. He was to be executed by 'the severing of his head from his body.' Royalists perceived that Charles gained in stature at his trial. He refused to be cowed by his accusers and maintained his stand for what he saw as the liberties of England. He did this by maintaining that the court had no legal power: 'For if power without law may make laws, may alter the fundamental laws of the kingdom, I do not know what subject he is in England, that can be sure of his life, or anything that he calls his own.' So his case was that the trial was illegal, and he was confident that there was no legal precedent for the extraordinary proceedings. But the accusers, men such as leading regicides Oliver Cromwell and Henry Marten, were to prevail. The court, representing the Commons of England, condemned Charles to be taken to Whitehall to be beheaded.

WILLIAM AND MARY'S 'GLORIOUS REVOLUTION'

The beginnings of British 'constitutional monarchy'

The reign of James II at the end of the seventeenth century was one of the shortest and most troubled that the British throne has seen. During the three years of his rule he alienated large numbers of his subjects, including many of the most powerful people in the land. Perhaps the most fundamental difference between James and the majority of his subjects was religion. James had converted to Catholicism in 1669 when he was Lord High Admiral and his brother, Charles II, was king. At first he kept his religion a secret, but when the news leaked out in 1673 he was forced to resign. Members of the Protestant aristocracy, fearful that a Catholic might become king, tried to exclude James from the succession. They were not successful and when Charles died in 1685, James became king. But in spite of his Catholicism, James promised at the start of his reign to defend and support the principles of the Church of England.

He immediately had to cope with a rebellion organized by the Duke of Monmouth, Charles' illegitimate son. Monmouth, who had been banished for plotting against James, landed at Torbay and raised his rebellion, by which time he had about 6,000 men behind him. But the professional troops of the royalists were too much for his unruly rabble, and he was defeated at the Battle of Sedgemoor on 6 July 1685. Monmouth was executed in London on 15 July. James sent his Lord Chief Justice George Jeffreys to the west country to deal judicially with the rebels. Over 300 people were hanged and some 800 were deported to the West Indies. The image of these 'Bloody Assizes' haunted people in the west of England for years afterwards. This, and the general opposition to Catholicism, made James obsessively fearful of opposition, and he began to appoint Catholics to leading posts in his government.

This was not all. In 1687 James proclaimed religious toleration for all faiths. Far from being the liberal measure that it sounds today, this was another advance for Catholicism. How tolerant James really was appeared in the following year when he continued his crusade for Catholic appointments. He attempted to give a Catholic the post of President at Magdalen College, Oxford. When the fellows of the college objected, they were expelled. There were other incidents that showed James' desire to outface the Protestant opposition. He entertained the Papal Nuncio, d'Adda, even though the recognition of Papal officials was illegal in Britain. James was acting as if he felt himself to be above the law.

The problem of the succession

The news that James' wife Mary Beatrice was pregnant galvanized the opposition. If a Catholic king was bad enough, the prospect of a Catholic succession was intolerable. For the second time in the seventeenth century a revolution seemed to be on the horizon. But it was to be a very different revolution from that in which Cromwell toppled James' father Charles I.

Meanwhile relations between James and his brother-in-law William of Orange in Holland were deteriorating. James, tired of trying to win support for his policies from William, demanded the return of six English and Scottish regiments from the Dutch States General at the beginning of 1688. The States General responded by disbanding the regiments and telling the troops that they were free to leave Holland if they wished. In general the Catholics amongst them returned home to James. But a substantial body of Protestant soldiers stayed in the Netherlands.

Meanwhile, rumours continued to circulate about the pregnancy of Queen Mary Beatrice. The Queen had suffered several miscarriages, and there were many opponents of James who refused to believe that the pregnancy was actually genuine.

In May 1688 James issued his Second Declaration of Indulgence, a document that expressed his intention to dismiss from his service anyone who would not cooperate with his policies. It was another indication that James wished to rule absolutely, without heed to any opposition. What was more, James insisted that his Declaration should be read out from every church pulpit in the land. When seven of his bishops protested, they were swiftly thrown into the Tower.

The next shock came on 10 June when Mary Beatrice gave birth to a son. A rumour was immediately started that the child had been smuggled by Papists into the lying-in room in a warming pan and that he was not Mary Beatrice's son at all. Potential Protestant witnesses, such as Archbishop Sancroft who was in the Tower, were conveniently absent.

In February 1689 representatives of the Commons of England brought to William of Orange a document called the Declaration of Rights. This outlined the problems caused by the policies of the later Stuart kings, who had claimed to rule by divine right. William accepted a role that was more circumscribed, but he was no puppet. He used the cabinet council to assess and influence the mood of parliament, through which he governed. Good channels of communication between king and parliament were essential for William, who was often absent from the country, either in his native Netherlands or on his longstanding military campaigns against the French. In spite of these absences William kept strong control over key areas of policy, particularly foreign affairs and the treasury.

But no rumours could detract from the fact that, as far as the laws of primogeniture were concerned his son took precedence over his eldest daughter, Mary, who was married to William of Orange.

But the trend was against James. At the end of June the jury acquitted the seven bishops. And immediately afterwards another seven men who took issue with the king sent a messenger to William, inviting the prince to come over and save their country. They expressed their commitment to William's cause, saying that they would stand by him when he arrived in England. And they assured him that nineteen out of twenty people in the country wanted a change.

For William, the idea of ruling England was attractive. He suspected that if he did not go to England, there might be a rebellion that would end in England becoming a republic. This might be a threat to the Dutch, as it had been in Cromwell's time. In addition, as joint king of England he would be able to count on the country's support for his campaigns against France, whereas it was unlikely that an independent republic would support him.

William's preparations

It was the threat of the French in the Rhine region and a French attack on Dutch trade that gave William the pretext for raising an army. The troops might be needed on the mainland as well as in England. So in July William began his preparations. He was in a good position. As well as the British exiles, he had regiments of French Huguenots, his own personal troops and a Dutch regular army. Together he had between 12,000 and 15,000 men behind him. There was also an impressive fleet of over 200 ships. This armada would carry an array of supplies and back-up equipment (everything from a forge to a printing press) as well as the soldiers and sailors themselves. The official word was that all these preparations were for fighting against the French. But enough people were in the know for the news to leak to England where, however, no one at court took the threat seriously.

With England relatively quiet, it was the French who gave William the pretext for action. On 27 September Louis XIV's army invaded the Palatinate and laid siege to Philipsburg. While doing this they could not attack Holland, and in any case most of the German rulers were on William's side. The way seemed clear for an invasion of England.

William landed at Torbay in November 1688. There was little opposition to his arrival and he marched quickly to London. James fled to France, leaving a vacuum behind him: how would the question of the succession be decided? A parliament, summoned in January 1689,

William and Mary

provided the answer. By fleeing to France, James had effectively abdicated: Parliament offered the throne to William and Mary, and they were crowned in April.

William and Mary came to the throne of England as the nominees of English politicians. But the joint rulers were not political pawns. They ruled as monarchs, although never again would the country fall victim to the sort of 'divine right' monarchy that it had experienced under James.

The constitutional monarchy

William and Mary took a coronation oath that put them firmly under the law. They agreed to govern in accordance with the statutes, laws and customs of parliament, and that they would uphold 'the Protestant Reformed Religion established by law'. This was in contrast to previous coronation oaths in Britain, in which kings had usually sworn to uphold the laws of their ancestors. The position of William and Mary was somewhat different: they were constitutional monarchs.

The way in which the monarchy was controlled was further set out in a Bill of Rights that was passed by parliament at the end of 1689 and was a version of the agreement William and Mary had signed when they accepted the crown. Amongst the bill's ways of limiting royal power were that it forbade the use of an Ecclesiastical Commission to govern the church; it banned of the levying of money in ways other than agreed by parliament or for longer periods than agreed; and it prevented the crown raising of a standing army in peacetime without parliamentary consent. The crown was not to suspend statutes and parliament should be freely elected. These were worthy guidelines for the monarchy, but they were not comprehensive enough to add up to a written constitution. The bill effectively suspended royal power 'as it hath been excersised of late' without rendering the crown impotent.

So William and Mary's 'bloodless revolution' was hardly a revolution in the modern sense. The British had prevented a Catholic succession and avoided the slide into absolute monarchy. But it was not clear exactly how the controls on the crown would work. The next decade and a half would make things clearer. In his wars against the French, William would have to make great demands on the exchequer

It soon became clear that parliament did have control over the purse strings and that parliament's role was crucial in negotiating the large long-term loans that were needed to finance the war. What was more, a substantial growth in the executive system was needed to administer these financial deals. In a way, these changes actually gave a strong ruler, such as William, more scope to run government the way he wanted to. But they also made it clear that Parliament was as important a force in government as the crown.

TAKING OF QUEBEC

A shaping force in the balance of power in Canada

The English-speaking people of North America remember above all the founding settlements of the first immigrants from England. But the French also played a key role in the exploration and settling of North America. The interplay between these two nations was a vital force in the formation of modern North America and has affected Canadian history to this day. And the final outcome of the conflict between Britain and France had still wider repercussions, opening up the way for the British to build on their expansion all over the world and create the empire that was to dominate so much of the planet in the nineteenth century.

French explorers had sailed up the St Lawrence river by 1535. In the following 200 years the French steadily built up their presence in North America. French fur trappers and missionaries spread out right across the continent, founding settlements that were destined to become great cities: Quebec (1608), Ville-Marie (later Montreal, 1642), Detroit (1701) and New Orleans (1718). As one can see from these names, the French occupied a huge tract of the continent, from Nova Scotia, across the Great Lakes and far west of them, and southwards down the banks of the Mississippi River. There were not very many of them, but they knew more of North America than any of the other Europeans.

Using this knowledge, the French settlers mastered the profitable fur trade. The wealth they gained from this alienated other settlers in the area (especially the Dutch and English on the east coast) and took away some of the livelihood of the native Americans (particularly the Iroquois). So there were conflicts from the start. As early as 1629, the English retaliated, attempting to take the important settlement of Quebec. In 1670 the conflict stepped up when England, under the auspices of the Hudson's Bay Company, started her own fur trade in earnest in the northern part of the continent. But it was not until the war of 1754–60 that the conflict was brought to a head.

The fighting began with skirmishes between Britain and France in their colonies. This state of affairs continued for two years, and then France attacked the British colony of Minorca. By bringing the conflict to Europe, the French had made a real challenge to British supremacy; Britain responded by declaring war.

The British decided first of all to go for the French West Indian island of Martinique. This was an important base and trading centre for the French. The British strategy was conceived by William Pitt, the Secretary of State, whose more than capable grasp of logistics was to help Britain eventually achieve victory with a minimum of losses. But the British were not to be successful in Martinique, largely because of the incompetence of the commander, Major-General Hopson.

The next British target, Guadeloupe, saw a different sort of campaign when Hopson died, to be replaced by his second-in-command, Colonel Barrington. He was able to force the French governor to surrender before his compatriots could send any reinforcements. A rich island,

which French privateers had used as a base from which to attack American trading vessels, had been taken. It was a significant blow, and it gave Pitt a useful bargaining point.

The next battle between the two powers was back in Europe. Prince Ferdinand of Brunswick, an ally of Britain, had retreated to the area of Minden, near the British king's possession, Hanover. He was threatened by two separate French forces, under the Marquis de Contades and Marshal Broglie. Together, the two French commanders had nearly one hundred thousand men, almost twice the strength of Ferdinand's army and the English soldiers that had joined it. Ferdinand had difficulty keeping the two French forces apart – his one hope of victory. He had to cope with the cowardice of Lord George Sackville, which deprived him of vital support, and in the end Hanover was only just saved for the British.

But Pitt knew that the real hope of defeating the French lay not in Europe or the West Indies, but in Canada. For this campaign he was fortunate in his commanders. Major-General James Wolfe was an intelligent strategist, brave in battle, but unpredictable and sickly. General Jeffrey Amherst was a dependable soldier, an excellent foil to the mercurial Wolfe.

The two men were to have different roles in the war. It was Wolfe's task to sail up the St Lawrence river and attack the crucial city of Quebec. Amherst, meanwhile, would head northwards from Albany. He would aim to cut off the communications of Montcalm, the French general at Quebec, with Montreal, leaving him nowhere to go if Wolfe defeated him. But in approaching the campaign in this way the British too suffered from poor communications. Amherst and Wolfe were split, and the distances involved were large. What was more, for the attack on Quebec to work, the army and navy

General James Wolfe

Knowing the geography of the area in which you are fighting is one of the most important assets in warfare. Wolfe learned this hard lesson in his difficult passage up the St Lawrence. He was to teach it to the French when he took his men up the Heights of Abraham, the cliffs near Quebec that the French had supposed to be unscalable. It was a difficult, indeed risky, exercise, the more so because it had to be carried out at night. But it gave Wolfe the advantage of surprise that he needed. In the ensuing battle the British general was killed. But he had taken his men to the point of strength that eventually led to Britain gaining domination of Canada.

would have to work closely together. Such close coordination could not be guaranteed in the eighteenth century. Another difficulty for Wolfe was that he only got an army of two-thirds the strength that he had expected. And to put further obstacles in the way of British progress, the start of Wolfe's passage up the St Lawrence was delayed by fog.

Nevertheless, the British ships made the difficult river journey. They were assisted in the passage by James Cook, who acted as pilot on this expedition and who was later to become yet more celebrated for his journey to Australia and New Zealand. When they finally got to Quebec they found the French troops waiting for them on the northern bank of the river and to the east of the city. The French clearly had superiority of numbers compared to the British, but seemed unable to press this advantage by entering battle. In actual fact Montcalm was anxious to save his resources since the French leaders were anxious that they should not be short of men for their European campaigns. This fact, together with a dispute between Montcalm and the governor of Quebec, made the French less strong than they must have appeared to Wolfe.

Wolfe was also worried about the weather. It was not just the fog. Autumn was approaching and the St Lawrence would freeze over. He had to tackle his opponents before it was too late. Landings and raids on the northern shore of the river only resulted in losses for the British. And then, to make matters worse, Wolfe fell ill of a kidney disease. It began to look as if the British would be defeated.

Wolfe knew that the end was near, for good or bad. He asked his doctor to do what he could to alleviate his pain for a few days. He sent men out on reconnaissance and came to the conclusion that he should land his troops above the city. They would disembark in a little cove called the Anse du Foulon at the bottom of the cliffs beyond Quebec. From here they could scale the cliffs via a steep path, hauling guns up behind them on ropes. They achieved their aim on the night of 12 September, so that the French awoke to find the British troops massed ready for battle on the Plains of Abraham. The French were forced to give battle and the British, in spite of inferiority of numbers, were victorious, using brief, controlled volleys of shots to tear through the French ranks. After the initial shooting, losses were kept to a minimum and French survivors ran off, pursued by Wolfe's men. But not by their commander: both Wolfe, and his opposite number Montcalm, lost their lives in the battle.

It was not the end of the war but it was the turning point. By 1763 the Treaty of Paris was signed. This granted Canada, and most of the rest of the French territories in North America, to England. Guadeloupe, together with Martinique, Bell Isle, Maria Galante and St Lucia were returned to France. The British domination of Canada was confirmed, although the strong French-speaking element was to remain. Elsewhere, Britain dominated India and was respected as a major military power in Europe. Britain itself was well defended, and would continue to build her influential empire.

PUBLICATION OF NEWTON'S PRINCIPIA MATHEMATICA

The transformation of our ideas about force, motion and gravity

The seventeenth century saw a revolution in science. Building on the work of astronomers like Copernicus, Galileo transformed the prevailing view of the universe and improved the telescope to the extent that it could be used to observe objects much more accurately than had previously been possible. In the field of philosophy, René Descartes was looking at nature in a radical way, laying a stress on epistemology, the science that examines the nature and limits of knowledge, and seeking to interpret the world in terms of mathematical laws. But perhaps the most influential of all was the British scientist Isaac Newton, whose achievements were wide-ranging, but whose work on gravity in particular changed the way we look at the entire universe.

Newton was an unusual scientist in that he worked for most of his life in isolation, shunning discussion and debate and doggedly pursuing his individualistic path. Even as an undergraduate at Cambridge he was quietly doing work that he would later develop into radical new theories and scientific laws.

His first important work was in optics, where he challenged the prevailing view of light. He was the first to perceive the significance of the way white sunlight turns into a coloured spectrum when passing through a prism. He showed that sunlight was in fact made up of a combination of all colours, which were split up by the prism. In other words phenomena like a rainbow were not caused because white light was *modified* in some way, as previous scientists had thought, but because the white light was being *analyzed* and its constituent colours exposed.

Newton made other important contributions to optics. For example, he created the first reflecting telescope. Newton used it to minimize as much as possible colour distortion, but similar designs have proved invaluable to astronomers for a variety of other reasons.

Gravity and motion

But Newton's most influential work was in the area of gravitation. Newton had long been fascinated by the phenomenon of attraction. Some chemicals will react only with certain others; some bodies are attracted together (by what we now know as static electricity); fluids exhibit surface tension; and so on. The scientist Hooke mentioned to Newton that it might be possible to examine attraction by studying planetary orbits. By looking at the way the orbits of different heavenly bodies are influenced by other such bodies, and by looking at the way bodies behave on earth, Newton was able to come up with a set of laws that show how such bodies behave. His conclusions were published in his most important book, *Philosophiae Naturalis Principia Mathematica* (*Mathematical Principles of Natural Philosophy*), published in 1687.

The book contained the three laws of motion that described how moving bodies behave: (1) that a body remains in its state of rest unless it is compelled to change that state by a force impressed on it; (2) that the change of motion (the change of velocity multiplied by the mass of the body) is proportional to the force impressed; and (3) that to every action there is an equal and opposite reaction.

Newton was also able to predict what force a planet would have to exert in order to divert a satellite from a straight path and make it follow a circular orbit around the planet. He showed what Hooke had supposed: that the centripetal force holding the satellite in orbit must decrease with the square of the satellite's distance from the planet. By comparing the behaviour of the Moon in its orbit around the Earth and the behaviour of an object falling to the Earth's surface, Newton was able to conclude that the same force was operating in both cases. He called the force *gravitas*, the Latin word meaning weight, from which we derive the word *gravity*.

Newton went on to express his findings in a universal law of gravitation, which states that: every particle of matter in the universe attracts every other particle with a force that is proportional to the product of their masses and inversely proportional to the square of the distance between their centres.

It was possible to explain a wide range of phenomena from Newton's findings, from the behaviour of tides to the paths of comets. Although he worked independently of his scientific colleagues, news of Newton's findings spread quickly around the world of learning once the *Principia* was published. His work was taken up in different ways by philosophers such as Leibnitz and Spinoza – Newton found himself at the centre of European thought. The general physical laws that Newton had put forward became the basis of a reorganization of western science; subsequent science was indebted to Newton, especially in the fields of optics and that of physics. Additionally, scientific academies were established in many European countries, and Newton's telescope became an important new tool for research.

For the wide-ranging importance of his work, Newton was made president of the Royal Society (which accorded him scientific recognition) and warden of the Royal Mint in London (which gave him a substantial income). His work on gravity was not superseded until the time of Albert Einstein.

Isaac Newton did most of his scientific work alone. He was fascinated by optics and was the first to explain correctly why a prism separates the colours in white light. His other fascination was with the laws of motion, symbolized by the story of the falling apple and borne out by extensive calculations.

CAPTAIN COOK'S VOYAGE TO AUSTRALIA

A new awareness of Australia and a new, scientific style of exploration

We know Captain James Cook as one of the heroes of seafaring and exploration. He successfully sailed his way to Australia and, in 1770, claimed the island continent for the British Empire and his sovereign, King George III. This was indeed an epoch-making event, and Cook's staking of the British claim was to shape the history of Australia, leading later to the creation of the penal colony to which Britain sent its convicts, and ultimately to the emergence of Australia as an English-speaking state in its own right.

But the voyage to Australia was not Cook's only achievement. His dietary methods led to the conquering of scurvy, the disease that had killed so many sailors deprived of vitamin C on long voyages. His work on navigation gave mariners a more precise method of calculating their position at sea. And his various voyages gave us more knowledge than we previously had of the Pacific, south Atlantic, southern Indian, Arctic and Antarctic Oceans.

James Cook of Whitby
Cook was the son of a farm worker from Yorkshire, England. He was apprenticed in his youth to a shipowner from the town of Whitby. Here, in the dangerous waters of the North Sea, Cook learned his seamanship. He did well, becoming an able seaman at the age of twenty-one, before being promoted to mate three years later and given his first command after a further three years. But instead of settling down to a life on the trading vessels of the North Sea, Cook offered himself to the Royal Navy. This meant starting again as able seaman. Advancement came quickly and, by the time he was twenty-nine Cook was master of HMS *Pembroke*.

During the Seven Years' War between Britain and France (1756–63), Cook distinguished himself, seeing action in the English Channel and the north Atlantic. As master of the *Mercury* he sailed to the

Captain James Cook

St Lawrence River in Canada where he charted the difficult waters and so contributed to the success of General Wolfe's later landing. His reputation as a navigator was already secure.

Preparation for the voyage
The 1768 expedition to the Pacific which Cook was to command was a scientific one, sponsored jointly by the Royal Society and the Admiralty. Cook, an obscure officer who held a non-commissioned rank until shortly before the expedition got underway, seemed an odd choice. But he had scientific credentials: in Newfoundland in 1766 he had observed a solar eclipse and had sent a report to the Royal Society.

Cook was to be accompanied by a group of scientists whose records, drawings and specimens were to change our picture of the world. Charles Green, assistant to the Astronomer Royal, was the most important of the team as far as the Admiralty was concerned. He would make astronomical observations which, it was hoped, would improve the accuracy of navigation. But of more interest was the gifted amateur scientist Cook took with him. Joseph Banks was wealthy: he put up

£10,000 towards the costs of the expedition and supplied some of the scientific equipment. He was also a botanist with the enthusiasm of a talented amateur, a member of the Royal Society and a devoted follower of the great scientist and father of scientific classification Carolus Linneaus. Banks took with him Dr Carl Solander, a pupil of Linnaeus, and two artists, Alexander Buchan and Sydney Parkinson. It was Parkinson in particular who was to give us our first idea of the extraordinary wildlife of Australia.

On board ship
The vessel in which Cook and his team sailed was the *Endeavour*, a converted Whitby collier less than 100 feet long and weighing some 368 tons. She was round-bowed, with a deep hull and a flat bottom, and was a decidedly unglamorous vessel for the ninety or so men who sailed in her. But she was solidly built: a ship designed for a hard working life on the North Sea could withstand a great deal.

The *Endeavour* sailed in August 1768. To begin with, Cook was far from popular with his men because of the strange dietary regime he insisted on. He reduced the allowance of salt meat and increased the intake of citrus fruit juices and items such as sauerkraut, mustard, grains and raisins. He also seized every opportunity to take on stores of fresh foods during the journey. The regime eventually won the respect of the crew as Cook had succeeded in combatting scurvy, the disease that had previously taken the lives of thousands of sailors on long voyages. There were only a handful of cases of scurvy during the whole of Cook's voyage.

The first stages of the voyage
Cook's first task was to go to Tahiti. Here, he would be able to observe the transit of Venus across the face of the Sun. By watching this event and recording it accurately it would be possible to make more

accurate calculations of the Earth's distance from the Sun, a measurement important in navigation. The transit had been observed before, or rather parts of the phenomenon had been observed from different places on the globe. The advantage of going to Tahiti was that Cook would be able to see the whole event from beginning to end and thus, it was hoped, make a more accurate record.

The observation was carried out, but only after Banks had recovered his quadrant from the islanders who displayed a penchant for pilfering everything they could lay their hands on. After an exploration of the island the *Endeavour* sailed southwest across the Pacific in the direction of New Zealand. The purpose was to discover the supposed continent, the Terra Australis Incognita. Cook also wanted to know whether places such as Van Diemen's Land (Tasmania) and New Holland (eastern Australia) actually made up the coast of the continent or were merely a group of islands. By circumnavigating New Zealand, naming coves and promontories as he went, and making uneasy contact with the warlike Maori, Cook proved to his satisfaction that he had come upon a pair of islands.

Approaching Australia

With the transit of Venus observed and the coast of New Zealand charted, Cook could go home with the feeling that he had more than achieved his target. He could return home by sailing eastwards, around Cape Horn, or he could go westwards, eventually rounding the Cape of Good Hope and sailing northwestwards up the coast of Africa towards Europe. Neither route was attractive. Winter at Cape Horn would be dangerous while the westerly winds around the Cape of Good Hope, against which Cook would have to sail, were a daunting prospect. Cook and his officers therefore decided to sail westwards until they fell in with the coast of

Banksia serata *(after Parkinson, 1770)*

New Holland, following the coast to the North or whatever direction it went. Eventually they would cross the Indian Ocean before rounding the Cape of Good Hope and sailing for home. Such a course gave them more opportunities for picking up provisions on the way, and more opportunity for exploration.

The *Endeavour* left New Zealand on 31 March, reaching the coast of New Holland on 19 April. Sailing north they picked out smoke rising from the headlands, indicating that the land was inhabited. A few days later they saw their first native Australians. They were soon to meet more of these people fishing in their bark canoes. To Cook's surprise the natives' reaction to the great ship and its occupants was neither the curiosity of the Tahitans nor the hostility of the Maori: they simply ignored the *Endeavour* and went about their business.

Later, when Cook and his men landed in small boats, the native Australians' reaction was different: some ran away, others stood their ground and tried to attack Cook, although they had little chance with their spears and stones as the Europeans were armed with muskets.

As they moved northwards and explored the bay where they had landed Cook and his companions made little contact with the local people, who ignored the gifts of beads Cook left them and wanted little to do with the Europeans. But the explorers did accrue a great deal of evidence about the natural history of the place where they had landed. Banks made notes and collected thousands of specimens, while Sydney Parkinson drew the animals and plants that they found. So rich was this scientific harvest that Cook named the place Botany Bay. The northern and southern points were named for the two scientists, Cape Banks and Point Solander.

Today, it is difficult to imagine the astonishment that these early explorers must have felt on first coming across the unique wildlife of Australia. Farther north flying foxes were sighted, and they saw and shot kangaroos. A picture of a large, empty continent with a sparse population of humans and bizarre animals had begun to emerge. On a social level, the difficulty of the Europeans' relations with the native Australians also started a pattern that was to continue far into the future.

It was on their journey northwards, inland of the Great Barrier Reef, that the explorers came nearest to disaster. On the night of 11 June the ship struck the reef north of what Cook was to name Cape Tribulation. Most ships of comparable

Joseph Banks

size would have keeled over, but the *Endeavour*, with her flat bottom, stayed steady. They had to throw items overboard – including the heavy cannons – in order to get the ship to move, and there were about four feet of water in the hull by the time this was achieved. But disaster had been averted and the ship was moved, beached and repaired. Ironically, a large piece of coral that had been forced into one of the holes in the hull probably did more than anything else to save the ship from sinking before she could be beached.

From here they sailed north again, passing up the coast to Cape York, the northernmost point of northeastern Australia. Here, they landed on the tiny Possession Island and formally claimed the whole coast of New Holland for the British, setting the seal on the colonization of Australia and the country's fate as a British colony and English-speaking state. From this point on Cook, his men tired and ill and his small ship battered and leaky, worked his way home. The ship was to reach England in July 1771.

Cook's achievement

James Cook was not the first European to reach the shores of Australia. That distinction must go to Tasman and Dampier, in whose wake Cook followed. Neither did Cook circumnavigate the new continent – he had no real grasp of its shape or size. But his explorations did give him a far surer sense of the Australian environment than anyone from outside had had before. He was able to distinguish the islands of New Zealand from Australia. And the work of the scientists who worked on the *Endeavour* gave a penetrating insight into the country's wildlife.

Nevertheless, Australia did not capture the British imagination in the way that Cook's other ports of call, the exotic Tahiti and New Zealand (with its fearsome occupants), were to do. What stuck in the mind most was Banks' description of a rather barren, bland landscape: 'It resembled in my imagination the back of a lean Cow, covered in general with long hair, but nevertheless where her scraggy hip bones have stuck out further than they ought accidental rubbs and knocks have entirely bar'd them of their share of covering.' Given such accounts as this, Australia was to slip from the European consciousness until the decision to solve the problem of British prison overcrowding by sending convicts to Australia to start a penal colony. It was a grim heritage, considering the spirit of optimism in which Cook's original voyage had started out.

But that optimism had other fruits. Since Cook's time very few voyages of exploration of any note have done without accompanying scientists. The work of Banks, Solander and Parkinson showed what science could achieve when taken to unexplored regions of the globe. Cook's team showed the world that exploration need not be a matter of arriving, looking round and conquering. It was more important to use the resources of science and art to observe, analyze and record.

*In April 1770, sailing NNE, James Cook and his crew aboard the
Endeavour sighted the coast of Victoria – their first view of the island
continent. Their journey had been inspired by the need for improvements
in navigation. They knew that measuring the angular distance of the Sun
from the Moon would enable them to work out their position using tables
published in the relevant nautical almanac. Their task was to observe the
transit of the planet Venus across the face of the Sun, allowing them to
work out more precisely the Earth's distance from the Sun and thus to
increase the accuracy of navigational calculations. Such measurements
and calculations were finally less significant than Cook's discoveries in
Australia. But the scientific rigour with which those discoveries were
recorded was perhaps most significant of all: it had a vital influence on
the way future expeditions were run.*

Cook's route around the world

JAMES WATT'S STEAM ENGINE

Improvements in technology that fuelled the industrial revolution

In the seventeenth century Britain had a thriving manufacturing industry and was mining more coal than any other nation. In the following years coal consumption rose further as the population increased. Soon the iron industry began to expand in response to the demand for a larger supply of this material for industry. The demands on resources, particularly of coal, were such that the deposits near the surface, which could be removed by open-cast mining, were soon exhausted. It became necessary to dig deeper to mine the underground seams of coal. But as the miners pushed down below the water table a new problem arose. Flooding in the shafts and tunnels made the new form of mining dangerous – and threatened to make it well-nigh impossible.

Miner's friends and others
Around the end of the seventeenth century engineers began to address this problem by designing pumps to remove water from the mines. One of the first to come up with a solution was Thomas Savery, who was probably a Cornish mining engineer. At the end of the century Savery was developing a device he called the Miner's Friend, a pump that used the combined effects of atmospheric pressure and steam to remove the water. He patented this device in 1698.

Savery's pump was a simple affair. It did not even have a piston. Steam from a boiler was fed into a receiving container. One pipe connected this to the water to be moved, another carried water out at the top. A flow of water outside the container cooled it, condensing the steam and creating a vacuum thereby sucking the water up the first pipe into the container. Steam from the boiler was used to drive the water through the second pipe at the top.

The Miner's Friend was ingenious but in practice severely limited. It would only pump water up some fifty feet, so if the system was to be used in a mine of any depth a series of pumps would have to be used to raise the water in steps. And the boiler technology was very primitive. Boilers often blew up as the pressure increased. It is not surprising, therefore, that Savery's invention saw more service pumping water in large houses than it did in mines.

The first person to come up with a practical improvement on Savery's pump was Thomas Newcomen. His steam engine, which appeared in 1712, was widely used in Europe, although its inventor died in 1715 and so did not profit from his work. Newcomen's engine was the first to have a piston. This was connected by a hook to one end of a large wooden beam. At the other end of the beam was a pump rod. The engine worked by injecting steam into the cylinder to force the piston up; then cold water was forced into the cylinder to condense the steam so that the piston dropped down and the pump rod at the other end of the beam moved upwards. Then steam was pushed back into the cylinder to begin the process again.

Newcomen's engine was a big improvement on the Miner's Friend. It could

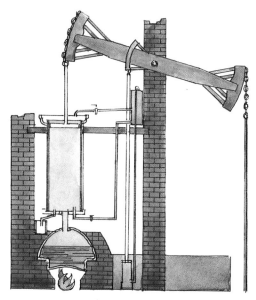

Newcomen's steam engine, 1712

pump water from much lower depths and the risk of the boiler blowing up was limited as it could work with steam at low pressure. It also had a clever mechanism that opened and closed the valves automatically. But the engine was still incredibly noisy and very inefficient – particularly because so much energy was used up alternately heating and cooling the cylinder during each stroke. As time went on various engineers made improvements to Newcomen's engine. John Smeaton was one such improver. His more precisely machined components made the engine more efficient.

Watt's pioneering work
But the most famous improver of the steam engine was the Scottish instrument-maker and inventor, James Watt. This pioneer is surrounded by myths. The most long-lasting is the story of Watt sitting in the kitchen watching steam lifting the lid of a boiling kettle and then inventing the steam engine. As we have seen, the steam engine had already been invented by the time Watt was born in 1736. But his were to be the decisive improvements that allowed the steam engine to play its key role in the industrial revolution.

James Watt was employed by Glasgow University as a maker and repairer of scientific instruments. One day in 1764 he was brought a model of a Newcomen steam engine to repair. Looking at this model set him on the decisive path. Watt realised that the main problem with Newcomen's engine was that the cylinder had to be alternately heated and cooled, wasting energy, losing efficiency and taking a great deal of time in the process. The solution Watt came up with was to have two cylinders. One would contain the piston and would be hot all the time, another would form a separate condenser and would be kept cold.

The steam engine as improved by Watt would use only a quarter of the fuel taken

Cugnot's steam carriage, 1771, an early use of steam power for transport

up by Newcomen's engine. It was an important breakthrough, but Watt, reliant on his relatively low income from the university, could not afford to develop it on his own, let alone manufacture it. So he formed a partnership with a businessman called Matthew Boulton. They proposed to manufacture steam engines from Boulton's factory, Soho Works, near Birmingham, England.

Improving the engine

The period after Watt's original patent saw numerous other improvements that made the steam engine a still better source of power for industrialists. One problem with early steam engines was that their parts – especially the cylinder and piston – did not fit together very accurately. Watt's partner Boulton expressed the difficulty by comparing Watt's trade of instrument maker with his own of ironworker. But help came from outside the partnership. The prominent Midlands ironmaster John Wilkinson had produced a special machine for boring large cannon barrels.

Wilkinson used his machine and his experience to produce better-fitting cylinders for the engine's pistons, thereby increasing efficiency. Watt and Boulton were enthusiastic about the result, noting that the fit was so close that you could not push a coin into the gap between the two parts. Appropriately enough, Wilkinson was one of Watt's first customers. His boring machinery, which was to produce artillery for both sides during the Peninsular War, was henceforward powered not by a water wheel but by steam.

Watt himself came up with further refinements. His 'parallel motion' kept the piston rod moving vertically. A new system of valves allowed steam to enter on either side of the piston to give a double-power stroke. And he came up with a particularly ingenious device called a governor to regulate the engine's speed. As the engine went faster, a pair of metal balls rotating centrifugally on arms were flung gradually higher. The movement of the arms pulled down a bar controlling the throttle, which in turn reduced the amount of steam supplied to the engine, slowing it down again. The way the governor vacillated as the engine ran meant that the speed could be kept constant.

Crucially, Watt was working on a way of converting the 'up and down' movement of the engine into a rotary motion that could drive machinery. His first solution was to use a crank. But one of his workers, knowing the system that Watt was developing, patented it himself. This forced Watt to find another way around the problem. His concept was the 'sun and planet' gear system. The rod on the opposite end of the beam from the piston carried a gear (the 'planet'). The wheel shaft (connected to the machinery the engine was to drive) bore another gear (the 'sun'). As the rod was pushed up and down, the planet circled the sun, making it rotate twice for every revolution of the engine. This doubled the effective speed of the engine and provided a viable way to drive machinery.

This was perhaps the most significant of all Watt's later improvements to the steam engine. The engine was no longer simply a pump with limited use outside deep mines. It could form the power source for factories everywhere.

Not surprisingly, Boulton and Watt soon had a successful business on their hands. They were providing exactly what Europe's expanding industry needed: power to pump water from mines and to drive machinery. No longer were manufacturers dependent on wind or water power to drive the increasingly complex machines that industry was using. Between 1769, when Watt patented his separate condenser, and 1800, when the patent ran out, Watt and Boulton built about 500 engines. This compared well with the 1,000 Newcomen engines that had been built by this time. When other manufacturers started to take advantage of Watt and Boulton's work, the numbers increased still more rapidly.

Other developments were taking place. In France in the early 1770s N. J. Cugnot was building his steam carriage, and in 1801 in England mining engineer Richard Trevithick announced a steam-driven vehicle, a concept which he had been developing quietly during the period of Watt's patent. Vehicles like these were the primitive ancestors of the railways which were eventually to revolutionize transport the world over and to have their own effect on the industrial revolution.

The coming of industrial change

So two key facilities had been provided for industrial expansion: the ability to tap an apparently unlimited supply of coal from deep mines, and a source of power that could be built anywhere. But the steam engine alone did not create the industrial revolution. In order for the great manufacturing expansion of the eighteenth and nineteenth centuries to take place, coal had to be not only obtainable but easily transportable. The development of widespread canal, road and, later, railway networks ensured that this would be the case.

There were further technological innovations that hastened the progress of industrial change. Particularly important amongst these were improved machines for manufacturing textiles. A succession of spinning and weaving machines appeared in the eighteenth century that made textile manufacture steadily faster and more automatic. So yarn and cloth were the most important products of the early factories.

But even technological developments like these were not enough. The social conditions had to be right, too. A culture was necessary in which enough people could organize the resources needed for production and take the risks necessary to

RIGHT *Watt the scientist knew little of the practicalities of the business that grew up in the wake of his improved steam engine. He was first and foremost a technical problem-solver who modified a model steam engine so that it would work more efficiently. His business partnership with Matthew Boulton gave him the security he needed to carry on his work, further modifying and improving the full-size engines built in their factory. The business was successful, with Watt's improvements turning the steam engine into a vital source of motive power in countless factories.*

ABOVE LEFT *Watt's model of a steam engine with a separate condenser*

get new industries going. They had to be committed and receptive enough to new ideas to carry on investing and expanding as the new technological changes came along. In many ways Watt and Boulton exemplify this pattern. Watt, the diffident inventor who would worry away at his steam engine to make it more efficient; Boulton, the manufacturer and businessman: they needed each other.

And behind these inventors and entrepreneurs there were the equally necessary armies of men and women who could mine the coal and operate the machines. In England in the eighteenth century there was the right balance between population rise and increase in literacy for this to happen. The industrial revolution followed in countries where a similar social pattern was emerging: the United States, France, Germany and Switzerland. Industrial production boomed. Between 1500 and 1750, before the effects of the steam engine and the other industrial inventions had made themselves felt, industrial production rose on average 0.2 per cent each year. Between 1760 and 1780 the annual rise was 1.5 per cent. During the following twenty years, the average annual rise steadily increased to 2.1 per cent.

For Britain and the other emerging industrial nations these increases in production meant better opportunities for international trade. By the beginning of the nineteenth century Britain's exports to most of her trading partners exceeded her imports in value. And this confirmed a pattern that would continue through the century, in which colonies around the

world were tapped for their raw materials and to a certain extent regarded as a market for goods, although a larger market was found in the industrialized west itself. Industrial capitalism had arrived in both Europe and America. For years it would be dominated by Britain, the country whose early start got the industrial revolution off the ground and whose expanding empire would continue to bolster it.

The industrial effects of the technological changes centred on the steam engine were obvious enough. But what of the social changes? There are many ways of measuring such changes. One way is to look at the way income per head increased during the period: the evidence is that it went up much faster, particularly in the nineteenth century, than it had done before.

But since wealth is not distributed evenly, and since inflation could eat away earnings, this is not an accurate indicator of how the majority of the population was affected. Another measurement is provided by the higher life expectancy of people in industrialized societies. People undoubtedly lived longer. But this could be as much the result of agricultural improvements that increased the food supply and of advances in medical technique as of the changes in industry.

It is difficult in short to say whether life for most people was any better. But life was certainly different. The number of people living in towns increased dramatically. And the factories provided a different style of work from agricultural labour, if equally arduous. Life had been changed across much of the world.

BATTLE OF YORKTOWN

Key conflict in the American revolution

By 1763 the British had gained control of most of France's territory in North America. But over the next dozen years, the American colonists grew away from their British overlords. They had found it easier to create what they saw as a fair society in America than in Britain. In America one could succeed through hard work rather than the accidents of birth. Land was plentiful and ownership did not depend on being born into a land-owning family. And the more the colonists could control their own affairs, the closer they could come to creating the kind of society they wanted.

Economically the American colonists were also breaking free of Britain at this time. Britain had aggravated the situation by imposing restrictions on colonial manufacturing and trade. But more decisive was the British decision in 1763 to establish a standing army in America (in itself another potential threat to the colonists' way of life) and to pay for it with taxes imposed on the colonists.

The British taxed Americans as heavily as they could and reasserted their power over the colonists. At each stage in this process, the economic threat was compounded by a political one. Apart from the standing army, in 1763 the British forebade settlement beyond the Appalachian Mountains. The rationale for this was that the British wanted to avoid war with the native Americans. But the effect on the colonists was to deprive them of a vast source of land, again threatening their way of life. It also imposed another economic restriction, depriving the manufacturers of the east coast a new market west of the mountains.

Another restriction on colonial freedom were the Navigation Acts and the Revenue Act of 1764. Together these laws put severe restrictions on colonial shipping and imposed taxes on commodities such as molasses brought to the colonies from the West Indies. Although the

George Washington

British reduced the impact by lowering the tax level, these Acts form an example of the way the colonists were affected both economically and in other ways by British policies. The Quartering Act of 1765, which compelled colonists to provide quarters, fuel, candles and beer for British troops, worked in a similar way. Further taxation, such as the Stamp Tax (1765) and duties on imports (1767), provoked increased objections and challenges from the colonists. In 1773 colonial concerns came to a head when people in Boston held the so-called Boston Tea Party, at which they boarded British ships and threw their cargo of tea into the harbour rather than pay duty on it. When the British responded by closing Boston Harbour, the colonists organized to protect their rights.

The Americans made their demands plain. At the First Continental Congress in 1774 they asked Britain to renounce her authority over Massachusetts and to stop taxing the colonists. A trade ban with Britain was instigated. At the Second Continental Congress, on 4 July 1776, they adopted the Declaration of Independence, provoking Britain to strong military action. But by this time the first

shots in what was to become the American Revolutionary War had already been fired.

At the outbreak of war, it was not clear which of the opponents would win. The British had professional soldiers (although the standing army was small) and a fleet forming a blockade in the Atlantic. They supplemented their forces with mercenaries, colonial loyalists and some native American supporters. They were also well financed. On the other hand, they were far away from home and getting extra supplies and troops across the ocean would always be time-consuming. The colonists had the advantage of plenty of manpower easily to hand and unrivalled local knowledge. Their militiamen (known as minutemen, because they were trained to act at a moment's notice) were supplemented by volunteers. To begin with, the colonists tended to have more soldiers than the British, but they were neither as well disciplined nor as effective. But as the war continued and the colonists gained experience they became a better match for their opponents. The colonists also hoped that Britain's other enemies (France and Spain) would support them.

The first years of the war

The opening shots of the war were fired at Lexington, Mass., in April 1775. Several hours later, at nearby Concord, English and American troops again fought, confirming that the incident at Lexington was not an isolated one. These events signalled the beginning of a war that would last eight years. Battles would be fought on a front stretching from Quebec and Montreal in the north to Florida in the south.

The first two years of the war saw Britain preparing by enlisting soldiers at home and hiring mercenaries in Germany. The naval blockade was also organized. After Lexington and Concord, the British withdrew to Boston. The colonists intended to attack Boston from one of the neighbouring hills and remove the British. But at the Battle of Bunker Hill (June 1775) the Americans were pushed back from their positions above Boston, a success the British paid for with extremely high casualties.

Bunker Hill confirmed the opinion of the colonists that they needed a unified army. It was one of the decisions of the Second Continental Congress to organize what was to become known as the Continental Army, and to select George Washington to command it. Other important events at the beginning of the war were battles at Montreal, where the colonists took this important city with no casualties at all, and Quebec, which they failed to take. They did better in the south, where the British governors of Virginia and North Carolina were forced to flee.

The middle years

The years 1776–78 saw varying fortunes for both sides. By 1776 the colonists had control of all the land east of the Appalachians. But the British had a plan that they thought would regain them the upper hand. In 1777 their leader Burgoyne would march south from Canada, intending to meet up with General Howe at the Hudson River. Burgoyne performed his part of the plan, arriving at the Hudson in August 1777. But Howe was distracted. He had left New York by sea and landed at Chesapeake Bay, where he met Washington at the Brandywine. The result was a victory for Howe, who took Philadelphia in September. But by this time Burgoyne was in trouble. He had met the colonists at Saratoga, east of the Hudson, suffered a crushing defeat, and was forced to surrender to the colonists.

Saratoga was the first turning point of the war. In itself it was a blow to the

'Minutemen' of the American army

British. And it had the additional effect of persuading the French to come into the war on the colonial side. But the British did not give in. In 1778 they scored a victory at Charleston; there was a further British victory at Camden in 1780. Early in 1781 the British fought heroically, but in the end unsuccessfully, at Cowpens. Every gunner was killed before the British artillery was silenced. The following year a further victory, at Guildford Court House in North Carolina, gave the British some hope, although casualties were very heavy.

Yorktown

The early months of 1781 saw the British General Cornwallis moving into Virginia and establishing a base at Yorktown, near the entrance to Chesapeake Bay. Yorktown lies on a low plateau overlooking the York River. Marshes, creeks and ravines cut it off from the surrounding land, and together with the river these features must have made it an attractive base that seemed easy to defend. Cornwallis was in a certain amount of confusion about the intentions of his British colleagues, receiving instructions from Clinton about various planned actions further north. So in the end Cornwallis decided to dig in at Yorktown. He set up two lines of defence, a minimal outer line composed of several redoubts, and an inner line that was intended to be more secure.

In May 1781, Washington and the French commander Rochambeau began to threaten New York City in the hope that Clinton would be forced to recall some of the troops from Virginia. But it was difficult to get into a good attack position and these operations did not come to anything. Meanwhile, the French admiral Grasse was on his way with twenty-nine ships containing about 3,000 soldiers. He was heading for Chesapeake Bay. In consequence, Washington and Rochambeau decided to march to Chesapeake to join up with Grasse and mount a combined attack on the British at Yorktown.

Washington showed his skill in logistics and organization during this extensive troop movement. Roads and bridges were repaired in advance and boats were found to transport the men down the bay. The colonists seemed to be ready for the attack. But all was not so well with the French. The newly arrived Grasse was unwilling to send his ships up the York River to cut Cornwallis off.

Washington pressed on with the the allied army, however. By the end of September they were sufficiently established around the town and sufficiently fearsome to make the British abandon

their outer defences. Short of food, the British also began to slaughter their horses. But they did not do anything to challenge the allied presence outside the town.

Scarcely able to believe the passivity of Cornwallis, Washington ordered his men

King George III of England

to dig in and to start constructing zigzag trenches to bring them gradually closer to the British lines. Working under cover of darkness they had constructed a trench only about 600 metres from the British by 6 October. This was soon supplemented by redoubts and communications trenches. The British at last responded, using their guns to threaten the allies. But Washington's gunners, especially those of his French allies, proved superior. The French claimed they could put six consecutive rounds in the same place on an enemy battery.

A few days later the allies constructed another parallel trench, this time only 300 metres from the British. This move was made partly by taking over some of the British defences. It now seemed impossible that Yorktown could be successfully defended. The British were tired and demoralized. Cornwallis knew he was defeated and started to evacuate his troops by boat across the York River. Then a storm put paid to further evacuations and it became clear that all Cornwallis could do was to prepare for surrender.

After Yorktown

The war was not over. There were further battles – mostly at sea – in which the colonists were given valuable help by Britain's enemies – the French, Spanish and Dutch. But after Yorktown it was only a matter of time before the American victory would be confirmed. It was at the Treaty of Paris in 1783 that the British finally acknowledged American independence. The first article of the treaty declared that 'His Britannic Majesty acknowledges the said United States ... to be

On 16 October 1781 Cornwallis started to withdraw his troops from Yorktown, across the river to Gloucester, in the hope that he could reassemble his army and attack New York. But the weather was against him and before he could ferry more than 1,000 men across the river a storm blew up and he knew it was pointless to continue. So the following day one of Cornwallis' officers was sent to Washington with a proposal for surrender. It only took a day to discuss the terms, and on 19 October, at two in the afternoon, the British marched out to surrender. In two years' time another document would be signed, the Treaty of Paris that gave the United States their independence.

free Sovereign and independent States.' It also established the boundaries of the United States: from the 31st parallel in the south to a line close to today's boundary in the north, and west to the Mississippi River. Florida was ceded to Spain. Fishing rights were granted; debts were to be paid; property confiscated by the British was to be restored. The British were to withdraw 'with all convenient speed' and there would be no further prosecutions or confiscations for action taken in the war. Britain also made peace settlements with France and Spain.

The American Revolutionary War resulted in the creation of the United States, the country that has influenced world history as much as any in the 200 years since its creation. It also confirmed the important position of George Washington, the commander in chief who was to preside over the Constitutional Convention in 1787 which drafted the constitution, set up the two-chamber system of government, and did so much to shape the history of the new republic. Not surprisingly, it was also Washington's fate to be unanimously elected the republic's first president.

FALL OF THE BASTILLE

The event that sparked off the French Revolution

The situation in France at the end of the eighteenth century was approaching a crisis. The ruling monarch, Louis XVI, and his extravagant wife Marie Antoinette were remote from their people; the king's main interests were hunting and eating. The rule of the king was absolute, and the power lay with Louis and his ministers.

The aristocracy resented this as much as anyone. Jealous of the power of the ministers, they did what they could to regain power for themselves. They clung for dear life on to the privileges that they still had – in particular the right to high office in the army, the church and the diplomatic service – in the hope that from these positions of influence they could reign in the absolutism of the king. But in turn, because of their privileges, the aristocracy were unpopular. Two particular causes of resentment were the fact that they could claim exemption from several taxes and their control over manorial courts.

Another unpopular and in many ways powerful group was the church. True, many churchmen were far from wealthy. But the church as an institution held more than one-tenth of the land in France, and the higher churchmen were extremely rich. This fact, together with a somewhat increasingly secular attitude, particularly amongst the better-educated members of general society, led to widespread anti-clericalism.

Lower down the social scale were the bourgeoisie, the urban middle class. Many of these people were well-off – often more so than their counterparts in the aristocracy. Yet they were barred from privileges and wanted to gain access to some of the rights – whether social or financial – of the upper classes.

In rural areas many of the peasants owned some land, but not enough to make a living. So they had to do paid work in addition to working in their own fields. Some also had to borrow livestock or equipment from larger farmers, who

King Louis XVI of France

claimed a large proportion of the peasant farmer's produce as a hire fee. There were also high taxes, together with feudal dues that had to be paid to the local lord. The workers in the cities fared a little better. But even here, although industry was expanding, wages were not keeping pace with the cost of living, and industrial unrest was not uncommon.

So there were a great many grievances amongst the people of France at this period, but little unity about what was needed to put them right. There was a split, in both town and country, between those who found it difficult to survive at all, and those who, while rich enough, resented the fact that they were barred from the privileges of the upper classes.

The beginnings of opposition
In the late 1780s, opposition focused on the king. In order to try to sort out France's deep financial trouble, Louis appointed a new Director-General of Finance, Jacques Necker of Switzerland. Necker, who arrived with the reputation of being somewhat of a financial genius, instituted loans to pay off the public deficit. But he failed to clear up the unfair system of taxation. Necker's successor,

Alexandre de Calonne, tried to solve the problem by introducing another land tax, which would be levied on all owners, irrespective of their social status. Indeed the new tax would hit the privileged hardest of all. It was also to be a tax which the king could impose without recourse to the *parlements*, who were generally supposed to approve measures of this sort.

And so, by trying to remove one source of grievance, Louis and his finance minister provoked another. The Paris *parlement* refused to let the new measures pass without the assent of the Estates General, a committee that had not met since 1614 and which was composed of representatives of the nobility, the clergy and the commons (or 'Third Estate').

Matters came to a head in May 1788 when the king refused to allow the Estates General to meet to discuss the taxation. The *parlements* were stripped of their power to oppose the policy of the king and Louis began to enforce the new measures. And so objections began to make themselves heard in less disciplined ways than they might in the *parlements*: violence began to spread around the country, and Louis' officials quickly realized that it would be impossible to collect the tax at all. Even the clergy assembled to condemn the actions of the government.

With violence rife and national bankruptcy a distinct possibility, it became clear that something had to be done. Louis was forced to call the *parlements* once again, to reinstate Necker, and to promise that the Estates General would meet next May. But there followed a dispute about the composition of the Estates General. In 1614 it had been made up of equal numbers from the three estates. The Paris *parlement* upheld the view that it should once more be constituted in this way. This meant that the nobility and clergy could always defeat the commons. Necker spoke on behalf of the commons and it was agreed on 27 December (in time for the elections in the new year) that they would have double the number of members granted to the other two estates. But the system of voting was not made clear.

As can be seen from the controversy surrounding the composition of the Estates General, the strife had focused on the differences between the privileged and unprivileged classes – the clergy and nobility against the commons. What was more, the *parlement*, by coming out on the side of equal representation for the three estates, was alienated from the mass of the bourgeoisie who wanted change. The Third Estate would, they hoped, be their true representatives.

Something of the grievances of the three estates can be seen from the *cahiers de doléances*, the lists of grievances drawn up for consideration by the Estates General. The absolutism of the king was condemned, and a constitution was requested which would provide for regular meetings of the Estates General at which taxes could be voted on. Individual liberty, press freedom, church reforms, government economies and financial and customs reforms were also requested.

But more than this, the members of the Third Estate felt that they would not have succeeded until they made the Estates General a more representative body. Soon the Third Estate was proposed as the representative body of the nation. All members of the Estates General who turned down an invitation to join the Third Estate would forfeit their right to act as representatives. They invited the parish priests to join them from the clergy hall and gradually, in spite of resistance from the nobility, some of the clergy did just that. As priests began to join it became clear that the group was to take on a broader role. On 17 June 1789 this was recognized when the group voted to change its name to 'National Assembly'.

The king proclaimed that the actions of the assembly were illegal and that they

should be prevented from meeting. Locked out of the hall, the members met in an indoor tennis court, where they swore the famous tennis court oath which declared that they would not break up until a constitution had been formulated and established. Meanwhile, the price of bread was going up and civil unrest was continuing. The king sent in the troops and removed Necker once more, but the crowds of Paris remained violent. There was a sense of escalating violence.

Events came to a head on 14 July. There were stories circulating that thousands of royal troops were being mobilized. Crowds of citizens demanded weapons and when these were not forthcoming they rushed into Les Invalides and took whatever arms they could find. They took large supplies of guns and some ten or a dozen cannon, but there was little ammunition. For this they went to the old fortress of the Bastille.

The Bastille, an imposing building with eight round towers and stone walls eighty feet high, had long been used as a state prison for people who, although not guilty of an offence under common law, were held by royal decree. It was thought that its dungeons contained many people in chains, but in fact the Bastille held only seven prisoners in July 1789.

When the crowd, now augmented by many who had joined along the way, arrived outside the walls of the prison, the governor of the Bastille tried to negotiate. But the people were impatient. Soon a small group of men managed to get into the Cour du Gouvernement, a courtyard that gave them access to the pulleys of the drawbridges leading into the prison. These were lowered, with the loss of one life as the great wooden drawbridges were dropped down on to the outer bank of the moat, and the crowd surged towards the fortress.

What happened next is unclear. One side, it is not now known which, began firing. There were two hours of bloody fighting, after which the Bastille was sacked and demolished stone by stone. The governor of the Bastille, the Marquis de Launay, was killed and his bleeding head was raised on a pike and carried through the streets.

That night there was much celebration on the streets of Paris. A detested symbol of the king's power had been taken and removed. There had been casualties (of the assailants, almost one hundred people were killed). But for the people it was a crucial victory, showing how they could act to remove the despotism of Louis. And the people in the provinces seemed to be with the Parisians. Around the country-

side there was rioting and burning of aristocratic homes, discontent no doubt fuelled by the fact that the previous year's harvest had been particularly bad and that the winter had been very hard.

On a more constructive level, the National Assembly began to pass measures that would attempt to limit the power of the king, to abolish feudal obligations and

Revolutionaries charge on the Bastille

privileges, and to define the 'rights of man'. The king refused to accept these measures until the march of the women to Versailles in October, when he was forced to capitulate. There followed a period of relative peace, during which the National Assembly undertook numerous reforms. Church lands were confiscated to stave off national bankruptcy, and the church, law courts and local government were thoroughly reorganized.

Clearly there were vested interests that opposed these changes. But the National Assembly pressed on with their implementation and in July 1791 Louis accepted the reforms and was reinstated. The members of the National Assembly considered that the revolution was over. They dissolved the assembly in September 1791. But strife within the Third Estate continued and there was a second revolution, in 1792, which led to the imprisonment of the king and, ultimately, to the foundation of the Republic of France in September of that year. Early in 1793 Louis was taken to the guillotine. The hated embodiment of absolutism was gone at last.

Even then, the troubles of France were far from over. The now infamous reign of terror, a repressive regime in which opponents were sent to be executed at the guillotine, was to follow during the years 1793–4. To begin with, a democratic constitution was put forward under the auspices of justice minister Georges Danton. But when various rebellions against the

It did not matter that the Bastille contained only a handful of prisoners when it was stormed in July 1789. With its massive walls and its history as a prison for the victims of the royal decree it was a potent symbol of the repression possible and indeed prevalent under absolutist rule. So the prison was a natural rallying point for the people, newly armed after their raid on Les Invalides. Although the taking of the Bastille was immediately hailed as a triumphant victory, with dancing around the tree of liberty and through the streets of the capital, it was just a beginning. Before long, rioting and the destruction of the houses of aristocrats would spread through the country and the National Assembly would push through reforms to calm the revolutionary fervour and bring France to order again.

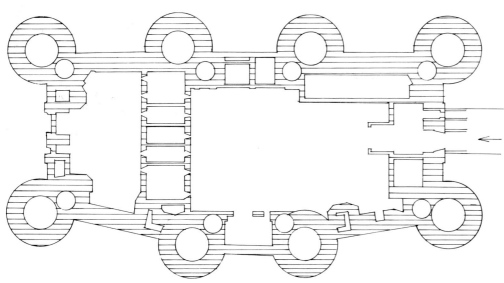

Ground plan of the Bastille

revolution continued, the influence of revolutionary leader Maximilien Robespierre came to the fore. It was under Robespierre that the army was sent to subdue the provinces and that the Revolutionary Tribunal sent large numbers of state prisoners to the guillotine. This was only to end when Robespierre and the other leaders of the terror were themselves executed.

The following years saw further attempts at establishing a workable constitution. The first of these, in 1795, established the Directory, an executive body that, although it prevented a return to either monarchy or the terror, was weak and short-lived. The second attempt, the constitution of 1799, established the Consulate, a three-man governing body led by Napoleon Bonaparte which paved the way for the First Empire in 1804.

The influence of the revolution

The fall of the Bastille can be seen as the key turning point in the French Revolution. It was the point at which the people realized that they could use violence effectively to further their opposition to the monarchy. In so doing they eradicated a potent symbol of Louis' power. It was the beginning of the end of an old feudal society and an absolutist monarchy. And it was the start of a search for a social structure to put in its place.

Although democracy failed in the years after 1789, France would never return again to a feudal monarchy. The power of the church was also undermined (indeed for a period churches were closed completely) and many aristocrats fled. And there was a redistribution of the vast wealth and land of church and aristocracy. To be sure, this redistribution did not go as far as it might: only the richer country farmers could afford to buy the newly available land. But the social balance of the nation was changed for good: the small farms that still dominate rural France could thrive.

And in spite of changes in government, the legal and administration systems set up during the early years of the revolution did prevail. Much of the revolutionaries' legal work was taken on board by Napoleon in his own legal code. So although the French Revolution brought about a period of great instability and bloodshed, a time typified by events like the fall of the Bastille, the seeds were also sown for future stability.

DECLARATION OF THE RIGHTS OF MAN

Statement of the principles of the 'free' world

The Declaration of the Rights of Man and the Citizen is one of the fundamental charters of human liberties. It was drawn up during the French Revolution and was first and foremost a reaction to the absolutist rule of Louis XVI and a summary of the tenets of the revolutionary movement in France. It was adopted by the French National Assembly in 1789 and was prefaced to France's first constitution in 1791.

But the declaration is more significant than its context suggests. In France itself it was reaffirmed by the constitution of 1958. But more than this, it enshrines key principles that governments and peoples in the 'free' world live by today. Its first article asserts that 'all men are born free and equal in rights' and that such social distinctions as are necessary should be based on the common good. Article two lists the essential rights of humans: liberty, private property, personal safety and freedom from oppression. The other fifteen articles cover such issues as freedom of religion and freedom of speech, the equality of citizens before the law, and the principle that no citizen should be arrested or punished without going through the appropriate judicial process.

The important concept of liberty is defined as freedom to do anything that does not harm others. Consequently, the power of the law is limited to forbidding actions that will harm society. The law is the expression of the general will of the people and should be equally available to all. All should also be eligible for high office and public employment. A public force is needed to maintain law and order and taxation will be necessary to pay for this. But this should be levied in accordance with the citizen's ability to pay. Public officials must be accountable to the people.

The Declaration reveals the interests of the middle-class revolutionaries who compiled it. In placing emphasis on private property and in opening up high office to members of the bourgeoisie, it is very much a document of late eighteenth-century France. Its pedigree is also shown in the influence of the philosophical writers of the eighteenth century, particularly the well-known Swiss philosopher Jean-Jacques Rousseau.

Jean-Jacques Rousseau

Rousseau's *Social Contract* had inspired revolutionary leader Maximilien Robespierre. The way it lays importance both on individual freedom ('man is born free but everywhere is in chains') and the general will is reflected in the Declaration. The idea of the general will is crucial to Rousseau. The philosopher takes it to extremes, asserting that the sovereign authority to make laws, for example, resides in the whole people, not in any individual or even elected representatives. Clearly this is impracticable for a whole nation, which cannot assemble together to make laws. So Rousseau's version of the general will could not be incorporated into either the Declaration or the subsequent Constitution, although it remained a vital influence on both.

Not surprisingly, the Declaration met with a stony response from the French king. Louis refused to recognize the document and the revolution had to pass through several bloody stages before many of its principles could be put into practice. Nevertheless, the Declaration was a major turning point in the Revolution, going a long way to defining what the people wanted and providing a political statement to match the great physical statements of the Revolution, like the storming of the Bastille.

The Declaration is not a charter for democracy. But to the democrats of the nineteenth century states its principles could be extended to apply to democratic government. And this was what happened. It took its place beside the other great charters – such as Magna Carta and the Bill of Rights – as one of the cornerstones of a new, democratic age.

As democracy increasingly became the preferred mode of government in the western world in the nineteenth and twentieth centuries, and as the franchise was widened to give more people a say in who governed them, the relevance of the Declaration became increasingly clear. The idea of the 'general will', far from Rousseau's conception of the entire nation, came to seem more and more relevant when there was universal suffrage. And although modern democracy has been shaped by several other forces (not least the older autocratic institutions that went before it), the declaration was a formative influence.

Liberty, equality, fraternity: the ideals of the French revolution lived on in the Declaration of the Rights of Man that the National Assembly adopted in 1789. Its first and guiding principle, that all people are 'born free and equal in rights' was inspiring to those who had survived the reigns of absolutist monarchs to look forward to a fairer society. And the principle has retained its relevance until the present day, as all know who struggle for the equal rights of everyone, irrespective of their race, sex or beliefs.

BATTLE OF TRAFALGAR

The beginning of British naval supremacy

After the instability of the revolution there was a need in France for a more stable government that would, nevertheless, carry on the policies of modernization begun by the revolution. The leaders of the revolution itself seemed unable to provide the sort of continuity that was required, with the frequent changes of government and constitution. Single-minded rule seemed to be the only way and, ironically, having ousted an absolute monarch the French seemed destined to be ruled by a dictator. The leader who emerged, in the dramatic coup of 18 Brumaire (the equivalent, in the revolutionary calendar of 9 November 1799), was Napoleon Bonaparte.

Napoleon ruled initially as first Consul and after 1804 as Emperor. And if many saw this return to a single autocratic ruler as a retrograde step, yet it cannot be denied that Napoleon presided over important reforms that would change France for the better. In the early years of his rule there were key changes in local government, an adjustment of the relationship between church and state, educational reforms, and the establishment of the legal framework, the *Code Napoléon*, which confirmed vital principles of equality and property rights that had been asserted by the revolution.

The domestic policies of Napoleon were important enough. But he is remembered even more for his aggressive foreign policy, which threatened to change the map of Europe and put the whole continent under French domination. For although France was at peace during the early years of his government, after 1803 there was continuous war for over ten years. He was a master tactician on the battlefield, perpetually outmanoeuvring his enemies to split their ranks before going in for the kill. Austria, Prussia and Russia would fall to Napoleon in this way. Poland and Italy would follow. Switzerland became a French protectorate. On

the mainland of Europe only Spain held out against the French. The other European nation that resisted Napoleon's advance was Great Britain.

The British had long known that the key to their political and commercial independence was the English Channel. The threat from France was obvious. The Revolution, with its declared enmity to all monarchies, had made things worse. The French envoy in London was therefore sent home in 1793 and the French responded by declaring war on Britain and Holland.

Admiral Horatio Nelson

By the time of Napoleon it was clear that the French had either to cut off British trade or gain military control of the English Channel if they were to beat their rivals. Napoleon knew of the importance of trade to the island race and put pressure on Britain by closing the European markets to British goods. He also attempted to weaken British trade by attacking Malta, Egypt and India. Meanwhile he pursued grandiose plans to invade Britain.

The French campaign in Egypt began

successfully, with a landing at Alexandria and a victory at the Battle of the Pyramids in July 1798. But Napoleon scarcely had time to consolidate his victory before the British navy, under Nelson, routed them at the Battle of the Nile on 1–2 August. It was a victory that brought the British several allies (Naples, Austria, Russia and Turkey), and the new coalition posed an immediate threat to French forces in Holland and Switzerland. But the French fought back and were in a strong position when Napoleon took over on the 18 Brumaire.

The first military success under the new regime was at Marengo, where Napoleon beat the Austrians. His victory was confirmed by the Peace of Lunéville in February 1801. It was now time for him to turn once again to his plans for invading England. His plans were outlined in a letter to Talleyrand in February 1802. France, Spain and Holland, together with some forces from Russia and Denmark, would be involved in the manoeuvres outlined in the letter. From England's point of view the most important plans were to draw the British fleet to Egypt, when the French would slip quietly across the English Channel with an invasion force. This would comprise over 100,000 men in some 2,000 small boats.

Napoleon's plans were spoiled by the collapse of the alliance between France, Russia and Denmark and the signing of the Treaty of Amiens in March 1802. This confirmed that Britain and Ireland were at peace with France, Spain and Holland. It was a blow, but it left France looking influential in Europe and it led to a strong majority in the plebiscite in May that voted Napoleon Consul for life.

In any case the peace was an uneasy one. The French continued their protectionism against British trade. The English refused to give up Malta (which she had agreed to leave under the terms of the treaty). The French refused to remove their garrison from Holland. There was peace in name for about a year, but at the beginning of May 1803 the situation had become too strained and England declared war once more.

The French had an advantage: although their fleet was smaller than the British, they held every port along the European coast from Texel to Genoa. This gave them many places to build new ships as well as shelter, and the ability to spread their fleet thinly along the coast. It gave the British fleet more of a problem in preventing the French from putting to sea, since it was difficult to blockade every port at once.

The British overcame this problem by making sure that, as well as blockading all the ports, they kept a substantial force in the western Channel. If one of the French squadrons did escape from port, the British ships that had been trying to blockade it would sail to the Channel and join the fleet already stationed there. The combined English forces in the Channel would then hope to prevail against the French. Napoleon initially concentrated his efforts on a flotilla invasion of England. This had little chance of succeeding while the blockade was in position, but it was still a threat to the British, who countered by raising extra troops. By December 1803 some 463,000 men had been enroled, a figure which continued to rise, showing the size of the British effort.

Meanwhile, the period between 1803 and 1805 saw further diplomatic measures on the part of the British to secure alliances against the French. An alliance with Russia, for example, was agreed on in April 1805 with the aim of opposing the French and restoring the balance of power in Europe. But by this time the French were already beginning an offensive against the British. The central character in the French offensive was Vice-Admiral Pierre Villeneuve.

Villeneuve was an aristocratic naval officer who had done well because of his courage, but who had a pessimistic attitude that made him a less-than-excellent commander of fighting men. He might have made a better administrator than a battle commander. The key British commander by contrast was Horatio Nelson – a more imaginative and inspiring leader of men and a figure who has become part of his country's mythology.

Nelson was a good enough strategist to know that he would soon have to fight a decisive sea battle with the French. So he began preparing the English fleet for the worst, reorganizing the manning of his ships and refitting the vessels as best he could under the circumstances. And the circumstances were difficult. He knew that he had to keep a close watch on Villeneuve at Toulon, but there was no secure British base nearby from which to do so. Most of the time he lay off Sardinia, from where water and provisions could be obtained, keeping a group of frigates watching Toulon. But Nelson was always at the ready for a movement from the enemy.

The first move in the events that led to the battle came on 30 March 1805 when Pierre Villeneuve broke out of the British

Vice-Admiral Pierre Villeneuve

blockade at Toulon. The French plan was that any of the ships that could break away from port should sail for the West Indies and rendezvous there, since none of the French ports were big enough to take a large number of battleships. Villeneuve accordingly picked up another squadron at Cadiz and sailed west.

When intelligence reached Nelson of Villeneuve's movements, the English admiral had to work out where his opponent might be going. First he thought they might be making for Egypt or Sicily, and when this did not seem to be the case, Nelson headed as quickly as he could westwards to Gibraltar. But Villeneuve was by this time several weeks ahead.

News from passing trading vessels and frigates gave Nelson the information he needed to gauge the direction in which Villeneuve was going. The French reached Martinique on 14 May; Nelson was at Barbados by 4 June. But a few days later Villeneuve sailed back east. Was he heading back to Europe? Nelson had no way of knowing for sure, but suspected that he was, and so sailed east himself before sending a fast sloop ahead of him back to England. The sloop overtook Villeneuve, its captain realizing that the French were sailing towards the Bay of Biscay.

By this time Nelson was gaining on his opponents, hoping to catch them at Gibraltar. The French, however, were taking a more northerly course towards Cape Finisterre. Their plans to link up with other French ships coming out of Brest were dashed by the British in the western approaches to the Channel, who had the advantage of intelligence from Nelson's sloop. When Nelson arrived at Cadiz he realized that the enemy must have gone north.

So at the end of July Nelson too sailed north, to join his colleagues Cornwallis and Calder and form a blockade in the Channel. There was now a solid blockade preventing Villeneuve's ships joining the rest of the French farther north. Without this blockade the French would have been ready to attack and invade.

All seemed well for England until news reached Nelson, by now in Portsmouth, that Villeneuve was sailing south again. On September 15 Nelson put to sea in pursuit of the French fleet, which had massed at Cadiz. It seemed to be another turning point. Nelson resolved to contain the fleet in the harbour until they were forced to come out and do battle. He had a bold plan. Instead of sailing parallel to the enemy fleet he would attack at right-angles, breaking up the enemy ships into three groups before destroying the individual vessels.

When Villeneuve was ordered to sail for Naples to support the emperor's new campaign, Nelson was ready. The English pressed towards the enemy in two divisions, hoping to break them into three groups as planned. The French did not try to escape, but stood their ground. Nelson signalled to his colleague Collingwood in the other line: 'I intend to pass through the van of the enemy's line, to prevent him getting into Cadiz.' As he pressed on, another signal appeared on Nelson's flagship, the *Victory*: 'England expects that every man will do his duty.' Within minutes of this patriotic call the English ships broke into the French line. The leading English ships engaged their chosen targets and fighting began. The vessels of the English rearguard then attacked the confused middle and rear French sections and soon there was little hope that the French rearguard would be able to fight back.

In the thick of the fighting the *Victory* became wedged tight between two French

ships, the *Redoubtable* and the *Bucen-taure*. From high on one mast of the *Redoubtable* a French marksman fired the shot that ended Nelson's life. But decisive victory would soon be in English hands.

The Battle of Trafalgar did not end the Napoleonic Wars or bring an end to the emperor's plans for expansion. But it did put a vital limit on Napoleon's power. From now on it was beyond doubt that Britain was the supreme sea power along the coast of Europe and would not be troubled in any way by invasion threats from France.

Nelson was well served by his flagship Victory *at Trafalgar. Although the ship was spacious by the standards of the day, there was little spare room for the 850 men aboard. She became wedged between two French ships during the action, as Nelson tried to push in amongst the French and break up the enemy formations. From this difficult position, her one hundred guns gave the crew the power to defend her well – most of the artillery was placed on either side of the vessel. After the English victory the flagship was in active service until 1812, after which she was transferred to harbour duties as a headquarters ship.*

DEVELOPMENT OF FOOD CANNING

The appearance of 'convenience foods'

'An army marches on its stomach.' So, we are told, said Napoleon who knew more than most about armies and had much cause for concern about provisioning his troops. Sending his men out to forage when supplies were low had almost lost him the Battle of Marengo in 1800. It was a scheme initiated by Napoleon to award large prizes to people with ideas to help French industry that inspired Nicholas Appert to carry on with his experiments in preserving food.

Of course, there were already some methods of food preservation available. Fish had been smoked for centuries. Generations of sailors had lived on salt beef. And the preservative qualities of freezing had long been known to those members of the upper classes who were lucky enough to have access to an ice house. But none of these methods provided an army on the march access to a reliable and varied food supply. Smoking and salting could only be used for a limited range of meat and fish. And ice houses were not portable.

Appert was a champagne bottler turned confectioner who lived at Ivry, near Paris. Champagne bottles gave Appert a starting point with the foods he began with. These were either liquids, such as stews, soups and milk, or small fruits, such as raspberries and cherries. He poured or packed the food into the bottles, inserted corks, and held these on with wire, just as if they contained the wine they were designed for. He then placed the bottles in a bath of boiling water, allowing the sterilizing effect of the heat to kill any bacteria, although Appert did not know that this was what was happening.

But he knew it worked. He soon moved to Massy and started a bottling factory employing some fifty workers. The army noticed when the navy took bottled peas, beans and soup with them in 1807. Two years later, Napoleon's Society for the Encouragement of Industry recognized

Appert's achievement, observing that foods bottled eight months previously were still in excellent condition. Appert was awarded one of the coveted prizes and published a book on his work.

Appert had thought of using other containers apart from champagne bottles for his preserved foods. But the bottles were strong, easy to pack and in plentiful supply whereas very little tin-plate was made in France. In Britain, where there was a flourishing tin-plate industry, it was a different story. A team of industrialists, headed by John Hall and Bryan Donkin, had bought the English patent rights to Appert's method. By 1813 Donkin and Hall had worked the idea out thoroughly enough to be able to send a package of tinned beef to the royal family, where it met with approval. Further publicity soon followed when Donkin and Hall's canned food was taken on expeditions to the Arctic and the northwest passage. By 1818 orders from the Royal Navy alone amounted to tens of thousands of cans.

But it was some years before canned food arrived in the shops. There was much less obvious need amongst ordinary people than there was amongst travellers or those organizing military expeditions. What was more, canned food was expensive. The cans had to be made by hand and the lids hand soldered in place, therefore only a limited number could be produced. In 1830 canned food finally reached the shops. In London, a can of salmon cost almost one shilling, nearly the price of a week's rent on a family house.

There was another limitation on canned food. It was difficult to remove the contents from the can in the early days; no one had invented a suitable design for a can opener. A hammer and chisel had to be used before the first simple can openers, consisting of a sharp blade at the end of a handle often decorated with a bull's head, appeared on the market.

It was to be some years before canned

food became food for the masses. And in 1845 it began to look as if it never would. Sir John Franklin took canned food on his Arctic expedition that year, and these provisions were the cause of the deaths on his ill-fated journey. Another blow to the canners came in 1855 when 5,000 cans destined for soldiers in China were opened and found to contain rotten contents. It was almost the end for the canners.

The reason for these early failures was that the food had not been heated to a high enough temperature to kill all the bacteria. It was known that the food had to be boiled to preserve it. Indeed it may be that the term 'bully beef' derived from the French *bouillir*, to boil, if it did not come from the bulls' heads on the can openers. But no one knew why. An improvement in the canning process, when chlorine salts in the boiling water helped raise the temperature enough to make sterilization quicker, did not solve the problem.

Canning had to wait until the twentieth century before it provided convenience foods for ordinary people. And it was then, with the trend away from household servants in the west, that convenience foods, together devices such as electrically operated kitchen appliances, came into middle-class kitchens.

We are used to thinking of canned food as food for the masses, produced on an industrial scale for consumption by anyone who can afford the relatively small purchase price of the tin and its contents. But it was not like this in the beginning. The process of canning was carried out by hand, with the packing, sealing and heating of the containers all very labour-intensive operations. And although labour costs were not so high as they are today, the resulting canned food was a luxury item, aimed at those who could afford the convenience or at soldiers or explorers planning long expeditions away from a regular food supply.

NAPOLEON'S MARCH ON MOSCOW

A disaster for France's unstoppable emperor

Most of Europe was under Napoleon's rule by 1810. Large areas were governed directly from Paris; other parts of the continent – Italy, Naples, Spain, Westphalia and Holland (the latter up to 1810) – were established as satellite kingdoms ruled by members of Napoleon's family. These kingdoms were useful to Napoleon as a source of money and of soldiers for his vast army. Then there were independent allied states such as Austria, Prussia and Denmark, all joined to the French Empire in alliances that favoured Napoleon. The Continental System, a blockade of trade with Britain, further bolstered his power, although it also caused discontent and encouraged opposition to the empire. Of the states outside Napoleon's control, Russia and the Ottoman Empire were the two largest examples. Like Portugal and Britain, however, they lay on the edges of the continent.

It was an awesome achievement, and it vested great power in the emperor and his family. But they were not the only ones to gain. In sweeping away the old feudal regimes and introducing a professional administration and the French legal system, the *Code Napoléon*, and by fostering at least a degree of local participation in government, the emperor did bring about social change for the better in many of the places he took over.

The roots of opposition

But this local participation could only go so far. When opposition and nationalism began to appear in Italy and Westphalia, and when Louis Bonaparte began to put the interests of his Dutch subjects before those of the empire, Napoleon tightened his grip and moved towards overall control from Paris. He also looked towards expanding his sphere of influence still further across Europe.

In theory France and Russia were allies. But there were too many conflicts of interest for the alliance to work in practice.

Napoleon on campaign

For one thing, the Russian emperor wanted to expand southwards towards Constantinople. Napoleon also cherished ambitions of moving into the eastern Mediterranean. Another problem was Napoleon's Continental System, which ruined the balance of trade in Russia.

It was too much for the Russian emperor Alexander, who allowed neutral ships into Russian harbours and, worse still, began to charge duty on French imports. Napoleon retaliated with diplomatic moves against Russia, for which he gained support from some, but by no means all, of his allies. It seemed that the only solution was to launch a military attack on the great power in the east.

Such a task should have awed Napoleon. Russia was a large power that would need the concentrated might of the French *Grande Armée* to subdue. But it was not easy for Napoleon to concentrate the power of his army. Its sheer size was one problem: it was probably the largest force ever raised up to that time. An army of some 600,000 men was potentially highly dangerous to any opponent. But that danger was dissipated when the army was difficult to control. The *Grande Armée* was made up of men from all over Europe. There were language barriers, cultural differences, and consequently it was difficult to enforce the required discipline. It was also difficult to supply such a vast force, especially when Napoleon's dependent states were not as cooperative with the needs of the empire as their ruler wished. Then there was the problem of disease. Infections spread through the army in the summer before the campaign.

The cards seemed stacked against Napoleon, but he had one good chance. He thought that the Russians would attack him directly, from the front, soon after he had crossed their borders. This was the sort of conflict that the *Grande Armée* could win. The French would draw their enemies towards them before using their vast forces to split them up and crush each section. Even with the illnesses of the summer, Napoleon's men would substantially outnumber the Russians and a victory would be ensured.

The journey to Russia

But even the first stage of the journey went badly. The march across the border into Russia, along appalling roads, went slowly. Supplies for the horses were inadequate and many died from eating unripe corn. The French had to cross the river Niemen, which divided the Grand Duchy

The Grande Armeé *on the march*

of Warsaw, one of Napoleon's dependent states, from Russia itself. Across the river was the Russian First Army, led by the Lithuanian general Barclay de Tolly, and the Second Army, under Prince Bagration. Together their strength was just under 200,000, enough for Napoleon to crush if he could engage them in battle quickly.

But the Russians would not be drawn. Both generals retreated, leaving the French to continue their depressing slog into Russia. They hoped to pick up supplies at Vilna (modern Vilnius), but when members of the army began looting the Lithuanians turned against them and Napoleon's men had to march on hungry. So they made for Smolensk, roughly halfway between Vilna and Moscow. Barclay de Tolly had arrived at this city ahead of Napoleon and resolved to offer some resistance. 16–18 August saw heated fighting, with the *Grande Armée* finally taking the city. But they did not gain much from the victory. The retreating Russians had set Smolensk on fire. Once again the problem of supplies was acute.

The first engagement
They marched on towards Moscow once more. As a result of the defeat at Smolensk, Alexander sacked Barclay de Tolly and replaced him with Kutusov, an able and popular man whose appointment raised the morale of the Russian troops. Kutusov, impressed by the apparent improvement of his army and urged on by Alexander, decided to challenge the French before they reached Moscow at the village of Borodino, some 115 kilometres (72 miles) west of the great city.

The two armies came together on 7 September. By this time Napoleon's front-line force was about 130,000 men strong, about 10,000 more than Kutusov's. But it was far fewer men that he had had at Smolensk, and the troops were demoralized, ill-fed and not really up to

complex battle manoeuvres. So Napoleon decided on a straightforward frontal attack on the Russians. The two sides thundered into each other for ten hours, until both sides were too tired to continue. It was the sort of battle in which there could be no real winners, the number of deaths running into tens of thousands. The vast numbers of the French and the extensive Russian casualties meant that Napoleon was able to carry on to Moscow, while his opponents could retreat with dignity.

Moscow: arrival and retreat
A week later the advance guard of the *Grande Armée* finally arrived outside Moscow. Napoleon was able to move into the Kremlin immediately. But his presence, and that of his large numbers of unruly troops, was too much for the Muscovites. The people of the city, led by the Russian governor, started to set Moscow alight. Fires that were started to destroy strategic targets like arms stores and markets soon spread and before long much of the city was ablaze. The population fled into the surrounding countryside and Napoleon and his men were left stranded.

Soon there would be the harsh Russian winter to contend with. Once more the native people had done what they could to cut off the invaders' supply lines. There was nothing to be gained from staying in the city. So on October 1812 Napoleon began an epic retreat back across eastern Europe. About 107,000 soldiers, their equipment, baggage and booty, plus thousands of civilians including most of the foreign population of Moscow set out, past Borodino (the field still littered with corpses) and towards Smolensk.

If things had seemed bad for Napoleon and his army before, now the difficulties really started. Just before they got to Smolensk, on 6 November, the snow began to fall. Kutusov kept challenging

the retreating army, attacking the flanks just enough to keep them marching westwards. There was no relief and little food in Smolensk and after a few days' rest it was back on the march again, with a diet of horseflesh and the prospect of disease and cold. Napoleon's huge main force (originally there had been 400,000 of these troops) was soon down to less than 100,000. The flanking army was also severely depleted.

And that was not all. Kutusov decided to halt Napoleon's dignified retreat and defeat his army. He hoped to cut the French off at the Beresina river, which they had to cross. The single bridge was destroyed before the French arrived, but Napoleon's engineers managed to construct pontoon bridges to allow the army to cross. Under heavy fire, some 50,000 French managed to cross the river before repeated breaches in the bridges made it impossible for more to escape. Many of those who were left stranded tried to swim across, only to lose their lives in the bitterly cold water.

As the Russians continued their attack, the French emperor heard bad news from Paris. There were stories there that he had died in Russia and monarchist plotters were trying to seize power. A demented general, Claude Malet, had tried to take over. With his army in ruins and the prospect of defeat at home, Napoleon left his men behind and rode away from the perishing Russian winter towards Paris.

The remains of the *Grande Armée* were in a dismal position. They were still being attacked, their numbers were dropping steadily, and the sub-zero temperatures were unbearable. By the time the French got to the borders there were only about 25,000 men left from the original main army.

The disintegration
Things were never the same for Napoleon after the defeat in Russia. Prussia ended

When Napoleon and his men paused outside Moscow before advancing on the city, it seemed at last as if they had reached their goal. But the emperor must have known deep down that there would be immense problems ahead. It would soon be winter and the prospect for getting adequate supplies was bleak. Soon his forces would face humiliation.

her alliance with France and in 1813 formed the Sixth Coalition with Russia, Britain and Sweden. But Napoleon was not beaten. He raised a new army and went to war against Prussia and her allies, defeating them at Lützen and Bautzen, before being overcome in the Battle of Nastions at Leipzig. Again, when the allies invaded France the following year, Napoleon put up a strong fight, beating back each invading army as it attacked Paris. But he could not sustain this success. To try and secure the succession and win time he abdicated (at first in favour of his son, later, when the allies insisted, unconditionally).

The final blow came in 1815 when the emperor returned to France and tried to defeat the allies. He met the Anglo-Dutch forces in what is now Belgium, and was decisively defeated at Waterloo on 18 June. On 23 June he abdicated once more and was exiled to Saint Helena. Although it was not his final defeat, the Russian campaign was the turning point for Napoleon. Once it was realized that the force of the emperor could be laid so low, opposition was fuelled against him. Dependent states knew that, for all the reforms that the emperor imposed, the real goal of his conquests was to foster the interests of France.

Moreover, there was an increasing interest in nationalism in Europe at this time which was hardly at one with the success of a great pan-European empire. It would be some decades before this movement would gel into the formation of modern nations such as Germany and Italy. But the roots of such important changes were here in the opposition to Napoleon, particularly amongst the leaders of that opposition. For the common soldiers it was a different story. Many were still loyal to the old aristocracies of their regions, or to the church. But they could see equally that French expansion was against the interests of their leaders.

And finally, the Russian débâcle must have had a marked effect on the morale of Napoleon's surviving soldiers. Already, in 1814, his men were deserting in larger-than-usual numbers. With such a crushing blow to morale, it is surprising that the French army survived as long as it did.

EMERGENCE OF THE SOUTH AMERICAN NATIONS

A continent begins to break away from foreign domination

The Spanish and Portuguese conquests in the New World resulted in waves of migration from east to west during the years between 1500 and 1800. There was much money to be made by Europeans, whether they were on the lookout for a quick fortune based on gold and silver to take back home, or whether they wanted to settle down and run cotton or sugar plantations or ranches. But although there was wealth, freedom was limited for the people of southern America. Rule was from Spain. Most of the population – those of Spanish descent who had been born in America, the local people, and the *mestizos* or mixed-race people – grew to resent this. The Spanish presence, as well as limiting the Americans' freedom, affected their economic well-being. Trade between the various colonies was restricted – initially they could only trade with Spain or Portugal.

Such restrictions as these helped to foster a spirit of independence and nationalism and to unite the diverse populations of the Spanish and Portuguese colonies. The scene was set in Haiti, away from the mainland, where a former slave, Toussaint L'Ouverture, led a successful struggle for freedom against France. Meanwhile, changes in Europe were reducing the strength of Spain and Portugal as world powers. For example, in 1807 Napoleon Bonaparte invaded Portugal. The following year he deposed Ferdinand VII from the Spanish throne and installed his brother, Joseph Bonaparte. It was clear that it was time for change in America too.

Brazil did not have to fight for its independence from Portugal. Pedro of Portugal, who ruled the colony as regent on behalf of his father John VI, became King Pedro I of the independent empire of Brazil in 1822. But the Spanish colonies, in the areas now occupied by Ecuador, Colombia, Panama, Venezuela and Bolivia had to put up more of a struggle to win their independence. It was a time that

Simon Bolivar

threw up both popular risings and great military leaders. One of the most important of the latter was Simon Bolivar, a rich young man who had been born in Caracas, Venezuela in 1783 and who on a visit to Europe in 1804 vowed to liberate his country from Spain.

By 1810, when Bolivar returned to South America, a group of rebels had already started the struggle for freedom. Bolivar joined them and soon emerged as their leader. They took Caracas in 1810 and declared independence from Spain the following year. But this was only the beginning of the story. Setbacks meant that Bolivar was forced to leave the country and reassert its independence on his return. In 1813 this was done with the establishment of the Second Venezuelan Republic. In 1817 he returned again, and this time his activities culminated in an important victory in Colombia (the Battle of Boyacá) and the foundation of the Gran Colombia in 1819. This was a federation of what are now Colombia, Ecuador, Panama and Venezuela. Bolivar was the first president of the federation.

However, the struggle was yet not over. Bolivar defeated the Spaniards at Carabobo, Venezuela, in 1821 before annexing

Ecuador. By 1823 he was also ruler of Peru. The final battle came at Ayacucho, Peru, in 1824. This finally ended Spanish rule in South America. The following year, when Upper Peru was made into a separate state, it was named Bolivia in honour of the liberator.

Bolivar was one in a line of inspirational South American leaders of this period. For example, San Martin and his Army of the Andes helped carry independence across Argentina and into Chile. These men became heroes of the nations they helped to found, although they also had their problems. Bolivar found the union of the Gran Colombia difficult to hold together. He eventually became dictator of the union, but only to see the component states withdraw until he ruled only Colombia itself. The tide had turned against him and he eventually resigned the presidency in 1830.

But if the union of states broke up, and if the liberal government of which Bolivar dreamed failed to materialize in South America, their founder was still a vital influence. On his early visit to Europe he had come under the spell of Enlightenment thinkers such as Rousseau, and his ideas about government had longer-lasting effects than his military victories. The constitution of Bolivia, for example, framed in 1826 was an important model for other South American states. And the Congress of Panama of the same year was the first in a continuing line of international diplomatic conferences that still shape our lives.

The influence of Bolivar stretches across the northern area of the South American continent – Panama, Ecuador, Colombia, Venezuela – and Bolivia. Bolivar helped to bring liberal thinking and western-style constitutions to these new nations, although his experience also showed how difficult it was to impose government on the European model in South America.

INVENTION OF THE POSTAGE STAMP

The post becomes an accessible and reliable form of communication

Communications have always been of central importance to humanity. The ability to send messages over long distances has always been one of the essentials of running a state or empire of any size. The Chinese were probably the first to develop an elaborate long-distance messenger system – a system that came to its height under the Mongols, although it started centuries before them. The Romans also had an elaborate network for carrying messages, the *cursus publicus*. This involved a system of relay stages stretching across the whole of the empire, and a sophisticated inspection, policing and administrative network that ensured that the system was used in the way intended by the government.

The *cursus publicus* was effective enough to survive in part after the fall of Rome, both in the east and in the west. But the changing monarchs and political alignments in medieval Europe did not bode well for such a system. The most effective medieval system was the one which began with the increase of trade, particularly in Italy, in the late Middle Ages. This commercial network even extended outside Europe for a while, linking the great centres of Venice and Constantinople.

The rise in educational standards, the arrival of the printing press, and the trend towards the formation of nation states changed matters at the end of the medieval period. More letters were being written, and more governments than before realised the importance of communications across the continent. And there were also people who could see a way of making large amounts of money from the post. Such a group were the Taxis family, originally from Bergamo in Italy. Under the aegis of the Habsburgs they built up an enormous international postal system using some 20,000 messengers throughout Europe.

Meanwhile, as the nation states were continuing to develop, national postal systems sprang up. Systematic public postal services were set up in France in 1627 and in Britain in 1635. These were state systems that combined security for the transmission of government documents with public access to carrying facilities. But private systems also appeared, flouting the theoretical state monopolies.

In the eighteenth and nineteenth centuries the use of stage coaches speeded up

Rowland Hill

the mail. The postal systems had come a long way, but there was still room for improvement. Rowland Hill, a reformer who had tried out his utilitarian principles on the education system by running a school designed to prepare its pupils for *laissez-faire* capitalist society, was the most prominent critic of the English postal system in the nineteenth century. He pointed out that the lack of a uniform postal charge made the system confusing and unfair to the poor; that the custom of collecting the postal fee from the recipient, rather than making the sender prepay was inefficient; and that the inefficiency of the service had led to numerous 'contraband' carriers who took business away from the Post Office.

Hill campaigned for several years to reform the system. He suggested that an across-the-board charge of one penny, pre-paid, would improve matters, and that the drop in revenue would be compensated for because more people would use the service. Objectors replied that people would not suddenly start to write more letters; that companies rather than the poor would benefit; and that management costs would increase.

But on 10 January 1840, Hill got his way. The penny post was introduced, bringing with it a uniform charge for a letter throughout Britain and the concept of the pre-paid postage stamp. The objectors were proved right, however, and net Post Office revenue went down taking some twenty years to recover. Hill spent the rest of his career with the Post Office locked in battle with his superiors and with governments, trying obsessively to protect his reforms. Meanwhile, other countries were adopting Hill's ideas. Switzerland and Belgium followed in 1843; other nations would quickly adopt similar systems. In spite of the initial problems, Hill had brought the postal service within the orbit of ordinary people. And the adoption of the postage stamp ultimately simplified the administration of the service. As the coming of the railways sped up the mail still more, the system that Hill devised was there in place ready to take full advantage of this burgeoning network. Hill was one of the begetters of our age of mass communications.

The Penny Black, the original postage stamp, became a well-known symbol of a cheap, reliable postal system: using it was as easy as walking to one of the numerous red post boxes that were appearing all over Great Britain. The fact that the stamp was of British origin was signalled by the universally recognizable portrait of Queen Victoria, whose empire was expanding around the globe at this time. To this day, British postage stamps are the only ones in the world not to bear a legend identifying their national origin.

INVENTION OF PHOTOGRAPHY

A new method of image-making transforms communications

Of all the inventions of the nineteenth century, few have had such a great impact as photography. The ability to create instantly a permanent, accurate image of any object, and to reproduce it at will, has transformed our knowledge of the world. Later developments, such as colour photography and motion pictures, have added still further to the importance of the new medium. It is now impossible to conceive of a world without the easy access to an almost infinite variety of images that photography has brought.

In brief, two technologies had to come together before photographs could be produced. There had to be a way of producing an image, and a way of recording the image was needed. The image-producing technology had existed for centuries. The *camera obscura* ('dark room') was a room or large box with blackened interior walls and a small hole in the middle of one side. Straight rays of light from a brightly lit subject would pass through the hole to produce an upside-down image of the subject on the wall opposite the hole.

Arab astronomers had used room-size *camera obscuras* to observe solar eclipses as early as the tenth century AD. By the nineteenth century the device had been made much smaller. There was often a frosted-glass screen in place of the wall on which the image formed, allowing one to trace off the image. The *camera obscura* had become a tool of the artist – Canaletto used a *camera obscura* to produce his highly accurate pictures of Venice.

It was this use of the *camera obscura* as an artist's tool that attracted the man who was probably the first pioneer of photography, Thomas Wedgwood. He wanted to make images of flowers, plants and architectural subjects that he could transfer on to dinner plates in his porcelain factory. He put a sheet of paper moistened with a solution of the light-sensitive chemical silver nitrate on the glass of his *camera obscura* and began to produce images. But

he could not fix the results – light continued to act on the paper until the image was obliterated. Wedgwood gave up.

The next person to develop the idea of photography was the Frenchman Joseph Nicéphore Niépce. He used a metal plate with a varnish of bitumen and oil as his light-sensitive material. In the darker areas of the image the varnish was left soft and Niépce dissolved it away with acid. The resulting plate was printed like an engraving. Niépce had found a way of creating a permanent image: one of his pictures, dating from 1826, is the earliest surviving photograph.

But Niépce's image was a far cry from modern photography. The result was blurred; the exposure took eight hours to make, even on a sunny day; and Niépce did not make the vital advance of producing a negative from which many copies could be made. But he did take one important step before he died without seeing his invention fully exploited. He went into partnership with a younger man, Louis-Jacques Daguerre.

Daguerre was a theatrical scene-painter with an acute sense of artistic composition and a talent for making money. He took Niépce's idea and spent some ten years developing it. He tried different light-sensitive substances before coming up with a sheet of copper, plated with silver and made sensitive to light by exposure to iodine fumes. This was kept in a light-tight container until the moment of exposure. Mercury vapour was used to develop the image, which was fixed with salt and chemically cleaned.

Daguerre's pictures were a great advance on those of Niépce. They were far clearer and sharper. Their polished copper surface gave them a special quality not seen in images before. And shorter exposure times meant that for the first time humans could be included in the frame and be recognisable in the final picture. Daguerre worked on his process for ten

years before he felt ready to make an announcement to the public in 1839.

Meanwhile in England, another pioneer was doing equally important work. William Henry Fox Talbot was a talented amateur scientist. His research followed closely in the footsteps of his compatriot Wedgwood. Like the porcelain manufacturer he used paper, made sensitive to light with salts of silver. But as he went on he conceived a rather more elaborate chemical process than his predecessor, and he also learned how to fix the images. The more elaborate process Fox Talbot called the calotype. It was a huge step forward because it involved *developing* the latent image on the paper. In other words, a much shorter initial exposure time was made possible with the image appearing in a subsequent process after the paper was removed from the camera.

Fox Talbot started by soaking the paper in salt solution and drying it. Next the paper was lowered into a silver nitrate solution. This reacted with the salt on the paper to produce silver chloride. The paper was then placed in one of Fox Talbot's *camera obscuras* and exposed to light. On removal from the *camera obscura* the paper was washed, first with another salt solution, then with potassium iodide. Sodium thiosulphite was used to wash away any remaining silver salt and fix the image.

The first photographic negatives were made in an English country house, Lacock Abbey, the home of amateur scientist William Henry Fox Talbot. Fox Talbot made simple experimental cameras consisting of a lens attached to a light-tight box that contained a piece of paper that had been made sensitive to light. To make his first surviving picture, Fox Talbot set his camera in front of one of the diamond-lattice windows of his home. The result was an instantly-recognizable pattern of light and shade.

Fox Talbot's early, pre-calotype, pictures were not as spectacular as Daguerre's. In fact the earliest example, first exhibited in 1835, is little clearer than the first surviving photograph of Niépce. But the images would soon improve in both detail and sharpness, and Fox Talbot's efforts, combined with his essays on his new techniques, caused a sensation in England. By the end of the 1830s, on both sides of the Channel, it was clear that photography had arrived.

Fox Talbot took photography one important step further. When he and Daguerre made their independent findings public in 1839 neither had found a way of producing subsequent copies of a photograph – each image was unique. It was the English inventor who came up with the negative-positive process, allowing numerous copies of an image to be made and giving photography its special reproducible quality that has been so important ever since. Fox Talbot's early negatives were in fact produced quite simply. He made his photographic paper transparent with wax. The image on the transparent paper could then easily be contact-printed on to another sheet of paper which had been treated with silver chloride. As with the original photographs, sunlight was used as a light source for this process.

Fox Talbot was a rich amateur who did not need to make financial profit from his inventions. Recognition was enough for him, and this came soon enough. In the right conditions the calotype allowed exposures as short as ten seconds, which meant that portrait photography of acceptable standards was possible. Images of Fox Talbot's family and servants in his work *The Pencil of Nature* (the first photographically illustrated book) brought him the fame he desired.

For Daguerre things were different. The French pioneer was a businessman, keen to exploit his work to the full. He

Joseph Nicéphore Niépce

secured the support of the French government for his work. And he wrote a booklet on the Daguerreotype which was published in more than thirty different editions and translations, all over Europe and America, within five months of its original appearance in France. Soon, it was all the rage to have one's portrait taken by Daguerre's process.

From this evidence it is clear that the impact of photography was immense. The French painter Paul Delaroche, on seeing one of the early Daguerreotypes, said 'From today painting is dead!' But it soon became clear that photography would have a different role from painting. It was not simply that it was more accessible to a wider range of people. People soon began to see roles for photography that could not be fulfilled by painting.

Fox Talbot himself foresaw that photography could be put to use by scientists, paying particular attention to the ways in which it might capture subjects under the microscope. By publishing the first photographically illustrated book he looked forward to the time when the reproducible quality of photography would be exploited by the communications media all over the world.

In the following decades such expectations would be triumphantly fulfilled. As early as 1857, Lady Elizabeth Eastlake wrote an essay on photography which treated the still-recent invention as a new mode of communication in its own right rather than an adjunct to painting. Soon a host of different developments would show how right she was.

In the 1870s the half-tone process, by which photographic images were broken up into a series of lines or dots of differing degrees of blackness, appeared. It would revolutionize the high-speed printing of images, enabling them to be used in newspapers, for example.

The same decade saw the fruition of the work of photographer Edward Muybridge. He used series of photographs to analyse the movement of people and animals. And in so doing he pioneered both the high-speed photography of moving subjects and, still more important, looked forward to motion picture photography, another invention that would change our view of the world.

During the next decade Jacob A. Riis would make the first experiments with flash illumination, taking photographs in dark places and, in so doing, revealing photography's great ability to document the lives of ordinary people in ways that were beyond the scope of the easel painter. And by 1903 the Lumière brothers had developed the autochrome, the first colour photographic process to appear.

It is now impossible to imagine a world without the easy access to images of absolutely anything that photography is capable of capturing. And the access does not stop with ready-made images. Photography quickly became so simple that anyone with a minimum of technical skill and a little money could make their own pictures. Even if the richness of photographic imagery available to us sometimes seems overwhelming, it can truly be said to have opened our eyes.

IRISH FAMINE

Poverty and emigration in the nineteenth century

Ireland in the early nineteenth century was heading for a crisis. After about 1740 the population started to rise quite quickly. For about eighty years Irish farmers would benefit from a high demand for their produce, both at home and in England, and the result was a rise in prosperity, too. But by the mid-1830s things had changed. Improved transport meant that the British could import meat easily from Ireland. But the bottom fell out of the Irish grain market as Britain turned increasingly to the European mainland to augment what her own farmers could produce. To make matters worse Ireland had little in the way of industry, and what there was was concentrated in the north.

In the meantime, the good grain crops of the foregoing years had put a great strain on the soil. So agricultural productivity was reduced, even though there was still a sizeable indigenous population to feed. When landowners saw this problem coming they reacted in their own interests: tenant farmers and peasants were removed from the land or forced to subsist on a tiny plot on which they could barely grow enough potatoes (the country's bland but nutritious staple crop) to feed their families. And the problem got worse because the population continued to grow. Although figures are uncertain, a population of around 6.8 million in 1821 had turned into one of roughly eight million by 1841.

It was this pressure that stimulated the trend towards emigration, which stopped the population growing even more. Thousands of Irish people, with little hope of prosperity – or even survival – at home left for Britain, Canada and the USA. There is also some evidence that people got married at a later average age in these less secure times, another fact that made the population rise less quickly than it might. And it is reasonable to suppose that the death rate would also have

increased in this period. Regular failures of the potato crop – vitally important for the rural Irish – occurred during the period: in over half the fifteen years leading up to the famine, the crop failed either partially or totally. This may well have caused many to lose their grip on life.

Some two-thirds of the population depended on agriculture for their survival. The rising population prevented most farmers from turning to more profitable cattle farming for export. And the exhausted soil and the fact that many farmers were cultivating holdings of no more than five acres meant that they were hard pressed to grow enough to support their own dependents. What was more, tenant farmers had rents to pay and, although these were not as mercilessly increased as

Irish emigrants on a ship to America

was once thought, they took away a vital portion of the meagre profits.

The coming of the famine

Then, in 1845 and 1846, disaster struck. The potato crop failed partially in 1845 and totally in 1846. A harsh winter immediately afterwards did not make things any better and, although there was a brief

respite in 1847, the next year the potato blight returned once more. Hunger and disease were rife. Typhus, relapsing fever, scurvy and dysentery became common amongst the rural poor.

The catastrophe was made worse by a change of government. From 1846 on the new Whig administration of Lord John Russell adopted a policy of *laissez faire*. To begin with the only aid for the starving, if one could call it aid, was to provide extra jobs on public works. This proved unsatisfactory because the works themselves had to be paid for out of the rating system. So by the end of 1846 even this provision was abandoned in favour of reliance upon the poor law, which effectively herded the poor together in workhouses or gave them temporary relief in soup kitchens.

Not surprisingly, many tenant farmers disappeared from their holdings at this time. A clause in the poor law limited relief to those who held less than one quarter of an acre. And landlords, liable for the rates of their tenants, were glad to get rid of those who could not pay. In one year alone, 1849, some 90,000 people were driven from their homes for these reasons.

But people did not simply lose their land. Many lost their lives. In 1845 the country's population had been about 8.5 million. By 1851 the total was about 6.5 million – and this was at a time after the population had been rising. About half of those who disappeared had lost their lives because of the famine; the rest had emigrated, mostly to Britain, North America or Australia. To most, it did not matter where they went: they had little to lose.

Emigration continued to be part of Irish life from the time of the famine onwards. Between 1841 and 1925 it had been estimated that some 4.75 million Irish people left for the USA alone. The substantial Irish communities here, in Canada and in Australia date largely from the famine period, or from the difficult years immediately before.

Irish society was mainly rural, the economy mainly agricultural. High rents and the lack of any alternative source of income meant dire poverty when the crop failed, as it did repeatedly in the 1840s. The fact that most Irish farmers had only a very small amount of land meant that there were no reserves to fall back on. The result was hunger and death for many, a decaying economy for those who survived.

The famine left a transformed Ireland behind. The tiny peasant farms of the earlier years all but disappeared. Landowners consolidated their holdings to make bigger farms. Whereas before there had been a split between the great aristocratic landowners and the rural poor, the dominant classes now were the aristocracy and a new rural bourgeoisie. The latter were survivors of the famine who, through improved education and larger landholdings, shared many of the interests of their richer counterparts. Later, the Land Act of 1881 would help to protect tenant farmers and make them more inclined to invest in their farms. In some ways this drew the two classes still closer together. A landless rural working class remained, but it was much smaller than it had been previously. It was largely from this group of people that the continuing flow of emigrations were derived.

Farmers tried as best as they could to adapt to the prevailing economic climate. The amount of land used for growing wheat decreased markedly. Non-grain crops and meadows in which animals could graze, by contrast, became more common. Grain crops such as oats (for animal feed) and barley (for distilling) held their own. This new policy was successful. Exports of beef, sheep and pigs increased. There was a limited prosperity to be found for those with enough land to contribute to this trade.

Emigration in a wider context

If the famine and population movements that followed it transformed Ireland, the changes were typical of a wider trend that can be traced during the nineteenth century. For, as transport improved and population pressures in Europe made themselves felt, peoples' horizons widened. For the increasing populations of the old European nations emigration became more and more attractive.

From Spain and Portugal people travelled to make new lives in South and Central America; from eastern Europe they wandered farther east across to the Steppes and Siberia. From Britain, colonies such as Canada and Australia proved popular. And for a vast number the USA, with its western frontier being pushed steadily back and its reputation for freedom and opportunity, claimed more immigrants than any other country.

In the century after 1815 some thirteen million English and Scots emigrated. Of these about sixty-five per cent settled in the USA, with large contingents going to Australia, Canada and South Africa. Germany, Italy and Scandinavia also sent large numbers to the USA, and there was a sizeable exodus from central Europe. By 1914 the world population was dominated in many areas by Europeans. As the expatriate Europeans settled down and raised families, one-third of the world's total population had its roots in Europe.

PUBLICATION OF THE COMMUNIST MANIFESTO

The book that defined the class struggle and inspired revolutions

When it first appeared, the pamphlet that was arguably to be the most influential publication of the nineteenth century was little noticed. But its authors, Karl Marx and Friedrich Engels, Germans working in England, were convinced the ideas it contained held the key to the way the world was going to develop.

The *Communist Manifesto* begins with the assertion that all human history is the history of class struggle. Everything else flows from these conflicts between the classes. In earlier periods, the antagonism was between a host of different social orders – in ancient Rome between patrician, plebeian and slave; in medieval Europe between lord, vassal, guild-master, apprentice and serf. In the authors' own era, the struggle was between the bourgeoisie (predominantly the new urban manufacturing middle class) and the proletariat (the army of workers needed to sustain the new manufacturing industry).

Marx and Engels trace the development of the bourgeoisie, showing how their political power steadily increased with their economic strength based on manufacturing industry. With the need for an expanding market for the products of that industry the bourgeoisie spread all over the globe, setting up trading networks. In so doing raw materials were bought up cheaply, thereby drawing huge areas of the world into the new bourgeois civilization. The bourgeoisie, meanwhile, tightened its grip on capital and its control of the means of production and exchange.

These changes led to the growth of a vast modern working class, the proletariat. Masses of factory workers, many of them unskilled and many of them women, were needed to fuel the forces of production. Even many of the lower middle classes, lacking the capital to compete with the industrialists, were absorbed into the huge class.

There was much scope for resentment amongst the growing proletariat. But to begin with, say the authors, any opposition they are likely to put up against their oppressors will be disorganized; it will also be severely punished. Eventually, the workers will organize to form trade unions to help keep the wage rate up. Occasional riots would still come to nothing and membership of a union would probably be illegal. But the workers would gradually build on their unity.

Finally, Marx and Engels predicted, a portion of the bourgeoisie would join the workers in a fight against the oppressors. At this point there would be a revolution. The old order would be swept away and a new, communist regime, taking into account the interests of the entire proletariat would take its place. In communist society private property would be abolished. The factories and other means of production would pass into state ownership, and the state would also control banking and the economy, communications and means of transport. There would also be a state-run education system. There would have to be heavy taxes to pay for this, but the aim would be to make the fruits of labour into well-being for the labourer rather than aggrandizement for the bourgeoisie. Ultimately, class distinctions would disappear anyway.

The *Communist Manifesto* was very much a work of its time. The way in which it speaks of history in terms of social class is typical of the nineteenth century. And it was written on the eve of the wave of revolutions that swept across Europe in 1848. The monarchy was abolished in France; Hungary fought to free itself from Austrian domination; a pre-parliamentary body was established in Germany; Italy saw liberal uprisings; there was civil war in Switzerland; Prague formed the centre of uprisings that resulted in the formation of a pan-Slavic alliance.

But the 1848 revolutions were not successful. These represented only an early stage in the development of revolutionary movements rather than a conclusion. They were not communist-inspired movements, but they did give scope for working-class elements in society to unite. And Marx did see in the French revolution of 1848 and the Paris Commune that followed it in 1871, a model for a proletarian state.

But Marx knew that the proletariat would take much longer to evolve into a unified enough force to sustain a truly communist revolution. This came much later, with the setting up of communist states in what became the Soviet Union and in eastern and central Europe. But even here, Marx would have been disappointed that the proletariat did not gain the power that he saw as its due, but that privilege and élitism continued to live on under the guise of equality.

If the rise of communism was not the success that its founders had hoped, the *Communist Manifesto* has had an enduring influence. Even if we do not accept its conclusions, the discussion here and in Marx's other works of the importance of economics, the way in which ideas have their roots in society, and the rejection of any political system that does not consider the good of the vast mass of the people, remains relevant.

The Communist Manifesto *was written against the background of great social change in Europe. The spread of manufacturing industry had led to the growth of a vast, urban working class or proletariat. Based in the cities, which had become the centres of industrial production, these workers could communicate and organize much more effectively than their counterparts in rural industries. And so it would be they, Marx and Engels predicted, who would eventually inspire the revolutions that would overturn the bourgeois factory bosses and hand over the means of production to the state.*

OPENING OF JAPAN TO WESTERN TRADE

The end of centuries of isolation, the beginning of a powerful new influence on the world

To most people from the west Japan was a land of mystery in the early nineteenth century. The Tokugawa shoguns had ruled the country from the seventeenth century. They distributed land amongst their vassals (known as the *daimyo*) in a way that gave them close control of the whole country. Daimyo who were related to the shoguns held the main cities, economic centres and military sites; unrelated daimyo held the rest of Japan, which was split up into autonomous domains.

After 1639 the Tokugawa shoguns kept their country almost totally isolated from the outside world. There was some trade with the Chinese and Dutch, but the Dutch were only allowed contact with Japan via an offshore island, so westerners were largely excluded. This was a policy that had kept Japan successfully isolated for centuries. But the nineteenth century, one of unprecedented change in the west, also saw new developments in Japan. The government of the shoguns was no longer as efficient as it had been. The shoguns and daimyo lived extravagant lives, while existence was hard for the peasantry, who frequently revolted. And although they had traditionally been despised by the ruling class, the merchants were becoming increasingly important, at least for trade within Japan itself. It was not be long before they looked outside their native land.

Interest from overseas

There was no lack of outside trading interest in Japan. Russia was one country that needed an eastern trading partner. As Siberia and Alaska were colonized it made increasing sense to look east for supplies. The British were another powerful force with their eyes trained on Japan. Britain was looking for international markets for the products of her expanding manufacturing industries.

Both of these powers seemed to have a good chance of opening trading relations with Japan. The British started to move into the area after China's defeat in the Opium War. A British missionary even settled in Okinawa in 1846. The Russians sent their Admiral Putyatin on the long voyage to Japan in 1852, with instructions to get the Japanese to agree to a trading treaty.

But it was the Americans who got there first. They had one immediate reason for their interest. They had a growing whaling industry that took American ships far into the Pacific. More and more, as American whaling traffic in the Pacific increased, shipwrecked sailors from the USA were being washed up on the Japanese beaches. Their reception was not always welcome on these notoriously isolated shores.

There were other reasons for the Americans' interest. They were already trading with China, and the usual route took them very close to Japan. And the opening up of California made Japan seem even nearer to the USA. Japan would be a new market, and if the Americans got there quickly they would keep ahead of possible competition from Britain and Russia. Then there was the expansion of the American steamship business. At least one New York businessman with an interest in shipping was putting pressure on Congress to do what they could to open up trade with Japan.

Pacific overtures

So the point had come when the Americans decided to make overtures to Japan. In 1853 President Fillmore sent a squadron of ships under the command of Commodore Matthew Perry to extract from the Japanese a promise to treat future shipwreck victims well; he also hoped to push them into a trading agreement with the USA.

Perry arrived with four ships in July 1853. The Dutch had warned the authorities of their arrival, so the shogun and his government were prepared. Amongst the rest of the population, Perry's ships, two of which were driven by steam, caused a sensation. But there was little public opportunity to see the occupants of the American 'Black Ships'. It was Perry's task to deliver the president's letter and leave, giving the Japanese government the chance to consider their response before returning in a year's time.

The shogun felt threatened by Perry's visit. For one thing, the Japanese could do little against the collective might of the American navy. The shogun's seat at Yedo (modern Tokyo) could easily have its supplies cut off by a sea blockade. The shogunate, fast losing power and in financial trouble could hardly put up much opposition. On the other hand, neither could the shogun afford to lose face completely by inviting the Americans in immediately.

It was difficult to decide what to do and the shogunal officials, known as the Bakufu, took the extraordinary step of asking the advice of all the daimyo and the Confucian scholars. This did not help as the advice they received was contradictory. Some said, drive the Americans away

Commodore Matthew Perry

now, for they will not give Japan another chance if any concessions are granted to them. Others advised that the foreigners be allowed in, because resistance was impossible and the Japanese could always learn the ways of the Americans and compete with them on their own terms. The final decision was a compromise. The shogunal officials would be polite but evasive towards any American request, meanwhile preparing to put up a defence in case the foreigners should turn violent.

When Perry returned in February 1854 he was prepared to be persistent. And, for all the Japanese resolve to stay independent, it did not take him long to secure the treaty he wanted. By the end of March the Treaty of Kanagawa was signed. It ensured protection for shipwrecked Americans, trading rights for the USA at two Japanese ports, Hakodate and Shimoda, and the right for an American consul to reside at Shimoda. It was not much of a concession. The two ports were far from the key cities of Kyoto and Yedo. But the Americans had their collective foot in the door. As the Japanese pessimists had predicted, it would be difficult to shift them.

Other arrivals

It was not just the Americans. The Russian admiral Putyatin was still in Japanese waters. He alarmed the locals by sailing into Osaka Bay in 1854 and, at the end of that year, got into trouble when a whirlpool caused by an earthquake wrecked his ship off Shimoda. To their credit the Japanese helped him, and a treaty between Russia and Japan was signed in February 1855.

The Crimean War also sent the British into Japanese waters, in search of Russian ships. Admiral Sterling took time out from his search for the enemy to come to an agreement with Japan in October 1854, winning the right of British ships to put into the harbours of Nagasaki and Hakodate to take supplies on board.

Traditional Japanese costume

One other western power reached agreement with Japan, this time at Japan's instigation. After Perry's first visit it became clear to the Japanese that they should investigate steamship technology, so they sent representatives to Holland to try to obtain steamships. The Dutch had few spare vessels, so they sent one steamship together with officers who could teach the Japanese the niceties of her design. Soon the Japanese would be using this knowledge to build their own shipyards, perhaps the first clear example of the Japanese taking on and developing western technology for their own benefit. In return the Dutch got their own trading agreement with the Japanese.

The road to modernization

In the 140 years since these treaties were signed Japan has been transformed from an inward-looking, backward glancing state to arguably the most successful economic power in the world with a trading network spanning the entire globe. Such changes could not have come in the way they did without the overtures of Perry and the rest, but Japan was changing anyway. The Tokugawa regime was tottering and the people who stood to gain most from its collapse were the merchants. This is not to deny the importance of the new links with overseas – they provided the essential impetus for change.

But the transformation of Japan did not go smoothly to begin with. The resistance to the foreigners was such that in 1862 the emperor issued an edict to the shogun to order the foreigners out of the country by June the following year. Oddly, the government, which could see that there was no turning back, told the foreigners that no action would be taken if they remained. But before the time was up fanatics had already used the edict as an excuse to attack the British legation.

When June arrived there was firing from Choshu on American, French and Dutch ships. The Americans and French put up armed resistance, and the British also joined in, in retaliation for what had happened earlier at their legation. The struggle was still going on in 1864 when the combined ships of the foreign powers attacked the hostile Chosu batteries and wrested from the government an agreement to keep the shipping lanes open. The government realized that their interests and those of the foreigners were identical.

The next important year in the history of Japan's modernization was 1867, the year in which Emperor Meiji came to the throne. Only fifteen in the year of his accession Meiji had, at first, a difficult time politically. But he was to rule for forty-five years, during which time Japan would blossom into a modern nation.

The new Japan

From this time on many Japanese travelled to the west to learn new skills.

American ships lay in Osaka Bay for some time while the terms of the treaty between Japan and the United States were negotiated. While they were waiting, the American seamen could see a variety of Japanese shipping sailing by, evidence that there was already plenty of commercial activity within Japan itself, and that there was a burgeoning merchant class who would soon be more than willing to trade further afield. But as they marvelled at the difference between the two cultures they could not begin to imagine the consequences of their visit: how Japan would soon become more westernized and how the country would gradually come to take a major political and economic position in the world.

Similarly, people from overseas would flood into Japan in response to the country's desire to acquire the benefits of modern western life. Railway engineers, shipbuilders, teachers, soldiers, financial experts – all found a valued place in the new Japan. By the 1870s, the Japanese even wanted to look like westerners. Western dress became increasingly common, as people abandoned the old ways and the skirt-like costume of the *samurai* began to disappear.

The changes soon bore other fruit. The facilities and institutions that were necessary for healthy trade with the west were quickly set up. There were banks, telegraph offices, printing works and post offices; harbours and dockyards were improved and lighthouses were built. Japanese international commerce was off to a flying start. The enthusiasm for western things soon went further than dress. Western foods – cereals, bread, and so on – and even cigars and cigarettes became popular. And the attraction of gadgets such as gas-lamps and cameras was extremely seductive.

But it was not only a question of trade and gadgetry. Japanese society was changed structurally. Feudal domains were abolished in 1871 and were replaced by a centralized, professional bureaucracy. Officials were recruited more and more from the new university-educated classes. New legal codes and a better educational system were soon introduced. The new administrative framework was in turn put to use in fostering commerce and economic growth. There were government subsidies for industries that could save imports. Quality-control systems were introduced for industries that were exporting goods. And there were even technical training schemes.

Imposed quickly and comprehensively (but still backed up by an economy that had efficient and intensive agriculture) this capitalism grew rapidly in Japan. First the textile trade, then heavy industries, grew and prospered. And Japan built on this economic success with political imperialism, again looking to the west and copying the expansionist policies of countries like Britain. At first, it was neighbouring islands that were taken over. Then, in a series of wars between 1894 and 1918, Japan increased her holdings on the mainland. This progression culminated at the Versailles Conference after the end of World War I, and the granting to Japan of a permanent seat on the Council of the League of Nations. Japan was a world power at last.

The trend begun by Commodore Matthew Perry took Japan back into world history and brought Europe and Asia closer together. It created an extra market for America, but had immeasurably greater impact on Japan herself. Japan's status as a world power – her role in world conflict and her domination of the world economy – dates from his time.

INDIAN REBELLION AGAINST THE BRITISH

The seed of Indian nationalism and a turning point in British policy

Since the middle of the eighteenth century, the British East India Company had gained control of much of the Indian subcontinent, first by trading, then by exerting political power, levying taxes, and taking over from some of the local princes. In 1757 the pre-eminence of the Company was confirmed when Robert Clive led the Company's forces to victory at Plassey. In 1774 the Company established Warren Hastings as its first Indian Governor-General. Soon the Company engaged in further wars to gain more Indian territory.

But although the Company came to dominate India, some things were left alone. Indian religion, for example, was allowed to continue. Hindu and Muslim holidays were faithfully observed. And there was no policy for educating the indigenous people.

The coming of change

By the beginning of the nineteenth century, however, things were starting to change. A new generation of British administrators had higher ambitions for, and in, India. They wanted to Europeanize the subcontinent, educate the Indians, and convert them to Christianity. They also suppressed some of the local customs that were repugnant to them, such as *Suttee*, the burning of widows.

This change coincided with the arrival of some of the trappings of modern western life in India. The administrators were keen to improve communications across their large and intractable domain and soon the railway and the telegraph started to appear. Such facilities, while useful to the administrators, were repugnant to Hindus, whose caste system forbade people of different castes from using, for example, the same railway carriage. It was another erosion of traditional values. Together with the suppression of *Suttee*, the introduction of western education and the promotion of Christian missionary

activity, it was bound to displease the conservative elements in Indian society.

Another discontented group were the Indian princes. As the East India Company continued to annexe new territory and to become more of a governing power and less of a trading one, it seemed more of a threat to local rulers.

But perhaps more significant still was the resentment of a larger class, the landowners. Many of these, particularly in the north, had almost the power of local princes. They were particularly strong in the northern province of Oudh, which was surrounded by East India Company territory in the early 1800s. They had fortified homes, armed guards, and high status. They paid little to the British in taxes. But gradually, they were being made to pay more, to pull down their fortresses, and to disarm their retainers.

To the British they were an obstacle to efficient government. They did little except collect rents and avoid paying taxes. So the British increased the taxes and stepped up the pressure to pay, thus forcing many of them to sell up, or to become dependent on the local moneylender. Amongst this class, discontent and anger with the British became steadily stronger during the first half of the nineteenth century.

Problems for the British

British foreign policy was in any case experiencing setbacks at this time. There was a defeat in Afghanistan in 1841. Soon the Sikhs of the Punjab were challenging the Company's rule, and three British regiments were defeated at Chilianwala in 1845 before the British were able to gain control once more by destroying the Sikh army.

There was a sense of crisis welling up, and this even affected the British army. The East India Company had to rely on local recruits for its army in Bengal. Many of these were Hindus from the north, and

often men of high caste had to serve beneath officers of lower religious rank. This led to poor morale and discipline. Grievances about pay and pensions were also rife.

So there was enough discontent in the army of the East India Company for one acute problem to lead to serious trouble. In the spring of 1857, such a problem emerged. A new Enfield rifle had recently been adopted by the army. Its cartridges had to be bitten before they were put into the gun, and it transpired that the shells were greased with fat from pigs and cows. The dietary laws of both Muslim and Hindu were thus being violated.

The Company stopped using cartridges that had been treated in this way forthwith, but the damage had been done. In April a group of cavalrymen in Meerut, northeast of Delhi, who would not touch the cartridges were court martialled and put in prison. They were also publicly humiliated by being stripped of their uniforms. One of the Indian officers warned his British superiors that there was a threat amongst the troops to take over the gaol and release the prisoners. No one in authority believed the story, but three whole regiments turned on their superiors, broke open the gaol, and let the prisoners go. The rebels were soon on the march towards Delhi.

The Indian rebels, sweeping through the streets of cities such as Delhi and Lucknow, took the British by surprise. In both these towns, the rebels had the support of large numbers of the local population, and were able to outnumber the British, and cause many casualties before the occupying forces retreated to wait for reinforcements. But if the British were caught unawares, the Indians underestimated their persistence. Extra troops were sent in and in the following year the British were able to claim India as their own.

Queen Victoria

The British were ill-prepared, both psychologically and in terms of numbers. They relied on the Indians for defence and had little chance of overwhelming them once they rebelled. And the rebels moved so quickly that they had the advantage of surprise. At Delhi they found the ammunition store guarded by two British officers and six men, who blew it up rather than surrender. The rebel response was to kill all the Europeans they could find and to proclaim the king of Delhi Mogul Emperor. In the coming months the British would gather on a ridge overlooking Delhi and wait for reinforcements before risking an attack on the city, which was filled with rebel soldiers.

Meanwhile, other towns were also experiencing the horrors of the conflict. Lucknow, capital of the nawabs of Oudh and seat of the British Residency, was a particular flashpoint. Henry Lawrence, head of the Regency Council established in the Punjab, prepared to defend the Residency. He had with him some 1,700 soldiers, many of whom were Indians who remained loyal to Britain. But they were a tiny minority. For in Oudh the local people joined the troops in rebellion, the result being a long, protracted siege.

In June and July, at Cawnpore, the British were also surrounded. This time the rebels rallied under a prominent, if dispossessed, local ruler, the Nana Sahib. The British were finally granted safe conduct out of the town, but were fired on as they left, and those who were not killed were taken prisoner. The prisoners were also killed and the British soldiers, when they finally took control of the town, replied with vengeance on the rebels.

Unrest continued at Lucknow in September. There were repeated British attempts to retake the city. After the first assault, the rebels laid siege to Lucknow, trapping the British inside. Then further trouble at Cawnpore took some of the British forces who were trying to relieve the city away. Only in March was Lucknow finally retaken. Fighting continued sporadically well into 1858, but by November the British regarded India as well under their control once more. In November of that year a proclamation was issued declaring Queen Victoria ruler of the whole of India. It was a turning point in British foreign policy.

The influence of the rebellion

The unrest of 1857 and 1858 was more than a military rebellion. Substantial parts of the local population were involved in some areas, and this was what gave the rebels their strength in places like Oudh. But the rebellion did not affect the whole of India. Some areas, such as the Punjab, where the Sikhs and Muslims had little in common with the Hindus who were the most prominent rebels, remained quiet. Nevertheless in Meerut and Delhi, Lucknow and Cawnpore, and further southeast in Allahabad and Benares, the rebellion posed a serious threat to British supremacy.

It also caused a violent response from the East India Company's forces. Such violence was fuelled by the massacre at Cawnpore, although this only confirmed a trend that had already begun. The force was soon quelled, with emergency laws passed to prevent indiscriminate violence against Indians. But the rebellion changed the way the British regarded India. The spirit of optimism and westernization that had prevailed in the early part of the century soon subsided. The British realized they could no longer so readily rely on their Indian troops to defend British interests. From now on Europeans would dominate the army, with a substantial Indian contribution of men from the loyal regions of the Punjab and Nepal.

The civilian attitude altered too. The British administrators were far keener to leave Indian society to its own devices. This meant withdrawing active support for missionary work. It also meant abandoning attempts to outlaw indigenous customs such as polygamy and child marriage. Many other aspects of the structure of Indian society were respected. The Indian princes found new favour – and responded with fervent loyalty to England's and India's sovereign.

But some of the developments of the earlier part of the century were allowed to continue. Education continued to receive support, as did the construction of public works. Such developments meant that at least part of the old programme of westernization was allowed to continue.

What happened after the rebellion thus set the agenda for much of India's subsequent history. England would retain a firm grip on its possession, realizing that only such a firm grip could unite the diverse factions and multifarious cultures that occupied the subcontinent. The administrators of the Victorian era saw little hope for an independent India. The people seemed to them too disunited and too tied to tradition to make a go of it on their own. Many seemed only too grateful for the security of foreign leadership and the chances that Britain offered for the country to develop.

However, in British policies of this period lay the seeds of future unrest and future change. Education fostered by the British gave the nationalist movement a chance to establish itself. And that nationalist movement would eventually look back to the rebellion as its earliest incarnation, even though the events of 1858 did not necessarily carry the whole country with them.

PUBLICATION OF THE ORIGIN OF SPECIES

A book that changed our view of the world

Charles Darwin's book *On the Origin of Species by Means of Natural Selection* was a turning point of modern science. It put forward a theory so revolutionary and so wide in its implications that no educated person could ignore it. It was controversial, but it was also of its time. And it has influenced scientific thinking – not to mention philosophy, religion and other branches of thought–ever since.

The author

The son of a doctor, and a descendant of the eighteenth century naturalist Erasmus Darwin, Charles Darwin seemed destined for a scientific career. Following the example of his formidable father he began a training in medicine at Edinburgh in 1825. His interest in medicine, however, was short-lived. At Edinburgh he met Robert Grant, who was later to become Professor of Zoology at University College, London. Grant stimulated Darwin's interest in zoology, but this was hardly an obvious career in the early nineteenth century. Instead, Darwin went to Cambridge University where he intended to take a degree in preparation for entering the church.

Although the church seems an odd career for the future theorist of evolution, the Church of England had a long tradition of nurturing naturalists – from Gilbert White of Selborne onwards. Darwin began to move towards this tradition by amassing a vast collection of beetles in his Cambridge rooms. But the most decisive influence on Darwin at this time was his friend J. S. Henslow, Professor of Botany.

It was Henslow who recommended Darwin for the position of naturalist on a forthcoming voyage of exploration. The ship was to be the *Beagle*, and the voyage was to take Darwin on a five-year circumnavigation of the world. It was to be a voyage that would open Darwin's eyes and sharpen his powers of reasoning; it would give him the opportunity to see an

Charles Darwin

extraordinarily wide variety of habitats and wildlife; and it would give him data to base much of his later work.

One example of the sort of information Darwin collected on the *Beagle* related to the fossil record. Fossils had a special fascination for the Victorians. As these most ancient traces were increasingly uncovered and classified it became clear that the Bible's account of the timing of the Earth's creation could not be taken at face value. It was against this background that important nineteenth century works such as Charles Lyell's *Principles of Geology* were received. Darwin made fascinating fossil discoveries in South America, on the Argentine pampas, including the remains of a massive elephant-like mastodon. A further discovery of another large quadruped called a mylodon (and later dubbed *Mylodon darwinii*) was made on the coast, south of Buenos Aires.

What was fascinating about these fossils was their similarity to current species. Received wisdom told Darwin that creatures like this had died out, to be replaced by new species. But the similarities opened up the possibility that some sort of gradual change might have been responsible for the replacement of one species by another.

Another pivotal observation by Darwin while travelling with the *Beagle* was made on the Galapagos Islands in the Pacific Ocean, southwest of Panama. This group of volcanic islands is isolated from the nearest large landmass – Central America. Each island in the group is also isolated from its neighbours by strong sea currents and a lack of wind. Consequently, the flora and fauna of each island have little chance of travelling beyond their home. What Darwin found was that each island had a distinctive but similar population. The most celebrated examples are the different species of Galapagos finches which are similar except for their different bills which seem fitted to the food supplies available locally. These facts suggest that the birds have somehow adapted independently to their particular environments.

Observations like these were pivotal when Darwin began to set down his theories about the origin and diversity of species. As he remarked in one notebook, he 'had been greatly struck . . . on character of South American fossils, and species on Galapagos Archipelago. These facts (especially latter), origin of all my views.'

Working methods

The voyage of the *Beagle* made Darwin into a great observer and an effective recorder of his observations. He continued writing in his notebooks in the same clipped, telegraphic style for years after he returned from the voyage.

But if, in this respect, Darwin was a model scientist, he was not a great experimenter. He did some experimental work to test his theories, for example breeding and studying different species of pigeons to investigate how characteristics are passed on from one generation to the next. But in the main he relied on correspondence and conversation with other scientists who had done more experimental work, persisting until he got the response

Woodpecker - finch
Camarhynchus pallidus
Tree species

camarhynchus holiobates
Mangrove swamps

Camarhynchus psittacula
Camarhynchus pauper
Camarhynchus parvulus
Insect eaters

Warbler finch
Certhidea

Camarhynchus crassirostris
vegetarian

Cocos Island finch
Pinaroloxias

TREE DWELLING FINCHES

Geospiza
magnirostris
Seed eaters

Geospiza
fortis

Geospiza
fuliginosa

Sharp-beaked finch
Geospiza difficilis

Geospiza
conirostris

Geospiza
scandens

Cactus eaters

GROUND DWELLING FINCHES

The Beagle *reached the Galápagos Islands in September 1835. It was here that Darwin was to observe the variety of species of finches that existed on the different islands of the archipelago. Darwin's finches, as they came to be called, could be distinguished by the different sizes of their beaks. They had apparently evolved independently in response to the similar conditions but differing food supplies on the various islands. The fourteen species include three main groups: ground finches (six species that feed mostly on seeds on the ground); tree finches (that feed on insects in trees and live in the moist forests); and a finch that feeds on small insects in bushes in both dry and humid regions. This phenomenon was to give Darwin one of his most important examples when he came to theorize about the origin of species. He saw that what had happened in the wild was something similar to what happens when breeders of domestic animals breed selectively to get the characteristics they want. In fact, Darwin studied and bred various types of pigeons as part of his experimental work on evolution.*

168

he wanted and, in his own phrase, 'pestering them with letters' until his queries were answered. These communications were clearly of vital importance to Darwin, although one tireless colleague, Hooker, reported that Darwin always seemed to give him more information than he had imparted to Darwin.

The evolution of the theory

Darwin suspected that, briefly and simply, when an individual emerged that was somehow different from the norm for its species, and when that difference assisted that individual's survival, it would pass on its success to future generations. Individuals that inherited this variation would survive better and the species would evolve in that direction, until it became the norm. The theory came to Darwin in a moment of inspiration in 1838. The principle of natural selection was born.

But Darwin did not jump to conclusions. He tested his theory, studied, corresponded with friends and colleagues, and refrained from publishing his findings until this process of testing was complete. Amongst his most helpful colleagues was Charles Lyell who helped Darwin classify his finds and discussed their implications with him. Sir Joseph Hooker and Thomas Henry Huxley were also confidants with whom Darwin discussed his findings.

In spite of all the observation, discussion and experiment on which Darwin's theory had been based, its author was still reluctant to publish. A theory at once so revolutionary and, to the God-fearing people of nineteenth-century Europe so contrary to belief, was bound to arouse controversy. In the end, events forced Darwin to publicise his views. In 1855, his book already well underway, Darwin read an essay by Alfred Russell Wallace, *On the tendency of variations to depart indefinitely from the Original Type*. Wallace's essay represented an independent discovery of Darwin's theory.

Mylodon darwinii

Darwin decided that the best approach would be for both his and Wallace's ideas to be put forward together at a meeting of the Linnean Society in London. It would then be clear that the two scientists had worked independently and that neither was claiming that the theory was his sole property. Thanks to the support of Lyell and Hooker, papers by Darwin and Wallace were read together in 1858. Given to a select scientific audience, they made little impact. But the publication of the *Origin of Species* in the following year took the intellectual world by storm.

Perhaps the most obvious religious objection to the book was that the Biblical account of creation could not be literally true if Darwin's theory was correct. Darwin's was not the first work of science to put forward ideas that made people question the account of the six-day creation of the world in Genesis – accounts of the geological discoveries of the nineteenth century dealt with time spans vaster than those discussed by Darwin.

Much of the controversy about Darwin's book was misplaced. Most of those who were upset by the theory of the origin of species were concerned about what it implied about humankind – that humans evolved like any other animal, and that we are little more than close relatives of the apes. This seems extraordinary today, since nowhere in his book does Darwin mention the origins of the human race. He was afraid that applying his theory to people would lead to a questioning of the Christian view of our unique place in the scheme of things. Darwin was quite right about this – though perhaps he was naïve to think that by leaving mankind out of his book he would stop readers making this connection.

There were also scientific and pseudo-scientific objections. Some of these were from more traditional scientists who rejected Darwin's use of the hypothesis as unscientific; they were already behind the times. Others came from those who were jealous of Darwin's fame and anxious to protect their own positions; they too were indefensible. Yet another criticism was that Darwin had plagiarized the theories of Lamarck, the scientist who had suggested that changes in the habits of a creature brought about evolutionary changes. This was a wanton misreading of Darwin.

Whatever the causes of the controversy, the *Origin of Species* rapidly became a bestseller. The first edition of 1,250 copies Darwin had thought too large. But his publisher, John Murray, was right to insist on a sizeable printing – the edition sold out immediately and by 1872 there had been five further editions.

Darwin's microscope

And not everyone was hostile. T. H. Huxley, as might be expected, reviewed the book warmly in *The Times*. This review did much to popularize the book and to ensure that it was taken seriously. Lyell, too, was finally convinced of the validity of the theory and incorporated it into a new edition of his *Elements of Geology*. And Hooker also made the theory work for him, using it to help explain the geographical distribution of plants in his book *Introduction to the Tasmanian Flora* (1859). Amongst the true scientists of the period, Darwin's theory gained acceptance. Future generations of scientists would find it equally useful.

The legacy

More recent scientists have found that the theory of natural selection has helped them in many ways, and their research has thrown light on the theory and modified it in detail. In paleontology, for example, much more is known now than in Darwin's time about the speed at which fossils evolved and the circumstances of their evolution. We can now see how the speed and nature of changes varied with alterations in the environment and ecology – organisms either failed to respond to these changes and died out, or changed by natural selection and lived on.

Twentieth-century science has built on and modified Darwin's work in many other ways. Field studies and ecology (disciplines that Darwin, with his work on the *Beagle*, helped to found) have led to new evidence about how organisms adapt to their environment; the science of genetics has progressed; the mathematics of selection have been studied; animal behaviour has been treated experimentally. The work that Darwin began goes on, opening up our view of our world.

AMERICAN CIVIL WAR

A decisive change in the political balance of the United States, and the abolition of slavery

Abraham Lincoln in 1860 called the United States 'a house divided . . . half slave and half free'. He was referring to the division between the eighteen 'free' northern states and the fifteen southern slave states that made up the Union. Slavery was not the only difference between the two sectors. The north was much more urban and more developed industrially than the south, which relied on plantation farming for its economy. The north was led by businessmen, the south by planters. Broadly speaking the leaders of the north believed in progressive democracy and industrial expansion. The prevailing ethos amongst the southern leaders was conservative and aristocratic.

These conservative southerners were hanging on to the advantages that slave ownership gave them. Not that every white family owned slaves in the south – indeed under ten per cent of white southern males were slave-owners. But slavery was seen as a unique southern right, without which life would be very different. Even non-slave-owners defended slavery.

The tensions between the two halves of the country had continued during the 1850s. They were particularly evident in disputes over new territories. Anti-slavery campaigners would try to keep slavery out of these areas, pro-slavers would dispute their right to do so. A case in point were the territories of Kansas and Nebraska. Slavery was barred from these territories until a senator pushed through the Kansas-Nebraska Act in 1854, allowing the territorial legislatures the right to decide whether slavery would be admitted in their areas.

One effect of this was to make the new territories, especially Kansas, into battlegrounds for the pro- and anti-slavery factions. Meanwhile, several northern states passed 'personal-liberty laws' to help discourage people returning fugitive slaves, something they were supposed to do according to federal law.

Abraham Lincoln

In 1860 there was a presidential election. The Democratic Party split into two sections, representing North and South, with rival candidates running under regional tickets. But it was their Republican rivals, with their candidate Abraham Lincoln, who won the election on a platform of anti-slavery measures and other sweeping reforms. Many southerners threatened that their states would secede from the Union if Lincoln was elected, but Lincoln countered that secession was illegal and that he would hold all federal possessions in the South in the event of any state's breaking away. It was a fight over just such a possession, Fort Sumter, Charleston, South Carolina, that began the American Civil War between the North (or Unionists) and the South (or Confederates). And so it was secession, not slavery, that was the immediate cause of the war.

Not all the slave states fought for the southern Confederacy. Eleven states would fight on the southern side, twenty-three on the side of the north. Both sides

began by appealing for volunteers. Initially there was a good take-up rate, but as the war progressed the number of new volunteers declined and the two sides had to resort to the draft. This was very unpopular – no less so because rich men could buy themselves out of military service.

Ironically, although prospective black soldiers in the North flocked to join the Union army and fight for their brothers' emancipation, the northern army originally refused to accept negroes. After 1862, black men were admitted to the northern army, although there was a period of two years before they were given equal pay with white troops.

The course of the war

Many northerners thought the war would be over quickly and that they would win it easily. They had the advantage of the nucleus of the United States army on which to centre their effort, and a larger population from which to draw fresh troops. But the first months of the war proved the northern optimists wrong.

The first inkling that the fight would be a long one came at the Battle of Bull Run (or Manassas) in July 1861. The Union forces, under Irvin McDowell, made several assaults on the Confederates. One Confederate general, Thomas J. Jackson, stood his ground so resolutely during one attack that he won the name of 'Stonewall'. Such tactics eventually allowed the southerners to go on the offensive against the exhausted Unionists, who finally fled in disarray to Washington.

It was to be a similar story in many of the other encounters of the early years of the war, with many southern successes. But there were problems for the southern leaders. Up to this point much of the fighting had not been far from the Confederate capital of Richmond. This was a great anxiety for the southerners, but there was a way out of the problem. Washington, the capital of the Union, was only some one hundred miles away from Richmond and was itself a frontier town. So Confederate general Robert E. Lee strove to shift the battle front from one capital to another, to pass the anxiety to the North and the initiative to the South.

To make best use of this advantage Lee needed to push his way over the Potomac River into the Union state of Maryland. But he was aware of the problems he faced. His army was much smaller than that of the Union, but even so there were difficulties in supplying it. Horses were difficult to come by because the Unionists were gaining ground in the principal horse-breeding states (Kentucky, Missouri, Tennessee and West Virginia). Raw materials and the products of industry were also in short supply because many of these came from the northern or border states. Even food was a problem. The North was blockading southern ports, and even if this strategy was not a complete success it held up supplies. Lee was well aware of his army's weakness. He wrote that his army lacked 'much of the material of war . . . the men are poorly provided with clothes, and in thousands of instances are destitute of shoes.'

The blockade had another effect, which the South felt might turn to their advantage. The trade in cotton from the South was cut off, depriving the English mills of their most important raw material. Southern leaders thought that this might bring England into the war on the side of the South. There was some likelihood of this, since relations between England and the Union were strained at the time. But events would conspire to keep England and France, another potential ally of the South, out of the war.

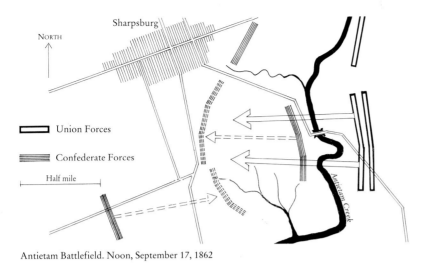

Sharpsburg

NORTH

Union Forces

Confederate Forces

Half mile

Antietam Creek

Antietam Battlefield. Noon, September 17, 1862

On the afternoon of 17 September 1862 battle was raging on either side of Antietam Creek. The incident shown here is the point at which the Unionist 9th Corps, under Burnside, pushed back the Confederate right wing. Burnside's men (shown in outline on the map) charged across the creek from east to west. The southern forces (shown as striped lines) were forced to retreat from the western bank of the creek towards Sharpsburg (at the top left of the map). The skirmish was representative of what happened in the battle as a whole: the Confederates were forced to retreat although there was not an out-and-out victory for the Union.

On 29–30 August Lee scored a second victory over the Union forces at Bull Run. This gave back virtually the whole state of Virginia to the South and sent the northerners in retreat to Washington. Here the forces of the North recombined, barring Lee from attacking Washington with any real hope of success. So Lee decided that he would manoeuvre his way towards Washington, in the hope at least of keeping the Union forces well away from Richmond – if possible out of Virginia. Accordingly, less than a week after the second Battle of Bull Run, Lee's army crossed the Potomac River to enter Maryland. Soon they would make a breach in the enemy's communications network by damaging the Ohio to Baltimore railway.

So Lee pressed on into Maryland. It was tough going. He thought he might find many southern sympathizers in the state who would join his army, but few were forthcoming. He soon discovered that the entire Union army had not retreated to Washington. There were small Union garrisons all over the area, particularly near the Potomac around Harpers Ferry. Lee knew he had to open up a line of communications in the area, but these garrisons proved difficult to shift. Lee began to conceive a plan to remove them.

He decided to divide his army up, sending Thomas Jackson with one force to take the Union posts along the Potomac River, while his other general, James Longstreet would cover him. Lee issued his orders on 9 September. But some time in the next few days one copy of the orders went astray. On 13 September a Union soldier found the orders wrapped around three cigars at a former Confederate camp site. Immediately they were taken to northern general George B. McClellan.

Antietam Creek

The loss of the orders was a blow for the south, but not perhaps as great a blow as it seemed. McClellan pushed forward toward Lee more quickly than Lee expected. Soon 100,000 Union soldiers had gathered near the small town of Sharpsburg, near the narrow stream known as Antietam Creek. Lee, his army divided, only had 18,000 men in the immediate vicinity with which to face them. Moreover, McClellan's troops were relatively fresh and well

supplied, while Lee's were tired, battle-scarred and ill-equipped. But there was one consolation for Lee. On the same day he received a message from Jackson. Harpers Ferry had been taken. This meant that Jackson could join Lee – and he would bring a large cache of captured arms with him.

Confederate officer

Still the two armies waited by the banks of the creek. Then, early in the morning of 17 September, McClellan's men began to fire at the Confederates. By six o'clock their heavy infantry was attacking the Confederate lines. By now Lee had amassed some 40,000 troops, but he was still heavily outnumbered. But, incredibly, Lee's troops stood firm and, helped by McClellan's tactical mistakes, were able to defeat the superior forces of the North in three separate onslaughts during a single day.

At the end of the day, when it looked as if Lee's right flank would finally succumb to the northerners, the final contingent of Confederate reinforcements arrived – only 3,000 men, but enough to give them extra strength they needed to resist.

By the end of the battle some 26,000 men had been killed, slightly more from the North than from the South. Even then, Lee stood his ground, trying to find a way of mounting another attack on McClellan. But the northern commander was all too aware of his losses and would not be tempted into another battle. Finally Lee,

his bellicosity satisfied, realized that nothing could be gained from advancing. So he led his men back over the Potomac River into Virginia, leaving Maryland to the Union once more.

The political initiative

McClellan was disappointed with his losses at Antietam, but Lincoln took a more positive view. At least the Confederates had been forced to retreat. And if, for the moment, there was no chance of taking a military initiative, Lincoln knew how to take a political one. He decided to seize the opportunity of the southern retreat to issue a declaration that would change the course of the war and of American history. Four days after the battle, Lincoln issued the Proclamation of Emancipation.

The Proclamation stated that as from 1 January 1863 all the slaves in the rebel states would be recognized as free: 'I, Abraham Lincoln, President of the United States...do order and declare that all persons held as slaves...are, and henceforward shall be free; and that the Executive government of the United States, including the military and naval authorities, will recognise and maintain the freedom of such persons.'

Lincoln knew that this Proclamation would not actually free the slaves in the South. But by making the announcement when he did he made it clear that slavery would be abolished in the event of a northern victory. The effect of this in turn was to bring slavery out into the open as an issue of the war. No longer would the South be allowed to fight simply for independence from the North: the North would be fighting for the liberty of a large proportion of the southern population. In the international arena, it would no longer be likely that either England or France would enter the war to fight on the side of slavery.

After Antietam, the war still had almost three years to run. There would be mixed fortunes, and in the end over a million lives would be lost. But Antietam, and Lincoln's proclamation which followed the battle, marked the turning point. From then on, the leaders of the North seized the political initiative; soon they would take the military initiative too.

FOUNDATION OF THE INTERNATIONAL RED CROSS

Nations come together for the good of humanity

In northern Italy, 1859 was a year of bloody battles. Cavour, prime minister of Sardinia–Piedmont, wanted to expand his power base in Italy, a move which was to lead eventually to Italy's unification. But to do this he had to ally with France against their mutual enemy, Austria. The new alliance could then march through Lombardy and push towards the states of Parma, Modena and Tuscany. And this they did, fighting horrific battles at Magenta (near the border of Piedmont and Lombardy) and Solferino (near the Lombard frontier with the territory of Venice). At Magenta, the blood flowed so freely that the origin of the name of the colour magenta is said to derive from this battle.

Solferino was even worse. The battle involved some 300,000 men, of whom 40,000 suffered serious wounds or died. The hand-to-hand fighting and rifle shooting went on for sixteen hours, and when ammunition ran out the rifles were used as clubs and men fought with hands, teeth and stones. Soldiers staggered over bleeding corpses to reach their adversaries and the Italians and French mercilessly chased the Austrians around four unsuspecting Italian villages, leaving death and destruction in their wake. The battle became so merciless that even the wounded were pounded with rifle butts. And when the French and Italians gained the upper hand they were not spared. The defeated could rescue only a few of their wounded men and many of those who had survived up to this point were gunned down even though it was clear that they had no chance in the fight.

Henri Dunant

In the quiet after the battle things only seemed worse. Medical supplies were limited. Indeed, supplies of any description were few and far between because the local people, poor and resentful of this barbaric invasion of their space, had

Henri Dunant

looted the soldiers' stores and knapsacks while the battle was in progress. And even for those who had managed to get through the ordeal unwounded, there was no water to quench their thirst after a day's fighting in the blistering heat.

The day before the battle a man arrived at Solferino who was to write a moving account of the carnage and its aftermath. His name was Henri Dunant, a Swiss businessman who was trying to get support from France for a venture in Algeria. He had found it impossible to get the civil service or the government to grant him the land he needed for his business, so he had decided, in desperation, to ask Napoleon III himself. As the emperor was fighting with the Italians, Dunant had to go to Solferino.

Dunant was shocked at what he saw. What medical care there was had a hopelessly makeshift character – men used handkerchiefs to bind broken limbs or dress wounds. And the lack of water meant that cleaning a wound was impossible. Dunant organized what relief he could. But he realized that he could do more good by publicizing what had happened. So he wrote and published a book, called *A Memory of Solferino*. In it he

described what he had seen and made suggestions about the best way to prevent such a horror happening again. In brief, he proposed that in every country a body should be set up specifically to provide medical aid for the armed forces. It should be a voluntary body that would be able to stand outside any conflict in which its country might be involved. But would anybody take up Dunant's call?

The Committee of Five

Clearly if such a proposal was to get anywhere – within Switzerland itself, let alone on a national scale – a number of different talents would need to come together. Organizational skills would above all be required; medical knowledge essential; political influence would be useful; and it would be helpful to have access to someone with extensive military experience.

One of the early readers of Dunant's book, the Geneva lawyer and philanthropist Gustave Moynier, was someone with the experience to pull such a team together. Moynier already had great experience of charitable work, striving hard to motivate people to help Geneva's disadvantaged – from orphans to alcoholics. When he read *A Memory of Solferino* he asked Dunant to come to a meeting of the Geneva Public Welfare Society and put forward his ideas.

That meeting, in February 1863, led to the formation of the five-man committee that was to create the Red Cross. In addition to Dunant and Moynier, one obvious choice was Dr Louis Appia. Appia was a military surgeon with extensive experience on the battlefield who had written widely on his subject. He had also advised Dunant on medical matters when he was writing *A Memory of Solferino*. The next member was a man with both a military and a political background, General Guillaume-Henri Dufour. At seventy-three, Dufour was also something of an elder statesman and gave added weight

Representatives of sixteen different nations came to Switzerland in October 1863 to sign the first Geneva Convention. In retrospect, now that 165 nations have signed the Convention, it seems a small beginning. But it was a unique event at the time. Never before had nations come together in this way to put their names to basic humanitarian principles. Without this gesture, and the commitment of the men and women who, since this date, have made the Red Cross function, the whole structure that now protects the casualties of war, prisoners of war and victims of famine and disaster would simply not exist. Above all, the foundation of an international body at a time when nationalism was such a strong emotion pointed the way forward to the global solutions to problems that have become increasingly important in the twentieth century.

and influence to the committee. Finally, another doctor, Theodore Maunoir, joined the team.

By now, it was clear to the committee that the scheme had to have a truly international quality if it was to succeed. So they planned an international conference in Geneva for October 1863. Persuading a significant number of countries to send delegates at relatively short notice was not easy. And up to the last minute Dunant and his colleagues were not sure exactly how many would attend. But they began to gain support from influential European figures. The king of Saxony pronounced that '… any nation which does not participate in this humanitarian work puts itself outside public opinion in Europe.' Soon many other rulers and politicians were agreeing with the king, and on 29 October 1863 representatives from sixteen different states came to the conference.

The conference met to agree on a document that has become known as the first Geneva Convention. This sets out the basic principles under which the relief organization should operate, and has operated ever since.

The Convention committed the signatory governments to care for the wounded in time of war. The most important condition was that the care should be for all victims, whether friend or foe. To protect doctors and nurses from attack on the battlefield, the signators accepted the Red Cross symbol to denote their neutrality and to identify vehicles and buildings which should not be attacked. The Committee of Five became the International Committee of the Red Cross. This would continue to be made up of Swiss citizens and would work from a headquarters in Geneva. The International Committee acts as an intermediary body between the various National Red Cross Societies, particularly in times of war.

The man who inspired the foundation of the Red Cross in the first place, Henri Dunant, passed into obscurity. The business problems that sent him to Solferino in the first place eventually left him destitute and forced him to resign from the Committee in 1867. For fifteen years he disappeared from public life completely. His pivotal work was eventually recognized, however. He was awarded the first Nobel Peace Prize in 1901.

Meanwhile, the work of the Red Cross was expanding. Revisions of the Geneva Convention involved the organization in caring for the casualties of sea warfare (1907), for prisoners of war (1929), and for civilians in wartime (1949). Later still, the remit of the Red Cross expanded yet further. The Red Cross now does much relief work that is not connected with war at all. This includes looking after the sick, the old, the disabled, orphans, and, in particular, helping the victims of disasters, from famines to chemical explosions.

The Red Cross also fosters important training activities. For example, twenty-five National Societies run some 240 schools of nursing; sixty of the Societies also offer training to nursing auxiliaries. And many of the nurses taught in this way are also instructed in the art of passing on their knowledge to lay people, so that the fundamental skills of health care are transmitted around the world.

To cope with this work, the Red Cross has expanded beyond the dreams of Dunant and his colleagues. The original sixteen signatory nations had grown to sixty-seven by 1948. Today there are over 100, including the Red Crescent organizations of the Islamic world. The size of the body is shown by the sheer scale of the prisoner-of-war problem in World War II: by the end of the war the Red Cross index of internees and prisoners of war contained thirty-nine million cards. The total worldwide membership of the Red Cross is now over 250 million. In addition, the original structure of the International Committee and the separate National Red Cross or Red Crescent Societies has been supplemented by the League of Red Cross and Red Crescent Societies, founded in 1919, a federation of National Societies which has the role of peacetime coordination.

The sheer importance of the health care provided by the Red Cross across all international borders and nationalities cannot be disputed: the organization has become a key element in the story of human survival. The Red Cross is also a remarkable embodiment of international cooperation, a unique demonstration of what the world community can achieve.

GERMAN UNIFICATION

The creation of a new and powerful nation from Europe's German states

The first half of the nineteenth century saw steadily accelerating moves towards the unification of the various German states. Sometimes there were literary rallying calls to places with a shared language and culture to unite. But there were also less visible, but highly important economic changes that paved the way for unification. The growing railway network brought Prussia and the other states nearer together. Increasing Prussian coal and iron production, together with the railways, allowed the north German state to build up her economic strength. And the formation in 1834 of the German Customs Union (*Zollverein*) also greatly helped pull the German states together. Crucially, Austria, the other dominant German-speaking power, was not included in the *Zollverein*. For four decades the Prussians would struggle to keep her out.

From about 1815, when the first loud voices in favour of German unification began to be heard, there was a split between those in favour of *Grossdeutschland*, a huge confederation of all the German-speaking states extending from the Baltic to the Adriatic and dominated by Austria, and those who preferred *Kleindeutschland*, a smaller amalgam excluding Austria and taking the lead from Prussia. To begin with, it seemed that the defenders of *Grossdeutschland* would win. In 1815, a German confederacy was formed over which Austria presided.

After 1848, the year in which revolutions swept across Europe and changed the political map, the future of Germany looked uncertain again. But if there had been political changes, the solid economic foundation of Prussia was a constant – indeed Prussia's economic dominance was clear by the 1850s. The northern state once more seemed set to dominate. When Prince William of Prussia became Regent in 1858 he made it clear that he wanted to unite Germany under Prussian leadership. But it was not to be easy for William.

Realizing that he had to strengthen his army, he found it impossible to get his new army bill passed through parliament. He appointed a new Chancellor, the brilliant Otto von Bismarck, to help the passage of the bill.

Bismarck, who was to become known as the 'iron chancellor', imposed a strong grip on Prussia. In 1864 he led the Germans (both Austria and Prussia) into a war with Denmark over the provinces of Schleswig and Holstein. After the German victory, when Austria tried to assert her independence from Prussia, Bismarck declared war on his erstwhile ally, defeating Austria in 1866 and forming a new North German Confederation. This new grouping took in Prussia, Westphalia, Alsace-Lorraine, Schleswig and Holstein.

Although Bismarck's iron will was essential in the formation of this union, the Chancellor was not acting in a political vacuum. He had to hold open the possibility that the remaining southern states could retain some freedom if and when they came into the union, while at the same time giving Prussia enough power to remain the prime mover. Nevertheless, the Prussian-led Confederation had considerable powers, particularly in the areas of foreign policy, customs, commerce, banking and civil law.

Meanwhile the economic strength of Prussia was being kept up. As well as the trade links with other German states through the *Zollverein*, Bismarck built up trading partnerships with England, Belgium, Italy and France. Independence from Austria was economic as well as political. The prospect of wealth through this trade – or poverty without it – soon drew the remaining southern German states (notably Thuringia, Saxony, Württemburg and Bavaria) into the Confederation. Bismarck was also able to exploit the political uncertainties surrounding the Prussian war with France to encourage these states to come into the union.

During the negotiations with the southern states, Bismarck was able to keep for Prussia most of the powers that would enable her to dominate a united Germany. The Prussian army would to all intents and purposes become the German army; the Prussian chancellor would become the German Prime Minister; finally, at the beginning of 1871, the Prussian King became the German Emperor. Germany had become a great world power.

After 1871 Germany's presence in the world had a higher profile. The new nation began to expand. Envoys were sent to Africa and the South Seas in the early 1870s. Merchants soon followed, swelling the German coffers, and soon administrators came in their footsteps, to protect German interests still further. It began to look as if Germany would expand in the way that Victorian England had done. However, German colonization was not an economic success.

While it is simplistic to see in the work of Bismarck the inevitable seeds of future German expansion, without him future attempts at German expansion and the rise of the Third Reich could not have taken place. The new reunited Germany of today also owes its existence to the work of Bismarck. Whatever our view of the effect of a large, united and powerful Germany on Europe as a whole, the influence of William's chancellor is clear.

It took a strong hand to bring the German states to unity as one nation and Otto von Bismarck, who became known as the 'iron chancellor', was the man with the strength to do the job. He was motivated by the desire to bring Germany under Prussian leadership, putting Austrian power into eclipse in the process. By 18 January 1871, when the German Reich was proclaimed at Versailles, he had attained his goal and Germany had attained roughly the size and boundaries it would have in the twentieth century.

LISTER'S DEVELOPMENT OF ANTISEPTIC SURGERY

Safer operations for millions of people

Surgery is one of the oldest medical disciplines. Even the earliest peoples carried out surgical techniques – from the staunching of wounds to the amputation of limbs. By the beginning of the nineteenth century surgery had advanced greatly. Anatomical knowledge had grown by leaps and bounds and the technical skill of surgeons was impressive. It had to be. There were no proper anaesthetics, so operations had to be done at great speed. Patients would be sedated with opium or intoxicated with alcohol; then they would be tied down and operated on at breakneck speed. Even a leg amputation could be done in five minutes.

Working in this way was perilous to the patient. Apart from the possibility of mistakes when operating at speed, there was also the risk of infection before the necessity of aseptic conditions in the theatre was understood. Many patients, although their operations had been carried out with technical correctness, died as a result of infected wounds. But the physicians of the eighteenth and early nineteenth centuries were at a loss as to the cause.

Joseph Lister
The man who was to lead the way in eliminating infection from the operating theatre was the British surgeon Joseph Lister. Lister was born in 1827. His father, also called Joseph, was a businessman and amateur physicist who made his own contribution to science – the development of an improved objective lens for the microscope. Young Joseph studied medicine in London before going to Edinburgh in 1855 to work with James Syme, the foremost surgeon of the period, at the Royal Infirmary.

Lister was very successful at Edinburgh, building up a substantial body of surgical knowledge and original research. He investigated the process of inflammation, noting the part played by minute blood vessels in the early stages and how

different substances irritated them. He researched skin-colour changes in the frog and showed how the action of irritants on pigment cells was relevant to his work on inflammation. And he did important work on the coagulation of the blood.

By this time surgery had been revolutionized by the use of general anaesthetics. Lister himself had been in the theatre when the first major operation in England under general anaesthetic was performed. No longer did the surgeon have to work at lightning speed. The scope for more accurate work, and for operations on new areas such as the abdomen, was suddenly far greater. However, the new techniques brought with them new problems. Infections were on the increase. The unpleasant phenomenon of 'hospital gangrene' led many to lose their lives after potentially life-saving operations. Lister and his colleagues asked themselves what was going wrong.

In 1860 Lister was appointed Regius Professor of Surgery at Glasgow University. Shortly afterwards he was also made surgeon at the Glasgow Royal Infirmary. It was here that he would do the work that would change the course of surgery. A colleague, Thomas Anderson, suggested that Lister should read papers by the French chemist Louis Pasteur. He it was who had worked on the process of fermentation, suggesting that it was caused by micro-organisms in yeast, an idea that went against the grain of chemical theory at the time. He soon extended his theory to putrefaction, suggesting that this too was the result of the action of micro-organisms.

Lister was not the only person to take notice of Pasteur's work. Spencer Wells, a surgeon and campaigner for 'cold water for cleanliness', pointed out the relevance of Pasteur's theories to surgery in 1864. But Lister was the first to actually take the theories and investigate them in practical

terms. He observed that cleaning the wounds and going one step further – keeping germs out of the operating theatre as much as possible – could hold the key to successful surgery.

Developing the method
The antiseptic that Lister tried was phenol, or carbolic acid. Lister had followed the work of F. Crace Calvert, Professor of Chemistry at Manchester, on the acid. Calvert noted that it had been applied to corpses, with the result that decay had been arrested for up to a month. Calvert began to supply surgeons in Manchester with the acid, which they used for cleaning wounds.

Lister himself tried the acid in 1865, first on a wrist operation in which he normally had a high success rate, and second on an operation on a compound leg fracture. Both operations were failures and Lister waited for several months before trying again. Clearly a period of thought was needed: it seemed that Lister had not yet decided on a consistent experimental method with which to assess the effects of the carbolic acid. Lister decided to concentrate mainly on compound fracture cases when using carbolic acid. The advantage here was that if the treatment failed the surgeon could always amputate the limb and save the patient's life – and without antisepsis this would have been the orthodox treatment in any case. Thus the patient gained the chance that his or her limb might be saved, while running the risk that Lister might have to resort to the usual amputation if things did not go to plan.

During the early months of 1866 the

The antiseptic spray and carbolic acid dressings formed a vital part of Lister's operations. Lister used them as part of a surgical procedure based on the killing of germs and their elimination from the operating theatre.

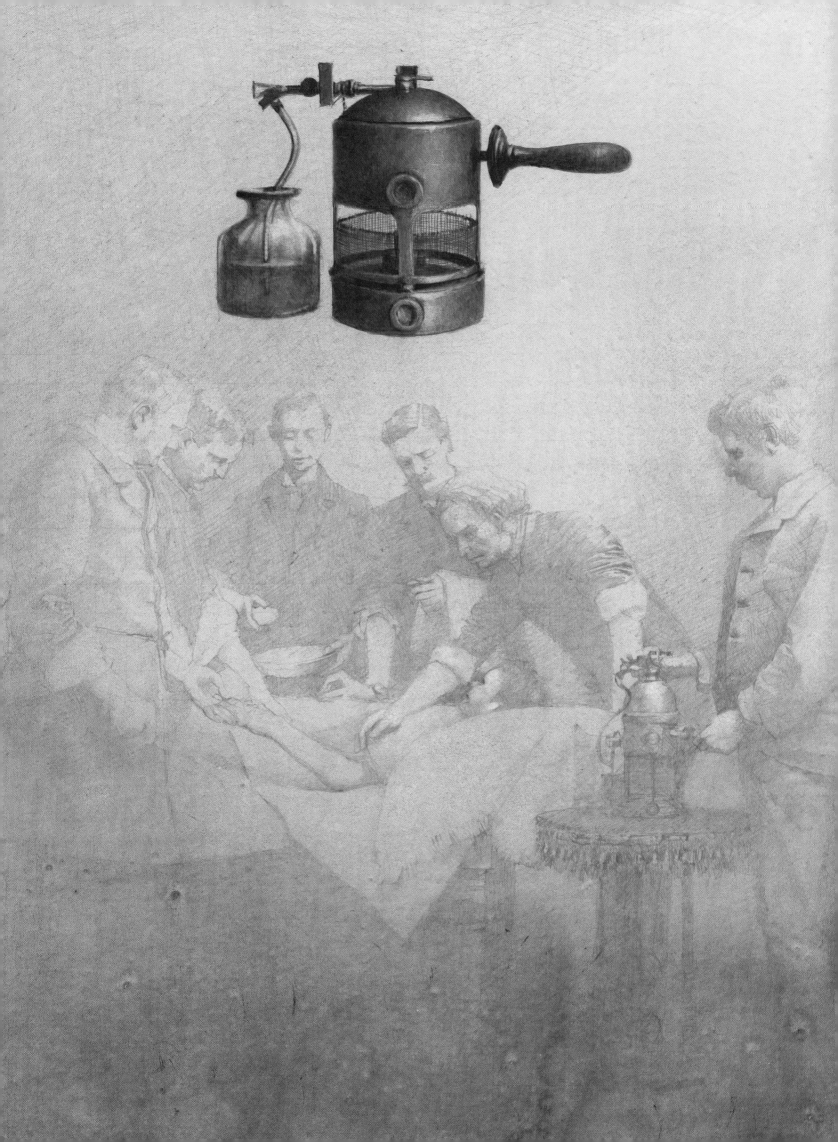

compound fracture cases began to come in. They were people who were victims of a range of different accidents but all came to Lister with the same expectation: the best they could hope for was the loss of a limb. A typical case was twenty-one-year-old John Hainy, a mould worker in a factory that produced iron castings. He was admitted with a broken leg after a heavy box containing a mould for an iron pipe had fallen on him. He was brought to Lister some three-and-a-half hours after the accident and the surgeon quickly cleaned and dressed the wound using antiseptic before setting the leg. Lister watched carefully as the scab turned to living tissue in the antiseptic conditions created by the continuously applied carbolic acid.

There was a setback when Hainy developed bed sores. These became gangrenous and Lister suspected the infection was transmitted from nearby infected patients. So he had Hainy moved to a different place in the ward and applied antiseptic treatment to the sores. It worked. Hainy was finally discharged in August 1866, completely cured.

Lister was proud of his success with Hainy, but he did not publish the results immediately. Other compound fracture cases were coming in and each one taught the surgeon more about the best methods to use. Lister continued to refine his working practices. He went public the following year printing a note about his work to accompany his application for a new job, the Professorship of Systematic Surgery at University College, London. Lister did not get the job (he lost the election by a single vote) but the occasion spread news of his work through his profession.

Meanwhile he was also working on the antiseptic treatment of abcesses. Again he was successful in bringing his patients relief, although he was not treating the underlying cause of the abscesses. He was alert to preventing infection re-entering the body from the discharge, as well as stopping germs rushing in with the air into the space left by the discharge.

Publication

It was also in 1867 that Lister formally published his findings, in a series of papers in the medical journal *The Lancet*. He began by putting forward the germ theory of infection, stating that germs, long since thought of as accidental accompaniments of putrescence, had been shown by Pasteur to be the actual cause of the condition. The surgeon's aim, therefore, was to kill these germs with a substance that would not affect the patient's health adversely.

His paper goes on to give detailed accounts of some of his most important

Joseph Lister

cases. Detailed descriptions of the dressings and the use of carbolic acid were given, so that other surgeons could follow Lister's methods. It was expected that others would follow these details rigourously, so careful does one have to be about the spread of germs. For example, Lister cautions about treating a probe with an antiseptic rag. Lest this seem overcautious Lister adds, 'If we could see with the naked eye only a few of the septic organisms that people every cubic inch of the atmosphere of a hospital ward, we should rather wonder that the antiseptic treatment is ever successful than omit any precautions in conducting it.' Indeed, elsewhere Lister made himself enemies in Glasgow by describing how unhealthy the atmosphere in his hospital wards actually was. In doing this Lister was simply trying to emphasize in the most practical way the need for germ-free conditions.

Lister did not only make enemies in Glasgow. Detractors elsewhere pointed out that the use of carbolic acid had been recommended elsewhere, particularly by the French writer Lemaire. But Lister was rightly resentful of such criticisms. They missed the point. Lister's originality was not so much in the use of carbolic acid as in the way he used it. Only Lister linked Pasteur's germ theory of infection to actual clinical practice in this way. As for Lemaire, many of his recommendations, such as the internal taking of carbolic acid for a range of disorders, were useless if not actually harmful. Lister's work, by contrast, actually saved life and limb.

The influence of Lister

In many places Lister's ideas and methods spread quickly through the surgical profession. As early as 1867, a Dr George Derby of Boston, Mass, was operating antiseptically using Lister's techniques. Soon there were other American converts to Lister's system. Antispesis also caught on rapidly in Germany. At least one German doctor came to Glasgow to watch Lister work. Others read his articles in *The Lancet*, followed his instructions with success, and wrote their own cases up in German journals. Surgeons from Russia, Austria and Denmark also reported success with antisepsis in the late 1860s. At home, acceptance was more gradual, although a group of close colleagues championed Lister from the start.

Those who had limited success with antisepsis probably failed to follow the details of Lister's instructions closely enough. This was partly Lister's fault, because the way he wrote about the subject laid more emphasis on the antiseptic itself – the carbolic acid – than on the need to create a totally aseptic, germ-free environment around the wound. So it was easy for lazy practitioners to use Lister's acid sprays and dressings without giving them a chance. But ultimately, as successes multiplied and as Lister himself continued to work to improve his techniques within the framework of his antiseptic method, few could remain unconvinced.

The evidence spoke from itself. The death rate from surgery had reduced from at least thirty per cent to nearer five per cent. What was more, the number of operations that were safe to perform had greatly increased as a result of Lister's work. Innumerable people owed their health – and their very lives – to Joseph Lister.

INVENTION OF THE TELEPHONE

The beginning of instant communications

For thousands of years people have tried to find some way of sending messages that does not involve an actual human messenger travelling from sender to recipient. The ancient Chinese used bonfires to warn their garrisons of approaching attackers on the Great Wall. The Romans flashed signals through the air using mirrors. Both systems, when backed up by the resources of a great empire, could send signals over long distances by using chains of signallers.

These methods of long-distance signaling were primitive. But the human race would have to wait until experiments with electricity got well underway before a really sophisticated message machine appeared. This happened in the nineteenth century, when a number of scientists began to investigate the power of electric currents to stimulate a mechanical action far away.

The pioneers were American scientists Joseph Henry and Samuel Morse, and British inventors William Cooke and Charles Wheatstone. Cooke and Wheatstone patented their first telegraph in 1837. In 1844 Morse sent his first message along a wire using his famous 'dot and dash' code. Wherever an organization of any size needed instant communications, the new telegraph systems caught on. Soon stock markets and railways, newspapers and armies were sending messages by telegraph. By the 1860s telegraph wires stretched from coast to coast in the USA.

Alexander Graham Bell

But the telegraph did not make instant communications as accessible as some had hoped. You had to be near a telegraph office to use the service. And the telegraph did not transmit the human voice. The person who was to make the leap to a voice-transmitting system was the teacher and inventor Alexander Graham Bell.

Bell came from a family of well known elocutionists and speech therapists. His father, Alexander Melville Bell, was the author of a manual, *Standard Elocutionist*, which was regularly reprinted in English. Alexander Graham Bell and his two brothers carried on their father's profession. Young Alexander's formal schooling was limited (although he had one year at Edinburgh University) and he was taught largely by his father. By the time he was twenty-one, in 1868, he was his father's assistant in London and had already begun his researches into sound. He continued these after 1870, when the family moved from England to Canada.

In Canada both father and son became well known as the advocates of a system devised by the elder Bell called visible speech. This was a way of representing different sounds by depictions of the vocal organs. Deaf people could imitate the positions of the organs shown and so learn to speak.

Bell's work with the deaf was crucial in his research towards the development of the telephone. It gave him a thorough grounding in the science of sound production. And it put him in touch with the parents of two deaf students whom he had helped and who were able to fund his research. As a teacher of the deaf Bell

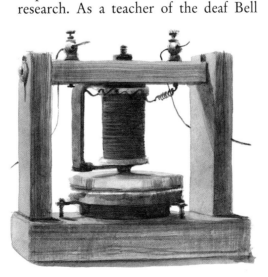

Bell's early telephone apparatus

knew something about sound and how it travels – that a sound consists of vibrations in the air, for example. He sought a way of reproducing these vibrations so that they could be transmitted over long distances.

During his work with the deaf Bell had seen a device called a phonautograph, invented by the Frenchman Leon Scott. This consisted of a membrane attached to a thin stick. On the end of the stick was a bristle which touched a glass plate. There was a cone on the front of the membrane. When you spoke into the cone the membrane vibrated, causing the stick and bristle to move, drawing a thin line on the glass. The pattern drawn on the glass differed with the sound spoken into the cone.

Bell took the idea of the phonautograph and wedded it to ideas from some of the scientists who had been working on electricity. Bell wound a long wire around an iron bar. One end of the wire was connected to a battery, the other to another bar at some distance from the first. Near to each bar he placed a membrane (on one end of a cone, to concentrate the sound). Speaking into one of the cones made its membrane vibrate. This made the metal move in the magnetic field around the wire, causing a fluctuating magnetic field and, in turn, a fluctuating current in the wire. This fluctuating current set up another fluctuating magnetic field at the other end, making the second membrane vibrate to reproduce the sound at the first membrane.

Bell got his telephone to work for the first time in March 1876. By June he was demonstrating the apparatus to a group of scientists and celebrities at the Philadelphia Centennial Exhibition. By the beginning of the following year he was sending telephone messages from Boston to Salem. And in July the same year he and a group of partners had founded the Bell Telephone Company.

Bell's company had its problems. Bell

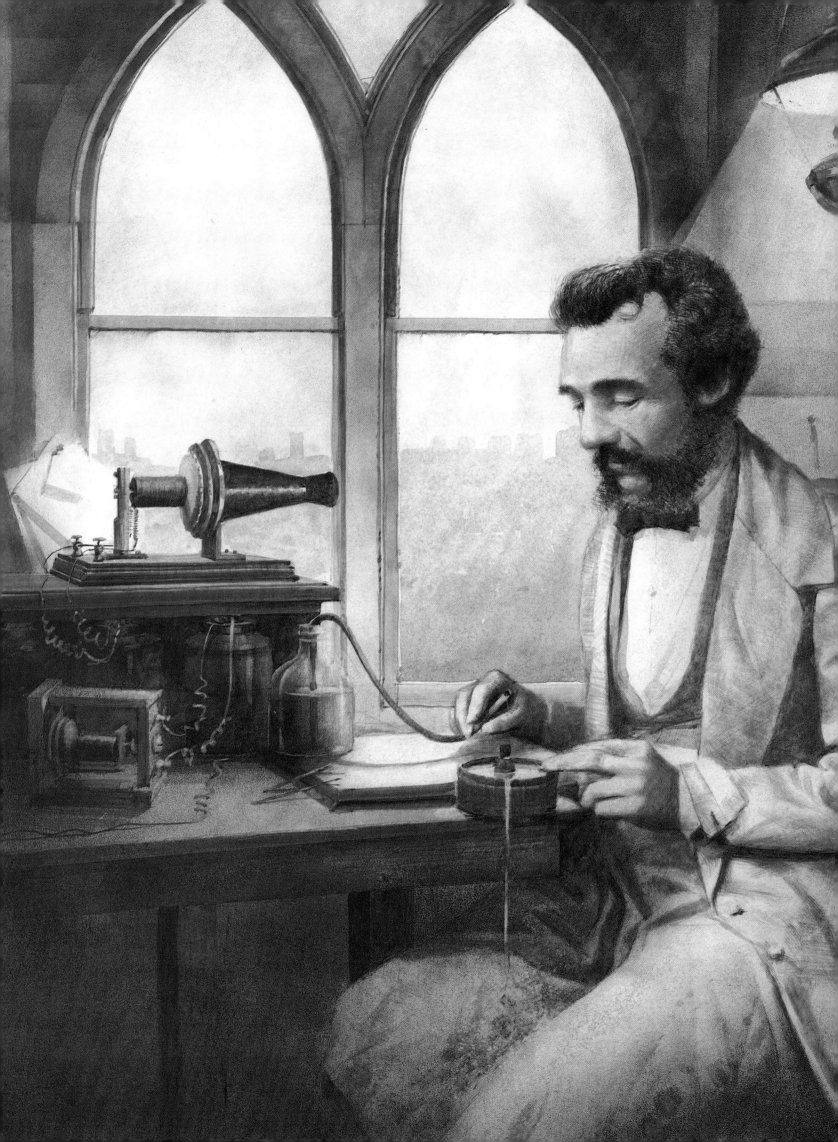

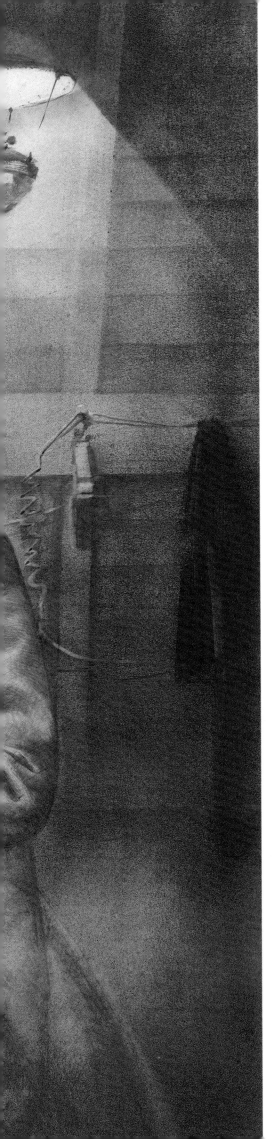

Bell's telephone brought together two pieces of apparatus that already existed, a membrane that vibrated as a result of sound waves and an electromagnet. Bell's insight lay in his way of using this equipment to transform a variable vibration into a variable electric current which could be sent along a line and translated back into a vibration at the other end. Like many influential inventions it was essentially very simple. The apparatus could be made with ease, and once Bell had refined the invention, telephones could be manufactured rapidly to satisfy the unprecedented demand. Bell soon found himself a rich man, and he used his money to finance further scientific projects.

was involved in countless legal suits for patent infringement, some very soon after the company was formed. These often involved much larger, better-established firms, such as the great Western Union Telegraph Company. But throughout all these disputes, which took their toll on the inventor's health, Bell's claim to be the true originator of the telephone was upheld.

The success of the telephone

The telephone proved a popular innovation. It soon outstripped the telegraph as a message-carrier that was comparatively cheap and easy to use. Bell's work seen in scientific terms was brilliant enough – it was a clever synthesis of ideas from different sources about acoustics and electricity. But his contribution was even more significant – he was the first to recognize the commercial potential of the telephone.

But there were still problems with the application of the new invention. Because every user had a terminal, and would want to be able to speak to any other user, the lines had to come together so that the correct connections could be made. This was the origin of the telephone exchange, the first example of which opened to serve twenty-one telephones in New Haven, Connecticut in January 1878. It had a bank of switches that enabled any one telephone in the system to be connected to any other.

People soon realized how useful and convenient the telephone could be. The number of users increased dramatically. By 1887 there were 1187 exchanges in the United States connecting over 150,000 subscribers to the system. The United Kingdom had 26,000 subscribers by this time, Germany 22,000, and Canada, Sweden, France and Italy all had more than 9,000. The telephones used on these networks were fairly primitive compared to modern instruments. There were no dials (calls had to be made via the operator). The same unit had to act as both mouthpiece and earpiece, so there were problems with sound distortion. But the advantages outweighed the disadvantages. The age of instant communication had arrived.

Bell's success brought him much money which he invested in further research and on teaching the deaf. He was involved in early work on a surprising range of subjects, from sound recording and sonar detection to manned flight and the hydrofoil. He was also an early president of the National Geographical Society, and the inspiration behind the founding of the Society's famous and respected magazine.

But the telephone remained Bell's best known invention, the achievement for which he was honoured in his lifetime and has been remembered ever since. Its influence on broadening communications, transmitting information, and making the world effectively smaller, is obvious. The early pioneers quickly saw its potential. Before the end of the nineteenth century, for example, the telephone allowed the development of pre-radio wired broadcasting systems. London, Paris and Budapest had such systems which were only phased out with the introduction of radio in the twentieth century.

PUBLICATION OF FREUD'S INTERPRETATION OF DREAMS

A new approach to how we think about ourselves

At the start of the twentieth century a book was published in Vienna that was to herald a new understanding of the human mind. Its author, Sigmund Freud, opened up an entire field of psychological study and espoused theories that would have an influence, directly or indirectly, on a remarkable range of fields, from science to literature, from religion to advertising. The book, which appeared in an edition of only 600 copies and was written by an author little known outside his own discipline, was *The Interpretation of Dreams*.

Sigmund Freud dedicated his life to ceaseless research into the human psyche. He chose to study medicine to find out about human nature rather than through a particular desire to heal the sick. By the time he was in his late twenties he was a lecturer in neuropathology. He did important research on the region of the brain called the medulla and on the effects of the drug cocaine.

But more important and influential still was his development of the techniques of psychoanalysis. This was a method of finding out about the patient's mind and treating the patient's neurotic ailments by questioning, suggesting, the use of 'free association' and sometimes hypnosis. The motive was to concentrate on a particular symptom and to throw light on its origins. Methods such as free association allowed Freud to perceive and at least partially overcome the patient's resistance to revealing repressed thoughts and memories, especially those relating to sexuality.

Freud's work with patients led him to some startling theories. Many of these have been modified by later work, but they have nevertheless been important in shaping opinions in the twentieth century. For example, Freud was struck by how often sexuality played an important part in neurosis. Patients would often tell him that one of their parents had attempted to seduce them as children; they would later reveal that these seductions did not in fact

take place – they were either fantasies or reversals of a role subconsciously desired by the patient. From these findings the idea of the Oedipus complex, in which a child wants to sleep with the parent of the opposite sex, emerged.

But perhaps Freud's most influential work was on dreams. *The Interpretation of Dreams* was the fullest account to date of psychoanalysis and Freud thought it was his most important book. It analyzes dreams to show their relation to unconscious desires and experiences, again often dating back to childhood. It shows how dreams can condense one subject into another and can displace one person on to another, so that the analysis of dreams must be done with great care and subtlety.

When it first appeared the book was little noticed, although there were some favourable reviews. But before long an enthusiastic circle of followers gathered around Freud, meeting at his home on every Wednesday to discuss psychoanalysis. This group included some of the other founders of modern psychology such as Alfred Adler and, later, Carl Jung. Freud's influence was not confined to his writings. His circle would gradually spread around the world, some members adapting and deviating from his ideas, others following the master more closely – all contributing to a change in the way we view ourselves.

Freud's other influence was his own psychoanalytical practice. Many of his books, including *The Interpretation of Dreams*, contain case studies drawn from Freud's own experience. As well as providing evidence for his theories the case studies make fascinating reading. They demonstrate dramatically how Freud had opened up the study of the mind, and how the apparent illogicality of dreams could acquire its own strange logic under the scrutiny of analysis.

Many practitioners no longer agree with Freud's conclusions, and some of his successors have somewhat modified his

original theories almost beyond recognition. Nevertheless, subsequent research has often built on his foundation, and our ideas about the human psyche would be entirely different without Freud. What is more, his writings and case studies continue to provide an absorbing source of information about the human mind.

But the influence goes much further. For example, Freud has had a profound influence on the arts of the twentieth century – always a useful barometer of the consciousness of a period. Many modern movements in painting have tried to explore the world of dreams and the unconscious, as too have numerous modern writers and film-makers. Even in more mundane areas, such as the imagery used in advertising, Freud has left his mark.

The most apparently straightforward advertising posters often contain images that are designed to pass half-hidden messages to the unconscious in a way that would have alternately angered and amused the father of psychoanalysis. His influence is all-pervasive. Concepts such as the Freudian slip, the Oedipus complex, the death wish, the phallic symbol, the family romance, have all become part of the way people think in the twentieth century. They all begun with Freud who radically and irrevocably shaped the way that we think about ourselves.

Freud's work opened up an entire area of the human psyche that had scarcely been given serious consideration before. The whole idea of the unconscious, how it can both mirror and contradict our conscious thoughts, how it can be glimpsed in the strange world of dreams, and how knowledge of it can be used to treat psychological disorders, is Freud's special legacy. Although, since Freud's death in 1939, his ideas have been modified or radically revised by subsequent researchers, few other thinkers have had comparable influence.

BOER WAR

The conflict that brought to a head the political future of southern Africa

In 1815 the British title to the Cape Colony in southern Africa was confirmed. From then on the British pursued a policy of anglicization that put pressure not only on the native peoples, but also on the other substantial group of settlers in the area – those of Dutch descent known as the Boers. Soon pressure from the British would lead to mass migrations of Boers into the northeastern part of the area, away from the Cape Colony towards the region surrounding modern Johannesburg. These movements of the 1830s, known collectively as the Great Trek and involving some 10,000 people, led ultimately to the formation of two independent Boer states, the Orange Free State and the Transvaal.

Could the British and the Boers live peacefully side-by-side, and what would become of the native peoples of southern Africa? The question was a difficult one. The British controlled the sea coasts of southern Africa, meaning that the Boers could not trade internationally without using British facilities and paying British tariffs. This became important in 1867 when diamonds and gold were discovered along the borders of the Orange Free State and in the Transvaal. Quickly the already difficult situation became complicated. There was unrest amongst the black workers and conflict amongst the mining interests. Britain tried to form a South African Federation and then in 1877 attempted to annex the Transvaal. Meanwhile, people flooded into the area in the hope of gaining wealth.

But, strengthened by wealth from gold, the Boers of the Transvaal clung to their independence from Britain. After the British defeated the Zulus, the Transvaal Boers rose against the British and won their independence with the Treaty of London in 1881. The appointment of President Paul Kruger in 1883 gave them a strong leader.

It was a changing political situation that marked great social changes in the area. Large, influential mining firms, such as Wernher Beit and Rhodes Consolidated Goldfields, had been set up. They had brought into the area many new skilled workers. The social make-up of many places had changed beyond recognition. Johannesburg, for example, only founded in 1886, quickly grew to a town of 50,000 people of whom only just over 6,000 were from the Transvaal itself. This left the workers in the mines of Transvaal in a difficult position. Many of them were foreigners, or Uitlanders; and many of these were British. They had no political rights, but their numbers were large and they could pose a significant threat if they were organized.

Paul Kruger

The British authorities were also in a difficult position. They had invested large amounts of money in the Transvaal goldfields. The Boers did not seem to want to develop industry but were glad to take the profit from the gold. Men like Cecil Rhodes, on the other hand, were British imperialists who had a huge stake in the area. Rhodes, the prime minister of the Cape Colony after 1887, had made a great fortune out of gold and diamonds. But he was also driven by a more abstract imperial ideal: a united southern Africa under British rule. So the British colonial secretary Joseph Chamberlain put diplomatic pressure on Transvaal – at least to give rights to the British workers there and at most to hand over sovereignty to the British.

But Kruger would not give in. A rising in Johannesburg was expected, but this failed to take place. Rhodes and the British planned to put up resistance to the revolt. But at the last minute the uprising was called off. The main British force held fire, but there was an abortive raid into the Transvaal led by Rhodes' friend Leander Starr Jameson, administrator of Rhodesia. Timed to coincide with the non-existent rising and intended to help put it down, the raid was abortive and an embarrassment to the British, who now appeared as the aggressors. Rhodes was discredited, and the British and the Boers were one step closer to war.

Meanwhile the Uitlanders were continuing to put on the pressure. In April 1899 a petition addressed to the Queen and signed by some 20,000 Uitlanders arrived in London. Britain responded by demanding that the Transvaal government give the vote to the British after five years' residence; they also restated the British claim to sovereignty. Negotiations continued but did not lead to agreement. The Boers prepared for war and feelings in Britain ran high as a result of the petition. The British authorities also gathered their forces, arranging for troops to be shipped in to augment Britain's relatively small army in southern Africa.

The start of the war

The Boers grasped the initiative, taking advantage of the small numbers of the British and crossing the border at several points with an army of 35,000 men – more than the British could muster immediately. They were well armed, with German artillery, and they knew the country. They were also mainly mounted soldiers, knowing as they did that the African grasslands would provide ample grazing for their horses. The British, by contrast, had more foot soldiers than cavalrymen.

Boer soldier

The Boers soon began to take the upper hand. Two British battalions were trapped and had to surrender at Nicholson's Nek before the Boers went on to surround and besiege a further 10,000 British men at Ladysmith, on the border with Natal. Mafeking, with its small British defensive force, and Kimberley, with its large civilian population, were the next towns to be besieged.

Soon reinforcements were arriving to assist the British. Britain, with a large and spreading empire, could draw on troops from all over the world, and detachments started to come in from Australia, New Zealand and Canada. At first, the British and their reinforcements had little success. The British commander-in-chief, Sir Redvers Buller, spread his troops too thinly to withstand the strong local opposition. The relief of Kimberley was attempted, but the British were repulsed by Boer rifles. The same happened in the northeastern district of the Cape Colony.

At Colenso in Natal there was also a Boer victory. Here British losses of 1,100 seem low by modern standards, but when they are compared with the Boer losses of only forty men, the size of the victory can be appreciated. A substantial amount of British artillery was also seized by the Boers at Colenso. Natal was an important target for the Boers because Kruger wanted to take control of Durban. This port would give him access to trade routes and avoidance of tariffs unknown in his hitherto landlocked state.

A new British strategy

British fortunes changed with the appointment of new commanders, Lord Roberts of Kandahar and Lord Kitchener of Khartoum. They quickly realized the importance of using larger forces at specific sites. So they massed their troops and concentrated on the Boer capitals, Bloemfontein and Pretoria.

They also turned their attention to the important mining centre of Kimberley. Here cavalry under General French were used. First there was a long encirclement, then French's cavalry took the town on 15 February 1900. From then on things began to improve for the British. Boer strongholds began to fall. Ladysmith, Bloemfontein, Johannesburg and Pretoria were taken with relative speed during the months between February and June. Meanwhile Mafeking, which had endured a siege for over seven months, was also relieved and Kruger and his army were on the retreat. On 27 August, the war's last pitched battle was fought at Bergendal. By this time the two principal British forces had joined up, and once more the British were victorious. The Orange Free State and the Transvaal were annexed by Britain, and the war was declared to be over.

But the Boers did not give up the fight. They launched a guerilla war, based on a campaign that stretched from northern Transvaal almost to Cape Town. The guerillas made sudden attacks on supply convoys and British camps, living off the booty they managed to capture. Kitchener responded with a scorched earth policy that was designed to take away the guerillas' shelter and sustenance. But they would not be defeated, pushing on with their campaign even while peace negotiations were in progress at Middelburg. In the end, Kitchener had to put up a network of thousands of corrugated iron block houses, fortifying the whole country and making it impossible for the guerillas to operate.

A peace treaty was finally signed on 31 May 1902. The Boers surrendered to the British but kept their personal liberty and property. They would be allowed to continue to speak Afrikaans, they would not be taxed for the war, and Britain would provide £3m for rehabilitation. There remained the question of the position of the indigenous population. The peace conference shied away from a decision on giving native black people the vote. The fate of southern Africa was sealed. By the end of hostilities 46,000 lives had been lost, including those of around 24,000 Boers, most of whom had died in refugee camps.

The peace at the end of the Boer War was designed to lead to a southern Africa in which British and Afrikaner interests would be served equally. What happened was that the marginalization of the native people set the tone for the history of South Africa until the late twentieth century.

British motives for the war

Why did the British go to war in Africa?

Lord Kitchener of Khartoum

The Transvaal has some of the richest natural resources in the world. It is easy to suppose that the British were protecting their claims on the wealth they could win from African gold and diamonds. But this is only partly true. The British, by virtue of their mining interests in the Transvaal and their control over trade from the landlocked state, were taking great commercial advantage of these resources before the war. There were also military reasons for hanging on to southern Africa. If the Suez Canal was threatened in a European war Britain would need other African naval bases. Cape Town was one obvious choice. The military objectives were clearly influential on Chamberlain at the time when the decision was made to go to war.

But there was a larger goal in mind. Above all, the British were fighting for empire, the ideal that had won them Canada, Australia and other vast areas of the globe. It was perhaps best summed up

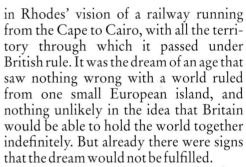

At Ladysmith, on the Natal border, the Boer troops surrounded some 10,000 British soldiers. Almost one third of these would die in the siege, which lasted for four months in 1899–1900. Such episodes typified Boer determination. These men knew the country, they took the initiative, and they stuck to the task. Only a policy of scorched earth and concentration camps could lead to their eventual defeat.

in Rhodes' vision of a railway running from the Cape to Cairo, with all the territory through which it passed under British rule. It was the dream of an age that saw nothing wrong with a world ruled from one small European island, and nothing unlikely in the idea that Britain would be able to hold the world together indefinitely. But already there were signs that the dream would not be fulfilled.

After the Boer War the British ruling class would never again assume that victory in the colonies would come easily or automatically. The tide was turning. The large colonial contribution to the British forces in Africa, and the coming global conflict, would begin the turn of the tide. Soon British leaders would be thinking less in terms of an empire, more of a commonwealth of equal nations.

The native reaction

During the period when the colonial powers were fighting it out in southern Africa, native people were rebelling against colonial occupation all over Africa. From the Ashanti rebellion in the Gold Coast (West Africa) to Somali resistance to the British and Italians in Somaliland (in the east), from struggles in Sudan to revolts in Rhodesia, Africa was not unresponsive to foreign rule at the end of the nineteenth century. Such movements, although they achieved little at the time, were part of the same questioning of the colonial presence as the Boer War and the peace that followed it. In many parts of Africa such resistance would eventually lead to strong nationalist movements and to the emancipation of the indigenous peoples. In South Africa, with the initiative of nationalism in the hands of the Afrikaaners, the story would be markedly different.

MARIE CURIE'S DISCOVERY OF RADIUM

A breakthrough in research on radioactivity

Our knowledge of radioactivity owes much to the scientist we have come to know as Marie Curie. Born Maria Sklodowska in Warsaw in 1867, she was the daughter of an impoverished teacher of mathematics and physics. From an early age she showed that she had a powerful intelligence and an unusually good memory, and she was soon supplementing the family income by teaching. In 1891 she went to Paris and enrolled at the Sorbonne. Three years later she had the best degree of her class and had married Pierre Curie, with whom she would work.

During the late 1890s physicists were fascinated by the work of Henri Becquerel on uranium. Becquerel had discovered that salts of uranium emitted rays similar to X-rays. Marie Curie decided to test other substances to see if they too gave off these rays and to establish what else she could find out about the rays. The initial stages of Marie's research were greatly helped by a discovery made by Pierre. Pierre Curie discovered the phenomenon of piezo-electricity – the generation of an electric charge when a non-conducting crystal is compressed. Pierre's piezo-electric quartz electrometer was a device that could detect the minute electrical charges Marie was looking for.

Such assistance was valuable to Marie. She was a woman working in an alien, male environment, and often found it difficult to get acceptance, let alone equipment. So she needed to begin her work with a series of simple experiments. She therefore tested as many different substances with the electrometer as she could lay her hands on. Thorium and its compounds, she quickly discovered, behaved in a similar way to uranium.

Marie then started to work on different compounds of uranium and thorium. She established that the electric current produced by uranium did not vary according to the state of the compound (whether it was wet or dry, in lumps or powder) but only according to the amount of uranium present. This was a very important piece of information. It suggested that the current did not come from some interaction between the molecules of the substance, but from the atom itself.

The mystery of pitchblende

One of the substances Marie was using in her experiments was pitchblende, a mineral containing uranium oxide. Pitchblende was interesting because it seemed to emit rays at a rate some four times greater than that of uranium. Could there be some unknown substance in the pitchblende which was causing this activity? Using measurement techniques that they developed together the Curies were able to announce the discovery of two new elements in pitchblende. These elements they named polonium (for Marie's native country) and radium. The phenomenon of electrical activity produced by uranium and the new elements they named radioactivity. Pierre also worked on the action of magnetic fields on the rays given out by radium, discovering that there were three different types of radioactive particles, positive, negative and neutral, which physicist Sir Ernest Rutherford would later call alpha, beta and gamma rays.

In 1903 the Curies and Henri Becquerel were jointly awarded the Nobel physics prize for the discovery of radioactivity. It was a triumph, but other forms of recognition were slow in coming for Marie. She still did not have a university appointment, for example. Only when Pierre died in 1906 was she appointed to her husband's old professorship, becoming in the process the first woman to teach at the Sorbonne. Marie's work was thus a breakthrough for women as well as for science. Entering physics had been difficult enough; now she had shown that women could enter the great European educational bastions. Although it would take decades for science and education to be opened up in the way suggested by her success, her achievement was nevertheless a significant pioneering one.

And Marie continued her work. In 1910 she isolated pure metallic radium for the first time. The following year she was awarded the Nobel Prize for Chemistry for her discovery of radium and polonium and for obtaining pure radium. She continued to work on the medical applications of X-rays and on radioactivity until her death (caused by exposure to the rays she had spent her working life studying).

Marie Curie made a unique contribution to the discovery of radioactivity and to research on the radioactive elements. She brought to light the element that offered many a treatment for cancer, as well as helping to develop the diagnostic use of X-rays. Her work also looked forward to that of her daughter Irène and son-in-law Frédéric Joliot. This second husband-and-wife team worked on nuclear fission and the production of nuclear energy. Finally, by doing what she did and gaining recognition for it, Marie Curie achieved much for the position of women in education and science.

It is not always the search for new knowledge alone that motivates a scientist to choose one area of research over another. Often the reasons are far less lofty. Marie Curie had limited equipment and resources at her disposal and so began a series of tests on substances that were relatively easy to obtain. It was this that led her to the mineral pitchblende, and it was pitchblende that led her to the concept of radioactivity and the element radium. But this is not to belittle her achievement. Marie Curie needed great determination to continue her work and rigorous scientific method to complete it. What was more it was work that would lead to significant achievements in the future, both from Curie's daughter Irène and in the wider scientific community.

WRIGHT BROTHERS' FIRST FLIGHT

The beginning of controlled, powered flight

For thousands of years people have dreamed that they could fly like birds. The classical myth of Icarus, whose father Daedalus made wings of feathers stuck together with wax that melted when he flew too close to the sun, shows how long this dream had been expressed. Nearer our own time Renaissance man Leonardo da Vinci drew designs for a helicopter and a device with flapping wings that was meant to carry a man through the air. And science fiction stories by Jules Verne were illustrated with further fascinating bird-like contraptions.

Many of these early ideas about human flight understandably involved attempts to imitate the overall structure and appearance of a bird. They also tried to make the pilot's muscles the source of power. But the first successful flights were made using a device that did not look anything like a bird at all. Flight for man and beast began in 1783 when the French brothers Joseph and Etienne Montgolfier made a hot-air balloon. First they sent up a sheep, a duck and a cockerel on an eight-minute flight above a park outside Paris. Soon after, the Montgolfiers had their first human passengers. Two friends risked the perils of the air while the brothers remained safely on the ground. The friends came safely back to earth and the history of ballooning had begun.

Gliding and hopping

For over a century, the hot-air balloon seemed to offer the greatest potential for flight. But towards the end of the nineteenth century there were numerous experiments with more bird-like structures, with varying degrees of success. Serious inventors knew that flapping wings connected to a human pilot's limbs would not give enough power for flight. But there were some significant experiments using steam power, the most obvious choice in the nineteenth century.

Two pioneers who did key work in this field were the Englishmen William Samuel Henson and John Stringfellow. Their so-called Aerial Steam Carriage, although it seemed at the time an eccentric design and contained a steam engine that was too heavy for flight, embodied several of the principles of powered flight. It had wings with curved surfaces to provide lift, it had a tail plane with adjustable control surfaces, and it had a three-wheeled landing gear. The model with a twenty-foot wingspan that Henson and Stringfellow built would, perhaps, have flown with a lighter engine. Its makers also conceived of an idea that would give powered flight its *raison d'être* – eventually, Henson predicted, worldwide companies would provide air travel to places all over the globe. He even tried to persuade the British parliament to fund an Aerial Steam Carriage Transit Company. The idea was simply too far ahead of its time.

To supplement the low power of their steam engines some pioneers took to launching their craft from a downward-sloping ramp. In fact, the first powered flight with a human on board was probably made in such a craft, in 1874. The craft was designed by French naval officer Felix du Temple de la Croix and was powered by a hot-air engine. It made its short flight at Brest. But the design was not taken up and du Temple's achievement languishes in obscurity. We know very little about his aeroplane. Together with other 'hops', such as those in aircraft designed in Russia by Alexander Mozhaisky and in England by Sir Hiram Maxim, this achievement did not have a great influence and is of interest mainly to historians of flight.

The first real achievements came with gliders. Amongst the most prominent pioneers were English baronet Sir George Cayley and German engineer Otto Lilienthal. Cayley made numerous designs and models and, towards the end of his life, produced a full-size glider that probably made a brief, uncontrolled flight. But Cayley was more important for his theories, pointing out, for example, that an effective flying machine should have separate mechanisms for propulsion, lift and control. Lilienthal was more successful in practical terms, making over 2,000 flights in various gliders before he lost his life when one of his craft crashed.

The death of Lilienthal and that of Percy Pilcher, a glider pioneer who died in the same way, meant that popular doubts about the future of flight were reinforced at the end of the 1890s. For many, the idea that it was simply unnatural for people to try to emulate the birds prevailed. It was not just a case of uncertainties about safety. There was no way of powering any of these early craft: a steam engine that would provide enough power to lift a person and an aircraft off the ground was still far too large and heavy. But some enthusiasts pushed on. The American Samuel Pierpont Langley, for example, built a miniature aircraft with a small steam engine. It flew for over a mile in 1896, reaching a speed of about twenty-five mph.

The American authorities were impressed with Langley's model and what it could do. The War Department were particularly interested. They offered Langley

Wilbur and Orville Wright

$50,000 if he could come up with a design that could carry a person. Langley took up the challenge. First of all he made more models, using a petrol engine for the first time, a decision that would turn out to be of vital importance. By 1903 he had a man-carrying craft ready for testing. He had worked with engineer Charles Manly, designer of the fifty-two horsepower radial petrol engine that powered the craft.

The design looked promising, the engine was powerful and the research on the models had been extremely thorough. In October 1903 a houseboat on the Potomac River was prepared as a take-off platform. But when the take-off was attempted the aeroplane hit part of the launch gear and dropped pathetically into the water.

It was the end for Langley. He had no more money to carry on his experiments, although his scientific attitude and his success with smaller crafts show that if he had persevered he would probably have succeeded. But in Dayton, Ohio, something was stirring.

The Wright brothers

Bicycle manufacturers Wilbur and Orville Wright were already coming close to the climax of their experiments with flight when Langley had his accident. They had started to fuel their enthusiasm for flight by gliding using several devices – a kite controlled by cables and more than one conventional glider – before turning to powered flight. Their background in the sort of light engineering needed to make bicycles undoubtedly helped them. This included the design and manufacture of precision parts, the use of a chain and gear wheels to transmit power, and in the experience gained in the control of a vehicle in more than one plane. None of these things were new to the Wrights. They also had the best possible approach to the problems of powered flight. They worked in small experimental steps, testing each

one on gliders and models before applying it to anything like a full-scale prototype.

But there were more skills to learn. The key was control, which had to be much more complex on an aircraft than on a bicycle. They started by trying to control their craft by warping the wings. But this was not enough. They realized that they also needed adjustable rudders to control the aircraft as it turned. So they tried a

The brothers experimenting with a kite

variety of designs, mounting sets of wings on one of their bicycles to test their theories. These tests continued as the brothers designed and built a fifty-foot kite to test the wing-warping control. This was followed by various piloted gliders. They also built a wind tunnel, to make their tests even more useful. They worked carefully, over a period of four years, with painstaking recording of data.

For 'live' tests of the various gliders the brothers went to the sand dunes of Kitty Hawk, North Carolina, where there was plenty of wind and slopes of the right gradients. The tests went well and eventually the brothers came up with the design that they thought would be capable of powered, controlled, piloted flight. The machine, which they named *Flyer*, was a

biplane. It had a single petrol engine which was linked to hand-carved, aerofoil-shaped propellers by bicycle chains. The rudders on the tailplane were controlled by the pilot, who lay down to fly the aircraft. It looked flimsy, but it had a good chance of working. The wings had the correct aerofoil section to give lift; the engine was light and powerful enough; the propellers were well designed; the controls worked, even though the front 'tailplane' design would prove less successful than the rear tailplanes of Henson and later designers. The hard work had paid off.

And so, on 17 December 1903, the brothers quietly went to Kitty Hawk to try *Flyer* in the air. Orville (who would pilot the aircraft), Wilbur and five others were the only people there. When *Flyer* travelled along its launch rail a brisk headwind was blowing and Wilbur anxiously ran alongside to steady the wing. But the curved wing surfaces did their job: *Flyer* lifted gently and flew straight for twelve seconds before catching on the sand. It was long enough for one of the Wrights' companions to record the occasion for posterity by taking a photograph. It was also enough to encourage the brothers to try further flights.

That day they tried three more times. The climax was a flight that lasted some fifty-nine seconds and took *Flyer* 852 feet across the dunes. But it seemed as if the triumph would be short lived. As the small party stood discussing what they would do next one of Kitty Hawk's brisk winds picked up one end of *Flyer's* wing and buffetted it across the sand. By the time they caught up with it the aircraft was ruined. Wilbur and Orville had to go back to Dayton and start building again.

But the brothers were not disheartened. They were not going to let the mishap spoil four years' work. And they knew they had a viable design. They built another, improved aircraft the following year and a third in 1905. By this time they had a machine that would stay in the air and could be controlled accurately by the pilot. It was capable of flights lasting up to thirty-eight minutes, covering some twenty-four miles. By 1906 they had filed patents and founded a company to build aeroplanes.

The Wrights had taken powered, controlled flight from idea to action, and from action to commercial availability. They had also shown that the best way to succeed in the air was to test, test, and test again. No longer would the haphazard approach of the first would-be airmen, with designs taken straight from concept to full-scale trial and all the risks to life that this entailed, be the preserve of aviation. Of all the pioneer aviators, Wilbur and Orville Wright were responsible for the dawn of the age of flight.

After the Wrights

The success of the Wright brothers, whose aircraft company did well at least until the death of Wilbur in 1912, inspired other designers and aviators. The search was on for more efficient aeroplanes that would take their pilots further and faster than the early Flyers. Among the most successful were the triplane in which British pioneer A. V. Roe flew in 1909 and the almost modern-looking monoplane that Frenchman Louis Blériot used in his famous flight across the English Channel in the same year.

Blériot's flight was celebrated for its length and for the fact that it showed the potential of aircraft for making sea crossings that could previously only be achieved by boat. It was also a signal of the invention's commercial potential: in the two days after his flight, Blériot received more than one hundred orders for aircraft. Clearly the day would not be far off when Henson's dream of international air travel would become a reality.

Another early vision of the aircraft's usefulness, in war rather than in peace, would soon come true. The US Army was not interested in the the Wrights' flying machine when the brothers contacted the military in 1905. But when war loomed in Europe, the opponents' views were different from this. No one could afford to ignore this new technology, and both sides in World War I quickly established training programmes for pilots and began to fund research into new aeroplane designs. The war undoubtedly did much to stimulate aeronautical research, although the actual aircraft used were still very basic. But they caught the imagination, the aviator became a popular hero and, by the time the war ended, the future of the aeroplane as a means of transport was ensured.

Perhaps the most celebrated of the aviator heroes was Charles Lindbergh. His aircraft *Spirit of St Louis* made the first non-stop flight from New York to Paris. Lindbergh heightened the achievement by flying solo and using an aeroplane with only one engine. By using an engine that was cooled by the airstream, Lindbergh saved weight. By filling up most of the body with tanks he had enough fuel to get through the 3,600-mile flight. Lindbergh was lionized after he made his flight successfully. It seemed that the ultimate had been reached. Airmen were truly the masters of the world.

It was a small band of people who gathered on 17 December 1903 on the sand dunes at Kitty Hawk, North Carolina to test the Wrights' Flyer. The brothers did not seek publicity, although they knew the design was very near to perfection. There were some twelve seconds of triumph for the brothers before the Flyer's *wing caught on one of the dunes, bringing the aircraft down. But the designers were not disheartened. They would soon have a viable aircraft and the world would have a new form of transport.*

MODEL T FORD

The principles of mass production applied to an item that everyone wanted

The motor car first appeared at the end of the nineteenth century. Amongst the numerous pioneers whose research made it possible, two men stood out, the Germans Carl Benz and Gottlieb Daimler. These men worked independently on the key technology that would make this type of powered transport possible: the petrol-driven internal combustion engine. From the 1860s to the 1880s, Daimler worked on a lightweight petrol engine and in 1885 he tried mounting it on a bicycle before progressing to trials with boats and carriages. Benz was working at the same time, and first demonstrated his three-wheeled car in 1885. Daimler's first car – a four-wheeler – followed in 1889.

It did not seem that these early vehicles would start a revolution in transport. They were slow, uncomfortable and difficult to drive. In particular the gearing of the early models was not low enough to handle hills: you had to get out and push. Breakdowns and accidents were a regular part of using the first automobiles. On Benz's first public demonstration of his three-wheeler he managed to drive it into a wall.

But the pioneers pressed on, improving the comfort and quality of their vehicles and, eventually, the speed. But cars were still built one by one, by hand, and so were only being made in small numbers. For some time, motoring would be the preserve of the rich, and would be more of a leisure activity than a reliable way of getting from A to B. It would not be in Europe that industrialists would first tap the potential mass-market for cars, but in the country that would become identified more than any other with the automobile – the USA. Probably the first person to exploit this market was Russell Olds, manufacturer of the Merry Oldsmobile, who produced 12,000 of these vehicles between 1901 and 1904.

But the man who did most to exploit the motor car in its early years was Henry

Henry Ford

Ford. In so doing he not only unlocked the potential of the automobile, he gave new mobility to thousands of Americans (particularly farmers living far away from the railroad) at whom his product was aimed, and he devised a system of production – mass production with a constantly moving assembly line – that was to be influential in industry everywhere.

Henry Ford was a farmer turned engineer who acquired his enthusiasm for cars early in the history of motoring. After a time in the fields he moved to Detroit, the town where he first saw an internal combustion engine. He built his first car, which he called the Quadricycle because of its four bicycle wheels, in 1896 in Detroit. For the next twelve years he would work away until he came up with a design for a car that would change the face of transport.

The association of cars with glamour and status was something that started early on in the history of motoring, with the rare and expensive products of the European manufacturers. But there was nothing glamorous about Henry Ford's vehicle. It was basic, ugly and only available in black paintwork. But it was also

solid, versatile, easy to mend and capable of transporting an American farmer across rough tracks with a load of feed. It was called the Model T, though it became affectionately known as the Tin Lizzie.

At $850 in 1908 the Model T was costly. But it was exactly what thousands of Americans – especially rural Americans – wanted. And compared to other cars it was not that expensive: most models that came anywhere near the specification of Ford's cost around $2,000.

Not surprisingly, the Model T became popular. Orders came in faster than Ford's factory could produce the cars. And Ford knew that if he could make the Model T cheaper, the market would expand even more dramatically. The answer was simple. Use the same facilities and the same workforce, but speed up production. He was already employing specialist workers to carry out separate parts of the production process. In other words, follow the example of the industrialists who had embraced mass production.

The rise of mass production

Mass production itself is older than the automobile industry. Back in the late eighteenth century, the American Revolutionary wars had stimulated the demand for rapidly made firearms. By 1800 Eli Whitney was making guns with many interchangeable parts, using employees who specialized in making specific parts and other workers who put the guns together. Simeon North was another arms manufacturer of the period who worked in a similar way.

The development of the mass production system was pushed forward in the second half of the nineteenth century when more sophisticated machine tools were developed. As items such as lathes and milling machines became more accurate, the amount of hand finishing required was reduced and production speeded up still further. Soon mass production

1913 Ford

spread from the arms industry to other areas, such as the manufacture of clocks, agricultural machinery, typewriters and bicycles. Items like shoes and textiles, although not assembled from parts in the same way, also had some of the skills of mass production applied to them, resulting in standardized products assembled quickly with a minimum of hand work.

It was not surprising that these techniques were used in the car industry. Russell Olds took the route to mass production after a fire swept through his automobile factory in Detroit. Because of the damage, and the need to get production going again quickly, Olds arranged for local engineering firms to make many car parts for him. These were then brought to the main production plant for assembly by Olds' workers. Trolleys of parts were wheeled from one worker to another and the cars were put together more quickly than before. In 1901 425 Oldsmobiles were built; the following year the figure had risen to 3,750; in 1903 it was 5,000.

Soon Olds was not the only car manufacturer using mass production methods. An important pioneer was the Cadillac company, which introduced totally interchangeable parts for its vehicles in 1908. This made true mass production possible, with parts made to standard specifications in a range of different specialized workshops being shipped to a factory that did nothing but assemble cars. A dramatic demonstration in 1908 proved how effective the method could be. Three Cadillacs were taken to pieces. The parts were then mixed with spares from stock and mechanics reassembled the cars successfully. Such a method made repairs much more straightforward too.

Ford's leap forward

But in 1913 Ford took mass production a vital step further than at the Oldsmobile and Cadillac factories. Ford's assembly line actually moved. The basic frame of each car passed along a slowly advancing conveyor belt which kept it at the right height and moved it at the correct speed. Workers on either side of the line added parts to the car which were brought to them by smaller conveyor belts. Thus each worker had a specific, specialized role, there was no wasted effort in trundling parts and half-finished cars around, and the production process speeded up accordingly. This was the crucial step in streamlining production, and Ford's methods soon spread to other industries, bringing goods that were hitherto expensive luxuries into the mass market.

Originally it had taken Ford's workers over twelve hours to build a Model T. With the moving assembly line a car could be put together in about an hour and a half. The savings in cost, the increase in sales, and the improvement in profits were all dramatic. It was a spectacular success for Ford, but his workers did not take to it. They were expected to produce more cars in the same time, and they were losing out in terms of job satisfaction as they struggled to keep up with the pace of the line.

One of Henry Ford's first cars

Soon they began to leave Ford's factory in droves.

Ford knew that this state of affairs could not continue. There was not an infinite pool of workers on which to draw – and the pool of workers willing to make Model Ts for about $2.50 a day shrank even more when the reputation of Ford's factory spread around. Unions did not help, since Ford had a ruthless, autocratic way with union leaders. Ford came up with a radical solution. The workforce was helping him to secure greater and greater profits. Why not give the workers a share in the profits they helped to create? Ford set aside ten million dollars for his profit-sharing scheme. Split between the workers it doubled their pay.

Most industrialists were doubtful about Ford's profit-sharing scheme. They knew of nothing quite like it and their instincts told them that it would not work. But Ford proved them wrong. The profit-sharing system gave the workers an incentive to put all their efforts into the arduous methods of production that their employer had devised. Numbers of vehicles produced increased yet again. And the new production methods paid off in another way. Ford could increase demand still further by cutting the price of the Model T. By 1916 you could buy a new Ford for a mere $360. Even Ford's own factory workers could afford one.

The Model T was perhaps the greatest success-story of American industry. In spite of the developments in automobile engineering that took place in the years after the introduction of the moving assembly line in 1913, Ford's factory continued to make Model Ts in great numbers. It was a winning formula. By 1925 half the cars in the world were Model Ts. By 1927, the year production finally ended, around fifteen million of the cars had been made. Only then did improved engines, starting systems, bodywork, suspension and the like oust the Model T.

And even after this Model Ts, rugged and easy to maintain, stayed on the roads – and the farm tracks – for decades.

Henry Ford was a pivotal figure in the history of America and the world. He took an already-existing invention and refined it to make the motor car and the independence that came with it available to millions. He developed a practical system of mass production that had a wide influence in many other forms of industry the world over. He gave American manufacturing a boost and a focus – car production would long be a mainstay of

American capitalism. And by giving Americans access to the car he gave them a special way of defining themselves. For the freedom of the road provided by the automobile, the ability to get up and go anywhere was something that appealed especially to the spirit of individualism in the American culture.

As the enthusiasm for the motor car spread through America, other car-producing firms began to prosper. It was seen that Ford's methods worked best with a large company and the consequent economies of scale. Already in 1908 William C.

Durant had founded General Motors by buying up a number of small car companies. Buick, Cadillac, Oldsmobile and several others were all absorbed into General Motors, which would eventually oust Ford in the 1920s as America's largest motor manufacturer. It is difficult to imagine this success coming so quickly without Henry Ford. Even the high car-ownership figures that still prevail in the USA can be seen as Ford's legacy.

The automobile was a product ideally suited to mass production. Once the parts had been standardized, it was mainly a question of working out a logical order of assembly. Then the part-finished cars could be rolled down an assembly line and further parts attached along the way. Here, completed chassis have been assembled on the ground floor of the factory while bodies and seats have been put together on the floor above. The bodies could then be lowered on to the chassis and bolted in place to make the finished cars. There were obvious advantages in that vehicles could be put together with unprecedented speed and with lower costs than before. Standardized parts also made replacement easier when faults developed.

OUTBREAK OF WORLD WAR I

The great war that changed the face of the world

The events of World War I are well known, at least in outline. The style of fighting – trench warfare – and the massive casualties to which it led are still better known, and have come to stand for the waste of human life and resources which war entails. What is less familiar is the way the conflict began, and how an apparently stable Europe erupted into conflict at the beginning of the twentieth century.

Balancing power in Europe

Bismarck, the chancellor who had presided over the unification of Germany in 1871, continued in office until 1890. During this time the German economy continued to prosper, and Bismarck carried on his policy of working with the other European countries to keep a stable balance of power in the continent while maintaining Germany's status and central position.

France was always a potential enemy of Germany because the new German nation incorporated the territories of Alsace and Lorraine. So for Bismarck maintaining the balance of power meant first of all isolating France from her European allies. It also meant creating an alliance with Austria-Hungary and Russia to preserve stability in eastern Europe. But although France remained isolated, Bismarck had less success with Austria-Hungary and Russia, whose interests were in conflict, particularly in the Balkan region.

Another powerful European presence was Italy which had, like Germany, emerged as a nation in the nineteenth century. Austria-Hungary, Germany and Italy formed a triple alliance in 1882, again with the avowed aim of preserving peace in Europe and keeping Germany secure.

Britain, although a considerable power with prospering industry and a growing empire, seemed less of a threat to Germany. Britain's energies were taken up with imperial expansion farther afield. Nevertheless, Britain too was drawn into various European peace-keeping alliances, notably with Italy, and then with both Italy and Austria-Hungary to preserve peace in the Mediterranean and Near East.

So by the time Bismarck left office in 1890 Europe seemed to be stable and Germany was certainly rich. But there were still threats to peace. France remained resentful over the German takeover of Alsace and Lorraine. The German alliance with Austria-Hungary, by excluding Russia, pushed France and Russia closer together in spite of the chancellor's attempts to woo Russia. And there was also tension between Germany and Britain as a result of Britain's success in colonizing Africa. The growth of Britain's empire, and the trade which resulted from it, depended on formidable sea power. It is not surprising, therefore, that the late 1890s saw the construction of a strong German navy. Such a fleet would deter Britain from attacking Germany. It might, so it was thought, also be used as a bargaining tool to gain Germany a share in British imperial possessions.

Meanwhile, Germany's economy was growing fast. An increasing population, a good early start in industry and the defeat of France in 1870–71 (giving Germany Alsace and Lorraine, where much of the industry was based) had stimulated a big increase in production. By 1910 Germany was producing seven times as much coal as France and four times as much steel. This success was also reflected in military terms. The Germans could produce more and better arms than her rivals. And her increasing population, together with the alliance with Austria-Hungary, could provide a massive army.

The Moroccan crisis

Germany's position seemed very strong. But in any game of diplomatic strategy the responses of one's opponents are difficult to predict. Eventually, Germany would get the balance wrong and the fragility of the system of alliances and re-alliances built up would become evident.

Something like this happened in 1905 when the Kaiser's ministers asked him to pay a visit to the Sultan of Morocco in order to confirm that the Moroccan ruler would give his support to Germany against French expansion. The Germans hoped that such an alliance would also have the additional effect of gaining British support against the French. But the effort misfired. As a result of the German intervention, France strengthened her position in Morocco and came to an agreement with Britain. Two years later Britain reached agreement with Russia about the two powers' involvement in Asia. The result was an alliance between France, Britain and Russia against Germany, Austria-Hungary and Italy.

Oddly, the Germans persisted with their attempt at intervention in Morocco, sending the gunboat *Panther* to Agadir in 1911. All this succeeded in doing was to stimulate Britain and France into further defensive preparations. Britain increased investment in its navy and took measures to defend the English Channel and the French coast. France made similar moves in the Mediterranean.

Archduke Franz Ferdinand of Austria, heir apparent to the throne of Austria-Hungary, was shot in Sarajevo, the Bosnian capital, on 28 June 1914. It seemed to many that the Archduke was tempting fate by appearing in public in Sarajevo on that date, the anniversary of the battle at which Serbia lost its independence, especially since he had already narrowly escaped a bomb attack earlier in the day. But when Franz Ferdinand was killed by a young Serbian, the result was far more catastrophic than the loss of one imperial life. Out of the panic that followed the Archduke's death came a far greater chaos that would engulf the entire world.

Balkan tensions

Trouble was also brewing at the other end of Europe. Germany's once-powerful ally Austria-Hungary, an empire made up of numerous linguistic and ethnic groups, was facing increasing pressure from some of its minorities. The Hungarians already had autonomy. Groups such as the Czechs, Poles, Jews and Serbs were beginning to press for power and independence.

Ironically, Austria-Hungary's position was made more difficult by the weakness of a neighbour, Turkey. Capitalizing on Turkey's decline, Austria-Hungary took control of two Turkish provinces, Bosnia and Herzegovina, in 1878. With them it acquired a vocal population of Serbs, more indeed than the total population of Serbia itself, which was also part of the empire. The result, as the national consciousness of the Serbs began to grow, was conflict between the minority and the empire. The Austro-Hungarian authorities began by imposing a trade ban on Serbian agricultural products (the so-called 'pig war'). When Serbia found markets elsewhere, Austria-Hungary formally annexed Bosnia and Herzegovina in 1908.

Serbian resistance went underground, but remained strong. Secret groups forged links between nationalists in Serbia itself and in Bosnia and Herzegovina. But the resentment of the Serbs was not only against the empire. In 1912 a Balkan League was formed, involving Greece, Montenegro and Serbia, with the aim of expelling the Turks from Europe. The success of this enterprise, entailing the participation of a large Serbian force, showed the empire, and Germany too, how strong the Serbian threat might be. It looked to the Austro-Hungarians as if they would have to crush Serbia in order to preserve the empire. Meanwhile Germany would try to prevent Russia from getting involved in the conflict and began assembling an army in Bosnia in preparation for an invasion of Serbia.

This was the position in early 1914 when the Austro-Hungarians decided to send the emperor's nephew, Archduke Franz Ferdinand, on a military and diplomatic mission to Bosnia. He would

Archduke Franz Ferdinand

inspect the imperial troops and see how the preparations for war were progressing while paying lip-service to the role he hoped the Serbian peoples could play within the empire.

One of the planned highlights of the visit was to be a ceremonial drive through the Bosnian capital Sarajevo. The date that was chosen for this, 28 June, was the date of a Turkish victory at Kossovo in 1389 when the Serbians had been deprived of their independence. The nationalists saw this as an inflammatory gesture and planned ways to cause as much disruption as possible.

In spite of poor security, the Archduke survived a bomb attack while driving through the streets of Sarajevo. It seemed that he would be safe and, although he was advised not to venture out later in the day, he set out once more to visit a member of his party who had been injured in the blast. It was on this second trip that, after his driver had taken a wrong turning, the Archduke was shot dead by a young Bosnian called Gavrilo Princip. Although he was a subject of the emperor, it appeared that Princip had been trained, sponsored and supported by Serbia. War now seemed inevitable.

The start of the war

The Austrians soon established that they would have full support from Germany. It was clear that Russia and France would then also join the war to fight against Germany, but Russia's strength was growing almost daily and it seemed to the Germans that to fight soon would give them a better chance. Also, the recent widening of the Kiel Canal allowed German ships to transit the North Sea, invaluable if Britain should enter the war too.

In fact, Britain made some efforts to stop the war. But British overtures for a joint appeal to Austria from France, Germany, Italy and Britain itself only made the empire move more quickly. On 28 July Austria formally declared war on Serbia; they attacked Belgrade the following day.

The Germans looked forward to a short war. But what was justly called by contemporaries the 'Great War' would last for four years. It would involve the whole of Europe, the Middle East, parts of Africa, and even the Far East, where German colonies were attacked and taken by soldiers from Australia, New Zealand and Japan. And the casualties would be unprecedented.

In turning from a European war into a world war, the conflict that was ignited at Sarajevo signaled a change in the way the world was perceived. The nineteenth century had been a great era of nationalism, seeing the foundation of many nations that have had important parts to play on the political stage. But while these nations were to remain influential, the twentieth century would become increasingly a period in which people would think of the world as a whole, or as dominated by great blocs of nations. The first global war influenced this new perception.

World War I also altered our ideas about war itself. Subsequent wars have been fought differently, with a less ruthless use of the common soldier as a target for the enemy, with more attention to the technological resources at the disposal of the generals. The war changed the perceptions of people outside the military too. It was not simply that the reality of war seemed to contradict the glorious calls to patriotic instincts. Rather that the great casualties and the appalling conditions of trench warfare inspired renewed questioning about the validity of war as a way of solving human problems. But if such perceptions are valid, World War I was not the 'war to end war' that many of its participants hoped.

EINSTEIN'S THEORIES OF RELATIVITY

All-embracing concepts that changed our perception of the universe

While the world's great universities and research establishments are responsible for much of the important scientific work that is carried out, sometimes new work is so original that it does not find a place within the establishment. This was the case with the early work of physicist Albert Einstein. In the opening years of this century Einstein was an obscure figure, working in the Patent Office in Berne, Switzerland. But while he worked on the patents he was also carrying out his own research which was to take theoretical physics into new directions.

In 1905 this work bore fruit in four papers. Amongst these were the publication that announced Einstein's Special Theory of Relativity and the paper that laid out the relationship between mass and energy. Together with the General Theory of Relativity, which Einstein published in 1915, these publications would revolutionize physics and radically change our view of the world. But to begin with, they were scarcely noticed. Einstein was not given a university post until four years after publishing the Special Theory. But by 1921 he was a Nobel physics laureate.

The Special Theory
Einstein's work related to light and the way it travels. Previous scientists had established that light travels from one point to another, as does sound, even though we cannot actually see this for ourselves. It therefore makes sense to talk about the speed, or velocity, of light. Some scientists had even gone so far as to attempt to measure the velocity of light, although an accurate measurement of the speed of light (about 186,000 miles per second) was not made until after Einstein published his General Theory.

Having established that light has a finite velocity, scientists felt it necessary to ask through what medium light travels. Sound was known to travel by creating vibrations in the air. Light seemed to be able to travel through space but, given that it seemed unlikely that it could travel through a vacuum, scientists theorized a medium called the ether through which light was supposed to travel.

Scientists in the nineteenth century clung to the idea of the ether and it took someone of the courage of Einstein to question its existence. But Einstein insisted that, in spite of scientists' efforts to prove its presence, the ether could not be detected. Einstein next noticed something about the velocity of light that sets it apart from other types of speed. Most forms of velocity are relative. We say that an object moves relative to something else. The effect of this on velocity has been shown by what happens when someone throws a ball from a moving train. If you throw the ball at 10 mph, it will move at that speed relative to you. But if the train is moving at 30 mph towards a bridge and you have thrown the ball in the same direction as the train is moving, the ball will be moving at a speed of 40 mph relative to the bridge.

Einstein perceived that light does not behave in this way. The velocity of light is constant relative to an observer – light always travels at 186,000 miles per second, irrespective of the observer's own motion. The velocity of light is absolute.

Albert Einstein

From his two postulates (that the ether cannot be detected and that the velocity of light is absolute) Einstein was able to make some extraordinary deductions about the universe. First, he made the surprising assertion that when bodies travel at very high speeds approaching the speed of light they tend to shrink and become heavier. When an object is moving in relation to an observer its mass increases the greater its velocity relative to the observer. What is more, no object can actually reach the speed of light – if an object did so it would become infinitely heavy and have a length of zero.

One thing emerged from the Special Theory that came to have an important bearing on the twentieth century: the idea that a very small amount of matter can be equivalent to a very large amount of energy. As we have seen, a fast-moving object has an increased mass; the object must also have increased energy as a heavier object has more energy than a lighter one moving at the same velocity. Einstein found the relationship of additional energy to additional mass, which he expressed in the famous equation $E = mc^2$. In this equation E is the equivalent energy, m the mass of the object and c the velocity of light. One result of the discovery of this relationship between mass and energy was the atomic bomb.

Another important result of the Special Theory was a change in our concept of time. Einstein described the time-dilation effect. This describes what happens when two observers move at a constant velocity relative to each other: it appears to each observer that the time processes of the other are slowed down. So to Einstein, time was no longer an absolute universal phenomenon but could flow at different rates for different observers.

Einstein presented his finding as theories, supported by mathematical calculations and equations. Subsequent scientists have shown his findings to be correct by

Albert Einstein was a scientist who took the entire cosmos as his subject. His theories of relativity could be applied to the universe as a whole, or to particles so tiny that they could only be measured decades after Einstein did his theoretical work. As well as changing our view of the universe, Einstein's work also led to the development of the atomic bomb, a fact that led the physicist to campaign for nuclear disarmament after World War II.

experimental means. For example, nuclear physicists have built apparatus that enables matter to be accelerated to very high velocities. They have found that the mass of protons (the nuclei of hydrogen atoms) travelling at some 177,000 miles per second does indeed increase dramatically. Even the time-dilation effect has been proved, using the rates of vibration of hydrogen atoms as a measure of time.

The General Theory
The Special Theory dealt with bodies that were moving at a constant velocity: it did not deal with bodies that were speeding up or slowing down. It was to this problem that Einstein addressed himself in his General Theory of Relativity. One of the central concepts of the General Theory is that of gravity. Einstein revised Newton's ideas about gravity. He asks us to imagine an elevator that is falling because of the earth's gravitational pull. If you drop a ball inside the elevator, it will appear to 'hang' in the air because the elevator is falling as quickly as the ball. From this example Einstein generalized the principle of equivalence: it makes no difference whether a body is acted on by gravity or by acceleration, the effect will be the same. Another way to look at the same idea is to imagine being inside an accelerating rocket. The feeling that the pilot experiences when accelerating is the same as that when the rocket passes by a planet and senses its gravitational pull.

This idea led Einstein to look at the way planets orbit the Sun. Newton had proposed that they have stationary elliptical orbits. Einstein showed that the ellipse rotates slowly in space. Another idea that comes out of the General Theory is that gravity has an effect on light. A beam of light can be pulled towards a planet as a result of gravity, just as we are pulled towards the Earth by the same force. This effect was proved experimentally by observing the effect of the Sun's gravity on rays of light coming from stars beyond the solar system.

The influence of Einstein's theories
The most dramatic consequence of Einstein's work was the production of the atomic bomb. Although a pacifist, Einstein felt compelled to tell the US government about the possibility of creating an atomic explosion when he saw that the rise of Nazism threatened to cause war in Europe. After the war Einstein continued to campaign for peace and understanding between the peoples of the world.

Einstein's theories also had an important influence on the way people looked at the universe as a whole. Einstein deduced from his ideas about how light rays could be bent by gravity that there could be no 'straight lines' in space since any ray of light would eventually be bent so that it would finally return to its point of origin. Similarly notional space explorers who could travel across the universe would eventually end up where they began. So Einstein's universe was finite, unlike Newton's infinite universe. Although these ideas have now been revised, they help to show the all-embracing implications of Einstein's work, from the behaviour of the smallest nuclear particles to the structure of the universe.

RUSSIAN REVOLUTION

The movement that led to the formation of the first communist state

The events that led to the formation of the first communist state in 1917 were complex in their causes and effects. Stereotypical pictures of the situations both before and after the revolution have become well known. So from one side we can still hear the rule of Tsar Nicholas II being described as a mercilessly autocratic oppression over a run-down country in which the workers and peasantry found it difficult to survive. While on the other hand the revolutionaries have been condemned for getting control of the empire by duping the people and offering them little more than they had before seizing power.

In fact, the situation in Russia in the years leading up to 1917 was grim. The imperial rule was indeed autocratic. There was no elected assembly and royal decree could overrule all other forms of government – a personality cult enhanced the emperor's power. The empire had a long way to go on the road to industrial modernization: Russia lagged far behind the countries of western Europe in this respect. Its vast size posed problems, too: improvements in transport were needed if the state was to function well, particularly as basic raw materials were scattered so widely.

In the northern portion of the empire the inhospitable climate made matters worse. And in the areas farther south, where the climate was more favourable to agriculture, the peasantry often had cause to feel let down by the difficulties put in their way when they tried to farm as efficiently as they could. Such difficulties ranged from simple problems in obtaining supplies to being prevented from owning land or acquiring additional fields to farm.

And yet there had been some economic progress. The railways (a large proportion of which were state-owned) were growing. The production of coal, iron and steel was on the increase. And even the hard-pressed Russian farmers were managing

gradually to increase their production of grain. The Russian economy was hardly advanced, but it was improving.

The working class, however, are rarely the first to benefit from economic growth. In the towns there was no choice for many factory workers but to accept a wage that was only just enough to survive on. Housing was also poor, with overcrowding common and facilities that were less than basic. In the country, rising rents often eroded any benefits that might have accrued from increased production, while local aristocracies often imposed very rough justice on any peasants who did not comply with the wishes of their landlords.

The combination of a slight upturn in the economy with continued injustice towards the poor was an obvious recipe

Tsar Nicholas II

for discontent. Towards the end of the nineteenth century the Russian government had to be on its guard against political opposition and industrial action. As well as workers, the intelligentsia also began question the prevailing methods of the government. Students began to object to the rigid hierarchies of the professions they seemed destined to enter or to be resentful at the high levels of graduate unemployment.

These sources of opposition began to be formalized with the formation (with great attendant risks to their members) of secret trade unions and a political party, the Russian Social Democratic Workers' Party. But in a climate in which membership of a union carried heavy penalties, in which Marxists were hunted down and persecuted, and in which association between workers and intelligentsia was difficult to achieve, it was hard to bring the two elements of the opposition together.

In 1905–4, however, a crisis looked near. The army's popularity took another nose-dive as a result of defeats in the war with Japan. And in 1905 a peaceful protest demonstration in St Petersburg advocating social and constitutional reforms led by the priest Georgi Gapon was fired on by troops. The setting up of a peasants' union, together with the structure provided by the original soviets (committees of workers' deputies) gave the government's opponents greater strength. In December 1905 there was an armed uprising of workers.

The following year saw the setting up of a compromise government that included a few of the Russian liberal leaders. The revolution was effectively crushed and the number of Marxist supporters fell dramatically in the ensuing three years. The troubles were alleviated by a series of good harvests and a pick-up in industrial production, although this was achieved at the expense of poorer conditions for the factory workers.

So the calls for change returned. In 1912 there were over 2,000 factory strikes, including one in which striking workers in the Lena goldfields were shot. By 1914, the number of strikes had escalated still further; there were more than 3,000 in the first half of the year alone. And they were accompanied by large demonstrations against the monarchy. Once more, crisis seemed to be looming. Then, in the summer of 1914, it seemed as if the monarchy might be saved. Russia entered World War I against Germany and the country began to unite behind the forces of the Tsar.

But war is expensive. The government had to put the bulk of its resources into the army – so much so that it was often difficult for farmers to buy tools as industry had switched over to producing equipment for the troops. This provided industry with work and a ready market – although even here, factories that did not get army contracts suffered as they could not get hold of raw materials for their 'inessential' work. And not enough of the wealth created by this work found its way back to the workers. Food shortages spread and prices went up. The strikes began again.

The year of revolution

As the workers continued their opposition it became clear that even the army were discontented with the government. 1917 was to be a year of revolutions. The first came in February when, deserted of support by all, including the army, Tsar Nicholas II was forced to abdicate and a new 'Provisional Government' was formed. This new government was dominated by the Constitutional Liberals (or Kadets), who strove to protect middle-class interests. But they also had to keep an uneasy peace with the masses. Many soviets were springing up, and numerous supporters of the Bolsheviks felt that it was wrong that a socialist government had not been set up as soon as the Tsar had been removed. But the bourgeois government of the Kadets was strong enough to hang on for a while.

The Kadets did not see it as in their interests to introduce the land reforms the peasants wanted. Handing over large tracts of land to the peasantry would have disrupted agricultural production. But the peasants had had enough. For centuries they had struggled to make ends meet under an autocratic regime. Now that regime had been swept away, they still did not own the land on which they worked. Soon after the February revolution, rioting began again. Exploitation of the workers continued in the factories and mills, with wage cuts being imposed and poverty and hunger spreading through the towns. And the cost of the war still had to be borne somehow. As opposition began to swell, the Kadets sought alliances with the socialist members of the soviets in order to quieten things down.

But the socialist party that was to be most influential in the coming months was hostile to the Kadets. The Bolsheviks, led by Vladimir Ilyich Lenin, continued to press for the transfer of power to the

workers by means of land reform, nationalization of major factories and banks, and immediate peace in the world war (after which, they believed, socialist revolutions would break out in Germany and elsewhere). During the summer of 1917, the popularity of the Bolsheviks increased in the factory committees and soviets.

An attempt by the Kadets and their allies in the army to set up a military dictatorship only served to alienate the people and push more support towards the

Vladimir Ilyich Lenin

Bolsheviks. By September, they were the dominant force in most of the soviets. And the revolutionary party began to take the form in which it was to be remembered, with figures such as Trotski, who was elected chairman of the Petrograd Soviet – coming to the fore.

It was Trotski who turned out to be the most influential of the revolutionaries during the next few months. Lenin's view was that the Bolsheviks should seize power straight away. But the Central Committee shared Trotski's opinion that they should delay. The power of the Provisional Government's leader Kerenski was on the wane. If they waited a little longer it would be still easier to take over. And the transfer of power could be timed to coincide with the opening of the second All-Russian Congress of Soviets, confirming the identification of the new regime with 'soviet power'.

Against a background of continuing discontent, with peasants rising against landlords and unrest in the towns, none of which could be quelled by the army, the Bolsheviks prepared for action. By the end of September, they had formally decided that the time for an armed uprising was ripe and had appointed a Military-Revolutionary Centre to oversee the Soviets' Military-Revolutionary Committee. Then they moved quickly. Plans were finalized concerning the takeover of the postal and telegraph networks, and the

rail links and food supplies to the capital. On 6 October a headquarters was set up in the Peter and Paul Fortress in the capital, formerly St Petersburg and now renamed Petrograd. The revolutionaries began to take strategic points. These included most of the bridges that connected the islands on which the city of Petrograd stands. The telegraph office was quickly taken, together with the central news agency and the Finland station. Soon ships of the Baltic fleet were also on their way to help the revolutionaries.

The next day saw the opening of the second All-Russian Congress of Soviets. Representatives from all over Russia had gathered at the Smolny Institute to decide where the revolution would go from here. Meanwhile in the city outside, revolutionary leader Lenin, who had been in hiding, had emerged to take command. Things were moving very quickly. More railway stations, the telephone exchange and the State Bank were swiftly occupied.

All the way through the period of the takeover Lenin realized the importance of communications. His announcement of the transfer of power to the Military-Revolutionary Committee was posted in the streets of the capital. The victory of the revolution was proclaimed at a meeting of the Petrograd soviet in the afternoon.

The Winter Palace

The Provisional Government – or what was left of it – was also meeting, in the Winter Palace, the baroque residence of the Tsars in the centre of the capital. By now, there were few to defend the palace – some detachments of Kadets and a women's battalion. And they were surrounded by revolutionary forces. At about ten in the evening a shot was fired from the cruiser *Aurora*. This was the signal for the revolutionary forces to attack the Winter Palace.

As they heard the footsteps of the revolutionaries approaching down the long corridors of the palace the members of the Provisional Government knew that their time was up. The Palace was taken with minimal resistance. After some scuffles in the corridors the ministers of the Provisional Government surrendered and were placed under arrest. There were only six casualties.

Consolidation

So the revolution had finally succeeded. The storming of the Winter Palace and the removal of Kerenski's government was followed by consolidation throughout Russia. Soviets swiftly became dominated by Bolshevik majorities. In the towns, people rallied behind Lenin's cry that

There was little resistance when the revolutionaries attacked the Winter Palace in Petrograd in October 1917. But the attack on the palace was important as a symbol of the revolution. It was not so much the defeat of the Provisional Government that was meeting inside the palace, but the symbolic defeat of the Tsar that was achieved. And the timing was right. News of the take-over spread quickly across Russia and the Bolsheviks were soon winning majorities in the Soviets. It was as if there had been a signal that the definitive revolution had taken place.

there should be 'workers' control' in the factories. In the country, people enthusiastically embraced his policy that land should become the property of the 'entire people'. And in the capital the All-Russian Congress was in control.

A Bolshevik government, called the Council of People's Commissars, came to power. Immediately a decree on peace was issued calling for an end to the war. Poland and Finland were granted independence. Nationalization and 'worker control' began. People looked forward to a period of industrial prosperity and to the breaking out of socialist revolutions all over Europe. Workers enthusiastically took up Lenin's instructions about supervising their managers – indeed they went further, often independently of the Bolshevik party itself, by taking control themselves. There was an air of optimism.

But the Bolsheviks had underestimated the massive damage to the Russian economy caused by the war, the policies of previous governments, and the unrest of recent years. The result was yet another

drop in industrial production, more unemployment and more food shortages. Matters in the country were a little better, with peasants relieved of their obligation to pay landlords rent for their land. But even here there were problems – little expansion in the actual amount of land available to farm, and a chronic shortage of equipment. The leadership of the Bolshevik (soon to be called the Communist) Party found ways out of this problem, first with armed repression of opponents, later with a revised economic policy. But it demonstrated how deep-seated the problems of Russia had become and how difficult it would be to impose rule on this vast, intractable country.

Other revolutions soon took place. Soviet republics were proclaimed during 1919 in Bavaria, Slovakia and Hungary, although they did not last long. Russian-inspired European communism was to dominate this region for much of the twentieth century, a state of affairs which the Bolshevik Revolution of 1917 made possible.

INVENTION OF TELEVISION

The true dawn of the mass media

Few people doubt the importance of the invention of television in the history of the twentieth century. The ability to send moving images directly into peoples' homes has transformed the way we view the world, at once opening up a vast fund of information and making possible the dissemination of opinion – and with it, propaganda – in a way that was unthought of before. If in the twentieth century a larger number of people are better informed about the world than at any time before, it is largely thanks to television. But any mass-communication medium has as much power for conveying distorted information as for telling the truth. Ironically, the very story of television's beginnings has been distorted in this way.

The person who is traditionally credited with the invention of television is the British pioneer John Logie Baird. He it was who in October 1925 produced on a tiny, flickering screen the first recognizable television image – the face of an office boy – which heralded the era of broadcasting as we know it.

How did Baird produce this image? Perhaps the greatest technical challenge was to make a device that would scan the subject along a series of closely-spaced lines, so that it could be turned into a single stream of information that could be sent along a wire or across the air. To do this, Baird used a device patented by the German scientist Paul Nipkow. This was a mechanical spinning disc, perforated with a spiral of holes. When turned, the disc scanned an object by splitting its image into small sections. The strength of light coming from each section was then picked up by photo-sensitive cells which turned them into electrical impulses. A second scanning disc could be used to turn the impulses back into an image of the subject.

Nipkow's scanning system was the one adopted by Baird. It had its problems. Because it was a mechanical system the speed of the scan, and therefore the clarity

John Logie Baird

of the image, was severely limited. By the time Baird began his work on television the answer had already been found, an electronic scanning system based on the cathode-ray tube. The cathode-ray tube was invented in the late nineteenth century by the German Karl Braun, but the scientists who pioneered its use for image scanning were A. A. Campbell Swinton (from Britain) and the Russian Boris Rosing. Although Rosing filed his Russian patent in 1907 and Campbell Swinton published his work the year after, Baird ignored them when he started his work on television in 1922. He stuck stubbornly to Nipkow's mechanical scanning system, meaning that the images on his 'Televisor' would always be blurred and that his system would eventually be superseded by one based on the cathode-ray tube.

For all these drawbacks, Baird's system was successful. Baird's dogged determination meant that, in spite of his limitations as a scientist, he managed to persuade people of the quality of his system. In 1925 he gave a demonstration of his equipment in London's Selfridge's department store. Although the results were poor by modern standards they stimulated a great deal of interest. What is more, Baird improved

his device during the later months of 1925, so that the crude silhouettes of the first images were replaced by recognisable faces – albeit rather blurred ones. These improvements and Baird's talent for publicity persuaded the BBC to let him use their facilities for regular broadcasts in 1929. In the next three years he sold about 10,000 of his 'Televisor' receivers.

Elsewhere in the world during the 1920s other pioneers were working independently of Baird. They included the Hungarian inventor D. von Mihaly and the American Charles Francis Jenkins who also used a mechanical scanning system, and a Japanese engineer called Kenjiro Takayanagi. Meanwhile the Russian scientists Paul Zworykin (working in the USA) and Boris Grabovsky were developing electronic scanning systems. These were to be the true ancestors of modern television.

But we still remember Baird and the effects of his vigorous promotion upon his invention. Only recently, the 'original apparatus' that Baird presented to the Science Museum in London has had its authenticity questioned – the machine in the form Baird presented it could never have worked. Presumably it was a reconstruction made by Baird's company as part of their publicity campaign. The power of television for publicity and persuasion was there from the beginning.

Baird's apparatus was crude and the image produced poor. A spinning disc perforated with holes in a spiral arrangement scanned the moving subject (the head of a puppet in this early experimental version). The resulting image appeared on the tiny screen in black and white, blurred and broken up into a series of broad bands. But it was a start. Although Baird's scanning system would soon be superseded by the electronic scanning of the cathode-ray tube, it did show the potential of television.

WALL STREET CRASH

The beginning of the great depression that transformed the world economy

To many Americans the great depression that came after the Wall Street Crash of 1929 was a bolt from the blue. America seemed to be doing well. The increased production capacity that came during World War I was put to use in peacetime making consumer goods and automobiles. Average wages rose steadily and unemployment was low, so demand for these new commodities could expand. An expansion of consumer credit fuelled demand even more.

But there were problems. Income was far from evenly distributed. Some sixty per cent of American families had incomes of less than $2,000 a-year – just about enough to buy the necessities for survival. There was a geographical division (people in the northeast and far west were comparatively better off than the rest of the population), and a split between urban and rural dwellers (city people got the best deal). And if wages increased, they did not keep pace with profits, meaning that the home market could not expand enough to satisfy the producers.

In addition, world trade was balanced very precariously. Europe, reconstructing after the war, relied heavily on loans from America. If the loans needed to be called in there would be a shrinking of America's European market and an immediate shortage of dollars for Europeans to buy American goods. Meanwhile, the European nations needed all the help they could get. France had a grave disparity between production and market capacities. while Germany had awesome inflation problems. These problems were magnified when seen on a world scale. Worldwide, there had been an expansion in production capacity but little increase in demand. Nevertheless, in general industrial economies were doing well, agricultural ones were suffering. Prices of food and raw materials declined.

The trigger for disaster came in America. A bull market in 1925–28, with stock market speculation reaching high levels, had pushed shares to what would be their highest prices for years – and far above their real value. People borrowed money to buy shares in the hope of a quick profit, and many feared that the upward trend would not last. The reaction came in October 1929. The method of reporting share prices lagged behind the actual sales, so that it was difficult on the New York stock exchange to know how much money you were making – or losing. As the tide turned and sellers began to outnumber buyers, prices seemed to be falling slowly. Thousands of people decided to sell, while the going was good. But the fall in prices was greater than people realised. The going was not good at all. Share prices tumbled and panic set in. On Thursday 24 October almost thirteen million shares changed hands, most at prices far below what their sellers hoped.

The financial establishment tried to intervene and prop up the market. But even the vast funds the bankers could throw at the market only briefly restrained the overall desire to sell. Funds were recalled from overseas in the search for liquidity in America. This led to a further collapse in the market. Fortunes were lost in a matter of hours. And share prices continued to fall steadily for two years. Unemployment rocketed. Prices fell, but few people held on to enough money to buy anything but the basics.

Europe was badly affected. What happened in America did not just stop the Europeans buying American goods, cutting world trade by more than half at a stroke: it also halted the post-war reconstruction process. In Germany, industrial production fell to about half of its previous level. There was financial crisis in Austria, Britain and France. Since most countries had no social welfare system to speak of, and since trade unions had little power, the scale of the human tragedy was enormous.

The Latin American countries, which had also been borrowing large amounts of money from the USA, were badly affected. The flow of foreign capital stopped, industrial production declined and violence broke out as baffled peoples turned against their rulers. Such difficulties often had the effect of radicalizing workers as people searched for a local political solution to their problems.

Elsewhere there was often a swing to the political right as some nations looked to a more rigorously controlled form of government as an answer to economic chaos. It was in 1933, with depression still raging, that Hitler came to power in Germany and Dolfuss in Austria. America itself chose a different path. Although socialism, badly split by the war and the events that came after it, was never influential in the USA, there was a move towards political liberalization and Roosevelt's famous 'New Deal'.

All these changes showed a disaffection with the forces of free enterprise: some sort of economic planning was seen to be needed. But deflation and austerity measures were not enough. In the end each nation had to fall back on its own unique resources to pull through. Britain strengthened links with its Commonwealth. America turned to public works. And Germany, Italy and Japan rearmed – war would offer its own set of goals and its own route out of the crisis.

Both urban and rural America were transformed by the Great Crash. In the cities, people who had made fortunes on the stock exchange were impoverished in a matter of days. In rural areas, already depressed, markets collapsed, wages nosedived and the familiar picture of depression America emerged. The optimism that had fuelled America's success turned into bewilderment. And the depression spread overseas, upsetting the delicate balance of world trade.

GANDHI'S SALT MARCH

A great step towards independence for India

By 1920 the Indian nationalist movement was being led by Mohandas Karamchand Gandhi. He it was who linked nationalism with traditional Hindu ideas and formulated the principle of non-cooperation against the British government in India. But by 1922 the policy seemed to have failed. Although non-cooperation had scored many successes, it had not been taken up in many parts of India and the self-rule that Gandhi had promised had not materialized. In March 1922 Gandhi was serving a sentence in a British gaol.

It seemed that Gandhi had got it wrong. Nationalist politicians reverted to negotiation and cooperation between 1922 and 1929. But the politicians who pursued this path soon realized that any limited concessions they might gain would only cause more unrest. There would not only be the demand for more concessions, but also struggles within the diverse Indian community to contend with. The tension between satisfying the indigenous population and remaining on negotiating terms with the British rulers was too great.

It was another influential Indian leader, Jawaharlal Nehru, who spoke out, demanding full independence. The respect he commanded as a result won him election to the presidency of the Indian National Congress party in 1929. In the following year Gandhi emerged again to launch a second campaign of non-cooperation. This time, widespread unemployment and worldwide depression brought many of India's disparate elements behind Gandhi.

In 1930 another meeting was arranged between Indian leaders and the British Viceroy, Lord Irwin. Gandhi was invited to the meeting, as was Nehru's father Motilal, another prominent nationalist. It was soon clear that only full dominion status would interest the nationalists – the meeting broke up. On 26 January, Congress proclaimed India independent, with Jawaharlal Nehru as its President.

The salt march

Congress also empowered Gandhi to take a stand. He focused attention on the Salt Tax. The manufacture of salt was a state monopoly in India. Everyone had to buy salt made under licence, even though many people could make it much more cheaply themselves. Gandhi instructed his followers to make their own salt from brine and refuse to purchase the state salt. For himself, he would undertake a symbolic march of 240 miles to Dandi, on the coast near Bombay, to take a pinch of free salt.

At first, the government in Delhi did not take Gandhi's gesture seriously. But thousands joined Gandhi's march. He was tracked every inch of the way by newspaper reporters, both Indian and overseas. And along the route local government officials resigned the service of the British to join the Indian cause. 'We are marching,' said Gandhi, 'in the name of God.' Once more, he had found a way of uniting the diverse views and religions of the people of the Indian subcontinent. But once more it was at the expense of imprisonment – this time for both the Nehrus as well as for Gandhi himself.

The Congress leaders were released in January 1931 so that they could once more meet the Viceroy. This time they at least drew up an agreement, the Delhi Pact, which marked the end of the civil disobedience campaign. But this was not the end of tensions in India. While Congress continued to press for independence, it proved very difficult for the Nationalist leaders to unite India.

Gandhi's withdrawal

By 1935 it looked as if the movement to independence might come about gradually and peacefully. The Government of India Bill introduced a democratically elected legislature, within which Congress could work. For much of the 1930s Gandhi withdrew from politics to let those in Congress plan the path towards true independence. After the war the British agreed on a date for independence. They approached the problem of disputes between Hindu and Muslim by partitioning India. Gandhi, horrified by the continuing fighting between the different religious groups, started a fast in January 1948. It was hoped that it would be another great unifying gesture. Promises of peace from the opposing groups began to come in. But on 30 January Gandhi was shot dead by a young Hindu fanatic. India, for a moment at least, was united in its horror.

The great events of Gandhi's life – the salt march, the fast, his very death – showed that India needed extraordinarily strong leadership for there to be much hope of unity. The British with strong and efficient colonial government had often managed to achieve such unity. Gandhi had managed it in inspired and inspiring moments.

The frail figure of Gandhi seemed an unlikely one for the leader who would best represent India in its struggle for independence from Britain. But it was exactly his small stature and frail form that provided such a clear symbol of the sort of leadership Gandhi stood for. He knew that India would not be able to stand up against the might of Britain by conventional military means. And he felt that such a stand would be wrong because it lacked the moral authority he was looking for. So a stand of peaceful, passive resistance was Gandhi's way. The thousands who joined him on the gruelling salt march showed by their actions how they agreed with him. By becoming a gesture that involved so many, the salt march also gave Gandhi publicity on a wide scale: it gave him sympathy all around the world – the sort of sympathy India would need if it was to make a go of independence.

I want world sympathy in this battle of Right against Might.

Santi MKGandhi

5. 4. '30

LONG MARCH OF CHINA

A great retreat that gave Chinese communism the strength it needed

From 1928 until 1949 China was ruled by the nationalist party or Kuomintang, at first under Sun Yat-sen, but mostly under Chiang Kai-shek. But there was also a strong communist presence in China, and it would eventually be this presence that would unite the country and transform Chinese life.

Sun Yat-sen collaborated with the communists. But in 1927 the commander-in-chief of the nationalist army, Chiang Kai-shek, took over in a military coup. He was concerned about the strength of the communists, who had recently taken the Chinese part of Shanghai. So he had the Shanghai leaders rounded up, and expelled the communist members from his government.

Setbacks for the communists
Things were looking black for the communists, but there was a glimmer of hope. On 31 July and 1 August 1927, part of the army based at Nanchang in Kiangsi province mutinied and declared themselves supporters of the communists. The mutiny was a failure and the nationalists soon retook Nanchang, sending the rebels fleeing. But the event was crucial in the history of Chinese communism, for it marks the formation of the Red Army (later to become the People's Liberation Army), giving the communists the power of arms for the first time.

But at this stage they did not have very much power. An operation to occupy the port of Swatow was a failure. At attempted uprising in Canton was put down by the nationalists. The Red Army was continually pursued and hounded by nationalist troops.

Another failure was the attempted takeover of Changsha, capital of the province of Hunan. This attempt was led by a communist who would come to have unparalleled influence: Mao Tsetung. When it became clear that they

were defeated, Mao and his followers retreated to the borders of Hunan and Kiangsi provinces where they hid amongst the mountains at Chingkangshan. In April 1928 the Red Army also came to Chingkangshan, and the two most dynamic elements in Chinese communism were united.

The new strategy
By this time Mao had worked out a new strategy by which to further the communist cause. He realized that the key to gaining power in China was not to take the cities but to win over the masses of the rural poor. There were millions of them, and if they were united they could resist the nationalists. The peasants wanted to be liberated from their landlords and to be left alone by the nationalist forces and authorities who were conscripting many of their number into the army and treating them badly as soon as they were in uniform.

Mao saw that these people represented the true spirit of China. It was thus a very different situation from the one that had existed in Russia before the revolution, where winning the support of the urban proletariat had been so important. China was overwhelmingly rural. And what attempts there had been at putting communist policies into effect in the cities (such as the ill-fated effort at forming a trade union in Shanghai) had been suppressed by the nationalists.

He also had different ideas about how any war should be waged. He saw that there was no point in risking his army in engagements with vastly superior forces. So if the nationalists attacked in their usual strength the Red Army would pull back, apparently breaking up in defeat but in fact reforming behind enemy lines so that the nationalists' communications could be cut off. Then, when their opponents were in disarray, the Red Army would go on the attack, assured

that, with the help of the local peasantry, *their* communications and intelligence would be intact.

The stronghold in Kiangsi
The new methods of the Red Army proved successful against the nationalists. Chiang Kai-shek launched a series of extermination campaigns against the communists, the first at the end of 1930, a second in February 1931. Neither of these was successful. They only served to swell the ranks of the Red Army, both with new local volunteers and with deserters from Chiang's army.

Nevertheless Chiang began a third campaign in July 1931. This time the communists were victorious at Kaoshing in Kiangsi province. At this point the nationalists had to withdraw to deal with Japanese aggression in Manchuria, leaving the communists control of virtually the entire province of Kiangsi. Here the communists set up their own government, the Kiangsi soviet.

As its name suggests, the Kiangsi soviet was run along Russian lines and led largely by men who had been trained in Moscow. Mao's role in the leadership is unclear, but he certainly remained a key figure in Chinese communism. It was clearly an embarrassment for the nationalists to have a communist state

Mao was not a well-known figure in international politics when he took part in the Long March in 1934. But the march greatly increased his fame and his experience as a leader. Here the marchers are seen crossing the Tatu River at the suspension bridge at Luting. This flimsy structure was the only way of crossing the deep gorge, and the nationalists had made the crossing still more perilous by taking away the planks on the bridge. But the marchers were able to replace the planks and get across to the next stage of their journey towards safety in Shansi province.

within the Chinese state, so they attacked the communists once more. Although they had some success against outlying communist communities, Kiangsi stood firm. The nationalists lost three divisions and had to retreat once more.

At this point Chiang sought advice from allies in Nazi Germany. The German generals told him what now seems obvious: that he was wasting his time with frontal attacks. So a plan was launched in October 1933 to blockade Kiangsi, cutting off the transport of vital foods and materials into the province, until the people simply could not survive any longer.

It was a vast operation, with guards posted permanently on every route in and out of the province and some 700,000 troops from the nationalist side involved. It looked set to succeed when a section of the nationalist army rebelled against their leaders and joined up with some of the more discontented nationalists. The rebels made overtures to the communists, but the Kiangsi soviet turned them down.

This turned out to be a mistake. The rebels controlled the coast at Fukien and could have provided supplies, arms and vastly improved communications. The Fukien rebels would also have benefited from the support of the communists. As it was, both movements failed. The rebellion fell apart in January 1934. And the communists, frustrated by the blockade, began to make frontal attacks on the nationalists who were surrounding them. By the summer of 1934 it was clear to the communists that they could not go on. Their attacks were not working. They either had to face extermination or to escape out of Kiangsi and beat a massive retreat. It was time for the long march to begin.

The long march

It was a desperate solution, but it could still be meticulously planned. Out and out victory would be unlikely, but at least a communist force might remain intact and skins would be saved. The communists broke out of blockaded Kiangsi in the southwest. From here they entered southern Hunan before entering the province of Kweichow, through which they marched until they reached Yunnan, the southwesternmost province.

This took them far away from the area ruled by the nationalists, into provinces governed by local war lords who had given only nominal allegiance to the nationalist government at Nanking. Some of the communists, notably the Second Front Army under Ho Lung, would march deeper into Yunnan before passing northwards through eastern Tibet. Mao's party turned northwards more quickly, passing just inside the eastern border of Tibet. Both were hoping to meet up with allies in northwestern China.

The distances involved were vast, but the comrades of Mao and Chu Te tackled it with aplomb. They marched thirty or forty miles every day –

Chairman Mao

sometimes even sixty or seventy miles. The nationalists had little chance of catching them up at this speed. Keeping up this pace they had little time for plundering or taking cities. And this was not their goal. They treated the people well in the areas they passed through, a fact that must have helped win many more of the rural poor to their cause.

But if they kept their enemies at a safe distance, the long march was not without other dangers. One of the most notable was the crossing of the Tatu River. This tributary of the Yangtze was bridged at Luting, where it flows through a deep gorge. The gorge was crossed by a suspension bridge, which consisted simply of a number of chains lashed together and covered with planks.

The nationalists, who knew that their opponents would have to come this way, had removed the planks, but had not been able to dismantle the chains. So they left the bridge guarded and hoped to ambush the marchers. The guards on the bridge itself were covered by nationalist machine gun placements on the sides of the gorge. So a group of twenty men had to swing along the chains to remove the guards, avoiding the blasts of automatic fire. Eventually the guards were overpowered, and the marchers triumphantly replaced the planks before crossing the bridge.

The Great Snow Mountains posed another enormous challenge to the marchers, this time a challenge of endurance. There was great relief when the marchers had crossed the mountains. They met up with their allies, the Fourth Front Army, in Szechwan province. The leader of the Fourth Front Army wanted to remain in Szechwan and establish another soviet, but Mao insisted on pressing on, leaving his allies behind and setting out across the grasslands of eastern Tibet.

These grasslands set yet another challenge to the travellers. The terrain was swampy and uninhabited and the weather was cold. What was more, there were nationalist troops waiting again as soon as the grasslands were crossed. But Mao pushed on, at last reaching his goal – the soviet area in Shansi province in the northwest. Soon the other contingents would join Mao in Shansi. The Second Front Army arrived, after a more southerly and westerly march, in October 1936. The two forces had a total strength of around 80,000. They constituted a real threat to Chiang Kai-shek once more, and were well protected amongst the mountains near Yenan.

But the Red Army could not claim a total victory. They had had to leave behind many of their number *en route*. And it was, when all was said and done, a retreat. It would be a long time before the communists could claim control of the whole of China. And for some years the main threat to Chiang would come from Japan. But the Long March had ensured that the communists survived. It cemented their attachment to rural China. And it brought Mao to prominence. In 1936 he became Chairman of the Central Committee of the Communist Party. For another thirteen years he would build up his base of support, becoming Chairman of the People's Republic of China in 1949.

SPANISH CIVIL WAR

A defeat for the left and the beginning of decades of dictatorship in Spain

By the end of the nineteenth century Spain was in decline. The last remains of the Spanish Empire were lost in 1898. Spain itself was backward. The bulk of the population was involved in agriculture and other rural activities, and both small farmers and landless labourers found it difficult to get a living out of the poor soil when high rents, debts and insecure leases were the norm. The church was still powerful and allied closely with the ruling classes, as was the army. A third powerful force were local politicians, who did their best to rig elections.

The Spanish monarchy was ill-equipped to deal with these problems. This fact eventually led to the success of a coup by General Miguel Primo de Rivera in 1923. He established a dictatorship and began to reform local government and to carry out a programme of public works. It was an ambitious attempt, but Primo de Rivera lost the support of the army and the king, who returned to the throne in 1930.

By this time the republican movement was gathering strength in Spain. At first it looked as if there would be a republican military takeover, but when the republican rising at Jaca failed on 12 December 1930, this threat subsided. Instead, the Second Republic was formed as a result of elections the following year, and King Alfonso XIII left Spain.

It was the aim of republican premier Manuel Azana y Diaz to create a modern democracy in Spain. But many of the old problems remained. The church was still a powerful influence for conservatism. Churchmen and the rich felt increasingly insecure under the leftists who dominated the government. Measures to legalize divorce, end state support for clergy salaries and dissolve the Jesuits only increased the tension. Then there was opposition from the regions, particularly from the Basque Catholics and from the more progressive nationalists in Catalonia. The army was another seed-bed of opposition.

Political opinion in Spain became still more polarized. By the 1936 election, the contest was between left-wing republicans and right-wing Catholics. To the former, it seemed that Fascism would take control if they lost; for the right-wingers, a defeat seemed to herald the onset of a Russian-style Bolshevik revolution. Threats to the republic gradually increased. The army was discontented. The Falange, a nationalist anti-Marxist group

General Francisco Franco

founded by the son of Primo de Rivera, was attracting support. There was rural unrest because of bad harvests and unemployment. The final straw came on 13 July 1936. Calvo Soleto, an anti-republican conspirator was assassinated by republican police in retaliation for a Falangist assassination of a republican. The army and the political right decided to act.

The course of the conflict

First there was a rising in Spanish Morocco and on the Canary Islands on 17 July 1936. Soon support for the revolt spread throughout Spain, but not as far as the leaders hoped. Navarre and Old Castile supported the rising, as did some of the large towns (particularly Seville, Cordoba, Valladolid, Sarragossa and Cadiz). But the republicans had promised autonomy to the Basque region and Catalonia, so these regions naturally supported the government. Barcelona, the capital of Catalonia, was a republican stronghold, and Madrid, the capital of Spain, was held by the government. So the rebels, who had hoped to be in control of the entire country within a week of the rising, had failed in their objective. Moreover, the government forces seemed equally strong. A long, drawn-out war looked likely, and both sides would have to look outside Spain for support if they were to gain the upper hand.

The republicans sought support first of all from France. This was not forthcoming as France and Britain feared a general war in Europe would result. So the republicans turned to the USSR. The rebel leader General Francisco Franco appealed successfully to the Fascist states of Italy and Germany. Soon, the organization of the International Brigades in support of the republic would give the war a still more cosmopolitan aspect.

But the ordinary people of Spain provided the basis of the armies. Workers, because of their crucial role in resisting the rebellion, became powerful in the republican area. Indeed, in cities like Barcelona old governments were swept away and labour organizations like the CNT took over. But there were many struggles within the republican movement. A Marxist revolutionary party, POUM, for example, launched a rebellion in Barcelona in 1937. This was suppressed by a new socialist government, which replaced the trade unions with political parties.

Yet it was not such disputes, but rather the organization of the republican army on a militia basis that led to Franco's early successes. Franco cut through the militia successfully, except outside Madrid. Help from the International Brigades and the USSR, plus the reorganization of the republican force into the Popular Army enabled Madrid to hold out longer. At the battles of Jarama (February 1937) and Guadalajara (March 1937) Franco's forces were defeated by the International Brigades. After these defeats Franco concentrated his attack in the north. By October 1937 he had the advantage of the republicans. The bombing of Guernica shocked republican supporters and battles in Aragon showed their weakness.

But Franco still could not take the capital. Only in March 1939, when internal divisions weakened Madrid, could he enter and take the city. By this time, with the evaporation of Russian support for the republic, the Nationalists had also taken control of Catalonia. Franco won because he was able to rally the Right behind him as leader, because he had more support from Italy and Germany than his opponents had from Russia, and because his organization was often superior to the that of the republican army – he found it easier to keep his supporters united.

The war condemned Spain to a long period of dictatorship. There followed an alliance with the Axis powers during World War II, and then neutrality when it became clear that the Allies would win. But Franco's fascism was not forgotten by western Europe, and it was an isolated Spain that emerged in 1945. As a struggle between Left and Right, the civil war also set the tone for much of the political scene after 1945.

Pablo Picasso painted his picture Guernica *in 1937, in response to the destruction of the Basque capital during the Civil War. The canvas forms the basis of the backdrop to the illustration below. It has become a symbol of the suffering caused by war and the anger of right-minded people that such suffering should take place.*

BOMBING OF PEARL HARBOR

The beginning of American involvement in World War II

Pearl Harbor was constructed on the Hawaiian island of Oahu, near Honolulu. It was the USA's biggest naval base outside America itself and, about one third of the way between California and Japan, it could be seen either as a deterrent to Japanese expansion or as a target for a possible Japanese attack. It housed the Pacific Fleet, and was defended by soldiers and airmen of the US Army.

In 1940 diplomatic relations between the USA and Japan were coming to a turning point. Both countries were examining their positions in the light of the war in Europe. The Japanese were intent on expansion. They sent their troops down the coast of China and secured the closure of an important supply line, the Burma Road. The Americans responded by putting a limitation on the export of army supplies to Japan. They also moved their principal Pacific naval base from San Diego to Pearl Harbor.

Following these moves there was a complex series of diplomatic negotiations between America and Japan. The most succinct summary of what the Japanese wanted was presented to the Americans in September 1941. They demanded that neither Britain nor the USA should interfere with their activities in Indo-China; that neither of those two countries should increase their forces in the far east; and that they should support Japan by supplying her with raw materials.

America refused to meet such demands. But intelligence sources told them that, if a diplomatic solution was not reached by 29 November 1941, the Japanese would launch an attack – although it was not known where they would strike. In the weeks after the Japanese demands, proposals and counter-proposals continued to fly between the two governments. The USA resisted Japanese expansion but did not threaten attack if Japan persisted.

Towards the end of November it was clear that neither side would give in. The Americans began to prepare for a Japanese attack. Warnings were sent to outlying commanders. The Americans thought that the biggest threat was from sabotage, and so grouped their aircraft together rather than dispersing them as they would to defend them from an air attack.

When the offensive arrived on 7 December, it was directed at Pearl Harbor and it came from the air. Pearl Harbor, arguably an obvious target, had received its warning late and was ill prepared. The first person to notice something amiss was a boatswain's mate who sighted a number of aircraft circling in the vicinity of the base at 7.30 in the morning. But these aircraft were not recognized as belonging to the enemy. At 7.55 the commander of the Pacific Mine Force on a mine-layer in the harbour saw a bomb fall. At first he thought that an American aeroplane had accidentally dropped one of its bombs. Then he saw the Japanese red sun symbol on the side of the aircraft and realized the truth. Quickly he contacted headquarters and the alarm was sounded.

By this time the bulk of the first wave of Japanese aeroplanes was approaching over the sea, undetected by American radar, to drop their deadly load. It was a formidable bombardment lasting about thirty minutes. It was followed by another wave of enemy aircraft.

But fortunately for the Americans neither of their two aircraft carriers were in the harbour, and so the worst damage, to aircraft as well as ships, was not inflicted. Nevertheless, ninety Japanese torpedo-bombers, fifty dive-bombers and fifty fighters, plus the second wave of another 170 aircraft, could inflict a great deal of damage. The battleship *Arizona* was sunk; *West Virginia* was badly damaged; *Oklahoma* capsized; *California* sank into the mud until only her superstructure could be seen. Many destroyers and light cruisers were also badly hit. The bombers also attacked the airfields and destroyed many of the closely-bunched aircraft. The American forces lost 2,403 men.

But Pearl Harbor was not the Japanese victory that it seemed. Above all, it immediately rallied the USA. The Japanese were now clearly the enemy and America could do nothing but declare war on Japan. What was more, the other Axis powers played into American hands after Pearl Harbor. The Japanese called on Germany to assist them against the Americans and Germany acquiesced with a declaration of war on America. Without this, the American administration might not have gained the support it needed to go to war against Germany as well as against Japan.

The Japanese argued that, in spite of these effects, Pearl Harbor was still a tactical and strategic victory. And it was followed by a number of other successes in battle. But tactically, they missed the two key American aircraft carriers at Pearl Harbor and many of the ships they damaged were soon repaired and ready for war. Strategically, the Pacific Fleet could not have stopped the Japanese advance into China anyway.

So if the bombing of Pearl Harbor inflicted losses on the American forces it did little in the long run for the Japanese cause. For the Allies, it provided a reason for them to unite with America to fight a worldwide campaign. And for the Americans, it stimulated popular support for involvement in the conflict, which had truly become a world war.

The Japanese bombardment of Pearl Harbor damaged the American military, but not as badly as the Japanese had hoped. As the dust cleared, it became clear that the absence of the American aircraft carriers from the harbour had saved much American hardware. The significance of the attack was enough to unite America with the Allies against the Axis powers, altering the whole course of the war.

D-DAY LANDINGS

The Allies take the initiative in World War II

By the early months of 1944 it was clear that the progress of World War II had reached something of a crisis. After June 1941, when the Germans attacked the USSR, there had been a string of German victories. The fortunes of the Axis armies turned in November 1942 in Africa, with the British victory at El Alamein, with Anglo-American landings in French North Africa, and when the Russians pushed through the German front at Stalingrad. By February 1943 the Germans had lost North Africa and their Sixth Army was surrounded near Stalingrad. In Italy things were also going better for the Allies. They had invaded Sicily in July 1943, while in Italy itself Mussolini was deposed and the new premier proposed an armistice.

But the Germans fought back. They restored Mussolini and put up a strong resistance to the Allied advance through southern Italy. They also held out against the Soviets. Meanwhile, much of Europe was under German occupation. The Allied commanders began to look for a way to take the initiative.

For some time the Anglo-American commanders had promised the Russians that they would create a second front in western Europe. Stalin was naturally keen that the Germans should be attacked from the west as well as from the east. There had been plans for an assault on Brest or Cherbourg in 1942, but these did not come to anything. But two allied conferences in 1943, in Casablanca and Washington, put plans in motion for an operation that would lead to the liberation of France.

The initial plans

It was realized that such an operation would have to be meticulously planned: the logistics were difficult and the coordination of the forces would need top-class leadership. After the Washington Conference in May 1943, Lieutenant-General Sir Frederick Morgan, head of COSSAC (Chief of Staff to the Supreme Allied Commander) took charge of the planning. He returned three months later with plans for Operation Overlord, which was set for 1 May 1944.

The substance of the plans was accepted, although Churchill increased the number of men involved by twenty-five per cent. Soon a Supreme Allied Commander was appointed, the little-known American Dwight D. Eisenhower. His command team was composed of some of the most experienced soldiers of the war.

General Dwight D. Eisenhower

Their first task was to look in detail at the COSSAC plans for the invasion. They realized that they needed to aim for places with adequate harbours to land large numbers of men and their often bulky equipment. They were also limited by the range of the Spitfire aircraft that would protect them from above. The latter restricted them to the coast between Flushing and Cherbourg. Within this strip, the area around Caen was relatively lightly defended and offered sheltered beaches and good land for potential airfields. It also looked easier than many areas to defend against counter-attacks.

An immediate problem was the sheer size of the invasion. COSSAC had asked for 3,323 landing craft, 467 warships and 150 minesweepers. When General Bernard Montgomery, who was to command the land forces in the first phase of the invasion, looked at the plans, he wanted considerably more ships in all these categories. To avoid removing craft from other theatres of war, it was decided to delay the invasion for about a month (the exact time would depend on tides and phases of the moon), so that more new vessels could be built. Even so, another planned operation in the south of France had to be postponed to make ships available. This would provide enough transport for the five seaborne divisions that it was planned to land on the beaches of Normandy.

The postponement of the operation had other advantages. The Allies had more time to make strategic bombing raids on Germany and on key targets to cut off German communications in the invasion area. The delay also meant that it would be more likely that the weather would be favourable for a new Russian offensive to keep the enemy continuously occupied on the eastern front.

Technological planning

Another key planning area was that of specialized armour and equipment. The British knew that they would need all the help they could get avoiding mines, breaking up the Germans' concrete defences and simply landing equipment in difficult conditions. So Major-General Sir Percy Hobart, the creator of the famous 7th Armoured Division (the 'Desert Rats'), was brought in to design new equipment. He came up with tanks fitted with flails to sweep mines, bridge-laying tanks, tanks adapted to attack concrete blockhouses and amphibious vehicles. Eisenhower was particularly impressed with the latter.

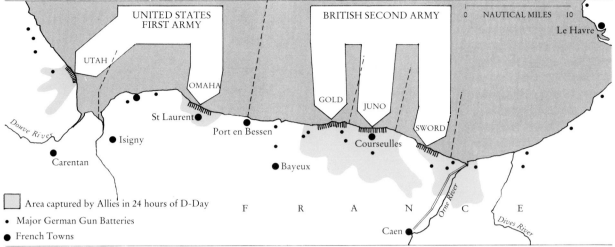

The D-Day Invasion Beaches, June 6, 1944

These were not the only daring technological solutions needed to support the planned invasion. The commanders knew that it would be impossible to take a major port like Cherbourg without damaging it; it would also be heavily mined. The Allies therefore planned to tow two prefabricated harbours across the Channel. These would then be anchored off the French coast to facilitate landing. Another problem with damage at the ports would be getting hold of a fuel supply for vehicles and aircraft. This was solved by laying PLUTO (Pipeline under the ocean). Fuel would be pumped along this line from the Isle of Wight to Cherbourg.

The situation in England

Security was obviously of prime importance. The invasion required vast troop movements and the stockpiling of arms and armour, ships and vehicles, on the south coast of England. British and Canadian soldiers were assembled in southeastern England, a huge force from the USA gathered in the southwest. During spring the force that assembled in southern England was awesome. Over 3.5 million men gathered along the coast. There were 4,000 assault craft, 1,200 warships and 1,600 merchant ships. Some 13,000 aircraft would also be involved.

It was vital that these movements and assemblies should be kept as secret as possible. Civilian movements in southern England were severely restricted. Visitors were kept away from the south coast. Civilian access was banned from large areas altogether. Even the communications of foreign embassies – telegrams and diplomatic bags – were delayed to stop intelligence getting out of the country. The command also spent some effort actively trying to deceive the Germans about their plans. They did what they could to suggest that they were planning to invade farther north, in the Pas de Calais, in July. Fake 'secret information'

and fleets of dummy ships in the southeastern ports certainly did much to confuse the enemy.

While the gathering of soldiers, the training exercises and reconnaissance missions continued, naval and military intelligence were gradually building up a picture of the beaches for which they were all aiming. Natural and military obstacles were assessed. Tidal oddities were observed. Everything was done to ensure that the force was as ready as it could be.

The opposition

Defending the French coast was a difficult proposition. The Germans were engaged in building a long concrete Atlantic wall to block out possible invaders. But the effectiveness of such a wall was always in doubt, and the Germans were also concentrating on defending key ports and the Pas de Calais region. It was this strategy that they hoped would enable them to push the British back before they could get too far inland.

But the Germans were not clear about how best to keep the British back. Rommel, who would in the event command the armies on the invasion coast, saw the necessity to fight the invaders on the beaches. But his Panzer divisions were not concentrated enough to give the swift blow needed: the Germans hoped to keep the British away from the beaches altogether. The Normandy coast was extensively mined with a host of different devices. There were also anti-tank gun emplacements and inland mortars. Then there were the mines on the beaches themselves. It would be a tall order to land at all.

Operation Overlord

The appointed day was 5 June, but the day before saw the sea lashed with gales and the beaches shrouded in fog. A short period of favourable weather was forecast for 6 June and Eisenhower decided to go. As the armada left England's southern

ports, troops of the British 6th Airborne Division prepared to be the first to land on French soil. Their gliders landed silently and accurately near Bénouville and quickly took bridges over the River Orne and the Canal de Caen. Soon further British Brigades landed east of the Orne to clear an area where seventy-two gliders carrying equipment, guns and transport could land in safety. At the same time American airborne divisions were carrying out similar manoeuvres on the western flank of the invasion area.

Meanwhile extensive Allied bombing of the Pas de Calais, together with radar-jamming, deceived the Germans. This was soon to be followed by a massive bombardment of the coastal defences in the true target area. By the time the boats started to arrive, at 6.30 in the morning, the Germans were hardly prepared.

The invasion army was split into five forces. The two American contingents, codenamed Utah and Omaha, would strike in the west, near Carantan and Vierville respectively. Three British forces, codenamed Gold, Juno and Sword, would land farther east, between Bayeux and Caen. The American Utah force landed quickly and successfully. They came to shore a mile away from their intended target, but they hit a poorly defended area so the mistake was turned to their advantage. The Omaha force was less successful. They had problems keeping their landing craft afloat in heavy seas and launched some of their amphibious tanks too soon. Those who got ashore did so wet, cold and under heavy enemy fire. Accurate fire from the ships saved them from complete disaster, but many lives were lost.

The British forces landed more successfully, well protected by Hobart's 79th Armoured Division with their specialized armour. They benefitted from the element of surprise and Hobart's eccentric vehicles. A total of 156,000 Allied troops had

227

The landing of the British troops on the beaches of Normandy was successful, although there were inevitably a number of wounded. Here members of the 1st South Lancashire Battalion help their wounded comrades ashore during their arrival at Sword Beach on 6 June 1944. They had been well protected: troops ahead of them had blown up bridges to impair German communications; there was also good air cover. If their American counterparts were less successful, the combined effort gave the Allies the initiative they badly needed.

landed by nightfall. Between the Orne and the Vire rivers a front of around thirty miles had been established. Caen had not been taken, but the Germans had no other cause for satisfaction. With limited artillery and no reserves in the area they were at bay behind the front.

A turning-point
The planning was impressive, even if all the ideas were not exploited as widely as the planners first thought. Hobart's eccentric vehicles, for example, were not employed on Omaha beach. The Omaha landings themselves were not the success they should have been. But otherwise the operation was a triumph, and it marked a turning-point in the war in Europe. In August, Operation Anvil would be launched by the Allies in southern France. Later that month Paris would fall to the Allies, who would then advance on the Ruhr from Belgium and Holland. Early in 1945 the final Allied assault would be underway. The D-Day landings would thus prove a crucial point in the war, during which the Allies seized the initiative, and after which German success was at best limited. It was the beginning of the end of the war.

INVENTION OF THE COMPUTER

The dawn of the information age

Of all the inventions of the twentieth century perhaps none has had the impact of the computer. The device has penetrated almost every aspect of life in the developed world – from the administration of government departments to controlling domestic appliances, from education to industry, from healthcare to warfare. But the computer is typical of so many technological developments: its invention cannot be tied down to one particular event or one specific person. The work of many scientists was involved and the computer took years to evolve into the forms with which we are familiar today. And it is still evolving.

Although the idea of calculating machines goes back centuries, the sort of ultra-high-speed electronic calculators that are modern computers have their origins in the 1930s. One of the most important pioneers was the British mathematician and logician Alan Turing. In 1936 he published a paper, 'On computable numbers', that envisaged a theoretical computer with an infinite capacity for data storage and an infallible process of calculation. It was a daring and brilliant concept and it, and its author's ability, earned Turing a place in British government intelligence during World War II.

Turing worked in secret at Bletchley Park during the war, with the team producing a computer named Colossus I, which was used in breaking enemy codes. The machine, which is now accepted as the first functional electronic computer, began operation in December 1943. Before the end of the war, nine other Colossus machines had been built at Bletchley. They could work at an awesome speed compared to any other calculating machines previously devised and so proved invaluable tools in code-cracking. The Colossus machines played a vital role in the analysis of Axis codes and thus made an important contribution to the Allied victory.

The war also stimulated American work on pioneer computing devices. The US Navy were looking for ways of calculating ballistics tables, and an American academic, Howard Aiken, was known to be working on a calculating device at Harvard University. His concept was an enormous electro-mechanical calculator controlled by sets of instructions fed to the machine on rolls of paper tape.

It was too large a project for the university to bear alone, but the IBM Corporation were persuaded to take an interest. The result was the Harvard Mark I, a vast machine that could perform calculations at the rate of slightly more than three per second (ponderously slow by today's standards but impressive enough at the time). It was useful enough to remain in operation at Harvard for some fifteen years, even though the secret work of the British with their completely electronic design made it instantly obsolete. By involving IBM in the computer field it could be said to have set a trend in computer manufacture and design that has continued to this day.

After the war, America continued in the forefront of computer development. By 1945 they had come up with a fully electronic design that, unlike the specialized British code-cracking machines at Bletchley, was intended for general-purpose calculation. Developed at the Moore School in Philadelphia, it was called ENIAC (Electronic Numerical Integrator And Computer). It was another vast machine containing around 18,000 valves, the heat from which had to be kept down with a special air-conditioning plant. It ran faster than its predecessors, and increasing the speed of computers was one of the things that would occupy computer engineers from then on.

Scientists were also working on some of the basic precepts for computer design. Turing and others were proposing the idea of using the binary number system, in which all numbers are represented by the digits 0 and 1. This chimes conveniently with the two states of a switch, on and off, allowing computers to represent strings of numbers by groups of switches. The concept of the program – the set of instructions that tells a computer how to behave – was also being developed. And another Philadelphia project, EDVAC (Electronic Discrete Variable Computer), was the first computer to be able to store its own programs.

Few people at this time realized to what extent computers would be used in the second half of the twentieth century, how people would be scared of computers, although even the most sophisticated are little more than elaborate calculating machines which blindly perform the instructions set them by their programs. Yet Turing, the visionary of the computer, aware more than anyone that no computer could think in the way that a human can, looked forward to the appearance of artificial intelligence. This is a concept that promises to make even greater changes to the world than the computers that have made its development possible.

Mathematician and computer pioneer Alan Turing stands in front of Colossus, the British computer used in intelligence during World War II. People communicated with these vast machines using media such as punched cards and paper tape, on which information could be stored in a form the computer could read. Operators had to be highly skilled and the hardware took up a huge amount of space. Such elaborate computers were only available to those with vast resources – the military and government departments. Today, with computers that tell the user what to do next, simple input devices like keyboards and touch-sensitive screens, and compact storage media, the processing power of a Colossus is within the reach of millions of people.

USE OF THE ATOMIC BOMB

A new power of destruction is unleashed, and the course of World War II is changed

In 1939 Albert Einstein, then a resident of the USA, felt compelled to write to President Roosevelt. The physicist explained that his work, and the work of others in his field, had led him to think that the element uranium might be turned into a new and highly powerful source of energy. The possibility was important because the research required might be done quickly and it might lead to the manufacture of a new bomb of awesome power. What was more, Germany might develop such a bomb before anyone else. Given the fact that Germany had already overrun Europe, the implications for world peace and stability were grave.

In fact, the fundamental work on which nuclear weapons were based went back some years. The pioneering work of Einstein himself on relativity had shown how a very large amount of energy could be contained in a very small mass. But physicists at first thought it unlikely that one would be able to release this prodigious energy.

One vital breakthrough came with the work of Ernest Rutherford between 1909 and 1920 on the structure of the atom. Scientists knew little about the atom, the basic building block of matter. Too minute to look at in the normal way, atoms have to be studied by bombarding matter with particles and then finding out how the particles have reacted. Before Rutherford, the atom was thought of as a sort of 'plum pudding', a positively-charged sphere containing negatively-charged particles called electrons. Rutherford was able to show that at the centre of the atom was a minute and very dense nucleus. This seemed to be made of positively-charged particles called protons, but these did not account for the entire mass of the nucleus. There had to be another type of particle, neutral electrically, which Rutherford called the neutron.

It was in the early 1930s that scientists finally tracked the neutron down. It emerged as a particle powerful enough to knock protons out of several different elements. Its electrical neutrality allowed it to penetrate matter easily. But even so, physicists doubted that it could be used to tap the formidable energy of the atom.

But extraordinary effects were possible when you bombarded atoms with neutrons. Variant forms of elements (called isotopes) could be produced. Sometimes even different elements appeared. The element that behaved most strangely when treated in this way was uranium. The most extraordinary effect of all was discovered in 1934 by Lise Meitner and Otto Hahn, working in Berlin. Bombarding uranium nitrate solution with neutrons, they found that the uranium atoms had split in two; the resulting fragments came together to form two different elements, krypton and barium.

They had discovered the process known as nuclear fission. Moreover they calculated that an immense amount of energy was released when the process took place. Now physicists could see that an explosive chain reaction might take place, with one neutron releasing two, two giving off four, and so on, at each stage releasing redoubled amounts of energy. Lise Meitner published the results of her and Hahn's work in 1939.

American response and the spread of nuclear weapons

Einstein's letter to the president was timely. The US government responded swiftly by setting up a team to develop the idea of a nuclear bomb. The team, based at Los Alamos, New Mexico, and working in secret, was an impressive one. It included Nobel prizewinner Niels Bohr who actually took news of Meitner's and Hahn's work to America, and Otto Frisch, nephew of Meitner who had worked with her on fission. In the lower echelons of the team was future Nobel physics laureate Richard Feynman. He later said that all science had stopped during the war except the little bit done at Los Alamos.

And fateful science it proved to be. In July 1945 the first experimental atomic explosive device was detonated at Los Alamos. In the same month a special commission recommended that the bomb should be used to quell the resistance of Japan to the Allies and to bring the war in the Pacific to a rapid end. First Japan was offered the chance at Potsdam to surrender or face destruction. She refused and on 6 August the first atomic bomb to be used in anger was exploded at Hiroshima. Three days later the city of Nagasaki was wiped out in the same way. Quickly, Russia joined the war against Japan and on 2 September, Japan surrendered.

Some 150,000 people lost their lives at Hiroshima and Nagasaki. The effect on buildings – and everything else on the ground – was devastating. For the first time the world knew the immense power for destruction that nuclear weapons had unleashed. The effect of such weapons in irresponsible hands would be terrifying. After the war there was heated discussion, particularly between Britain and America, about how nuclear weapons should be developed, and by whom. The outcome was that America jealously hung on

The dropping of the atomic bombs on Hiroshima and Nagasaki was devastating for the Japanese. The Americans judged that destroying two cities in this way would hasten the end of the war, and they were right. What they also did by using the weapons was to show the world the immense potential for destruction of which humanity had become capable. Once people had seen this, it became clearer how important it was that such weapons should not be used in the future. But it did not stop the post-war proliferation of nuclear weapons, something which peace campaigners are still struggling to contain.

to her nuclear capability, excluding Britain from joint research in 1946.

But this decision did not deter the British from pursuing their own programme of nuclear weapons development. Nor were the Russians discouraged. The Soviets had achieved a nuclear test by 1949; Britain followed in 1952. Although in these early years America would remain the supreme nuclear power, the nuclear programmes of Britain and the USSR were gradually to catch up with America's in terms of scientific development if not, in the case of Britain, in sheer numbers of weapons. Moreover France would join the nuclear powers in 1960, China in 1964, and various other countries, though not established nuclear powers, either have the capability to produce nuclear weapons or are believed to have secret nuclear capability.

This proliferation of nuclear weapons was made more threatening by other post-war developments. First there were political developments, such as the Cold War between east and west that threw an artificial frontier across Europe and made Russian weapons a threat to western Europe. Then there were technological changes, such as advances in rocketry, that made it possible to send nuclear weapons further across the globe than before. The launch of the Soviet satellite Sputnik I in 1957, for example, did much to equal out the forces of Russia and America. Now both nations could strike each other with nuclear force – from this point the missile was the most threatening nuclear weapon.

A further technological change was from fission reaction to hydrogen or fusion bombs. In such weapons an atom bomb is used to create the extremely high temperature required to set up a further reaction in a layer of hydrogenous material surrounding it. The result is an even more devastating explosion than with a fission bomb. The first fusion bomb was tested by the Americans in 1952. By 1958 all three nuclear nations had these highly destructive weapons.

Finally, the development of nuclear power for peaceful use brought its own problems. First there was the threat to the environment of nuclear power stations, a subject which is still the cause of heated debate. In addition, the spread of nuclear power stations around the world also resulted in the spread of nuclear technology and of radioactive materials that might also be put to use in war.

Disarmament and control

The horror of the utter destruction caused by the first two nuclear bombs, and the subsequent race to develop other nuclear weapons around the world caused justified alarm. It seemed that humankind had unleashed an unprecedented power for destruction. As it was not possible to 'uninvent' the bomb, people began to talk about ways of dismantling the nuclear weapons that already existed and preventing their future reconstruction and use.

Diagram of a nuclear fission reaction

The Americans and the Russians, who were to be the key nuclear powers in the post-war period, emerged with different answers to the problem. Bernard Baruch, American representative on the UN Atomic Energy Commission, proposed that atomic energy should be used only for peaceful purposes. From this proposal came discussions about internationalizing nuclear knowledge, so that the Americans and Russians would share their atomic secrets. But the two superpowers did not trust each other enough to proceed with this plan. The Soviet delegate on the Commission, Andrei Gromyko, came up with a counterproposal: nuclear weapons should not be used or constructed and current stocks should be dismantled. This was rejected because there was no provision for inspection or verification of the procedure.

Although this fundamental lack of trust between the USA and USSR would remain, it was clear that any meaningful decision about nuclear arms had to be taken internationally. With this in mind, the UN set up a disarmament commission in 1952. The goal was to be 'general and complete disarmament'. This meant that all countries should be involved and that all weapons, conventional as well as nuclear, should be done away with. A climax was reached in this series of talks when, in 1955, the Soviets presented a paper to the Commission that accepted most of the western proposals, including the vital one of international inspection and control. But again, the two superpowers were too suspicious of each other to agree: America refused to accept Russia's proposals.

The year 1955 proved a turning point. Discussions after this date tended to concentrate on more limited aims – on arms *control* rather than complete disarmament. There were hopeful signs. 1958 produced an agreement banning nuclear tests, but this was soon broken, first by the Russians in 1961. The next year saw an eighteen-nation disarmament conference, but neither France nor China were present. Nevertheless such partial talks did lead to some improvements in the international situation – notably to another ban on tests, the exclusion of nuclear weapons from space and the introduction of 'hotline' communications between Washington and Moscow.

Since the 1960s there have been a host of international conferences on peace, all of which have concentrated on aspects of arms control rather than general disarmament. Their success has been limited, with relatively little actual disarmament when the size of the world's stockpiles of warheads is taken into account. But they have fostered a slowdown in arms proliferation and have done something to further international understanding.

But this concentration on nuclear weapons has left much out of the picture. Nuclear war has become our horrifying image of apocalypse – and a very potent one it is too. But this should not blind us to the immense destructive power of the other types of weapons also available: the enormous stocks of conventional arms, and the curse of chemical and biological weapons. Such a diversity of weapons, held so widely, highlights what is perhaps the real lesson of the production and explosion of the first nuclear bombs in 1945. Our capacity for destruction is now vast, and it can be accessed easily and quickly and imposed on any part of the world almost instantly. War has become a truly global problem. Peace should become a global aim.

FOUNDING OF THE UNITED NATIONS

An international initiative for peace

The two world wars of the twentieth century were so devastating that, after both, there was a general feeling that such all-embracing conflicts should be avoided in the future. War no longer seemed like a way of solving problems that could not be solved in other ways, but a problem in itself. After World War I the League of Nations was formed to promote peace. At first it was an important element in the diplomatic scene, but it failed to function well in the 1930s, when the events that led to World War II gathered pace.

So after World War II a new body, the United Nations, was set up. Again, its main aim was to promote international peace and security. It was officially formed on 24 October 1945 and its charter was ratified by fifty-one original members. Its declared aims were: to prevent war; to foster good relations between the world's states; to work for human rights and fundamental freedoms; and to bring about cooperation in solving the economic, social and cultural problems of the world.

The San Francisco conference that led to the founding of the UN was sponsored by four states – China, the Soviet Union, the United Kingdom and the USA. A fifth, France, was invited to be a sponsoring power but refused. It was these five nations that became the permanent members of the Security Council. It was at first envisaged that this group, the victors in World War II, should act together to keep peace in the world. They would pool their resources to form permanent 'peacekeeping' forces that would be sent to the world's trouble spots.

But these five states were not the only members of the UN. Membership was also open to those other states who had fought against the axis powers in World War II. Thus there were a total of fifty-one founder members of the organization. Other peace-loving nations that were prepared to abide by the charter, subject to the recommendation of the Security Council and a vote in the General Assembly, were free to join.

The original idea of membership was very much that each member should be committed to the principles of the charter: there was to be no room for nations that were not truly 'peace-loving'. But as time went on it became clear that, if the UN was to be able to act decisively in the world arena, it would have to include all, or almost all, of the nations of the world. So membership grew, particularly with a large number of admissions in 1955, and the UN is now truly a world organization. A notable exception is Switzerland, a traditionally neutral country where the belief prevails that involvement in the use of collective force against aggression would be a violation of neutrality.

Within the UN six departments, or 'organs', were established to help it achieve its aims. The General Assembly would be the main debating body of the UN and would include representatives from all the member states. The Security Council would have the main responsibility for maintaining peace and security. The Economic and Social Council would coordinate the work suggested by its title.

The emblem of the United Nations

The Trusteeship Council would deal with trust territories (those preparing for self-government). The International Court of Justice would receive cases under international law. And the Secretariat, under the secretary-general, would carry out the day-to-day work of the UN.

The working of the United Nations

The General Assembly controls the UN's budget and expenses and runs elections to the three councils. In some areas it acts if there is a recommendation from the Security Council. These include the appointment of the secretary-general and amendments to the UN Charter. The General Assembly can also debate, make recommendations, and commission studies on matters that fall within the brief of the UN as a whole.

The Security Council consists of representatives of the five permanent members plus ten (originally six) other countries. The permanent members normally hold the right of veto on Security Council decisions. Non-members may also take part in debates, although their proposals can only be voted on if a member of the Council requests it. The members of the Security Council, especially the five permanent members, thus have unique power within the organization. This is strengthened because the General Assembly has no power over the Security Council.

The other two councils operate under the authority of the General Assembly. The Economic and Social Council is the largest of the Councils, having fifty-four members (originally eighteen). It has initiated a large amount of work in the social and economic areas and made many policy recommendations. It also coordinates the work of the specialized agencies that the UN has set up, and handles UN relations with non-governmental organizations. The Trusteeship Council is now responsible for only one trust territory.

The International Court of Justice sits

The origins of the United Nations were firmly rooted in the aftermath of World War II. There was an understanding amongst the nations who considered themselves great powers at the time that the victors of the war should make themselves responsible for maintaining world peace. The nations that were therefore most influential in the setting up of the UN were the USSR, the USA and Britain (represented here by leaders Stalin, Eisenhower and Churchill), together with China and France. It was these five nations that would become the permanent members of the UN Security Council, the organ of the UN that has the greatest responsibility for maintaining peace, and the greatest power. The effectiveness of the UN in bringing about peaceful solutions to world conflicts has been limited, but many politicians and peace campaigners alike still look to it as a potential base on which peace and world governance might be built.

at The Hague but may convene elsewhere if necessary. It consists of fifteen highly qualified judges. It deals with cases between states, although no states are obliged to bring cases to the court for settlement.

The Secretariat is made up of international officials who are responsible only to the UN and whose actions should not be governed by the interest of their 'home' country. They are recruited for their skills and their potential for integrity, irrespective of their national origins, although there is also an attempt to recruit officials from as wide a range of states as possible.

The specialized agencies

In addition to the six organs of the UN, specialized agencies have also been set up to deal with specific areas of UN work. These divide roughly into two groups, those concerned with international communications, such as the Universal Postal Union and the International Telecommunications Union, and the welfare agencies, such as Food and Agriculture Organization (FAO) and the United Nations Educational, Scientific and Cultural Organization (UNESCO).

These bodies, set off from the centre of the UN, have done some of the organization's most significant work. The World Health Organization (WHO) the Children's Fund (UNICEF), the FAO, UNESCO, the High Commissioner for Refugees (UNHCR), and the rest have all done invaluable work in health, food distribution, disaster relief and the welfare of children and refugees. And they provide object lessons in how supranational organizations can really work.

The importance of the UN

For all its influence, there has been much disillusionment with the UN in the second half of the twentieth century. The Cold War between east and west, and tensions between the affluent north and the impoverished south, have worked against it. Most obviously, it has failed to prevent war and to impose arms limitations. The permanent peacekeeping force that was envisaged, failed to materialize.

And there are grave doubts about the UN's effectiveness as a representative body. For example, in the General Assembly each member has a single vote, in spite of the widely differing populations of the world's nations, while the important Security Council is dominated by five already influential states. Moreover, because of the superpower domination of the Security Council, the UN finds it difficult to act in conflicts in which one of the great powers is involved (notable examples were American involvement in Vietnam and the Soviet invasion of Afghanistan). Other failures of which the UN is often accused include the continuing confusion and injustice of international trading arrangements and the continuing gap between rich and poor.

And yet, as many statesmen have pointed out, it is the only United Nations we have got. It does provide a coming together of people from widely differing backgrounds. It does foster international understanding. And it has saved lives. This alone justifies its existence. If it could be made a more representative organization it would stand an even better chance of doing these things more effectively.

DISCOVERY OF THE STRUCTURE OF DNA

The scientific breakthrough that revealed the basis of our genetic make-up

How does heredity work? It is a question that has long puzzled scientists. People have always noticed that their children seem to inherit some of their own characteristics. Yet it is difficult to establish a pattern that will predict *which* characteristics will be passed on. The first scientist to do significant work on this subject was an Austrian monk in the nineteenth century, Gregor Mendel. In 1856 he began a huge ten-year experiment, breeding some 28,000 pea plants in his monastery garden at Brünn, Moravia. He analyzed the way in which certain features, such as long or short stalks and different flower colours, were passed on.

Mendel found that there were patterns to his results. For example, all the dwarf plants produced dwarf offspring; but of the tall varieties only about one third reproduced true to type. Crossing tall and dwarf plants produced tall plants; while crossing the hybrids produced a mixture of tall and dwarf. Mendel evolved statistical rules that governed in what proportions the characteristics were passed on. His work provoked little attention in his lifetime.

Although Mendel's work showed the results of genetics in a particular species, it did not explain why these things happened as they did. The next major advance in our knowledge came in the early twentieth century with the work of W. L. Johannsen. Johannsen identified chromosomes and genes as the hereditary material in living tissue. But it was not known even then exactly what this material consisted of or just how it worked.

DNA: the search for its structure

For this information, science had to wait until the 1950s, when various scientists were working on the substance deoxyribonucleic acid or DNA. Each cell of living tissue contains chromosomes, and each chromosome contains many molecules of DNA. These molecules are small and have

to be highly complex in order to carry the genetic information that they do. But all DNA molecules, whether they come from humans, other animals or plants, have basically the same structure. But what exactly was the structure, and how did DNA work? These were the questions that a number of researchers in Europe and America were addressing in the early 1950s.

Foremost among these scientists were American geneticist James D. Watson and British biophysicist Francis Crick, working in Cambridge. They worked closely on the chemical structure of DNA, using molecular models as an aid to figuring out how DNA is made up. In this work they were partly inspired by US chemist Linus Pauling's use of models and work on other molecular structures. Indeed Pauling himself was working in America on the structure of DNA. Two other scientists who were also deeply involved in the search for DNA's structure were Maurice Wilkins and Rosalind Franklin, who worked in London with X-ray studies of the molecule. They bounced X-rays off DNA and recorded the patterns made by the rays on photographic plates.

In the end it was Watson and Crick who came up with the solution to DNA's structure. They were sharing an office in Cambridge with Peter Pauling, Linus Pauling's son, who told them that his father had already established what he thought to be the structure of the molecule. When news reached Cambridge of Pauling's proposed structure for DNA, Watson and Crick were impressed – indeed what Pauling proposed was rather like one of their own earlier suggestions, a helical shape made up of three chains with a backbone running down the centre. Watson and Crick had for some time believed that a helix or spiral would be the basic shape of the molecule, although the number of chains and the way they were held together remained unknown.

But Watson instinctively felt that there was something wrong with Pauling's hypothesis. In particular, the hydrogen atoms in the molecule did not seem to make sense chemically. Consultations with Cambridge chemists suggested that Watson was correct and that Pauling had made a basic error. This fact put pressure on Watson and Crick. They believed that as soon as Pauling found out his mistake he would devote all of his considerable abilities to solving the structure of DNA. In the minds of Watson and Crick the search turned into a race with Pauling.

Meanwhile Wilkins and Franklin had been carrying on their work with X-rays. Wilkins showed Watson a new photograph that again suggested a helical structure. Watson resolved to press on with model building, using two chains rather than Pauling's three. But he stuck to the idea of keeping the backbone of the helix in the middle.

Later, Watson admitted that the reasons he persisted with the central backbone were not truly scientific. As well as the backbone the molecule was known to contain four substances known as *bases*: thymine, adenine, guanine and cytosine. These compounds have different shapes and sizes. This does not matter if they are on the outside of the molecule. But if they are on the inside, making up the link between the two chains, then their different sizes make an unruly set of links

It took a vast amount of discussion, calculation, model-making and checking before the combined work of Watson, Crick, Wilkins and Franklin came up with the solution to the structure of DNA: the now-famous double helix molecule. But this work was only a beginning. The way the different parts of the molecule interact with each other, and the precise manner in which characteristics are passed on, continue to absorb scientists and to suggest new areas of research.

between the two rungs of the molecular ladder.

The breakthrough came when Watson and Crick realized that an adenine-thymine pair held together by two bonds of hydrogen was exactly the same shape as aguanine-cytosine pair, also held together by two or more hydrogen bonds. This would make an orderly set of links. Watson and Crick quickly set about getting their laboratory's model-makers to provide them with the parts they needed to build a complete model of their proposed molecule.

Naturally they wanted to do this as quickly as they could. First, there was the competition with Pauling: Watson and Crick wanted to get there first. Second, other scientists were working on other problems connected with DNA. If Watson and Crick had solved the problem of its structure, the other researchers would need to modify their work accordingly.

So they made the model and checked their way through it to see if it was as convincing as they had thought. It was. They showed their results to Wilkins and Franklin, and it seemed to square with their X-ray data. When Pauling saw the results, he too was convinced. The riddle had been solved.

Their work on DNA won Nobel Prizes for Watson, Crick and Wilkins. Watson and Crick continued their work, both carrying out research into the working of the genetic code. Wilkins also stayed in the same field for some time, checking and rechecking the results of Watson and Crick's work until it was clear that the double helix in all its details was the correct model for the DNA molecule. Rosalind Franklin, whose X-ray work was so impressive, also carried out further important work in the field before an untimely death at the age of thirty-seven.

The structure and work of DNA

The molecule that Watson and Crick described looked as beautiful in its model form as it was fascinating. It is made up of two long strings, each held together by cross-pieces and twisted to form the famous double helix shape that has also been compared to a twisted rope ladder.

DNA is made up of six basic substances. The sides of the ladder consist of alternating parts of the sugar deoxiribose and phosphate. The rungs comprise the four bases. Each rung is made up of two bases and these are attached only to the sugar units of the sides of the ladder. The order of the bases in a particular DNA molecule gives the genetic code. It is transmitted from one generation to the next, governing not only the basic attributes of the species (so that horses, for example, give birth to horses), but also individual traits, such as eye colour.

As an organism grows, its cells divide to form new cells. When this happens, the DNA also divides. The ladder uncurls and splits along its length, the paired bases of each strand separating, before rejoining other free bases to form new DNA. The way this happens, each new ladder is an exact duplicate of the organism's original ladder – the DNA molecules in each cell of a particular being are identical.

But what is the nature of the genetic information carried by these strings of sugars, phosphates and bases? The form taken by each cell, and thus the form of the entire organism, is determined by proteins, and these are made up of substances called amino acids. These amino acids link together in different ways to form different proteins. And the DNA contains the information about the order in which the amino acids should link up.

DNA is assisted in controlling protein structure and production by another, similar substance called RNA. This is made up in a similar way to DNA, but contains a different sugar and one different base. RNA acts as a chemical messenger, copying the genetic blueprint of DNA and acting as a mould to make the amino acids link together to form the right proteins. Scientists are still some way from understanding exactly how the four bases of DNA and RNA convey instructions about the make-up of a protein chain containing twenty amino acids. The work of cracking the code by which this information is transmitted goes on.

The science of genetics

The story of DNA did not end with the discovery of its structure. It has opened up the science of genetics, making possible genetic engineering, perhaps the most significant step that biological science has made in recent decades. This new discipline began in the early 1970s with the work of two scientists from California, Stanley Cohen and Herbert Boyer. Cohen took a single gene from a cell of a toad and transfered it to a bacterium. The gene was reproduced in each descendant of the bacterium.

This first step revealed the possibility of creating new organisms by combining gene in different ways. It is a process so radical that it has asked new questions of scientific ethics – to what extent has a human being the right to play god in this way and what is the nature of the scientists' responsibility for organisms so created? Questions such as these raise such difficult problems (quite aside from the technical challenges of the work) that experiments have been limited.

But there have been notable advances. Some of these have been in the area of creating new drugs to combat diseases that were once incurable or difficult to cure. Still more breakthroughs are hoped for in the field of disease prevention. Already genes from bacteria that are able to wipe out plant viruses have been transferred to the DNA of certain plants. Another gene, transferred to potato plants, deters harmful crystals from growing on the crops and destroying them. A further project has manipulated the DNA of nitrogen-fixing bacteria to make them more efficient, thus allowing farmers and growers to cut down their use of costly fertilizers.

There are hopes that such illness prevention may one day extend to humans. The most important work in this field is probably the analysis of the vast amount of data contained in human DNA. This concentrates on mapping the incidence of the four chemical bases that make up the key active ingredients of DNA. Every individual has some 100,000 genes and each has thousands of these bases in a unique combination. It is the combination that provides the individual's genetic fingerprint. Looking at the patterns in these genetic fingerprints should lead scientists to the causes of many diseases and the reasons for many human attributes. The analysis of all this data will take decades, but they will be very revealing decades for biological science. If the potential for illness prevention and food-crop improvement are realized, significant inroads could be made into problems of both disease and famine.

LAUNCH OF SPUTNIK I

Exploration goes beyond Earth

On 4 October 1957 radio receivers at research establishments around the world began to pick up an insistent bleeping from outer space that was to change the way we perceive the universe. For that was the date of the launch of Sputnik I, the first artificial satellite. Russian scientists had been doing research on space travel for years. As early as 1910, K. E. Tsiolkovsky had outlined most of the fundamental principles of space travel and had designed the sort of multi-stage rockets that would be needed to push a spacecraft clear of the Earth's atmosphere.

Other pioneer countries were less forward-looking when it came to space technology. In Germany, for example, there was an important programme of research into rocketry in the 1930s, but the knowledge gained from this was channelled into work on the V2 weapon with which Hitler attacked Britain in 1944. In the United States, although there was at least one important pre-war pioneer (Robert H. Goddard), sustained work on rockets really only gained momentum when German scientists began to arrive after 1945. Even then, the first space project was not begun until ten years later.

In view of the state of space research in the west, then, it was natural that news of a Soviet satellite should be greeted at first with scepticism and then, when the launch was confirmed, with astonishment. In the 1950s, people in the west were simply not prepared to believe that the USSR, hidden behind the iron curtain and in many ways technologically backward, was capable of a feat that seemed to belong to the realm of science fiction.

The initial achievement

What had the Soviets actually achieved? The Sputnik I satellite was a shiny metal sphere some twenty-three inches in diameter, weighing about 184 pounds. To launch it into orbit it needed a rocket about ninety feet long weighing four tonnes. The satellite reached an orbit between 140 and 580 miles above the Earth's surface. Atmospheric drag at the lower end of the orbit was quite high, so it was only a matter of months before the satellite fell back to earth. But the initial barriers – producing enough thrust to get out of the atmosphere and positioning the satellite accurately enough for it to stay in orbit – had been broken. A response from the USA, the other emergent 'space power', was eagerly awaited.

But before the Americans could respond, the Russians pulled off a yet more astounding feat: the launch of Sputnik II, a much heavier satellite (1,120 pounds) with a higher orbit and a cargo that included the first living being space, a dog called Laika. Sputnik II stayed in orbit for six months and was large enough to be seen in the night sky. It confirmed the pre-eminence of the USSR in this new field of research.

The American response was unspectacular. The launch of the satellite Vanguard I failed in late 1957 when the rocket caught fire. Success for the Americans came on 1 February 1958 when they successfully launched Explorer I, a satellite lighter than Sputnik II but with a higher orbit. It was followed by Vanguard I which finally got into space on 17 March 1958. The midget among the first satellites, this six-inch diameter sphere had a still higher orbit (varying between 140 and 2,470 miles above the Earth). The satellite still remains in this high orbit, a tiny memorial to the early days of what came to be known as the 'space race'.

The benefits

Today we are used to hearing justifications of space exploration in terms of the benefits it brings to humankind. Although the first Sputniks were intended primarily to test the feasibility of getting any sort of object (and with the space dog Laika, any sort of 'higher animal') into space at all, it is perhaps surprising how soon tangible benefits became evident. The commitment of both the USA and the USSR to space travel is reflected in the fact that by late 1958 the National Aeronautics and Space Agency (NASA) had been formed in the USA, while the USSR's first man in space, Yuri Gagarin, orbited the Earth in April 1961.

By this time, the scientific gains from space exploration were clear. Satellites were telling us a great deal about world weather patterns – the science of meteorology has continued to gain from weather satellites. Another obvious gain has been in communications. The first example was the four-tonne rocket the Americans put into orbit in December 1958. This spacecraft broadcast a Christmas message from President Dwight D. Eisenhower. Far more sophisticated communications satellites were to follow, their role becoming well known due to the rise of satellite television broadcasting, although there are many other applications. Yet another use for satellites has been in navigation. Ships can receive signals from satellites that enable them to calculate their position accurately.

Hidden benefits

Perhaps more fascinating are the scientific discoveries that have resulted from this type of exploration. These may not have any obvious immediate benefit to humankind, save that of expanding our knowledge of the Earth and its surroundings, but any information that we can glean about our environment is likely to help our survival and that of our planet. Even the early satellites, with their minimal instrumentation, could tell us much about space, the upper atmosphere, and the Earth – simply from the way they behaved. For example, as a satellite in an orbit lower than 200 miles succumbs to the effects of atmospheric drag, observations of its movements can tell us something about the density of the air in the upper atmosphere.

When satellites with instruments began to go into orbit still more interesting results were obtained. For example, the radiation levels in the space around the Earth were detected and the amounts of radiation could be measured accurately. One of the most surprising discoveries was the exact shape of the Earth, which could be measured accurately for the first time. Astronomers found that our planet was slightly pear-shaped, while the flattening of the Earth near the poles was less pronounced than had been believed from the terrestrial measurements.

Manned spaceflights

Perhaps the most publicised of the many early efforts of space exploration was the announcement by President Kennedy in 1961 of the project to put a man on the Moon by 1970. The ensuing manned Mercury (1961–63) and Gemini (1965–66) projects gave much initial experience and information. This was used in the Apollo programme, a series of manned flights culminating with Apollo 11, which put astronauts on the Moon for the first time in July 1969.

The vast amount of data collected about the Moon, the Earth, and space itself seemed to make the enormous expense (many billions of dollars) justified at the time. The numerous technological 'spin-offs' – items that could only have been made as a result of space research – provided a further justification. These items ranged from increasingly miniaturized electronic components to non-stick coverings for saucepans.

Since the 1960s the economic pressures on space research have been much greater. Putting people into space has been less of a priority than creating a reusable spacecraft (the space shuttle) and sending unmanned probes towards our neighbouring planets. Meanwhile, the importance and usefulness of satellites, the far more sophisticated descendants of the early Sputniks, has never been greater. For communications and for the gathering of scientific data we have never relied on them more.

A tiny sphere with a cluster of antennae circling the earth, the first Sputnik was an unassuming object. But it opened up a new era in exploration and communications.

242

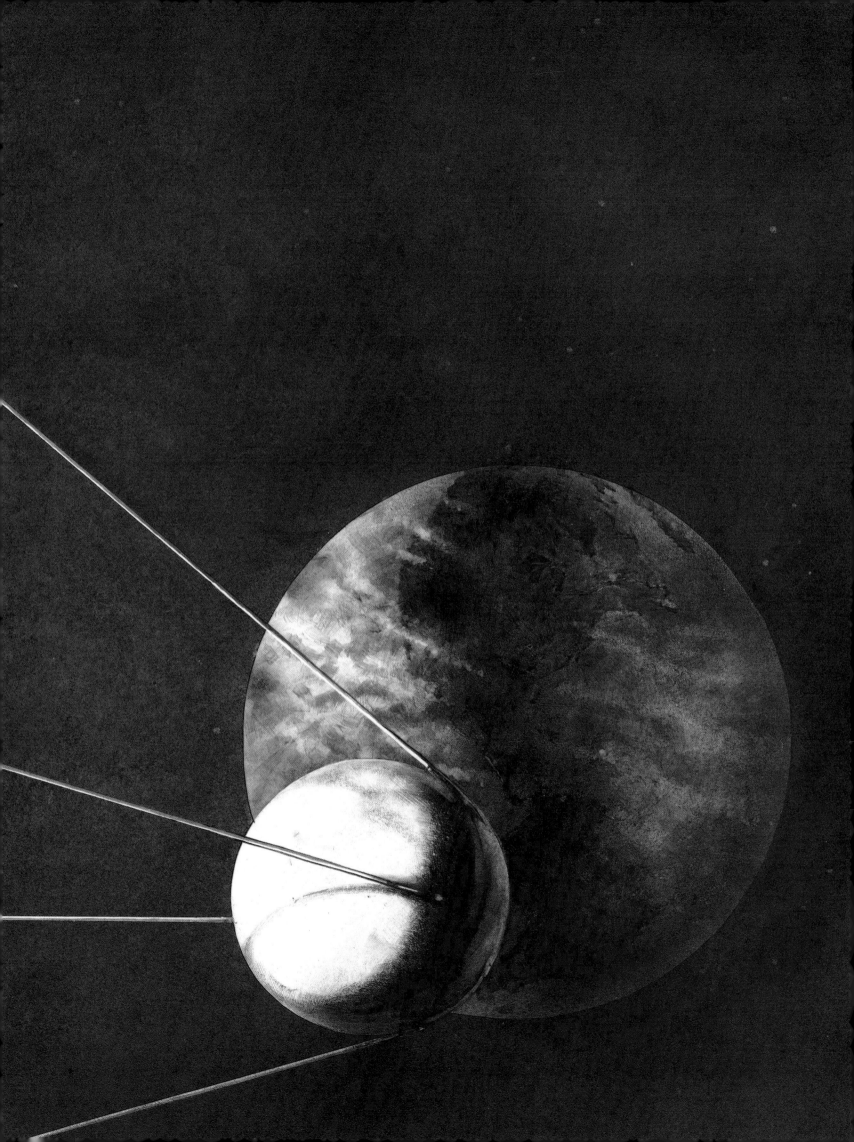

MARTIN LUTHER KING'S 'I HAVE A DREAM' SPEECH

Martin Luther King's 'I have a dream speech'

The movement for the rights of black people in the United States was the work of many – indeed it could have achieved what it did only with the active support of a large number of people. But one man above all has come to symbolize the black civil rights movement: Martin Luther King Jr.

Martin Luther King Jr was born in Atlanta, Georgia in 1929. His father, the pastor of a Baptist church, had a great formative influence on King, showing him the importance of both church and family in holding together the often precarious black community. He saw how a church leader could become a leader of the black community, organizing the registration of voters and working for civil rights organizations such as the National Association for the Advancement of Colored People.

As well he might. Although slavery had been abolished in 1865, black people in the USA, particularly in the south, had little power. They had to contend with segregation laws that kept them firmly to one side – the inferior side – of a 'color line'. The aim was to keep blacks in a position where they would constitute a source of cheap labour, and where they would have neither the freedom nor the education to fight for anything better.

A key episode in King's life, which shows his beliefs and methods clearly, was the bus boycott in Montgomery, Alabama, in 1955–56. It was a struggle against the concept that blacks should be considered equal to, but kept separate from, whites. One example of this was that seats on public transport were segregated, so that half the seats on buses were allocated to blacks, half to whites. Since blacks made up the majority of passengers, but could not sit in unoccupied 'white' seats, the situation was doubly absurd.

The black community of Montgomery organized a boycott of the buses as a challenge to the segregation policy, and King emerged as the main spokesperson and leader of the boycott. The move was a success. It worked firstly because of the massive support from the black community, second because King insisted on a policy of non-violent resistance to white opposition. This combination of collective action and non-violence was to characterize the other protests in which King was involved.

But the boycott in Montgomery was not as influential as many black leaders had hoped. Other boycotts did not follow across the south. More significant were the activities of the civil rights movement in Birmingham, Alabama, a hotbed of racism of the most violent and vicious kind. Here the whites had put up a solid resistance to any reforms, and the Ku Klux Klan had an appalling record of violence against black people. A ruthless, racist chief of police made things worse.

Although he had a strong team King's aims in Birmingham, to get the local authorities to start out on the path to desegregation and to enlist the help of the federal authorities in this, seemed difficult. The authorities secured injunctions against demonstrations and King was arrested. But on release he was able to mobilize massive and unified support from the black community. The police used dogs and high-pressure water hoses to keep the demonstrators at bay, but they could only unite them still more. In the end, with white opinion mobilized by television coverage, the president and attorney general intervened to force the locals to give in to some of the demonstrators' demands.

King's instinct was to take the Birmingham protest further, to mobilize a national movement for black civil rights using non-violent direct action to achieve more sweeping changes. The result was a march on Washington in August 1963, with around 200,000 people converging on the Lincoln Memorial to support a civil rights bill. This was the occasion on which King's famous speech, outlining his hopes for racial harmony, was made:

'I have a dream that one day this nation will rise up and live out the true meaning of its creed, "We hold these truths to be self-evident, that all men are created equal." I have a dream that one day on the red hills of Georgia, sons of former slaves and sons of former slaveholders will be able to sit down together at the table of brotherhood. I have a dream that one day even that the state of Mississippi, a state sweltering with the heat of injustice, will be transformed into an oasis of freedom and justice.'

A civil rights act followed soon afterwards. It was far from the end of racism in the USA. In particular, King continued to be shocked by the fact that even in the North, racism was rife. And continued black disenfranchisement remained a shameful problem. Indeed it is possible to criticize King as a conservative who played into the hands of the whites and achieved comparatively little. But King's work was a crucial beginning. It made civil rights recognizable as a national issue in the USA. And it brought international attention to problems of race, influencing many working for the cause of civil rights all around the world.

Martin Luther King saw his political speeches, his part in the Montgomery Bus Boycott, and his other work for human rights as 'just one aspect of a worldwide revolt of oppressed peoples.' His 'dream' was specifically of an America free from racial discrimination, but more generally of an entire world in which oppression, colonialism and all other forms of domination of one people by another would be eliminated. In this goal, King was representative of a whole movement, an ongoing struggle that continues to try to transform the modern world.

WOODSTOCK

A festival of music and peace

In February 1969 a meeting took place between four men who were to create an event that would become the hallmark of its era. The men were two entrepreneurs interested in doing something unusual with their money, John Roberts and Joel Rosenman, and two men from the music business, Michael Lang and vice-president of Capitol Records Artie Kornfeld. The event they were to stage was the Woodstock Music and Art Fair, known to posterity simply as Woodstock, the biggest rock concert ever to take place.

Michael Lang wanted to build a recording studio in Woodstock, in upstate New York. He and the others also had the idea of doing a series of concerts in the same area, a place where many of the country's leading rock musicians lived or had connections. The three-day festival at Woodstock was originally conceived as a curtain-raiser for the studio, a promotional event that would involve some of music's top names and publicize the new enterprise. But it quickly took on a life of its own.

The producers were united in their wish to have as impressive a line-up as possible for the concert. And they managed to attract some of the foremost folk and rock musicians of their time, from Joni Mitchell to Janis Joplin, The Who to Jimi Hendrix. But Woodstock was to be more than a concert. It was a product of the peace and youth culture of the late 1960s: 'Three days of peace and music,' promised the publicity. And in the USA at this time, for all the naïveté of the hippie culture, there was a very real feeling that opposition to the establishment – especially to the country's involvement in the Vietnam War – was necessary. Such a mixture of naïveté and commitment to a cause gave the Woodstock festival much of its unique character.

The organization was amateurish. One participant described it as a 'semi-organized disorganization.' One site had to be abandoned after extensive preparations had been made because the local authority refused permission. Others referred to the youth and lack of skill of most of those doing the preparation. And yet these same qualities meant that everyone was prepared to work incredibly hard to get ready for what promised to be an event of unprecedented size.

That size became apparent when some of the specialist contractors got to work. The electrical installers compared their job to wiring up a city. The sound man compared his task to the inauguration of the US President – an event he had also worked on. Refuse disposal, catering, telephones – all posed similar challenges on the rural site. The number of people employed turned into a small army, the amount of money invested amassed into a small fortune.

But even this did not prepare anyone for the numbers who turned up to watch. Even on the Wednesday before the weekend of the festival thousands had arrived at the site. By the following day the narrow roads near the venue began to block up and it became increasingly clear that the audience figures would far outnumber the 25,000 or so that the producers had at first hoped for.

Yet the vast numbers did not solve the financial problem of the producers. Many came without tickets and were camping on the festival site before the gates could be secured. And more and more were arriving. Eventually the number was near to 400,000. In the end the producers had to declare Woodstock officially a free festival. It seemed like financial suicide but it helped to preserve the atmosphere of peace and cooperation.

Even the musicians found it difficult to get in, so crowded were the roads. Many had to arrive by helicopter. But in the end the music began, a reflective folk-based Friday followed by two days of more strident offerings from the world of rock that were heard for miles around.

As the power chords resounded, however, one final blow descended on Woodstock. A storm drenched the audience and turned the ground to mud. Even this did not dampen the ardour of those present. In a way it helped. It only increased the need for people to share resources and help each other out.

And that was perhaps the significance of Woodstock. It showed a generation that often felt itself powerless in the face of international politics and war-mongering what they could do if they tried. It showed that what for some seemed the empty rhetoric of the peace movement and the counter-culture could represent a true commitment to get things done. And it demonstrated how in spite of bad planning, traffic, a lack of food and appalling weather a potential unruly crowd of thousands could become a group of people who wanted to make the world a better place to live in.

Canadian singer-songwriter Joni Mitchell was in her mid-twenties at the time of the Woodstock festival and was very much a member of the Woodstock generation. The words of her song 'Woodstock' emphasize the importance of peace and the coming together of a whole generation to assert their own view of the world. As such, she summed up what Woodstock was about. Her song continued to celebrate the importance of the festival long after the event, not only in the version recorded by Mitchell herself, but in other records by the bands Crosby, Stills, Nash and Young in the USA, who also played at Woodstock, and Ian Matthews' Southern Comfort *in the UK.*

FALL OF THE BERLIN WALL

The beginning of a new political era in Europe

Towards the end of World War II the troops of the Red Army began to take key centres in central and eastern Europe. Romania, eastern Hungary, Poland and Czechoslovakia steadily saw the advance of the Russians. Their vital role in the defeat of fascism was reflected in Communist influence in the provisional governments that were set up in the area immediately after the war – and they were helped by the fact that fascists and those who had collaborated with the Nazis were outlawed from these popular fronts. Through good organization, skilful use of propaganda, and ruthless employment of security and intelligence networks, the Communists further strengthened their hold. Soon all the countries of what became known as the 'eastern bloc' had become single-party communist states.

World leaders knew what was happening. By the time Churchill in 1946 publicly referred to an 'iron curtain' being drawn across Europe, it was clear that the continent would be divided. Rigged elections in Poland and Hungary in 1947 made this clearer still. Since then the injustices of the regimes in central and eastern Europe have been well documented in the west. Attempts at change and reform also became well known, but few in eastern or western Europe predicted the changes that occurred in 1989 and 1990 or the speed with which they happened.

European Communism had to contend with a long series of objections and demonstrations, which often amounted to little more than an expression of the desire for reform within the existing system, but which leaders felt they had to suppress – often with violence – in order to maintain the status quo. 1953 saw demonstrations in East Germany, which led to shots being fired at demonstrators. Still worse was 1956 when demonstrators were killed in Warsaw. In the same year came the Hungarian uprising, another attempt to withdraw from the Warsaw

Pact and end one-party rule. It led to suppression as the Soviet tanks rolled in.

Not all who feared or hated these regimes tried to change them. Some simply escaped to the west, favouring the route through the divided city of Berlin. The eastern response to this, in August 1961, was to erect the Berlin Wall, the clearest symbol of the separateness of what people had begun to see as the two Europes and an efficient way of keeping the east away from the west. It would be almost thirty years before East Germany would again seem to offer a very different way out of the Communist system.

Meanwhile the Soviets tightened their grip on other parts of the bloc. First there was Czechoslovakia where the 'Prague Spring' 1968, an attempt by local leaders

Mikhail Gorbachev

to make Communism more human, was suppressed ruthlessly, again by the Soviet army. Then there were strikes and demonstrations in Poland in 1980 which led to a change of leadership and paved the way for the rise of the trade union Solidarity.

From the point of view of the west, things also changed. In the 1960s and 1970s the West Germans pursued 'Ostpolitik', a policy that led to West German recognition of the western borders of the

Warsaw Pact countries and to a thaw in relations between Bonn and Moscow. America, western Europe and the USSR meanwhile pursued 'détente.' This was another policy that aimed to bring east and west closer, particularly in matters of boundaries, human rights, security and economic cooperation. Economic pressures forced the USA and USSR to continue talks about arms reduction through the 1980s, leading to agreements to reduce and balance weapons holdings. The 1980s also saw the premiership of Mikhail Gorbachev and the rise of the policy of openness (peristroika) that made it more possible to question how the system was working and to suggest improvements.

Such movements brought eastern and western Europe slowly closer together. In the late 1980s some of the eastern European states began to steer themselves away from totalitarian rule and in so doing to become more westernized too. This happened particularly in Hungary and Poland. In Hungary, Janos Kadar was the party leader who had been installed after the events of 1956. Kadar was a hardliner, but no Stalinist. He had to face mounting opposition, particularly from intellectuals and the press, and saw the growth of discussion groups that sought to air new ideas about reforms.

A party reform movement was established to try to make the party more responsive to public opinion and to put legal restraints on communism in Hungary. Then in early 1988 a party conference was held at which Kadar was removed and a new leader, Karoly Grosz, installed. The government of Grosz undertook to be open to major reforms. With the formation of the Hungarian Democratic Forum and the new openness of the government to change, the pre-1956 leader Imre Nagy was rehabilitated. With this rehabilitation also came a recognition that the country should work towards the radical changes that Nagy stood for.

In Poland the changes began with unrest in the shipyards of Gdansk, where the Solidarity union came to prominence. The union was formed against a background of government resistance against the idea of a large, powerful, national trade union. In 1981 martial law was declared and the suppression of Solidarity was attempted. But this backfired. The USA imposed economic sanctions on Poland and the union received support at home. Further protests led to further suppression by the security forces and, although supporters lost their lives, the union was very much alive in 1988. Polish leader General Jaruzelski realized that he would have to come to some sort of agreement with Solidarity, and his discussions led to elections that gave Poland the first non-communist leader of an eastern bloc state.

In 1989 the movement towards change shifted to East Germany. Presided over by party leader Erich Honeker, this country had perhaps the most successful economy of the eastern bloc countries. But there was still a painful difference between the living standards here and in West Germany. So in 1989 citizens once more decided to vote with their feet. With the Berlin Wall blocking an exit to the west, East Germans were travelling to West Germany via Hungary, Czechoslovakia, and the West German embassy in Warsaw. As the numbers increased and it became clear that these states were not going to stop the emigration, the movement led to two months (August and September) of acute embarrassment to the East German government. By October, with no let up, ill and ageing leader Erich Honeker resigned in favour of the younger Egon Krenz. It was a signal that the party, under its new leadership, could introduce reforms without losing face.

But Krenz's reforms were not enough. Protest had gathered momentum and it now seemed that nothing would satisfy the protesters except the overthrow of communism. At the beginning of November the pressure was at its most intense. On 7 November the government resigned. On 8 November the entire Politburo followed the government. On 9 November protesters made the first breach in the Berlin Wall, the structure that had represented the isolationism of the East German government from the west, and the totalitarianism of the regime that had seen eighty people die rather than cross it.

This first breach in the wall was both a great symbolic act and a signal for people to act. Before long further holes were being hacked out of the apparently impenetrable concrete and parties were being held on and around the wall. By the early hours of 12 November the East German army were accepting the inevitable. They too began to open up holes in the barrier. The effect was overwhelming for the people of the divided city. Easterners and westerners alike flooded through the gaps, in the hope perhaps of meeting long-lost relatives, of sampling life on the other side, above all of savouring the experience of free passage from one side of the city to the other.

But it was difficult to gauge the political effect of the breaches in the wall. Krenz and the Communists were still in power. The Stasi, the East German secret police, still inspired terror. What was more Krenz himself was a Stasi chief deeply implicated in falsifying the results of the elections in 1989 which seemed to show that his party, the SED, was still the choice of the people. It was inconceivable that he would introduce radical reforms. But the pressure for change was great from the people. The Central Committee responded on 10 November with a programme that promised free elections, and a new criminal code. But it was clear that the government's authority was limited.

On 3 December the whole Politburo resigned again, and three days later Krenz resigned as Chairman of the Council of State and Chairman of the National Defence Council. The SED leaders were now desperate for their party's survival. Changing the name of the party and

Amongst the graffiti on the wall, a new political slogan emerges to capture the essence of the times: 'Live alone and free, like a tree, but in the brotherhood of the forest.' Since the removal of the wall, Germany has moved on to reunification, at first in a spirit of heady optimism, then with feelings of the enormous difficulties, as the pressing needs of the east and the elusiveness of a speedy solution to them become clear. Many Germans from the east are finding that that the road to tree-like freedom is a long one, even when the brotherhood of the forest has been given official recognition.

changing the personnel of the leadership once more, failed to disguise the fact that radical changes were unlikely to be forthcoming. Eventually, at the end of January 1990, a Government of National Responsibility was formed, which was an openly provisional body that would run the country until free elections in March. From then on, there would be a steady move towards reunification of Germany and facing up to the huge social and economic differences between the two parts of the 'new' nation.

The end of 1989 also saw revolutions in other countries of central and eastern Europe. In Czechoslovakia there was the peaceful 'velvet revolution' that saw the replacement of the communist regime with the opposition coalition Civic Forum. In Romania, a bloodier conflict was necessary to remove dictator Nicolae Ceausescu. And in Bulgaria the departure of communist leader Todor Zhivkov paved the way for the formation of new political parties.

Already the revolutions of 1989 and 1990 have transformed the lives of many Europeans and have had implications beyond Europe as nations adjust their attitudes to the newly democratic European states. But it is impossible to assess the implications of these astonishing changes so soon after the event. Nor is it possible to predict what will happen in the USSR, where the policies of Mikhail Gorbachev have stimulated those who press for further changes. All one can say for certain is that changes will continue – and continue to be reassessed through the perspective of time.

INDEX